Psychoanalytic Crisis Work with Adolescents

Psychoanalytic Crisis Work with Adolescents: An Independent Approach offers a clinical and theoretical examination of the seemingly omnipresent and ever-growing mental health difficulties and crises that teenagers face today.

The book starts by grounding the reader in a contemporary perspective on adolescent development, exploring the adolescent mental health crisis as it is experienced today. Integrating psychoanalytic and sociocultural perspectives, it explores adolescent crises and risk-taking behaviours, including suicidality, overdose, and self-harm by cutting. The book then outlines practical ways of working clinically with the adolescent, alongside their parents, carers, and educators. Core themes throughout the chapters include the primacy of identity and belonging in adolescence and the impact of the external world on internal emotional reality, such as peer relations, the media and internet, family, and wider political and social realities.

This book is essential reading for psychotherapists and psychoanalytically trained clinicians working with teenagers struggling with these difficulties, as well as other health professionals and parents looking for guidance on handling troubling behaviour.

Maria Papadima is a child and adolescent psychotherapist based in London, UK. She trained at the Independent Psychoanalytic Child and Adolescent Psychotherapy Association (IPCAPA) and works in an NHS crisis adolescent team in London, as well as privately, with young people and their families.

Rachel Acheson is a child and adolescent psychotherapist based in Holywood, Northern Ireland. She trained at the Independent Psychoanalytic Child and Adolescent Psychotherapy Association (IPCAPA).

Nikolaos Tzikas is a child and adolescent psychotherapist based in Athens, Greece. He trained at the Independent Psychoanalytic Child and Adolescent Psychotherapy Association (IPCAPA) and is a member of the Association of Child Psychotherapists (ACP) and the Hellenic Child and Adolescent Psychoanalytic Psychotherapy Society.

Independent Psychoanalytic Approaches with Children
and Adolescents series
Series Editors: Ann Horne and Teresa Bailey

For more information about this series, please visit: www.routledge.com

'This book provides a most welcome and admirable addition to the Independent series and should reach audiences far beyond those already involved in offering psychologically-informed treatment to troubled adolescents. In a way that is often scholarly but always accessible it considers adolescence from many different viewpoints, offering new ideas about risk, self-harming behaviours, and how to help the young person and their families engage with those offering services in a way that enhances their capacity to think and be less destabilised by the struggles of adolescence. The authors state "Psychoanalytic work in this field requires two things that at first glance appear opposite: immediacy and depth". The ideas contained in this book, brought vividly to life through composite vignettes, show this principle in action. While taking a wider, systemic approach, recognising that culture, language, and social pressures shape the form crises take, this book is firmly rooted in psychoanalytic thinking, yet many of the chapters will also be inspirational to those working with adolescents in a wide variety of settings.'

Dr Janine Sternberg, *child and adolescent psychotherapist*

'This is psychoanalytic psychotherapy at its best – creative, grounded in clinical experience, and grappling with the many urgent problems that adolescents bring to the clinician. The papers are written in the main by psychoanalytic child and adolescent psychotherapists who draw on the Independent psychoanalytic tradition to develop new ways of working. The urgency of the risk-laden problems that their patients bring to the consulting room, make the depth of understanding and experience that come from the psychoanalytic tradition all the more significant.

These are clinicians working within the severely overloaded Child and Adolescent Mental Health interdisciplinary teams of our times, but still managing to find new ways of helping their patients and their families.

This ground-breaking collection of papers is a major contribution to clinical practice which will be enormously helpful to clinicians for many years to come.'

Monica Lanyado, PhD, *child and adolescent psychotherapist*

Psychoanalytic Crisis Work with Adolescents

An Independent Approach

Edited by Maria Papadima,
Rachel Acheson, and Nikolaos Tzikas

Routledge
Taylor & Francis Group

LONDON AND NEW YORK

Designed cover image: Photodisc & ImageDJ / Design Master

First published 2026
by Routledge
4 Park Square, Milton Park, Abingdon, Oxon OX14 4RN

and by Routledge
605 Third Avenue, New York, NY 10158

Routledge is an imprint of the Taylor & Francis Group, an informa business

This work was supported by Wellcome [205400]. The funders had no role in study design, data collection and analysis, decision to publish, or preparation of the manuscript.

British Library Cataloguing-in-Publication Data
A catalogue record for this book is available from the British Library

ISBN: 978-1-032-97225-1 (hbk)
ISBN: 978-1-032-97223-7 (pbk)
ISBN: 978-1-003-59277-8 (ebk)

DOI: 10.4324/9781003592778

Typeset in Times New Roman
by Apex CoVantage, LLC

Contents

Editors

Dr Maria Papadima trained as a child and adolescent psychotherapist at the British Psychotherapy Foundation (IPCAPA) after completing a PhD on trauma and psychoanalysis. She has worked for a number of years at an NHS crisis adolescent team in London, where she holds a senior psychotherapy position. She has a longstanding interest in assessment and therapeutic work with adolescents and their families and has developed, with her colleagues, a model of brief psychoanalytic work with parents and adolescents in crisis.

In addition to her clinical work, Maria has taught on psychoanalytic ideas and adolescent development in various contexts, including at the UCL Department of Psychoanalysis, the IPCAPA Training in child and adolescent psychotherapy, the London Institute of Psychoanalysis, and the Sino-British training. She is a doctorate examiner for the Tavistock training in child and adolescent psychotherapy and was, for many years, one of the editors at the *Journal of Child Psychotherapy*. She has published widely in the field of adolescent development and has presented her work in conferences both in the UK and internationally. She is currently undertaking additional training towards the Advanced Standing Qualification in Couple Psychoanalytic Psychotherapy at Tavistock Relationships.

Dr Rachel Acheson is a child and adolescent psychotherapist trained at the Independent Psychoanalytic Child and Adolescent Psychotherapy Association (IPCAPA). Since qualifying, she has primarily worked with adolescents and has experience running a therapy service in an independent boarding school, as well as working within the NHS in crisis adolescent, generic, paediatric, and inpatient CAMHS teams and voluntary sector services. Her doctoral research focused on silence in adolescent psychotherapy, and she has published on this topic, as well as on work with adolescents and infant observation. She has taught on MSc courses at the Anna Freud Centre, Birkbeck and the Tavistock and is the editor-in-chief of the *Journal of Child Psychotherapy*.

Dr Nikolaos Tzikas trained as a child and adolescent psychotherapist within the Independent tradition at the British Psychotherapy Foundation (IPCAPA) in London, UK. He is a member of the Association of Child Psychotherapists (ACP) in London and of the Hellenic Child and Adolescent Psychoanalytic Psychotherapy Society.

He currently works in private practice in Athens, Greece, and is conducting research on a psychoanalytic tool he has developed to measure play both qualitatively and quantitatively in children aged 4 to 8 years.

Prior to this, he worked in private practice in London and in an NHS crisis team for adolescents and their families, offering both long- and short-term psychoanalytic therapy as well as group work. He has taught infant and young child observation seminars and worked for several years in an NHS specialist looked-after children (LAC) team in London. He has published research and presented his work at conferences in the UK and internationally.

Contributors

Dr Flavia Ansaldo is a child and adolescent psychotherapist trained at the British Psychotherapy Foundation (IPCAPA) and is a full member of the Association of Child Psychotherapists. Alongside her private practice, Flavia has been working across NHS Child and Adolescent Mental Health Services and third sector organisations for the past 15 years and has experience working with young people with a variety of moderate to severe emotional and behavioural difficulties, including anxiety, depression, eating disorders, self-harm, attachment difficulties, and neurodevelopmental conditions. Flavia also offers psychotherapeutic interventions to parents and carers, aiming to support them in their parenting role and in their understanding of their child's emotional needs, in the context of the wider family relational dynamics. Flavia is passionate about teaching and currently holds a senior lecturer's role within the child psychotherapy doctorate at the British Psychotherapy Foundation and University College London. Alongside her clinical practice and teaching, Flavia has a keen interest in research and has completed a doctorate in psychosocial studies at Birkbeck University.

Dr Eftychia Apostolidou is a child and adolescent psychotherapist trained within the Independent tradition (IPCAPA) at the British Psychotherapy Foundation (BPF) and the Anna Freud Centre (AFC). She is currently working in both a Looked-After and Adopted Children (LAAC) team and a Generic Team across two outer London Child and Adolescent Mental Health Services (CAMHS). Before training as a psychologist in Greece, Eftychia originally trained and worked as a nutritionist-dietician, where she developed a strong interest in eating disorders and the psychodynamics of eating and feeding. She worked as a researcher in the field of dietetics and later as both a researcher and a clinical assistant at the Anna Freud Centre, before completing her doctoral training at University College London (UCL).

Paul Bell is a consultant child and adolescent psychotherapist and the founder and clinical director of the Anchor Practice, a multidisciplinary child and adolescent private practice in Edinburgh. Paul trained in child and adolescent psychotherapy at the Tavistock and Portman NHS Foundation Trust in London and worked in a variety of specialist and community CAMHS teams across North London for 10 years, as well as in the charity sector, before moving into independent practice. In addition to his clinical work, Paul is a visiting lecturer in the Department of Psychology at the University of Edinburgh, and he also provides psychoanalytic consultation to a variety of schools across Edinburgh and the Lothians.

Rebecca Bolam is a child and adolescent psychotherapist who trained at the Tavistock and Portman NHS Foundation Trust. She currently works in a generic CAMHS team in Oxfordshire and teaches on the Perinatal, Child, Adolescent, and Family Work: A Psychoanalytic Observational Approach course, also at the Tavistock and Portman NHS Foundation Trust. Her doctoral research focused on the experience of child psychotherapists working with risky adolescents in generic CAMHS teams. Prior to becoming a child psychotherapist, she worked with unaccompanied asylum-seeking children (UASC), alongside a very different career as an ecologist, where she spent her time surveying grasslands as well as monitoring bat and amphibian populations.

Catherine Campbell is a child and adolescent psychotherapist who trained at the Tavistock and Portman NHS Foundation Trust. She has a particular interest in working with adolescents and is currently a senior psychotherapist at SAFE, the adolescent crisis team within Enfield CAMHS. She also works in private practice. Previously, she worked in a generic CAMHS team, in schools, and at Open Door, a voluntary sector therapy service for adolescents and young people.

Dr Jocelyn Catty is a child and adolescent psychoanalytic psychotherapist and a member of the Association of Child Psychotherapists (ACP) and co-lead for child psychotherapy at Bromley CAMHS. She has a DPhil in English literature and was the research lead for the doctoral training in child psychotherapy at the Tavistock Clinic from 2013 to 2023. She was a senior research fellow on the Wellcome-funded, interdisciplinary study Waiting Times from 2017 to 2023.

Victoria Hayward is a principal child and adolescent psychotherapist and parent service lead at Open Door, a voluntary sector mental health service for adolescents and young adults, in Haringey, London. She gained an undergraduate degree in social and political sciences from the University of Cambridge prior to training as a child and adolescent psychotherapist with IPCAPA at the British Psychotherapy Foundation. Over the last 14 years, Victoria has worked in community and specialist CAMHS teams, the charity sector, schools, and private practice. Working with parents of teenagers with mental health difficulties is an area of particular clinical interest – both as a practitioner and as a supervisor – and she is currently engaged in a research study to investigate the efficacy of an intervention for parents who feel they need support in understanding their adolescent's mental health when the adolescent themselves is not receiving any treatment. Victoria continues to be involved with the training of new child and adolescent psychotherapists, on both the IPCAPA and the Tavistock trainings, and additionally lectures and offers consultation to those in other professions who work with children and adolescents with complex emotional needs.

Kate Mills trained at IPCAPA (BPF). She has taught and supervised on both the clinical and pre-clinical stages of training and has published in the *British Journal of Psychotherapy* on experiences on menarche and menstruation, and in the *Czech Review of Psychoanalytic Psychotherapy* on the use of Anna Freud's diagnostic profile. Kate is particularly interested in the areas of identity, sexuality, and gender in work with adolescents, and in the treatment of complex trauma. Kate is the co-lead for psychotherapy at Bromley CAMHS and works in private practice at 10 Windsor Walk and at University College School.

Hillel Mirvis is a senior child and adolescent psychotherapist and service supervisor at Dunstable CAMHS and in private practice. He qualified at IPCAPA (BPF), where he is a training supervisor and a member of their training advisory group. He has a particular interest in working with adolescents struggling with developing their sense of identity, about which he has published several papers.

Fembe Nanji-Rowe is a child and adolescent psychotherapist in doctoral training at the Independent Psychoanalytic Child and Adolescent Psychotherapy Association (IPCAPA) and a trainee member of the Association of Child Psychotherapists (ACP) and British Psychotherapy Foundation (BPF). Fembe is in a full-time clinical placement across Enfield generic CAMHS and Enfield Service for Adolescents and Families (SAFE) (2022–2026). She has an active interest in cross-cultural phenomena and processes of mourning.

Dr Victoria Nicolodi is a child and adolescent psychotherapist who trained at the Independent Psychoanalytic Child and Adolescent Psychotherapy Association (IPCAPA) and the Anna Freud Centre (AFC/UCL). In addition to her qualifications in the UK, she previously trained as a clinical psychologist in Brazil. She is the founder of the Latin American Psychoanalytic Hub (LAPH). Over the years, Victoria's clinical practice has spanned across diverse therapeutic settings, and currently, she works in the community by supporting adoptive parents and their toddlers and holds a position within the NHS, working with care-experienced children and young people.

Ruth Schmidt Neven, PhD, is a child and adolescent psychotherapist and clinical psychologist. She trained at the Tavistock Clinic in London and worked in adult and in child and family mental health services in the NHS for close to 20 years. She was a pioneer in parent support as joint director of the national charitable organisation Exploring Parenthood in the UK. Ruth now lives and works in Melbourne, Australia. She was the inaugural chief psychotherapist at the Royal Children's Hospital, where she established a child psychotherapy clinic and developed in-house training for paediatricians, as well as a clinical development programme for mental health professionals in the community. In her current role as the director of the Centre for Child and Family Development, she offers clinical services as well as professional training and consultation carried out throughout Australia and overseas. As a prolific author, her papers and books on child development and psychotherapy are reading texts in university courses and training institutions. Her earlier publication *Emotional Milestones: Development from birth to adulthood* was published by the Australian Council for Educational Research and Jessica Kingsley in the UK. *Rethinking ADHD*, of which she was the lead author, was published by Allen & Unwin and also translated into Japanese. Ruth's recent publications include *Core Principles of Assessment and Therapeutic Communication with Children Parents and Families* and *Time-Limited Psychodynamic Psychotherapy with Children and Adolescents*, both published by Routledge. Ruth has a lifelong commitment to disseminate information about child and family development in the wider community and is the presenter of the podcast series Talking Child Development.

Preface

Working with adolescents in crisis, while keeping the therapeutic spirit alive, demands more than simply applying established mechanical methods, safety planning, or risk protocols. It requires openness, flexibility, self-containment, and the capacity to think alongside young people, their families, and their networks during times of acute difficulty, when things can change from one moment to the next. Psychoanalytic approaches, with their emphasis on meaning, relationship, and unconscious communication, offer a framework that can hold these complexities while still responding to the urgency of crisis work.

This volume brings together contributions that illustrate how psychoanalytic thinking can inform assessment, therapeutic intervention, and collaboration with the wider network around young people in crisis. The authors, all psychoanalytic child and adolescent psychotherapist at different stages of their professional careers, share clinical accounts, theoretical reflections, and service-based perspectives. Together, the chapters in this book convey not only the challenges but also the *possibilities and pleasures* of working psychoanalytically with adolescents in crisis.

The book will be of value to new and experienced clinicians alike – psychoanalytic child and adolescent psychotherapists foremost, but also psychologists, psychiatrists, and other professionals working with young people and families in distress. It might also be of interest to those concerned with the broader social and institutional contexts in which adolescent crises unfold.

Maria Papadima trained as a child and adolescent psychotherapist at the Independent Psychoanalytic Child and Adolescent Psychotherapy Association in London, UK, after completing a PhD on trauma and psychoanalysis. She works in London with adolescents, young adults, and parents at an NHS team and privately. She has a longstanding interest in therapeutic work with adolescents (brief and long-term), including parent and adolescent work during crisis. Maria teaches and supervises at the IPCAPA training and other institutions and has published widely on clinical work with adolescents.

Rachel Acheson trained as a child and adolescent psychotherapist at the Independent Psychoanalytic Child and Adolescent Psychotherapy Association (IPCAPA) in London. Since qualifying, she has specialised in work with adolescents and their families, working within the NHS, voluntary, and schools' sectors. She now lives in Northern Ireland and continues to work clinically, teach, and supervise. She is Editor-in-Chief of the *Journal of Child Psychotherapy*.

Nikolaos Tzikas trained as a child and adolescent psychotherapist in London, UK. He has worked in NHS specialist services for looked-after and adopted children, as well as in an NHS team supporting adolescents and families in crisis, alongside his private practice. He now lives in Athens, Greece, where he works privately and holds a postdoctoral fellowship dedicated to developing and researching a psychoanalytic tool for assessing play. His longstanding interest lies in working with children and adolescents, particularly in exploring how play and playing manifest across different ages.

Acknowledgements

We are very grateful to all the authors who contributed to this volume for their generosity, insight, and commitment to this shared project. Their work has made this book possible, and their ideas on how to work therapeutically with adolescents in crisis continue to inspire us every day in our work.

We would like to thank the series editors, Ann Horne and Teresa Bailey, as well as the publishing team at Routledge, for their patience, encouragement, and editorial support.

All three of us want to acknowledge and thank our colleagues (and ex-colleagues, for those who have left) at the SAFE adolescent team in Enfield CAMHS, from whom we have learned so much over the years. Working in this excellent adolescent crisis team has been like a second training for each of us. In particular, we want to thank Catherine Young, Liz Doherty, Dr Raj Sekaran, Dr Mark Nathan, Angela Marsh, and Catherine Campbell, without whom the adolescent service we have all worked in would not have been the same.

We want to extend our deepest gratitude to our adolescent patients. It is through their trust, openness, and courage in sharing their thoughts and experiences that we have continued to learn and grow. This book is, first and foremost, for them – a reflection of the journeys we have shared and the meanings we have sought to build together.

We are grateful to our partners, families, and friends for their support and for the many discussions that helped shape this book as it developed.

This book is dedicated to our parents, Mahi, Yannis, Alison, Brian, Dimitris, and Theodora.

Introduction

*Maria Papadima, Rachel Acheson,
and Nikolaos Tzikas*

Like other authors and editors who have contributed to the Independent
Psychoanalytic Approaches with Children and Adolescents series before us, we
often turn to one of Winnicott's most resonant passages from 'The aims of psycho-
analytical treatment' (1962):

> I enjoy myself doing analysis and I always look forward to the end of each
> analysis. Analysis for analysis' sake has no meaning for me. I do analysis
> because that is what the patient needs to have done and to have done with. If the
> patient does not need analysis then I do something else.
>
> (Winnicott, 1962/1965, p. 166)

In working with adolescents in crisis, the paradox of 'doing something else' – or,
in truth, 'doing (at least) two things at once' – becomes central. The urgency of a
crisis and the distress it can cause both the adolescent and adults around them add
immediate pressure, while our task of holding meaning and sustaining a therapeutic
atmosphere – a space where meaningful conversations can happen, where we can
think rather than react – remains.

Psychoanalytic work in this field requires two things that at first glance appear
opposite: *immediacy and depth*. It demands, in the moment of crisis, attentiveness to
unconscious processes, alongside a capacity for practical, responsive engagement
with families, schools, and services – while always being aware of the sociocultural
and peer contexts in which the crisis unfolds. The authors and editors of this book
try to hold this set of paradoxes seriously yet lightly, showing how we can work
well within them.

This book brings together clinicians who have all worked with adolescents
and their families in crisis, from a range of perspectives and settings. While all
contributors – including the three editors – are psychoanalytic child and adolescent
psychotherapists, the chapters in this volume reflect the diversity of contexts in
which crisis work takes place: from public sector (NHS) teams to schools, from
research to work with parents, and from the consulting room to the broader social
frameworks that shape our understanding of crisis.

DOI: 10.4324/9781003592778-1

Part 1 opens with broad reflections on adolescence itself – how adolescents live today and the contexts within which their crises occur. *Flavia Ansaldo* (chapter 1) offers a developmental view of adolescence at the meeting point of inner and outer realities, drawing on both classical psychoanalytic and contemporary developmental thinking. *Rachel Acheson and Maria Papadima* (chapter 2) explore the formation of adolescent identity within today's 'mental health crisis', discussing how diagnostic language has become an ordinary part of adolescents' sense of self. *Jocelyn Catty* (chapter 3) brings a temporal lens to suicidal crisis, proposing that adolescence may be understood as a crisis of time itself, and arguing that psychotherapy offers containment through time.

Part 2 turns to foundational clinical concepts crucial to crisis work: crisis, risk, self-harm, and suicidality. *Maria Papadima* (chapter 4) traces the cultural and historical meanings of these terms and the ways they inform clinical understanding. *Hillel Mirvis* (chapter 5) looks in depth at the multiple and sometimes unexpected meanings of adolescent overdose, often reduced in the existing literature to a single phenomenon. He proposes that, instead, we can think of adolescent overdose as an unconscious communication worth deciphering. *Maria Papadima* (chapter 6) returns to the theme of self-harm, situating cutting as a contemporary symptom that can be understood both psychoanalytically and socioculturally. *Nikolaos Tzikas* (chapter 7) offers a psychoanalytic framework for assessing suicide risk, which he names the 'TIER' model. It integrates crisis formulation and psychodynamic understanding of what may lie beneath the surface.

Part 3 expands the frame to include the wider networks within which crises emerge and are held – parents, schools, teams, and institutions. *Ruth Schmidt Neven* (chapter 8) argues for reconfiguring adolescent–parent psychotherapy, placing the parent–adolescent relationship at the heart of crisis work, rather than an afterthought. *Victoria Hayward and Paul Bell* (chapter 9) bring experience from Open Door, and adolescent and young adult mental health service in London, showing how parent work can be transformative when the adolescent refuses direct engagement. *Rachel Acheson and Catherine Campbell* (chapter 10) explore therapeutic collaboration with schools in order to help adolescents remain connected to education while supporting staff by working closely with clinicians. *Rebecca Bolam* (chapter 11) examines how an adolescent's and family's crisis reverberates within NHS CAMHS teams, themselves under significant strain. *Eftychia Apostolidou, Victoria Nicolodi, and Nikolaos Tzikas* (chapter 12) focus on looked-after adolescents, offering a way of thinking about crises as 'cries' that often express earlier trauma and entangled network dynamics.

Part 4 brings together contemporary psychoanalytic perspectives on individual adolescent crisis work. *Maria Papadima, Catherine Campbell, Nikolaos Tzikas and Fembe Nanji-Rowe* (chapter 13) describe a pilot study of brief psychodynamic psychotherapy for parents and adolescents in crisis, developed within an NHS crisis team in London. *Kate Mills* (chapter 14) reflects on how to maintain lightness and playfulness in psychotherapy with high-risk adolescents: how can play survive – or even emerge for the first time – under the shadow of fear and risk? Finally, *Nikolaos Tzikas* (chapter 15) closes the volume by reflecting on the therapist's function in using countertransference, reverie, dreaming, and metaphor in work with adolescents at risk.

Across these sections, certain themes recur: the need to balance urgency with depth; the importance of creating time and space to think (and feel) rather than only react; the value of engaging not only with the adolescent but also with their families, peers, and institutions; and the recognition that cultural background, language, and social pressures shape the form crises take.

A central idea of this volume is that adolescent crisis can be understood not merely as a problem to be eliminated but as an opportunity for meaning-making and communication. All the chapters share a psychoanalytic sensibility: attention to unconscious communication, to the meanings embedded in symptoms, and to the possibility of change and communication even in acute states of mind.

In line with the Independent tradition within which this volume sits, all contributions are inspired by Donald Winnicott's and other Independents' emphasis on meeting the adolescent where they are, on pragmatism, and on attention to both internal and external realities. The work we do with adolescents in crisis is not 'standard analysis', if there is such a thing. But despite its applied nature, we believe it is profoundly psychoanalytic.

We hope this collection conveys the texture and aliveness – and even the pleasures – of psychoanalytic engagement with adolescents and their families in crisis, and that it will spark renewed reflection and practice in this field. We believe in the vital contribution psychoanalytic clinicians can make in this area, particularly within crisis teams, and in the value of relational, developmental approaches to adolescent crisis – rather than a purely diagnostic or symptom-based checklist approach. It is in this spirit that we share these ideas.

Reference

Winnicott, D. W. (1962/1965). The aims of psycho-analytical treatment. *The Maturational Processes and the Facilitating Environment: Studies in the Theory of Emotional Development*, 64, 166–170.

Part 1

Chapter 1

Adolescence at the intersection of inner and outer realities

A conceptualisation

Flavia Ansaldo

Introduction

This chapter explores key developmental features of adolescence and how they manifest in psychoanalytic psychotherapy. My aim is to reflect on adolescence as a dynamic intersection between internal psychic life, traditionally the focus of psychoanalysis, and external sociocultural influences, which increasingly shape the adolescent's experience. John Keats (1818), in the poem *'Endymion'*, described adolescence as a 'space of life between', which highlights its transitional nature and fluidity. We might begin with a simple but fundamental question: how do we define adolescence? Can we even offer a universal definition? And does adolescence, as a concept, exist in all times and cultures?

Definitions

It seems clear that adolescence is not a fixed phase but a socially and culturally shaped process. While this chapter is grounded in a psychoanalytic and developmental framework, it acknowledges that adolescence is a *psychosocial* construct – one that reflects and responds to the wider cultural, historical, and relational contexts in which it unfolds.

In many ways, adolescence mirrors the society in which it takes place, while also shaping it in return. Here is how this happens: the adolescent mirrors him-or herself and is shaped by social processes. In turn, society is shaped and deeply affected by adolescent processes. Later in the chapter, I will refer to Winnicott's ideas on how the ways that society understands and responds to the manifestations of adolescence reflect the state of health of the society itself (Winnicott, 1961). The World Health Organization offers a comprehensive definition of adolescence that touches on its key features, including physical, cognitive, emotional, and social aspects:

> Adolescence is the phase of life between childhood and adulthood, from ages 10 to 19. It is a unique stage of human development and an important time for laying the foundations of good health. Adolescents experience rapid physical, cognitive and psychosocial growth. This affects how they feel, think, make decisions, and interact with the world around them.
>
> (World Health Organization, n.d.)

DOI: 10.4324/9781003592778-3

To this definition I would add that the adolescent process not only interacts with the external environment but is also influenced by the societal frame surrounding the individual. This societal context significantly affects the adolescent trajectory.

My perspective is informed by my clinical work as a psychoanalytic psychotherapist in the UK, and I recognise that this context inevitably informs the way I conceptualise adolescence and its presentations in clinical settings. Systemic and psychosocial thinking can helpfully contextualise our intrapsychic understanding of every period of life, impacting how we can reframe and respond to adolescent manifestations and *what can be done*.

Another important question when conceptualising adolescence is: what are its time and space boundaries? Where does childhood end, and when does adulthood begin? While the WHO describes adolescence as 'the phase of life between 10 and 19 years old' (WHO on adolescent health), there is no universally agreed duration of adolescence, given that its time boundaries are primarily socially constructed and thus fluid. In some cultures, adolescence refers strictly to the period of time during which physical maturation occurs: once this is completed, so is adolescence. In other cultures, such as our own contemporary Western context, it is increasingly common to view adolescence as extending well beyond the teenage years and the completion of physical growth – into the early or even late twenties.

In our Western societies, contemporary adolescents could be seen as, in psychoanalyst Peter Blos's words, 'late bloomers' (Blos, 1979): the gap between biological and psychosocial maturation is getting wider, and adolescents tend to feel and behave like adolescents until later and later in their twenties, as mentioned. At the same time, in our society we are also witnessing the exact opposite trend, an 'early blooming' – with children being exposed from younger ages to sexualised content and images (particularly through social media), which we can speculate has an impact on their sense of self and their maturing bodies and minds. These are only some of the many cultural and social particularities when it comes to *what adolescence is*.

Early, mid-, and late adolescence

The time boundaries of adolescence can thus vary enormously depending on a number of different factors. I've noted already that within Western cultures, adolescence seems to extend nowadays beyond the end of the teen years, well into the mid- to late twenties. Despite this fluidity in boundaries, still, it is useful to distinguish developmental stages within this prolonged period: early, mid-, and late adolescence.

Stephen Briggs (2008) offers a helpful 'two phase' model: 'early' adolescence, beginning with puberty, is marked by intense physical, emotional, and cognitive change. Then mid- to late adolescence reflects the transition into young adulthood, shaped as much by social context as by internal processes. To these I would add 'young adulthood' as a distinct but closely related phase. Holding these stages in mind helps us to understand the adolescent's psychic tasks and difficulties in a nuanced way and, thus, is a key part of the wider developmental focus of this chapter. In order to understand emotional development in adolescence, we can start by looking at the emotional processes during infancy, as the way these unfold lays the foundations for how adolescent processes are negotiated and for what the outcome may be. Let's start with a summary of the relevant theory on early emotional processes, mainly through a Winnicottian and Anna Freudian lens.

A Winnicottian and Anna Freudian conceptualisation of early emotional development

The body, which is *centre stage* in the adolescent drama, previously, at the beginning of life, also held centre stage. In very early life, the infant is still undifferentiated from their environment. Anna Freud (1958), and before her Sigmund Freud (1923), presented the idea of a *bodily* ego at the start of life, which offers us an image for this undifferentiated state.

In one of her developmental lines (Anna Freud, 1963), Anna Freud presented the child's transition from physical towards mental pathways of discharge: at the beginning of life, every form of stimulation, physical or mental, goes through the body. In the first year of life, the infant mainly responds to internal and external stimuli through bodily responses. Gradually, supported by a *facilitating environment* (Winnicott, 1965), the young child develops increasingly sophisticated and symbolic pathways for mental discharge. This typically happens in the second and third years, as symbolic play and speech develop.

The facilitating environment

But what did Winnicott mean by the facilitating environment (1965)? The responsive and attuned caregiver (which Winnicott often referred to as the 'ordinary devoted mother' (Winnicott, 1949)) *is* the infant's facilitating environment (Winnicott, 1965) and provides the scaffolding for the developing ego.

Even though Winnicott mostly referred to the role of the mother-environment, nowadays it makes more sense to refer to the concept of maternal function, which transcends the caregiver's biological gender and encompasses the object's containing, ego-supportive function. Any future reference to 'maternal' will thus refer to the concept of maternal function in this broader sense, much like the concept of paternal function, which refers to any person (or institution) in the child's life that promotes healthy separation and internalisation of boundaries and societal rules, irrespective of their gender. Winnicott drew our attention to the importance, during infancy, of a repeated occurrence of body care experiences provided by the good enough parent. Concepts such as holding and handling refer to the ability of the caregiver, who is in identification with the infant's needs, to provide repeated, attuned experiences of meeting the infant's physical (bodily) and emotional needs in a timely and adaptive way, leading to increasing ego strength.

On the contrary, failures in maternal adaptation can lead to a lasting sense of the body as a foreign object that cannot become integrated into the psyche and which can feel alien and disconnected, becoming a source of anxiety instead of pleasure.

Continuity of being

Maternal adaptation to the infant's needs allows an experience of continuity of being, facilitating the development of the illusion of having created the object (the breast) out of need, through an act of primary creativity. At this early stage, the object is subjectively perceived, meaning that it is not differentiated from the subject and is located within the arena of omnipotence. Emotionally and developmentally, it needs to be perceived in this way. The ordinary devoted mother (Winnicott, 1949) intuitively fosters the infant's illusion of omnipotence for long enough to allow the ego to develop and strengthen. Any premature awareness of the separateness of the other, such as when the infant's needs are not met consistently enough, constitutes an impingement and a fracture in the infant's experience of continuity of being.

Over time, as the infant's ego grows stronger and maternal adaptation lessens, the object can gradually be perceived as separate and as distinct from the self, and this is the start of more mature object relationships. The gap between self and other, between inner and outer realities, can not only be survived but also be used as a cornerstone of future emotional development, particularly the development of symbolic functioning and our ability to live within the intermediate arena of transitional phenomena (Winnicott, 1958a). Where the awareness of separateness is introduced gradually and with enough ego strength, the infant is able to make use of the temporary absence of the object to their advantage, with the 'gap' between self and other being filled creatively and symbolically. The classic example of this would be the child's ability to 'create' their first transitional objects (e.g. a special stuffed animal or blanket) and derive comfort from this. According to Winnicott and Anna Freud, these more sophisticated, symbolic pathways of expression that we see, for example, in the child who communicates through words and play, go hand in hand with significant developments in ego strength and integration. The ego can now derive pleasure (instead of being overwhelmed) by instinctual gratification and can perceive external objects and reality as separate, governed by principles of time and space. In Freudian terms, we can think of this as the transition from the pleasure principle to the reality principle, laying the foundations for emotional regulation. Emotions that are symbolically represented in the psyche can be 'digested' and thought about. In contrast, early environmental failure and trauma can cause feeling states and experiences to remain unrepresented and unrepresentable and thus to be expressed via the body. The capacity for symbol formation enables us to enjoy a creative life, including connection with and enjoyment of our physical body. This underlies our capacity for fulfilling relationships, play, work, artistic creation, and all other cultural expressions. The adolescent task involves a renewed process of symbolisation, including a symbolic appropriation and integration of the mature body (Levy, 2018; Ruggiero, 2011), and a gradual transition from the vocabulary of action to the vocabulary of thinking and dreaming (Nicolò & Ruggiero, 2016).

In what follows, I will discuss adolescent development from a psychoanalytic perspective and will then address the developmental challenges adolescents face in regard to identity formation, body representation, and object relations.

Adolescence within the classic psychoanalytic perspective

Adolescence constitutes by definition an interruption of peaceful growth.
(Freud, 1958, p. 266)

Throughout her life, Anna Freud placed emphasis on studying, as a priority, ordinary child development. Only by deepening our understanding of ordinary child development, she thought, can we make progress in understanding the causes and treatment of pathological conditions.

So a solid understanding of normality in adolescence offers us the benchmark that we need to understand those adolescents who deviate from the norm. Inevitably, this benchmark is by no means universal and varies enormously across social and cultural contexts. But we do find some general patterns that are worth keeping in mind.

The psychosexual developmental stages

Historically, classic psychoanalysis paid limited attention to the study of adolescence as a developmental phase in its own right. Anna Freud noted this omission and sought to address it.

There were some exceptions to this tendency. For example, in 'Three essays on the theory of sexuality', Sigmund Freud described the onset of puberty as the moment when: 'changes set in which are destined to give infantile sexual life its final, normal shape. The sexual instinct has hitherto been predominantly auto-erotic; it now finds a sexual object' (Freud, 1905, p. 207).

From a classical psychoanalytic perspective, adolescence corresponds to the gradual establishment of what Freud named the genital phase of psychosexual development. Thus, the transition from latency – the routine-based and calmer period of the primary school years – leads to the genital stage, where the genitals become the dominant erotogenic zone.

After the tribulations of the pre-Oedipal and Oedipal phases – the time of early childhood passions – in latency the intensity of the child's drives usually lessens, though recently this view has been challenged, and it has been argued that within latency, too, there are important developmental shifts and storms (Maroudas et al., 2023). In ordinary circumstances, children during latency expand their developmental focus and grow socially and intellectually, while becoming increasingly able to adapt to reality and to internalise social rules and expectations. There is an overall sense of instinctual calmness during this phase, perhaps the calm before the storm of adolescence.

According to this classic psychosexual developmental model, the establishment of puberty places the genitals at the centre, as the dominant erotogenic zone. The phase-specific tasks during this period include the definition of new sexual aims (female or male) and the seeking of sexual objects outside the family.

Freud described this period as involving a gradual reawakening of the drives, both libidinal (sexual) and aggressive, alongside visible bodily changes and hormonal fluctuations, with new sensory and sensual experiences and the appearance of secondary sexual characteristics. All this is unsettling for the young adolescent. He or she is faced with the complex task of psychic reorganisation – revisiting previous phases, including pre-Oedipal and Oedipal material, but from the standpoint of a maturing body that is now (potentially) physically able to actualise Oedipal wishes, both sexual and aggressive, as well as having a shifting social position.

But adolescence is more than a revisitation of previous developmental stages. It involves new psychological achievements and challenges – a point that later psychoanalysts would more fully develop.

Continuity and discontinuity

Contemporary psychoanalytic thinking views adolescence as a unique and transformative phase. It carries powerful developmental forces, the result being more than the sum of its infantile parts. There are thus elements of both continuity with earlier development and discontinuity – the emergence of something fundamentally new. We can think of adolescence as a catalyst: it activates latent aspects of the psyche, creating both turbulence and opportunity for growth. Thus, the adolescent wants to move forward while, at the same time, craving the safety of earlier life.

In classic psychoanalytic thinking, because of the initial exciting discoveries around infantile sexuality, adolescence was relegated to the role of the 'step child', a developmental stage whose task is to finalise the shape of the psychosexual development that begins in infancy. But adolescence involves much more than simply shaping infantile sexuality into its final form.

Contemporary thinking has broadened the focus to encompass what is unique to adolescence, seeing it as a crucial second opportunity for growth, healing, and recovery. Recent advancements in neuroscience underline the profound neurological changes happening in adolescence, particularly the heightened neuroplasticity.

The transformative developmental tasks of adolescence include integrating the sexed and changing body into the personality, renegotiating attachment to, and separation from, parental figures, and achieving individuation, all while mourning the loss of childhood and its bravado and omnipotence. Gradually, aggression becomes integrated, needing to be rebound with libido in the service of development and culminating ultimately in the establishment of a separate identity. These tasks require not only psychic resilience but also a holding environment – both internal and external – that can support the adolescent in managing new and unfamiliar anxieties.

Adolescent identity – Sturm und Drang

The study of adolescence is a fairly recent object in psychology. Stanley Hall's first published book on adolescence in 1904 (Hall, 1904) marked the beginning of viewing adolescence as a complex developmental construct, encompassing biological and psychological dimensions. Described as a period of passion, suffering, confusion, and idealism, adolescence is an age of 'storm and stress' (Sturm und Drang) (Hall, 1904).

Identity formation and wider culture

A central developmental task in adolescence is the formation of a coherent, adult sense of identity. Erik Erikson (1968) described this as the core developmental conflict of adolescence: identity versus role confusion. But identity is not shaped in a vacuum; individual identities are rooted within biographical, social, cultural, and relational context.

For example, in contemporary Western societies, individualistic tendencies prevail. Adolescents are encouraged to 'find themselves' independently, yet this expectation – and the resulting tension between individual and collective needs – can create friction (Briggs, 2008). Recognising that identity formation is rooted in societal processes highlights the crucial impact of factors such as ethnicity, gender, and sexual orientation (Institute of Medicine & National Research Council, 2011). The more culturally diverse a society, the wider the repertoire of identities the adolescent can draw upon to embrace or discard. This process can be particularly tumultuous for young people from minority backgrounds, who may feel caught between the cultural and religious values of their family of origin and the value system of the society where they live and socialise.

Case example

Alyssa, a 15-year-old girl from a Bangladeshi background, was referred to a CAMHS team by her school following escalating difficulties at home. Her parents, first-generation immigrants from a Muslim background, had moved to London as young adults. Alyssa attended a large, inner-city state school, surrounded by peers from a wide range of cultural backgrounds.

As adolescence set in, the family began to experience high levels of conflict. In response, her parents adopted an increasingly authoritarian approach — imposing stricter rules, limiting her freedom, and responding to defiance with punishment. The situation reached a crisis point, at which point Alyssa ran away from home. She was missing for several hours, triggering understandable panic within the family and wider community.

During the assessment, Alyssa spoke of feeling caught between two conflicting realities. On the one hand, her parents' expectations were clear and rigid: she was to behave in a respectful, modest, and 'adult-like' way – calm, responsible, and compliant. On the other hand, Alyssa was immersed in a peer culture where adolescence was expressed through experimentation, rebellion, and boundary-testing. She described this cultural split as deeply confusing, saying she felt 'torn, misunderstood, and lost'.

Her parents, meanwhile, felt helpless and frightened – unsure how to contain her behaviour and increasingly afraid they had somehow failed. Their fear was not only personal but also culturally amplified: in addition to their worry about Alyssa, they were concerned with how the extended family and community would view her behaviour and, by extension, their parenting.

This case vividly illustrates how identity formation becomes more complex when adolescents have to navigate multiple cultural frameworks. For Alyssa, the conflict was not simply between adolescence and authority but between belonging and betrayal – of her peers, her family, her background, and her emerging self.

Therapeutically, I felt it was essential to offer Alyssa an individual space where she could safely voice her ambivalence and begin to explore a more integrated identity. Equally important was to offer her parents a parallel space to reflect on the cultural gap between their own adolescent experience and that of their daughter and to begin reframing Alyssa's struggles not as disobedience but as part of a developmentally appropriate process unfolding in a very different social context.

As a White therapist, I was also aware of the initial mistrust Alyssa's parents expressed toward me – a perception that, because of our difference, I might be aligned with their daughter or unable to truly appreciate the significance of their cultural values. Building trust and fuller engagement with them took time. Gradually, it became possible for them to experience that, although I came from a different background, I was able to hold both perspectives in mind – appreciating the depth and meaning of their position while also maintaining a developmental lens on Alyssa's needs. This bridging of perspectives was, in itself, part of the therapeutic task.

Cultural frames and rites of passage: an unpredictable collective frame

More generally, I have also wondered whether ideas around separation, individuation, and the instability of identity are more pronounced in Western societies, where adolescence takes on a distinctive form as a process towards separation.

Encyclopaedia Brittanica (n.d.) notes:

Historically, many societies instituted formal ways for older individuals to help young people take their place in the community. Initiations, vision quests, the Hindu samskara life-cycle rituals, and other ceremonies or rites of passage helped young men and women make the transition from childhood to adulthood. An outstanding feature of such coming-of-age rites was their emphasis upon instruction in proper dress, deportment, morality, and other behaviours appropriate to adult status.

This captures the paradoxical nature of adolescence. Such rites of passage, which many adolescents in Western societies might view as restrictive – challenging their individuality – may nevertheless provide a clearer, more certain collective frame compared to the uncertainties of Western societies.

As discussed, previous generations went through adolescence within a clearer, more predictable collective frame: the normative trajectory from childhood, through adolescence, and into adulthood usually involved a series of pre-defined steps, mostly within the heteronormative context of marriage and parenthood. Now, the emphasis in most Western cultures is on the individual's right to self-determination, expression, and actualisation, meaning that identity formation takes place among countless opportunities and possibilities. While in some ways a sign of progress, these changes can bring about a protracted transition from adolescence to young adulthood, filled with opportunities as well as uncertainties and anxieties.

Erik Erikson (1968), as part of his description of life's psychosocial stages, introduced the idea of a 'psychosocial moratorium' – a socially sanctioned pause between childhood and adulthood, between the biological transition in early adolescence (puberty) and the actual taking up of adult roles in society. This liminal space, for a few years, allows adolescents to try on the different identity 'hats' available on the societal shelf without having to commit prematurely, until they are developmentally ready to settle on a firmer trajectory. But the fluidity and uncertainty of this identity 'moratorium' can also be a period of confusion and anxiety – a challenging developmental task both for individuals and society.

The satisfactory resolution of this period hinges largely, though not solely, on how earlier developmental phases were negotiated. So as I've already discussed, to understand adolescence fully, we have to understand the early emotional building blocks of development. As such, before delving further into an exploration of adolescence, I will now summarise the main principles of early emotional development underpinning the theory and practice illustrated in this book.

The adolescent ego is first and foremost a bodily ego

If adolescence were a theatre, the body would be centre stage. Behind the scenes, we would find a tumultuous relationship between psychic structures and drives. This backstage activity is largely (although not entirely!) responsible for the onstage actions of the main character (the adolescent) and the rest of the actors (his object world, both old and new). The audience, metaphorically representing society, is a crucial component in the unfolding of the adolescent drama, shaping its course with its mirroring, emotional responses, attitudes, and expectations.

The loss of the fantasied ideal adult body

This section looks into the adolescent centre stage – the body – and its intricate relationship with the backstage: the ego and the superego. In early adolescence, marked by the onset of puberty, a main developmental task involves the gradual psychic integration of the sexually mature body. As the pubescent body enters the scene, the young adolescent embarks on a tumultuous process of reorganising self and other representations, both evolving dramatically. Feelings of awkwardness, shame, clumsiness, and dissatisfaction with the changing body are common experiences for the young adolescent. While the child still holds out hope for their fantasied, ideal adult body, young adolescents are faced with the real, imperfect body that doesn't match their infantile fantasies. This can lead to feelings of disillusionment and loss (Levy, 2018).

With the surge of drives during adolescence, lapses in the young person's ability to firmly grasp reality and to rely on symbolic functioning occur. The adolescent's body may once again feel alien and even out of control. The intellectualised latency child now leaves the stage, giving their place to the unruly adolescent, who may often replace words (and thought) with action, sometimes presenting impulsive and risk-taking behaviours. Blos (1967, p. 174) refers to this as the 'action language' or 'body language' of adolescence, driven by the ordinary regression of ego states.

The ego under pressure

Anna Freud, focusing on the ego as the 'seat of observation' (Sandler & Freud, 1980), explored adolescent development, noting the reawakening and intensification of drive activity after a 'truce' during latency, when the drives had calmed down. This resurgence includes pregenital and new genital urges, together with the hormonal and physical changes at the onset of puberty. Given the growing sexuality and strength of the pubertal body and the resurfacing of pregenital fantasies – which now have the potential to be actualised, particularly Oedipal ones – the ego can feel under pressure. All these shifts lead to what Anna Freud described as the 'inevitable interruption of peaceful growth' (1958, p. 267).

The ego attempts to accommodate the changes that are happening and to integrate more mature forms of sexuality – including the sexually mature body itself – into the existing structure of the personality. She writes:

> [T]hreatened with the anxiety by the drive development, the ego, as it's been formed in childhood enters into a struggle for survival, in which all the available methods of defence are brought into play and strained to the most.
>
> (1958, p. 257)

In ordinary development, the extreme use of defence mechanisms tends to be temporary. It leads to the eventual establishment of a mature, well-integrated personality. In pathology, defences continue to be clung to, making it hard for the adolescent to enter adulthood with enough ego strength and integration. While it is normal for the ego and id to feel at war, and for defences to be employed to manage the resulting anxiety, their excessive use can lead to pathological presentations in adolescence.

A symbolic re-organisation

Looking at all this together, we can say that the developmental task of adolescence demands a gradual adaptation to the reality of the changing body, integrating this acceptance into the adolescent's personality structure. However, this process can generate significant anxiety and can fracture the adolescent's continuity of being. Successful integration of the pubescent body into the psychic structure largely depends on how the pre-pubertal body was experienced and represented internally, influenced by the quality of the relationship with primary objects (Levy, 2018). When there has been a lapse in symbolic function, the adolescent is required to reinstate and reconstruct their self, including body representation, within the symbolic realm.

The psychic work of symbolic reorganisation of the body, starting with puberty (Levy, 2018), continues throughout later stages of adolescence. It involves a transition from perceiving the body as a concrete, foreign object to symbolically appropriating it as belonging to the self. Before this transition is complete, the dramatic bodily changes may lead to a perception of the body as belonging simultaneously *inside and outside the self* – at the border dimension of being and having (Ladame & Perret-Catipovic, 1999). Achieving a sense of 'being in the body that one has' underlies the successful integration of mind and body, contrasting with the experience of merely *having* a body. The latter carries the risk of a split between psychic and bodily experiences, whereby the adolescent may experience their body as foreign and alien. This experience, in some cases, could persist beyond the normative turmoil of adolescence.

So what happens when anxiety is so intense that these ordinary developmental processes are disrupted and the ego becomes overwhelmed?

Developmental breakdown: the body as battleground

Moses and Eglé Laufer (2018) offered a psychoanalytic understanding of 'developmental breakdown' in adolescence. For them, pathology at this stage reflects a breakdown in the capacity to synthesise the changes of puberty – particularly the sexual body – into the self.

In healthy development, the adolescent comes to experience the body as libidinally invested, owned, and experienced as unified. In developmental breakdown, by contrast, the body is experienced as alien, a forceful, threatening, even persecutory object, to which the adolescent has to submit passively. The body is felt to be external rather than internal, leaving little room for age-appropriate exploration (both in terms of masturbation and first sexual experiences), potentially leading to a psychotic-type break from reality, sometimes manifesting in behaviours that attempt to omnipotently regain control of the body, including self-harm and suicide attempts, but also eating disorders and substance abuse. In seeing self-harm and suicide as attacks on the body, we see that the adolescent tries to reverse the passive relation to the body into an active one, with them now being in charge. Underlying this frantic activity, the adolescent may hold a fantasy of preserving their body in its prepubescent state, rendering it harmless in both its pregenital and genital urges. Even though this negation of the body is likely to be rooted a long way back developmentally, originating at the Oedipal or even pre-Oedipal stages, the conflict we see in adolescent breakdown becomes active as a result of the physical and sexual maturation of puberty.

Case example

Flora was nearly 14 when her parents contacted me for an initial consultation. In the consultation, they expressed their worry about Flora's seeming depression. She appeared withdrawn recently; in addition, they had just discovered that she was self-harming by cutting her forearms with a blade.

Flora was an only child, and her parents' relationship had broken down a long time ago, without a formal separation. Flora had always been closer to her dad, with the relationship with her mother being a lot more conflictual. Since Flora started self-harming, the parents commented on how she tended to cover her cuts with a visible bandage, drawing attention to them, while apparently 'hiding' them. At times, Flora allowed her father to change her bandages, clean her cuts, and apply a soothing cream to her healing skin.

This vignette illustrates some of the concepts discussed in this section on psychosexual development in adolescence. While the origin of Flora's distress was multifactorial, I focus on how aspects of her stunted Oedipal development clashed with the onset of the adolescent process, contributing to a developmental breakdown. There is no doubt that Flora's tense home situation, and her parents' broken-down yet unresolved relationship, had created shaky developmental foundations for the turbulent processes of adolescence.

In this family landscape, with Oedipal dynamics so alive and present, one could assume that Flora's sexually developing body represented an enormous threat in her mind, making room for Oedipal wishes to become potentially actualised, with Flora's mother representing a defeated yet lingering Oedipal rival. Flora's cutting could be seen as an attack on her sexually maturing body, with the associated omnipotent fantasy of being able to stop her body from further growth and development, and from feeling alien, out of control and potentially 'dangerous'.

The changing of the bandages and the treatment of her cuts by her father can be thought about as a type of infantile body-care experience, which lured Flora into a false sense of security, while internally her anxieties and growing impulses continued to wage war. This is an example of how unresolved Oedipal scenarios can exacerbate the turmoil of adolescence and create a rejection of the sexually maturing body, leading to a breakdown of ordinary developmental processes.

To-ing and fro-ing: object relational progression (and regression) in adolescence

> I take it that it is normal for an adolescent to behave for a considerable length of time in an inconsistent and unpredictable manner; to fight his impulses and to accept them; to ward them off successfully and to be overrun by them; to love his parents and to hate them; to revolt against them and to be dependent on them; to be deeply ashamed to acknowledge his mother before others and, unexpectedly, to desire heart-to-heart talks with her; to thrive on imitation of and identification with others while searching unceasingly his own identity; to be more idealist, artistic, generous, and unselfish than he will ever be again but also the opposite: self centered, egoistic, calculated. Such fluctuation between extreme opposites would be deemed highly abnormal at any other time in life.
>
> (Freud, 1958, p. 275)

Object relations theory in psychoanalysis maintains its focus on drives and impulses, but it brings to the fore the relational aspects of intrapsychic phenomena, which is what I will focus on in this section.

Regarding object relational development in adolescence, we witness a 'recapitulation' of earlier developmental phases. The adolescent ego is put under strain not only from the surge of pubertal drives but also from the regressive pull toward infantile object relations, coupled with a simultaneous push away from them (Blos, 1962). This back-and-forth, push-and-pull movement significantly contributes to the weakness and fragility of the ego in adolescence, requiring a comprehensive renegotiation of the young person's self in its entirety.

From an object relations theory perspective, the adolescent experiences a second 'separation-individual process' (Blos, 1967), the outcome of which heavily relies on how the initial process of achieving separateness between self and other was negotiated. The first separation-individuation period (Mahler & Furer, 1963) concludes in toddlerhood, around the end of the third year of life, at which point the toddler establishes a more defined sense of self, separate from primary love objects. This leads to the emergence of the individuated self with clearer boundaries between self and other representations. Blos (1962) described the main developmental task in adolescence as a revisiting of this process, resulting in the typical contradictory behaviours marked by high levels of ambivalence, with the adolescent's simultaneous urge to push away and hold onto parental objects. We thus witness alternating progressive and regressive pulls taking place at once.

What implications does this hold for the adolescent's development of a distinct sense of self and identity? For them, 'there is not yet a capacity to identify with parental figures without loss of personal identity' (Winnicott, 1963/1965, p. 244). The urgency is to be different.

Understandably, this can lead to a developmental impasse, where old solutions for identifications are left behind and rejected, while new ones are yet to be discovered. This situation can lead to the ordinary emotional instability of adolescence as along with the 'doldrum' feelings described by Winnicott (1961): boredom, emptiness, futility, stuckness. However, the search for authenticity is such that tolerating feelings of boredom and futility becomes preferable to adopting 'false' solutions.

Furthermore, during this time, the adolescent revisits early infancy, in terms of the transition from experiencing the object as subjectively perceived (the subjective object) toward a position where the object can be objectively perceived (the objective object). In this process, eventually, the object can be located outside of the adolescent's magical control (Winnicott, 1969).

Greenberg (1975) points out that in ordinary adolescent development, the young person unconsciously reconnects with the omnipotence of early childhood and renegotiates its gradual relinquishment. Sometimes, though, there are instances where adolescents defensively cling to these infantile omnipotent strivings, attempting to ameliorate the fractiousness and upheaval of change and the uncertainty inherent in this developmental phase. The adolescent's fantasised omnipotence may sharply contrast with the reality of faced limitations, including their own mortality and the fallibility of previously idealised objects, mainly parents.

To restore the now-threatened omnipotence against all odds, the adolescent employs what Greenberg terms a 'magical manoeuvre' (1975). This involves placing an 'all-powerful other' on a pedestal, a tendency that can be seen in the idealisation of a best friend, a love interest, or a 'hero' (think movie idols, pop stars, and nowadays, social media influencers). It can also be evident in the adolescent's involvement with political, philosophical, or ethical ideas.

The peer group gains enormous significance from both drives and object relations perspectives, serving as the ideal displacement of the dependence previously directed towards parents and easing the threat of merger (Greenberg, 1975; Blos, 1979). Within the group, the adolescent finds abundant gratification for their instinctual urges: from extreme expressions of aggression and sexuality in the typical 'gang' scenario to more sublimated forms in shared social, sports, artistic, or intellectual endeavours. The group identity, as emphasised by Greenberg (1975), fulfils the adolescent's omnipotent strivings by offering the illusion of mightiness and strength, including identification with the group leader.

Generally speaking, forming a passionate attachment to an idealised 'other', whether an individual or a group, allows the adolescent to temporarily heal the narcissistic injury of the 'lost paradise' and can gradually consolidate feelings of identity and belonging. Omnipotent strivings operate as a necessary defence to fill the void left by the decathected primary love objects (Greenberg, 1975, p. 234).

The adolescent's quest for omnipotence and engagement in delinquent, unruly behaviour is considered ordinary and developmentally sound, contributing to separation, individuation, and the shaping of new identities (Horne, 2004, 2009). But these behaviours can become pathological when protracted, or they can lead to destructive outlets, such as serious offences, like assault, theft, and vandalism. Psychoanalytic literature, including works by Peter Wilson (1999) and Ann Horne (2004, 2009), discusses delinquency in adolescence, highlighting how it represents the extreme end of the spectrum within which the adolescent's quest for omnipotence manifests.

The roots of such behaviour often trace back to early environmental failures, causing disruptions in the infant's continuity of being during the time of absolute dependency and, in extreme cases, to experiences of trauma and abuse. In the latter cases, the illusion of omnipotence never occurred or did not occur frequently or consistently enough. Thus, the infant's ego may not have come fully into being and may not have acquired the capacity to tolerate frustration and manage internal and external realities effectively. In his writing on delinquency in adolescence, Wilson (1999) describes offending adolescents as operating in a highly narcissistic mode, including marked omnipotent functioning. He also explains how the libidinal investment of the self (including the body self) can be thought about in terms of an attempt on the part of the ego to defend against feelings of helplessness and vulnerability (Wilson, 1999).

Delinquent activity serves as an unconscious attempt by the troubled adolescent to rid him- or herself of unwanted painful thoughts and feelings that end up being located – via projection – into others. These others are at the receiving end of the adolescent's troubling actions. In many cases, delinquency has at its root a serious narcissistic injury, due to the hurt derived from early environmental failure, which has led to repeated experiences of humiliation and rage. The antidote to the narcissistic mortification is sought via fantasies of omnipotence and grandiosity, and when these are challenged, violence may erupt.

Delinquent activity can also be viewed as an unconscious attempt to address feelings of injustice and deprivation. Winnicott describes the actions of antisocial children as driven by deprivation and loss (Winnicott, 1956/1958), with delinquent activity unconsciously aimed at reclaiming something they once had – a good-enough experience of being cared for, which was then lost or taken away. Persistent and extreme delinquent behaviour contains elements of despair and rage, directed at those perceived as responsible for the suffered injustice and deprivation. But Winnicott suggests that delinquency also harbours hope (Winnicott, 1967a). Through the protest, some of what has been lost can be restored and reclaimed.

The persistence of an omnipotent type of psychic functioning can be explained by the sustained illusion of omnipotence in infancy. In such cases, efforts for complete maternal adaptation may too closely try to meet the child's needs. Winnicott cautioned against the dangers of 'too good mothering', as explored by Juliette Hopkins (1996), which can deprive the infant of developmental opportunities to navigate experiences of imperfection, frustration, and a perception of the object as both loved and hated simultaneously. A baby who is mothered 'too well' is essentially deprived of experiences of the object as separate from oneself – an object that can be loved, hated, and eventually retained as a stable feature in their object world. Hopkins (1996) elaborates on the risks here, describing how, in cases where the mother's complete adaptation persists instead of lessening over time, the infant eventually rejects her or lives in a non-adaptive state of regression and dependence. Hopkins explains that the rejection of the mother becomes necessary for the child to feel real and separate, with any further experience of closeness and intimacy leading to a fear of engulfment.

In adolescence (as well as in adulthood), the overly mothered or 'too-well-mothered' individual may oscillate between a state of dependence and merger and a state of rejection and alienation from the object. These dynamics strongly resonate with the 'core complex' presentation (Glasser, 1992) that we frequently observe in our clinical work.

Psychoanalytic treatment in adolescence: therapy as an extension of *mirroring* and *holding*

> The analytic treatment of adolescents in a hazardous venture from beginning to end, a venture in which the analyst has to meet resistances of unusual strength and variety.
>
> (Freud, 1958, p. 261)

The adolescent upheaval is not merely ordinary but essential. We should be more concerned about adolescents who do not behave like adolescents, continuing to be 'good' compliant children to their parents rather than embracing the age-appropriate revolt against childhood love objects. The 'too good' adolescent might be stifled by rigid defences against drive activity, erecting barriers that impede the natural unfolding of maturational processes during adolescence (Freud, 1958, p. 266).

Let us return to the opening quote of this chapter, but in its more complete form: 'Adolescence constitutes by definition an interruption of peaceful growth which resembles in appearance a variety of other emotional upset and structural upheavals' (Freud, 1958, p. 266).

If an 'interruption of peaceful growth' is expected during adolescence, how do we discern between ordinary adolescent upset and pathological manifestations? It's crucial to hold in mind that, as highlighted in the quote, ordinary development in adolescence often closely resembles the emotional upheaval seen in psychopathology. Winnicott believed that, in most cases, conflicts and anxieties in adolescence resolve over time (Winnicott, 1961) via the spontaneous progression of maturational processes, with therapeutic intervention necessary only in a minority of cases.

From an object relations perspective, offering regular psychoanalytic therapy (or any other type of therapy) to adolescents may contradict their developmental task of moving towards independence and establishing a new, separate identity. The offer of psychotherapy in adolescence invites a degree of dependence on the therapist, a centripetal pull that moves against the centrifugal push away from dependency on parental and transference objects.

The traditional setting of psychoanalytic psychotherapy, with once-weekly sessions (or more) for as long as needed, may thus feel threatening to the adolescent, who is developmentally grappling with ambivalence. Intimate experiences with a therapist and dependency on them may unconsciously invoke a regressive merging with the object, and a worry about losing their still-unstable autonomous self.

Holding this developmental perspective in mind, a flexible approach is necessary, respecting the adolescent's need to regulate closeness and intimacy while providing a robust and reliable therapeutic space. What does this look like in practice? It might involve understanding that there may be occasional missed or delayed sessions, and accepting to some degree that the adolescent should maintain some control over the therapeutic process and the intimacy with the therapist they can allow.

This is not consistently acknowledged, though. Unfortunately, punitive institutional responses, especially in resource-challenged NHS services, often allow little space for all this and fail to engage developmentally appropriate ambivalence. This can result in labelling an adolescent patient as 'not engaging' after a few missed appointments, potentially leading to discharge being discussed.

With all this in mind, recognising the value of brief or time-limited psychoanalytic work for adolescents, such as Short-Term Psychoanalytic Psychotherapy (STPP), is crucial. It can often be the right solution for the ambivalent teenager. Demystifying psychotherapy as not exclusively intensive and long-term is particularly important with adolescents, who are caught up in their emotional and developmental struggles. Brief work, for them, can offer containment and relief and be exactly what they need, without threatening their quest for autonomy and distance.

Winnicott, in his therapeutic consultations, brought to life the enormous potential of brief work. In this book he described the value of one-off initial consultations, offering the opportunity to make meaningful contact between patient and therapist, which can sometimes work and may at times be enough to release a developmental 'knot':

> [T]he very great confidence which children can show in myself (as in others doing similar work) on these special occasions, special occasions that have a quality that has made me use the word sacred. Either this sacred moment is used or is wasted. If it is wasted the child's belief of being understood is shattered. If on the other hand it is used, then the child' belief in being helped is strengthened.
>
> (Winnicott, 1971, pp. 4–5)

Pursuing this line of thought further: when considering psychoanalytic treatment in adolescence, how do we meet young people where they are developmentally? How much interpretation of the unconscious and the transference can their fragile ego tolerate and make use of? Ann Horne cautions (2009) against rigidly applying traditional psychoanalytic techniques, especially with adolescents lacking ego structuring and prone to acting out. Anna Freud's perspective on the use of the transference in analytic work with adolescents suggests that the 'live' emotional struggle adolescents are engaged in, and the task of navigating ambivalence in their object relations, leaves little or no libido to be invested in the analyst or in revisiting the past (Freud, 1958, p. 270). This suggests that focusing the treatment on interpreting the transference may be developmentally 'off-the-mark' during adolescence.

Technically, keeping analytic interpretation minimal initially or avoiding it altogether may be necessary. Ego-supportive interventions, such as those described in Hurry's 'Psychoanalysis and developmental therapy' (2018), can promote ego strength by supporting adolescents to recognise and name their feelings, thus making sense of the thinking and emotional states underlying their behaviour and gradually achieving greater emotional regulation.

This is a crucial stepping stone before embarking on more insight-based work, where interpretation of the unconscious and transference relationship might become possible. Premature analytic interpretations can overwhelm fragile egos and lead to unintended effects. They could, for example, be perceived as retaliatory and humiliating (Lanyado & Horne, 2013). A dogmatic interpretation, offered too soon, perhaps in an attempt to appease the therapist's analytic superego, can lead to two possible scenarios, as described by Winnicott (1991, in 'Playing and reality'): it can either be accepted as propaganda, or be rejected as useless, thereby discrediting the entire therapeutic process in the patient's mind.

When thinking about technique, Winnicott's ideas around the therapeutic effect of holding and mirroring are important (Winnicott, 1967b). These concepts were initially intended to describe relational processes between mother and infant. In the case of adolescents, these therapeutic processes can help compensate for problems resulting from early environmental failure, helping to achieve attunement and offering developmental help, with traditional analytic work and interpretation coming second (or, at times, never!).

The focus in Winnicott's work above and beyond all else is to meet the patient's developmental needs. His adaptations of technique are grounded in developmental considerations, in line also with Anna Freud's ideas on analytic work with children and adolescents, as well as Ann Hurry's later developmental therapy (Hurry, 2018; Winnicott, 1967b). Much like the idea that the mother's face is the infant's first mirror, the therapist's words (and face!) reflect back to the patient 'what is there to be seen'. I would add that this has to happen at a pace that the patient can tolerate and make use of. If this process goes well, the patient is enabled to see himself, find himself, and feel real: 'I am seen, therefore I am'. The repeated experience of this leads eventually, and hopefully, to improved ego integration and a better negotiation of the differentiation between self and other and inner and outer realities.

The adolescent psychotherapist often needs to preserve a capacity for reflection, without always directly sharing those reflections with the adolescent, and to resist being pulled into a sense of urgency and pressure for immediate change (from parents, school, or other professionals).

The essential therapeutic elements of mirroring and holding during psychoanalytic psychotherapy centre on the quality of communication between therapist and patient. This can be crucial particularly in cases where previous experiences of communication with the most significant attachment figures failed or broke down. Communication is always intended as the creation of a bridge between self and other. In the therapeutic encounter, this means feeling held and understood (Lanyado, 2012).

Winnicott says, 'Psychotherapy is not making clever and apt interpretations; by and large it is a long-term giving the patient back what the patient brings', enabling the patient to find his own self in the therapist's reflection and begin to exist and feel real (Winnicott, 1967b, p. 117). Feeling real is fundamental for the adolescent's exploration of their new identity, and this is demonstrated in their determination to avoid false solutions, leading to the mixture of defiance and dependence typical of adolescence (Winnicott, 1961). For the patient to be enabled to feel real, the therapist must become a real, live object, which Lanyado (2004) has referred to as the therapist's presence. The therapist needs to be a lively, attentive, interested, and receptive developmental object. This includes their ability to find a personal, creative, and spontaneous way of relating to adolescents, without resorting to verbal interpretations when they can't be tolerated. Non-verbal communication, including facial expressions, tone of voice, humour and lightness, and the therapist's spontaneous or impulsive gestures, to use Winnicott's terms (Winnicott, 1941), all play a crucial role, allowing them to meet the adolescent patient at the right level, communicating with them without overloading their fragile ego.

I am reminded here of a 15-year-old adolescent boy, whom I shall call Justin, with a serious narcissistic disturbance, rooted in his early experiences with primary objects who had made him feel special only to then drop him suddenly. Justin had continued to function, as an adolescent, in an omnipotent mode that made his behaviour hard to manage both at home and at school. In his sessions with me, it was clear that directly naming the unreasonable quality of his expectations and demands on other people ran the danger of further narcissistic injury and a disregard of me and the sessions. Instead of answering with words, I started making humorous 'eye rolling' expressions in response to his dramatic statements, and Justin became gradually more able to tolerate his omnipotence being questioned, explored, and thought about. He would look at my facial expressions with a mixture of amusement and curiosity, and eventually, one day, he asked me, 'What are you thinking about?' This offered me a mandate to gently share my thoughts.

Winnicott warned us of the pitfalls of a 'too good therapist' (1958b), depriving the patient of an experience of finding his own meaning and feeling understood over time. Overly early interpretations, resembling magic and witchcraft, can take away from the therapeutic and developmental value of the analytic encounter. I am thinking here of adolescent patients who are in the grips of a serious regression and who present with dependent tendencies. Receptivity to the therapist's interpretations may mask compliance and passivity in the transference. There can, in those cases, be a tendency to take the therapist's words as absolute truths with magical connotations.

I am reminded here of a severely depressed 16-year-old girl, whom I shall call Poppy, with incredibly low self-esteem. She was going through a 'developmental breakdown', no longer attending school. Early in the treatment, it seemed encouraging that despite her difficulties, she attended sessions regularly and seemed to accept my interpretations about her state. I gradually became aware, though, of the elements of compliance and passivity in the transference, and how I was placed on a pedestal, while she continued to think lowly of herself. The idealised quality of the transference emerged vividly at the beginning of each session, when she would compliment me (usually about my clothes). This contrasted with her view of herself as messy, sweaty, or unkempt. It seemed crucial to relinquish my own omnipotence as the 'too good therapist', offering timely interpretation, and to begin allowing Poppy to gradually discover herself, becoming able to survive the frustrations of me as a fallible yet real developmental object.

> The infant can actually come to gain from the experience of frustration, since the incomplete adaptation to need makes objects real, that is to say hated as well as loved. . . . [E]xact adaptation resembles magic and the object that behaves perfectly becomes no better than an hallucination.
>
> (Winnicott, 1958a, p. 238)

The too-good therapist, particularly in the psychotherapy with adolescent patients, also risks colluding with the adolescent's omnipotent defence, creating a scenario where omnipotent fantasies are located into the therapist and producing a regressive/submissive state in the troubled patient. As a result of this, insight from the therapist is stripped of any value or usefulness, and the therapeutic encounter can become 'no better than a hallucination' (Winnicott, 1958a).

To conclude, it's important to acknowledge that psychoanalytic psychotherapy may not always be the treatment of choice for all adolescents, especially those who engage in criminal activity or are prone to acting out. There are cases where the best possible intervention is at the level of what Winnicott described as placement, with environmental interventions and strong ego support being crucial (Winnicott, 1958b).

The therapist's role, in this applied work, includes consulting with parents, professionals, and networks to provide a balanced and developmentally focused understanding of the young person. Professional networks can often unknowingly mirror the polarities and extremes (either harshly punitive or not concerned enough/ denial) typical of adolescence, at the expense of the ability to think (Horne, 2018) instead of acting impulsively.

With all this in mind, what is the aim of psychoanalytic treatment with adolescents? I think it primarily involves guiding the adolescent back onto a healthier path of development and growth, helping them understand the reasons for unconsciously 'choosing' the path of pathology, 'a pathology that destroys the ability to love and experience love through relationships and through the ownership of a sexual body' (Laufer, 1996, p. 519).

Adolescence and society

> Is it not a sign of the health of a society that its teenagers are able to be adolescent at the right time, that is to say, at the age that covers pubertal growth?
>
> (Winnicott, 1961, p. 148)

I have so far focused on the intrapsychic and object-relational aspects related to adolescent development. Let's broaden the focus to include the societal and cultural frameworks that shape today's adolescents. I suggest that understanding adolescent processes relies on an exploration of the societal contexts in which adolescents operate. I see this as a dynamic, two-way interaction whereby adolescence is, to some extent, moulded by society, and vice versa. By considering societal processes, I account for the dominant responses, attitudes, discourses, narratives, and available identities that envelop the concept of adolescence in our time. These elements collectively contribute to defining and shaping the very essence of adolescence. Winnicott's famous statement '[T]here is no such thing as a baby' (Winnicott, 1960) can be extended to young adults: 'there is no such thing as an adolescent', therefore. This reframing shows that we need to think of adolescents within their specific social context and recognise their dynamic, evolving relationship with it.

A relevant question here is: what is it about adolescence that stirs up intense reactions? This phase is notorious for evoking particularly strong responses. Horne has outlined the presence of a 'harsh societal superego' (Horne, 2013), reminding us that society feels threatened by the wild, turbulent, and unpredictable adolescent. In response, there may be attempts to impose harsh and punitive measures, aiming to restore control and order. Horne has further described the contradictory emotions adolescent behaviour provokes in parents and society at large. There can be anxiety, helplessness, confusion, even envy. These paradoxical and polarised adult responses, swinging between praise and idealisation, criticism and indignation, echo the ambivalence and polarisation within the adolescent's own internal object world.

Society's ability to engage with and tolerate the uncertainty, contradictions, and intricacies of adolescence, without hastily resorting to premature actions, foreclosure, or rigid definitions, serves as a measure of the health of that society. This is what Winnicott captured so eloquently in the opening quote of this section. Considering that the 'cure' for adolescence is, in most cases, the passage of time (Winnicott, 1961), society's role in this maturational process should not be to aim to cure it but, rather, to tolerate and meet it. Winnicott's reflections on adolescence are contextualised and factor in societal elements; at his time, these included the aftermath of the Second World War, which had left adolescents without the structure and predictability afforded to previous generations, who had not been as deeply involved in military service and action.

Considering adolescence as a social construct involves recognising that the contours and outcomes of the adolescent process are dependent on the prevailing societal responses, views, and attitudes towards adolescent behaviour. A socially constructed view of adolescence as an inherently vulnerable time, potentially leading to enduring difficulties in adult life, may give rise to polarised perspectives of adolescents, casting them as either 'actively deviant' or 'passively at risk' (sometimes simultaneously) (Griffin, 1997). Various degrees of risk are associated with different societal groups, depending on factors such as gender, race, and social class (Briggs, 2008). For example, active deviance is stereotypically associated with seemingly aggressive males, often assumed to be from lower-income households or ethnic minorities, while passive vulnerability is predominantly associated with females.

The question is: in our society, with its dominant focus on diagnosis and pre-defined pathways for treatment, are we *meeting* and tolerating the turmoil of adolescence, or are we creating and medicalising it?

The conceptualisation of adolescence by society, including in the definitions of normality and pathology, influences identity formation and the development of identifications during this critical period. During the psychic reorganisation adolescents go through, old parental identifications will be relinquished and new, separate models of identification will be sought. The identity instability typical of adolescence means that there is a search outside the family for other identities to fit with what they feel to be their true sense of self, giving meaning and shape to their unsettling experience.

But what available identities does society offer adolescents? What are the dominant narratives and discourses around adolescence?

Modern society seems predisposed towards emphasising pathological discourses in adolescence, rather than emphasising the ordinary developmental processes. The dominant narratives seem to be around pathological manifestations in adolescence and how to formally diagnose and cure them. Ordinary language around feeling states and behaviour associated with developmental processes has been replaced by the ascendency of mental health language and self-diagnosis, which has become an increasingly common occurrence.

Of course, there are situations where focusing on pathology and treatment plans is appropriate. The advancements in our understanding of child and adolescent mental health in recent decades have led to improvements in our ability to understand and address psychopathology. However, these developments have been accompanied by an increasing emphasis on formal assessments, frequently leading to the offer of a diagnosis and pre-defined care pathways. Unfortunately, information – and sometimes misinformation – regarding the criteria for meeting mental health diagnoses in adolescence have spread literally (and virtually!) everywhere, and in particular on social media platforms.

At the same time, with this expansion of knowledge and interest, the extended waiting times for assessment in Child and Adolescent Mental Health Services (CAMHS) in the UK often compel families to invest enormously in the promise of a diagnosis. This promise often takes on a perceived significance akin to an omnipotent, magical solution to challenges. I would go as far as to say that, within public services, receiving a diagnosis can feel to a lot of young people and families like being offered a special status, or in other words, an identity.

I don't intend here to take an anti-diagnosis stance; on the contrary, I recognise many ways in which diagnoses in childhood and adolescence can offer a valuable framework for understanding a young person's challenges, generating acceptance and affirmation, and opening possibilities for additional support in school and funding for interventions.

The caution I present here is twofold: firstly, diagnoses in childhood and adolescence often fail to account for the crucial maturational and developmental processes discussed in this chapter. This oversight risks crystallising something that is still unfolding along a developmental trajectory into a permanent form. This can, at times, lead to foreclosure, disregarding the necessary exploration of the meaning underpinning feeling states and behaviours. While acknowledging the seriousness of the risks in adolescence, the goal should be to reveal the symbolic meaning of the symptom as a form of communication, to restore containment for the young person and wider system, and to avoid a reactive standardised response driven by anxiety.

Secondly, we ought to reflect on the impact of mental health diagnoses in offering a possible identity, albeit a pathologised one. Such identities can elicit care and affirmation in society, bypassing the developmentally ordinary feelings of uncertainty and instability associated with identity formation. An example of this would be the many adolescents I see in my clinical work with ADHD diagnoses – one of the most prevalent diagnoses in childhood and adolescence today. I am always struck by how profoundly this diagnosis permeates these children's identities, providing a reliable yet static framework through which they explain any difficulty they face. What comes across, sometimes even in young people's use of language, is that *being* ADHD replaces *having* ADHD, with the label becoming an all-encompassing tool of self-understanding and identification.

Another strong influence on identity formation in adolescence is the quality and nature of their social relationships. As previously mentioned, the adolescent is developmentally oriented outwards – moving away from parental figures and toward the peer group and the onset of romantic/sexual relationships. This centrifugal drive supports the process of separation, individuation, and the formation of a new identity. Given the enormous developmental weight of social relationships during adolescence, it's worth thinking about the way these connections are formed in modern society.

I am referring here to the use of social media, which now constitutes a substantial proportion of social interactions among today's adolescents. Making and sustaining friendships via social media is no longer an exception but the norm, representing a new and unprecedented standard, the full impact of which we are yet to fully grasp. Social media, by definition, is a platform used to form and foster social connections – mainly with peers, but also with people removed from the adolescent's immediate reality, such as famous actors, singers, or influencers.

For many adolescents, the social promoting function of social media undoubtedly exists, enhancing and extending their connections, allowing them to share experiences, test identities, and find communities that might otherwise remain inaccessible. However, there are also flip sides to these connections that can be thought about in terms of both hyper-connection and disconnection (Recalcati, 2019), the effects of which may not always favour the adolescent developmental task.

Hyper-connection refers to the aspect of social media use that leads to a constant virtual connection with others, without interruptions or gaps. This brings to mind the developmental value of the gap between self and other in the Winnicottian sense, and the idea that it is in the absence and temporary loss of the other that the potential for symbol formation and creative living emerges. So what happens, developmentally, when the gap is absent? When used sensibly, for some adolescents, as mentioned, online spaces can provide a creative space in which thoughts, feelings, and identities can be tentatively explored before being brought into the external world. As such, could some forms of virtual relating serve to mediate the gap – helping young people navigate separations and anxieties that may otherwise feel unmanageable?

As for disconnection, here it refers to the idea that connection through social media, as real as it may feel to the adolescent, is nonetheless a *virtual* connection. This poses the risk, in some cases, of replacing or distorting the perception of connection in real life with live objects, confusing virtual and real experience, and potentially leading to a lapse in symbolic functioning – which, as we know, is already fragile in adolescence. Psychoanalytically, this fusion of the virtual into the real can be referred to as a hallucination (Recalcati, 2019), contributing to magical thinking that may conflict with the adolescent's task of relinquishing omnipotent strivings and establishing a firm sense of reality.

Earlier, I discussed the centrality of the body in adolescence and the arduous task of integrating the sexually mature forms of the developing body into the psychic structure. This process has a strong social component, as the adolescent inevitably compares their changing body with those of others around them, mainly within their peer group. Acceptance or rejection of the body is not exclusively driven by internal factors but is also influenced externally, such as by the prevailing body images and standards of beauty promoted in society.

What unfolds in this process when today's adolescents constantly measure themselves not only against real bodies but also (at times *mainly*) against *virtual* bodies, as portrayed on social media? Ordinary narcissistic imbalances in adolescence may become exacerbated by the steady flow of perfect, filtered body images populating their newsfeeds. And what happens to self-esteem and self-worth when they are concretely measured in terms of 'likes', 'followers', and 'retweets'? The gap between self and ego ideal is bound to become larger and larger, at the expense of a healthier narcissistic balance. Yet it is also true that social media offers opportunities for reclaiming and diversifying representations of the body – for challenging rigid ideals and creating spaces for inclusion, activism, and shared vulnerability. In this sense, online culture can at times mirror a collective working-through of shame and difference, even if this process remains uneven and fraught.

As such, thinking about adolescence necessitates taking into account the virtual social reality that runs parallel to the real context. For some, this duality enables experimentation with identity and belonging, functioning as a contemporary extension of the adolescent's creative and transitional space. For others, it may become a site of withdrawal, where the wish to escape from reality paradoxically coincides with entrapment and a serious developmental impasse.

To conclude, what does the adolescent see when they look at themselves in the societal mirror? The outlook presented to young people can often appear bleak, reflecting global anxieties about war, inequality, and climate change. Acheson and Papadima (2023) note the lack of a convincing and hopeful collective narrative around adolescence at a societal level, pointing to the individualistic tendencies in our society, which emphasise inward self-focus at the expense of outward engagement. Yet paradoxically, it is precisely through these contemporary challenges – and through the creative uses of technology – that many adolescents are constructing new forms of meaning, solidarity, and action.

It would be helpful if the societal mirror could respond to the contradictions and challenges posed by adolescents not by merely reflecting back a harsh punitive superego (Horne, 2009), or a diagnostic manual of pathologised identities, but instead by wondering 'what is there to be seen' (Winnicott, 1971), namely, the tumultuous and gradual unfolding of complex yet ordinary developmental processes.

References

Acheson, R., & Papadima, M. (2023). The search for identity: Working therapeutically with adolescents in crisis. *Journal of Child Psychotherapy*, 49(1), 95–119. https://doi.org/10.1080/0075417X.2022.2160478

Blos, P. (1962). *On adolescence: A psychoanalytic interpretation*. Free Press.

Blos, P. (1967). The second individuation process of adolescence. *Psychoanalytic Study of the Child*, 22, 162–186.

Blos, P. (1979). *The adolescent passage: Developmental issues*. International Universities Press.

Briggs, S. (2008). *Working with adolescents and young adults: A contemporary psychodynamic approach*. Palgrave (2nd edition).

Encyclopaedia Britannica. (n.d.). Adolescence. *Britannica.com*. Retrieved May 11, 2025, from https://www.britannica.com/science/adolescence

Erikson, E. H. (1968). *Identity, youth, and crisis*. W. W. Norton & Company.

Freud, A. (1958). Adolescence. *Psychoanalytic Study of the Child*, 13, 255–278.

Freud, A. (1963). The concept of developmental lines. *Psychoanalytic Study of the Child*, 18, 245–265.

Freud, S. (1905). Three essays on the theory of sexuality. In: *The Standard Edition of the Complete Psychological Works of Sigmund Freud* (Vol. 7, pp. 123–124). London: The Hogarth Press and the Institute of Psycho-Analysis.

Freud, S. (1923). The ego and the id. In: *The Standard Edition of the Complete Psychological Works of Sigmund Freud* (Vol. 19, pp. 1–66). London: The Hogarth Press and the Institute of Psycho-Analysis.

Glasser, M. (1992). Problems in the psychoanalysis of certain narcissistic disorders. *The International Journal of Psycho-Analysis*, 73(3), 493.

Greenberg, H. R. (1975). The widening gyre: Transformations of the omnipotent quest during adolescence. *International Review of Psycho-Analysis*, 2, 231–244.

Griffin, C. (1997). Troubled teens: Managing disorders of transition and consumption. *Feminist Review*, 55(1), 4–21. https://doi.org/10.1057/fr.1997.2

Hall, G. S. (1904). *Adolescence; its psychology and its relations to physiology, anthropology, sociology, sex, crime, religion and education*. New York: Appleton.

Hopkins, J. (1996). The dangers and deprivations of too-good mothering. *Journal of Child Psychotherapy*, 22(3), 407–422.

Horne, A. (2004). 'Gonnae no'dae that!'1 the internal and external worlds of the delinquent adolescent. *Journal of Child Psychotherapy*, 30(3), 330–346.

Horne, A. (2009). From intimacy to acting out. In: *Through Assessment to Consultation: Independent Psychoanalytic Approaches with Children and Adolescents* (p. 110). Routledge.

Horne, A. (2013). On delinquency. In: *Winnicott's children* (pp. 186–202). Routledge.

Horne, A. (2018). Keeping the child in mind: Thoughts on work with parents of children in therapy. In: *Work with parents* (pp. 47–63). Routledge.

Hurry, A. (2018). Psychoanalysis and developmental therapy. In: *Psychoanalysis and developmental therapy* (pp. 32–73). Routledge.

Institute of Medicine (US) & National Research Council (US) Committee on the Science of Adolescence. (2011). *The science of adolescent risk-taking: Workshop report* (Chapter 4, The psychology of adolescence). National Academies Press. https://www.ncbi.nlm.nih.gov/books/NBK53420/

Keats, J. (1818). *Endymion*. Taylor and Hessey.

Ladame, F., & Perret-Catipovic, M. (1999). *Adolescence and psychoanalysis: The story and the history*. London: Routledge.

Lanyado, M. (2004). *The presence of the therapist: Treating childhood trauma*. Routledge.

Lanyado, M. (2012). What is therapeutic about communication? In: A. Horne, & M. Lanyado (eds.), *Winnicott's children*. London: Routledge.

Lanyado, M., & Horne, A. (2013). The therapeutic relationship and process. In: *The handbook of child and adolescent psychotherapy* (pp. 66–83). Routledge.

Laufer, M. (1996). The psychoanalyst of the adolescent. *Psychoanalytic Study of the Child*, 51, 512–521.

Laufer, M. E., & Laufer, M. (2018). *Adolescence and developmental breakdown: A psychoanalytic view*. Routledge.

Levy, R. (2018). Adolescence: The body as a scenario for non-symbolized dramas. In: *Psychosomatics Today* (pp. 93–109). Routledge.

Mahler, M. S., & Furer, M. (1963). Certain aspects of the separation-individuation phase. *The Psychoanalytic Quarterly*, 32(1), 1–14.

Maroudas, C., Wiseman, H., & Harel, J. (2023). The 'wave-particle' child: Reconnecting the disconnect in the concept of latency. *Journal of Child Psychotherapy*, 49(3), 412–431.

Nicolò, A. M., & Ruggiero, I. (2016). *La mente adolescente e il corpo ripudiato*. FrancoAngeli.

Recalcati, M. (2019). *The Telemachus Complex: Parents and children after the decline of the father*. John Wiley & Sons.

Ruggiero, I. (2011). Corpo strano, corpo estraneo, corpo nemico: Itinerari adolescenziali tra corpo, psiche e relazione. *Rivista di Psicoanalisi*, LVII(4), 825–847.

Sandler, J., & Freud, A. (1980). Discussions in the Hampstead index on 'The ego and the mechanisms of defence': I. The ego as the seat of observation. *Bulletin of the Anna Freud Centre*, 3, 199–212.

Wilson, P. (1999). Consultation in residential care. In: M. Lanyado, & A. Horne (eds.), *The handbook of child and adolescent psychotherapy: Psychoanalytic approaches*. Psychology Press.

Winnicott, D. W. (1941). The observation of infants in a set situation. *The International Journal of Psycho-Analysis*, 22, 229.

Winnicott, D. W. (1949, Autumn). The ordinary devoted mother and her baby. *Nine Broadcast Talks*. (s.l.); 1999. Accessed May 2, 2025.

Winnicott, D. W. (1956/1958). The antisocial tendency. In: *Through paediatrics to psychoanalysis: Collected papers* (pp. 306–315). London: Tavistock.

Winnicott, D. W. (1958a). *Transitional objects and transitional phenomena in collected papers*. London: Tavistock.

Winnicott, D. W. (1958b). *Collected papers: Through paediatrics to psycho-analysis*. London: Tavistock.

Winnicott, D. W. (1960). The theory of the parent-infant relationship. *International Journal of Psychoanalysis*, 41(6), 585–595.

Winnicott, D. W. (1961). *Adolescence: In the family and individual development*. Routledge, 2012.

Winnicott, D. W. (1963/1965). Hospital care supplementing intensive psychotherapy in adolescence. In: *The maturational processes and the facilitating environment*. London: Hogarth Press.

Winnicott, D. W. (1965). *The maturational processes and the facilitating environment: Studies in the theory of emotional development*. The Hogarth Press and the Institute of Psycho-Analysis.

Winnicott, D. W. (1967a). Delinquency as a sign of hope. In: *Home is where we start from: Essays by a psychoanalyst* (pp. 90–100). WW Norton & Company.

Winnicott, D. W. (1967b). *Mirroring role of mother and family in child development: In playing and reality*. London: Tavistock.

Winnicott, D. W. (1969). The use of an object. *The International Journal of Psychoanalysis*, 50(4), 711–716.

Winnicott, D. W. (1971). *Therapeutic consultations in child psychiatry*. London: Karnac.

Winnicott, D. W. (1991). *Playing and reality*. Psychology Press.

World Health Organization. (n.d.). *Adolescent health*. Retrieved May 2, 2025, from https://www.who.int/health-topics/adolescent-health#tab=tab_1

Chapter 2

The search for identity

Working therapeutically with adolescents in crisis[1]

Rachel Acheson and Maria Papadima

Introduction

This chapter presents some thoughts on what we have observed in our work with adolescents in recent years. We have both worked with adolescents in various settings. For two years, during the Covid pandemic, we worked together in the same NHS high-risk adolescent clinic, where we first started considering what we explore in this chapter.

Our clinical work at this service consisted of demanding caseloads of young people referred with complex and concerning difficulties, often self-harming or feeling suicidal. Our service, like most public-sector services in the UK, had experienced unprecedented levels of referrals and had felt, at times – particularly during the years of the pandemic – very stretched. During the years of Covid, taking our masks off to have lunch together after back-to-back appointments, we began sharing our thoughts with each other about the young adolescents we were seeing.

The young people we saw, mainly girls, had symptoms indicating an alarming level of disturbance. They unsettled and frightened their families and schools. Self-harm, overdoses, crisis line calls, ambulances, and A&E visits were weekly occurrences. Their parents would often appear distressed and helpless during initial meetings, as we, of course, would have done in their position.

Yet we also started noticing that there was a significant subset of these young people whose behaviour and feelings – even though needing close care and attention as signs of great distress – were not expressions of enduring mental health disturbance. Given a supportive environment and coordinated therapeutic care within the network, their initial symptoms sometimes shifted fairly quickly, with more ordinary, yet still troubling, concerns emerging. There was thus a significant difference we noticed between the manifest difficulties – high-risk presentations and descriptions of self-labelled mental health problems – versus the underlying difficulties these young people struggled with.

We started thinking that a large number of young people today experience the turmoil of early adolescence in a particular, new way. Under the influence of cultural and social conditioning – online and offline – and arguably, the lack of a containing cultural narrative, some young adolescents today may express their

DOI: 10.4324/9781003592778-4

very real but ordinary distress through the formation of an alarming, 'unwell' identity that helps them give shape to how they feel. We suggest that what is being framed as an 'adolescent mental health crisis' may be more accurately termed an 'adolescent crisis', expressed through mental health language.

We thus wonder whether aspects of the current widespread 'mental health crisis in adolescence' may involve developmentally expected adolescent turmoil, which young people have to get through, exacerbated by the particular challenges of the cultural context in which it is experienced, where mental health language is a common frame of reference. It is worth noting that, alongside the type of adolescent patient this chapter focuses on, at the same clinic we also saw other young people with presentations indicating enduring mental health problems (see Masterson, 1967, on adolescent diagnosis). There are, of course, different types of self-harm and suicidality, all requiring individual thinking and therapeutic work. Sometimes, longer-term therapy is indicated. At other times, as with the young people we describe in this chapter, shorter-term, psychoanalytically informed work can have a significant positive effect. This will depend on the young person's resilience and creativity, wish for change, and the coordinated support of their whole environment – family, school or workplace, friendship circle, and us as therapists.

Our particular contribution as adolescent therapists is threefold: to help young people and families navigate the complexity of adolescent turmoil, which is not easy at the best of times; to help differentiate transient from more enduring problems; and finally, to work preventatively so that adolescent problems don't persist into adulthood.

This chapter explores what we have come to understand about some adolescents expressing their experience through this 'unwell persona', which 'fits' and makes sense to them. We discuss this from a developmental perspective, seeing this presentation as a form of regression – part of the adolescent separation process and the emergence of sexuality. We also see these difficulties as part of the ordinary, necessary, and useful development of narcissism in adolescence. We consider the cultural context in which young people today come of age, online and offline, and we suggest that the ways the adult world tends to respond to these problems may be misdirected, despite good intentions.

Acknowledged within our work is the sad reality that long-term psychotherapy is not an option for the majority of cases referred to the UK public sector, and we imagine this is the case in other countries too. However, putting aside the problems and restrictions of that reality, it is also true, we believe, that long-term psychotherapy is not usually developmentally appropriate for adolescents who present in the way this chapter describes. This is for a number of reasons that we will touch briefly upon, illustrating with clinical material.

We have been inspired in our thinking by psychoanalytic ideas, attending to the underlying meaning of a crisis (often expressed in bold mental health language or alarming symptoms). We have also been informed by the ideas of developmental psychologist Urie Bronfenbrenner (1979) and, more recently, by child psychotherapist Ruth Schmidt Neven (2016), both of whom emphasise the system of relationships within which young people's behaviour needs to be understood for change to occur. We think that change for adolescents is only possible when these networks are taken into account, not when the focus is on the individual.

Despite the bleak nature of the material – self-harm and suicide are, after all, a parent's worst nightmare – we want to offer a hopeful picture about the work that can be done, often briefly, with these young people, as well as their parents and schools. The young people's resilience, creativity, and drive for life are at the centre of this work. For us as therapists, this work can be rewarding and enjoyable, and we feel it draws on our key skills as child psychotherapists.

Identity formation in adolescence and the 'unwell persona'

In adolescence, we question, and eventually discover, who we are, what we believe in, and in what direction we want to move. We also come to terms with sexuality as our bodies change, which can be unsettling. There are frequent shifts in this era of our life in who and what we idealise, and who and what we denigrate and leave behind. The search for an ideal identity – *the right identity* – is paramount and normal, to feel we have a place in the world. Julia Kristeva (2007) has said that the adolescent 'is striving for ideal models that will allow him to tear himself from his parents and meet the ideal partner, get the ideal job, and 'turn himself into' an ideal being'. Gradually, our wish for an ideal identity settles into more realistic constellations.

The process of searching for new ideals

To consider this process of identity formation, we turn to the classic work of Peter Blos, a German American early psychoanalyst who collaborated with Erik Erikson and Anna Freud. Blos (1967) argued that the adolescent search for the 'ideal' is a regressive wish, aiming to replace the previously idealised parents from whom young people are trying to separate. Adolescents' well-known passion and idealism – and the flip side, the inflexibility these involve – are normal stages we all go through.

Young people's search for an ideal identity also serves wider society through its clear, black-and-white thinking, high energy and drive (see Greta Thunberg), but equally, it serves adolescents by giving them an abrupt push towards external models to emulate and strive towards, moving away from the safety of parents, the first loves of their childhood.

In this journey, we can expect that teenagers reject parents to a degree while still needing their guidance and support. This back-and-forth movement – rejecting and needing adults – puts us as therapists in a difficult position. Adam Phillips (2011, p. 188) says:

It has not escaped anybody's attention who tries to 'treat' adolescents that just when they are trying to get away from those experts on life called their parents, they find themselves falling into the hands of another set of experts called their therapists.

We, as therapists, seen as 'mental health experts', despite our intentions, can end up being idealised or rejected too.

The 'unwell persona': an identity that fits

The teenagers we focus on here, presenting with this 'unwell persona', are typically referred to our clinics around age 13 or 14, reporting short histories of distress that have only recently come to the attention of those around them. They feel disconnected from the hobbies, friendships, and ways of life that had felt satisfying only a short time before. Their earlier passions now seem childish; they see their parents as uninteresting and sometimes as 'uneducated' in mental health or politics. They often think of their generation as quite separate from the generations that came before.

Replacing their previous interests, they come to us with a new, intense identity – that of *the mental health patient and advocate*. This identity makes sense to them: it offers words for how they feel. It drives their behaviour, both in the symptoms they exhibit and in their communication with those around them – parents, friends, school, therapists.

Young adolescents talk about their struggles in language that is well-versed in mental health definitions, which the internet has allowed them to explore and learn about. They often see no point in life and think about suicide. Many self-harm, a phenomenon that has significantly increased in recent years in the UK. They are interested in the diagnostic language found in the DSM[2] and have read extensively about the field, wanting to understand, with our help, what is happening to them.

We find ourselves, at times, in a strange, paradoxical position as therapists, as if our roles with our patients are reversed: adolescents come to us with fully formed mental health identities and diagnoses, which we ask them to question and open up, slowing them down to try and understand what all this means. It is thus adolescents themselves who are suggesting the possible diagnoses, while we therapists often try to speak in a non-psychological language.

Teenagers, like all of us today in the online world, are able to find information about their situation and sometimes self-diagnose. Because of the way the internet works, this can lead to likes and followers for those who want to communicate their thoughts online. Indeed, self-diagnosis and an expanded interest in mental health are strong recent trends on TikTok (Caron, 2022; Foster & Schmidt Neven, 2022), and social media algorithms make such posts grow exponentially.

This trend, we think, may be exacerbated by the limited access to widespread, preventative, low-key mental health support in countries such as the UK and the United States; but that does not explain the whole picture. There is also the reality that on platforms such as TikTok, adolescents find knowledge and community. They can share their stories of self-harm with peers, talk about 'being clean' when they stop cutting, and record their progress on apps. They sometimes take part in online suicide discussion groups, where they find understanding and don't feel alone.

This identity of the mental health patient and advocate, and the diagnoses that accompany it, can feel to the young adolescent as stable as life itself: a psychic raft to cling to, a convincing way to understand oneself, a language that can describe their struggle with a growing body that now feels alien, and their changing relationship with parents.

Mental health knowledge in internet and friendship communities

The internet has brought about a flattening of earlier hierarchies associated with information access, meaning that therapy appointments with these young people are often overlaid with terminology – ADHD, BPD, bipolar, anxiety, depression, dissociation. It takes time in the therapeutic relationship to discern meaning from these descriptive terms that young people use.

The friendship group and the wider online peer group are ever-present: they provide the needed support that young people have lost as they separate from parents. The turn from parents to the peer group was always a feature of adolescence, but today it takes particular forms. Their texting conversations with friends sometimes involve expressions of suicidal risk and subsequent offers of therapeutic help, with young people oscillating between the roles of patient and therapist, the phone as the umbilical cord between them. In a recent article (MacGregor, 2022), one contributor was quoted as saying:

> My friends all talk about mental health really openly. Some of them have a couple of panic attacks a week, or a couple a day on bad days.

Another says, even more concerningly:

> I turn to social media. . . . If I use a hashtag like #DepressionTok on my videos, I start to find other people that relate to me. It's nice to know you're not on your own.

The traditional psychoanalytic concept of hysteria (Freud, 1895) has fallen out of fashion today, due to its undertones of misogyny and its maligned history, yet it may have relevance in some adolescent self-harm presentations. Papadima (2019) writes that hysteria 'involves an unconscious but symbolised idea expressed via conversion through prevalent forms of 'mental illness' available to the sufferer within a particular social milieu' (p. 7). It is both a psychic structure and a way of relating and communicating with others (Bollas, 2000), which for adolescents can include parents, teachers, peers, and mental health professionals.

While in this chapter we are thinking about adolescents presenting in crisis with suicidal thoughts and engaging in self-harm, the frequent 'epidemics' of specific symptoms spreading within groups are not new phenomena, with laughing epidemics or group fainting episodes in schools being reported historically (Flanagan, 2012). The novel 'The virgin suicides' (Eugenides, 1993) describes this process well. The symptoms, ever-changing according to social context, mask the underlying affect linked to the originating trauma and so may be maintained in order to avoid addressing conflict.

Thinking in terms of hysterical, socially spreading presentations guides us to look at what an adolescent may be *doing* through their symptoms, rather than being too focused on the symptoms themselves. The symptom is thus to be understood, in this way of thinking, as a communication. It needs to be taken seriously (as such a symptom can be severe), but curiosity about its meaning is also essential. Without that, what looks like validation for a symptom and a concerning presentation actually neglects and dismisses the adolescent's real distress and their need for help in making sense of their struggle for identity.

The fact that sexuality has historically been a central factor in hysteria may go some way toward explaining both its prevalence in adolescents, whose sexuality is developing, and why it has fallen out of favour as a concept. André Green (1995) documented a wider progressive move away from an interest in sexuality within psychoanalysis, noting a tendency to think of our patients as sexually undifferentiated babies. We would argue that within what has been described as a 'hypersexualised society' (Kammeyer, 2013), the disturbing effect that sexual development can have on an adolescent can be easily overlooked or underestimated. In reality, the emergence of sexuality in adolescence can be experienced as a significant upheaval and even a trauma (Papadima, 2021). In our experience, thinking with an adolescent about this part of their life can be helpful in addressing underlying conflicts and the behaviours that follow.

We also have in mind the concept of social contagion, which refers to culturally communicated clusters of mental health presentations becoming prevalent in certain times and places (Hacking, 1998). There are links between the concepts of hysteria and social contagion, as individuals more open to suggestion (which adolescents in search of identity undoubtably are) can be vulnerable to both. The symptoms that emerge offer

a seemingly perfect solution: a nameable, concrete 'disease' firmly places the problem outside the self. The problem is then placed at a safe distance from one's underlying confusing, unnameable distress, and also outside of what is conceived of as personal responsibility.

(Papadima, 2019, p. 11)

There have been numerous reports over the years of ways mental health symptoms can become widespread among groups of adolescents. This tends to happen mostly with girls, but not exclusively: boys too have their group identities, changing from generation to generation. We concentrate, though, on females in this chapter because of their prevalence in the presentation we describe.

STEER's 'Young people's mental health in the UK' report (2022) reveals that girls aged 11 are now 30% more likely to suffer from poor mental health than boys of the same age, and by the time girls reach 18, they are more than twice as likely to experience poor mental health than boys of the same age. Young women tend to present more often in crisis – for example, thinking about suicide, planning, or attempting it (all dangerous and serious in themselves) – while boys tend to behave in more internalised ways, keeping their feelings to themselves and having a higher risk of completed suicide (Miranda-Mendizabal et al., 2019).

Why the interest in mental health?

We can speculate about the various reasons for young people's interest today in the language of mental health. The widespread individualistic tendency in our societies may be part of the explanation (focusing on individual rather than community explanatory frameworks for understanding pathology) (see Hari, 2018, for more on this).

In addition, the ordinary and needed passage through adolescent narcissism – an important turn inwards to establish a solid adult identity – requires young people to look for a 'special' status or 'label' to identify who they are. Adding to this, the wider cultural focus on identity as a major concept structuring progressive politics nowadays feeds into the ways identities can be seen as solid and final rather than transient.

Further, we know that adolescents today tend to have more internalising problems rather than externalising ones, with mental health symptoms such as self-harm, intense anxiety, and suicidality taking the place of the transgressions of previous generations, such as over-drinking, running away, or behaving in more obviously delinquent ways (Patalay & Gage, 2019).

Our own adult emphasis on psychiatric diagnoses, genetics, biology, and medication to understand human distress also forms part of the picture – including how we think of the role of psychotherapy. American psychoanalyst Nancy McWilliams (2015) points out the shift in our societies of moving from psychotherapy formulated as a healing relationship addressing complexity and meaning to one viewed today as a set of tools and strategies to treat distinct, clearly delineated mental health conditions, similar to broken bones or infections.

Open, less-stigmatised media discussions on mental health also play a role, with definite benefits; but our culture's intense interest in mental health has drawbacks too. Today's adolescents, like the young women described in Freud's time (1895), may unconsciously imitate but also mock the adult generation, forcing us adults to confront the limitations and inadequacies of our medicalised model. Adolescents are drawn in by the answers we, the adult generation, offer them: we have told them that the answer to human distress involves a mental health diagnosis and psychiatric medication. But as the passionate, questioning young people they are, they take our medicalised model to its caricatured extreme and expose its absurdity, challenging us to reconsider our beliefs about what makes a good life.

The new forms of delinquency and breaking boundaries

Delinquency and breaking boundaries are also relevant concepts here, yet they can be hard to name. The underlying communication of the delinquent – *'please notice me and offer me care, which I need'* – is noted in research from France (Le Breton, 2017). This study highlights the counterintuitive 'social logic' of self-harm as a form of boundary-breaking. Self-harm in adolescence, pragmatically, offers access to more support during a challenging time of life. The author concludes that self-harm and suicidality may nowadays be a necessary rite of passage, strongly influenced by culture.

This very normal need for care and support is ignited in part by the adolescent's changing body, an emerging, fully sexual body which, however, still needs care. Often, self-harming young people visit the school nurse, who cleans and bandages their wounds, reminding us of an infant cared for by an attentive mother. There is a bind here we can all relate to if we think back to our own adolescence: the adolescent wishes for physical care, but it's shameful to request or receive this from parents in a growing, sexual body. So we can speculate that the self-harm or talk of suicidality can unconsciously become ways for needs to be met and support to be offered, with adults and the friendship group helping.

The rapid onset of these problems can feel baffling to parents, who may try to reassure themselves that *'this is just a phase'* or (more angrily) that *'it's attention-seeking'*. These reactions leave young people feeling misunderstood and patronised, risking a deterioration, with risk escalating sometimes until they feel heard. Our task is to respect and accept the adolescent's identity while at the same time working with them to loosen and explore it.

Suicidality and self-harm in adolescents

A recent psychiatric study (Uh et al., 2021) identifies two distinct groups of self-harming adolescents at age 14:

a 'psychopathology' pathway, associated with early and persistent emotional difficulties and bullying; and an 'adolescent risky behavior' pathway, whereby risk taking and external challenges emerge later into adolescence and are associated with self-harm.

The main point in this research is that the subgroup of self-harming young people who don't present with severe psychopathological traits and who may be going through adolescent turmoil is much larger and requires a different form of treatment. This treatment can be shorter-term, focusing on adolescent processes, peer relations, and family functioning, rather than assuming these young people will end up with enduring borderline features, deep persistent depression, or self-destructiveness lasting into adulthood and attributed to longstanding trauma.

This doesn't mean that some young people's difficulties *don't* persist into adulthood – some may, as James Masterson has shown (1967). But there is much that can be done to prevent this stabilisation of symptoms, and there is important work in differentiating the manifest symptoms, including mental health language, from the underlying concerns.

Suicidality in adolescents comes in many guises. In our experience – and as the preceding research shows (Uh et al., 2021) – the adolescents presenting with an 'unwell persona', through which they understand their distress, in most cases don't want to die but are trying to find a good reason to live – which can be hard. By 'wanting to die' we mean the adolescent's suicidal wish to 'kill off' themself, their body, or the 'other' within them. The adolescents we refer to feel completely stuck and overwhelmed, looking desperately for an exit route. They often think, 'What's the point?', or report feeling 'fed up', and in exploration they talk about not being able to 'find a way out' from how they experience life. The language of suicide provides this exit route. They are looking for a way to alert their family, friends, and school to their need for additional support and for a radical change in their circumstances.

We have found, in our own work, that explicitly opening up and exploring the meaning of suicidal thoughts can help. Together with our patients, we conceptualise the symbolic function of their symptoms, and in so doing we have a chance to treat the cause rather than the symptom of their distress. This is a theme we will return to.

In young people with the 'unwell persona' presentation, we have noticed that self-harm doesn't tend to be that regular or habitual. With good support, respect, and care, self-harm may either stop entirely or continue infrequently, usually in response to something that has happened in the adolescent's life. Our approach has been to focus not so much on the self-harm itself but, rather, on understanding what it means to the adolescent. This is only effective, however, if the underlying problems are understood in the context of their whole life, building together with them an explanation that makes sense and 'fits'.

We will now share some general thoughts about the cultural context in which adolescents come of age today.

The cultural context: the 'ecological niche' in which young people come of age

Ian Hacking, philosopher of science, has explored the importance of the cultural context in which specific mental illnesses evolve. He says:

> Transient mental illnesses can best be looked at in terms of the ecological niches in which they can appear and thrive.

(Hacking, 2006)

Young people come of age today in a cultural context that may be, in certain ways, unsupportive of their development of identity and of the normal processes of separation and negotiating sexuality. In the news there is continuous information about global unrest, authoritarian movements increasing their power worldwide, and the climate crisis as a frightening background. Young people are often told they are set to inherit a broken system and a dying world.

This is a world where resources are stretched for most families, inequality is increasing, achievement is prioritised, and relationships and community can be undervalued, while the individual tends to be the focus. In this context, at least in the United States and the UK, we argue that we lack, nowadays, a realistic and convincing collective narrative around adolescence and the route to a satisfying adulthood.

Of course, there was never a time in history where problems didn't exist. Arguably, though, the difference today is the non-stop bombardment of news and information via digital sources and social media – the 24/7 news cycle that we all have to grapple with. This can be understood as one of the 'nested circles' around the individual that psychologist Urie Bronfenbrenner delineates (1979), the 'ecological niche' (Hacking, 1998) in which adolescents come of age. Psychologist Paula Durlofsky (2020), amongst others, documents the complex ways mental health today is affected by social media and the online world.

We can speculate that for the average child from a 'good enough' home, there is a current paradox: a relatively easy life with limited responsibilities, alongside a wider, complicated, and unequal world available to be witnessed online 24/7. This compromises emotional development, particularly when it comes to the development of healthy narcissism, aggression, sexuality, and identity formation.

In an earlier draft of this chapter, we went to great lengths to outline statistics about how life has changed for adolescents in the last 20 years. While a detailed look at these changes is, we decided, beyond the scope of this chapter, what we found was that the two places where adolescents spend most of their time – home and school – are, on average, now under considerable pressure. Both have access to fewer resources, alongside greater public expectation of their responsibilities.

Sexuality: a risky arena in the modern world

Despite more open societal discussions on sexuality, including school sex education, the public fears around paedophilia, sexual abuse, online grooming, and pornography create today the perception of an unsafe environment. This perception of risk has been documented over a number of years. In addition, young people nowadays learn about sexuality not just through their experiences with each other and with their own bodies but also through online content. Previously extreme sexual behaviours may thus be normalised nowadays through online porn.

So even when children today don't experience poverty, abuse, disability, or parental illness, current social changes make it harder to have a 'good enough' childhood – one with adequate ordinary risks to build independence and resilience, and with sexuality feeling a safe and exciting arena to explore. Research, indeed, shows that, when asked, children report being less happy in multiple areas of life than even ten years ago (The Children's Society, 2022).

We see the evidence of this perception of unhappiness in the steep rise of referrals to children's mental health services. We can surmise that the currently prevalent views of adolescents' emerging sexuality as potentially risky and dangerous may be part of this unhappiness, explaining to some degree young people's tendency to retreat to the online, at-home world, exhibiting fewer outwardly risky behaviours.

It would be fair to say that it's a confusing time to be a child or to raise one.

The search for identity: psychoanalytic ideas

What drives the feverish search for identity in early adolescence? Donald Meltzer (1967, p. 12) says 'the centre of gravity of the experience of identity shifts – and in the adolescent it shifts wildly and continually'. These constant shifts in the 'centre of gravity' explain the instability, splits, and diffusion we observe in this age group.

Blos (1967) highlights parallels between the 'second individuation' process in adolescence and the separation process in infancy and toddlerhood, as described by Margaret Mahler (Mahler et al., 1975). He sees regression as potentially productive in this process, while adolescents restructure and consolidate their character:

> The adolescent longs for the comforts of drive gratification but fears the reinvolvement in infantile object relations. Paradoxically, only through regression, drive and ego regression, can the adolescent task be fulfilled.
>
> (Blos, 1967, p. 170)

The normal and expected regression in early adolescence includes a frequent return to action rather than verbalisation. There may be a pull towards merging and idealisation, and activity as a defence against feelings of loss. In this process, the young adolescent often disempowers and rejects the parents, as can be expected, and it is important for parents to maintain their connection with their teens: if the relationship with parents really breaks down, the adolescent finds themselves in a void, with too much actualised power. There is now no parental authority for them to fall back on (Schmidt Neven, personal communication).

This is a paradoxical bind: without parental authority, the young person achieves the much-longed-for freedom and power, setting the terms of the dialogue with adults, who may feel they are 'held hostage' by the risky behaviour. Yet on the other hand, emotionally the adolescent is now more alone than ever, treated like a much younger version of themselves, monitored continuously, but not really heard and understood.

The diffusion of identity

Meltzer (1967) wrote about the 'diffusion of identity' in early adolescence and described the experience of self as 'a feeling of limitation akin to littleness, tinged with loneliness' (Meltzer, 1967, p. 13). Young adolescents, of course, wish to evade these vulnerable, destabilising feelings. One option, in their regression, is to identify with the 'unwell persona' – the mental health labels – we have described. This achieves much of what Blos (1967) talked about: feelings are enacted through self-harm; merger and idealisation operate within the peer group; and frenetic online and offline activity defends against loss. Without meaning to, the surrounding adults end up reinforcing these defensive actions as they try to closely attune to and monitor the adolescents as if they were infants. We have been struck by how many parents end up sleeping in the same room as their adolescents to monitor risk, or take away their doors. We have also been struck by how schools react to adolescents who present in this way – giving them passes to leave class frequently, or even accepting sharpeners used for self-harm in class. These allowances, seen as a response to mental health risk, would never be made for young people with more traditionally 'behavioural' issues.

We wonder whether this is a version of Ferenczi's 'confusion of tongues' (1949), where the symbolic, metaphorical function of adolescents' symptomatology is not recognised. The adults, scared and uncertain, take it as a given that young people's difficulties must be as disturbing as their words and behaviour. Their responses befit deep pathology – ambulances, risk assessments, one-on-one vigils. On a surface level, these responses validate the adolescent's powerful wishes, but more meaningfully, they leave them unheard and alone. The danger is that the adolescent's regression becomes actualised, risking a breakdown in their development, rather than supporting it.

The turbulent passage into adulthood

Blos (1967) describes how deficiencies in early ego development are laid bare during the second individuation process that occurs in adolescence: even the kindest childhood includes innumerable opportunities for emotional injury. Evans and Evans (2021) have explored the possibility that some young people with sudden-onset gender dysphoria may be nursing 'hidden grievances' against their parents.

Given the complications and challenges of a normal childhood nowadays, we see much that teenagers could be protesting about more widely. We thus wonder whether the ideas of Susan and Marcus Evans (Evans & Evans, 2021) could be expanded to help us understand the frighteningly large number of suicidal and self-harming adolescents we see today.

Adolescence represents an opportunity for 'normal childhood trauma' to be reworked; but what we have observed is how hard it is for such difficulties to be viewed as part of a developmental struggle and a protest against the limitations of modern life, a meaningful but often only temporary regression, as described by Blos. Instead, these experiences often come parcelled within the 'unwell persona' identity, running the risk of becoming more permanent.

It is clear from all this, we hope, that the adult network's response is key in whether the adolescent's unwell identity becomes entrenched or is left behind, followed by a more ordinary, satisfying developmental path.

We will now describe some clinical material to illustrate our thoughts. What we present is an imagined, composite case study. It isn't based on any real scenario or case that either of us has worked with. The material is inspired by our overall experience of working with adolescents. The way this case unfolds attempts to describe the work we, as child and adolescent psychotherapists, may do with young people and families with such difficulties.

Clinical material

The referral

In mid-October, our team receives a GP referral for a 14-year-old girl. We will name her Meera. The referral tells us that she has struggled with her mental health since starting Year 9 in September, with symptoms of anxiety and depression. Her parents are concerned as she no longer wants to go to dance classes, which she used to love. When they try to encourage her, she becomes angry, alluding she is too anxious to go. She spends increasing amounts of time online and protests when her parents try to limit this, telling them this is her main source of social contact. Her sleeping habits have changed. Her mother and teachers have seen evidence of self-harm on her arms.

The referral also tells us that Meera refuses to talk about any of this, other than to tell the GP she wants to be dead.

I[3] offer an appointment in ten days' time.

A crisis at school

Soon after, before the date of the appointment, our team gets an urgent call from the school. Meera's head of year, Ms Lacey, tells me, worried, that Meera has approached her to disclose acute suicidal thoughts, including intrusive thoughts about jumping off a bridge. As per school policy, Ms Lacey has called the parents and asks us whether she should call an ambulance, as the school day is coming to a close.

In exploring the circumstances in which this disclosure arose, Ms Lacey offers some background. Meera has been suffering panic attacks in class for some time. A while ago, she was given permission to use a pass to leave lessons when she can't manage, and the school has arranged a rota of staff to support her. Recently, however, there has been a shift in the school towards stricter guidelines and less of a focus on mental health. Staff have been told they need to question pupils when they use the pass to leave class, only allowing them a brief period of time in designated spaces before being accompanied back to class. Ms Lacey wonders whether this firmer stance might have played a role in Meera's worsening state. She knows that certain students, including Meera, disagree with these new rules, thinking they don't work. At the same time, she can see that Meera wasn't being challenged to expand her comfort zone and manage to stay in class and was using her pass quite frequently. As a result, her academic work had suffered, adding to her distress: so the right balance between attention to Meera's mental health and the school's rules has been hard to strike. Ms Lacey feels frustrated by what seems to her an impossible conundrum.

We puzzle over what might have triggered the situation that arose specifically today. Ms Lacey remembers that this morning Meera approached a staff member, after leaving class, and as per the new rules, fairly inflexibly, she was encouraged to return to her lesson or consider going home instead. Meera felt desperate, reporting that she did not want to go home, but equally couldn't face going back to class.

We acknowledge how frustrated and increasingly despairing Meera might have felt with the new rules and, at the same time, how frightening it had been for school staff to witness this. Ms Lacey shared the guilt she felt, no longer feeling she had permission to spend as much time with Meera as she used to. She knows, she said, that Meera is angry about all these changes – other pupils are, too, and feeling unsupported. We wonder whether Meera's deterioration today was the result of all these things piling up, with today's 'stuckness' and frustration the triggers to this desperate disclosure, which had perhaps appeared as the only way for Meera to express how she felt and to be heard.

We think about the next steps. I suggest that when Meera's parents arrive at school, they could all meet together and discuss the difficult feelings that came up today, including the change of policy around using the pass, which was so important for Meera to manage school life and have some space. I assure Ms Lacey that hospital is an option should things remain stuck, but I also offer to see Meera and her parents the following day at the clinic, which might be more containing than a hospital.

As we end the call, I reflect on how Ms Lacey used the time on the phone to slow down and think through what had happened, making sense of Meera's words in the context they had arisen. As such, she was able to move slightly away from the language of risk and from the school policies designed to manage this. I am struck by how well Ms Lacey seemed to know Meera; she was well aware of the pressures Meera faced at school, some of which Ms Lacey herself was facing, with changing policies and piling pressures.

A team administrator called the family later the same day and confirmed an appointment the following morning.

Meeting the family and Meera

The next morning, I meet for the first time with Meera and her mother, Katrina.

Katrina appears slightly dishevelled. It's clear she has been anticipating this meeting. I notice and acknowledge that dad hasn't come to the appointment. The first ten minutes of our time together are dominated by Katrina describing, in a pressured voice, how the last few months have been dominated by uncertainty and various family pressures. Syed, Meera's father, is going through a period of unemployment, and there are health issues in the wider family. For both reasons, they have been considering whether to return to their home country or whether to remain in London for now. Katrina tells me she's not sure how, or if, these things have affected Meera, as she doesn't talk much. Meera squirms, as if uncomfortable, when her mum says this, and frowns, her eyes looking downward.

Katrina continues talking quickly; at times Meera appears ready to jump in but stops herself. While keeping my attention on Meera, I listen in these introductory minutes to Katrina, who appears tired and overwhelmed.

I steer the discussion to what brings them here today and suggest that Meera, too, may have been struggling recently, adding another pressure to the family – I mention that, of course, I am aware how hard yesterday, for example, was for Meera, leading to this urgent meeting today. Katrina slows down, as if taken aback, and acknowledges after a pause that Meera has indeed had a tough time recently: 'It is awful to be a teenager', Katrina says. 'Hormones are flying around; I remember that stage well'. Meera tries to jump in again – and I can see that the reference to 'hormones' hasn't gone down well with her. But before she manages to speak, Katrina wells up with tears and says that she really wishes Meera would tell them what has happened to her to cause this change in behaviour: 'You never talk to us anymore!', she says, turning to her. 'And then we get all these phone calls from school! We don't know what to do!'

In our discussion, it is acknowledged how hard it is having to deal with so many changes – Meera having all these worries on her mind and not feeling able to talk to those around her about them, but also how hard it is for Katrina, having to deal with so many different things. Meera is invited more directly into the conversation, with a mention of the toll the pandemic must have taken, right at the time she was turning into a teenager.

Meera, with her head still down, agrees with this with a faint nod but doesn't add anything further. Katrina says what she finds the hardest is that Meera's behaviour increasingly dominates family life. She explains that school has recommended they keep monitoring Meera. An edge of anger creeps in, which I notice Meera has seen too. Katrina turns to Meera abruptly and says, 'We keep searching your room for blades and keep checking on you. Do you have any idea how hard that is for us? How worried we are?' Meera suddenly speaks rapidly, protesting about how far this surveillance has already gone, before even seeing mental health professionals: her parents have installed an app to track her movements, with alerts if she leaves school or moves location unexpectedly: 'I hate it! I'm not a baby!' she cries out. She turns to me and adds, 'My parents keep nagging me about sleeping more, but night-time is my time, the only time they're not checking on me!'

After this exchange, which has led to stony but anxious silence from Katrina, Meera goes back to being withdrawn and non-communicative.

As this part of the session comes to a close, I thank Katrina and explain that I will now see Meera alone for a bit, and next week, I will meet with Katrina again. Katrina, before leaving for the waiting room, says she's glad Meera can talk in private, as she says so little at home. She turns to her and says, 'Please be open! Tell the therapist what's on your mind, be truthful!'

Meera's individual space

In our individual time together, initially Meera is silent. I reflect on what her mother has said in our joint time, commenting that it sounds like things have felt unstable in the family recently, and that can't have been easy. I also acknowledge the disagreement they clearly have about the version of events, and how normal that can be in families – we all see things differently. Meera's body relaxes a bit; she shifts to sit more comfortably in her chair. She tells me that she can't stand all this sudden attention and monitoring.

As the conversation unfolds, we discuss Meera's school experience. I say that she may know I spoke with Ms Lacey yesterday, who shared some information with me, which I'm aware Meera had agreed to – I know that Meera had disclosed she considers killing herself sometimes. I get a sense that this link between Ms Lacey and I, in Meera's mind, has softened things. She smiles tentatively and tells me that if it weren't for Ms Lacey, she wouldn't be managing at school. I'm aware that things have felt unstable at school, too, with changes happening there, like at home, and Meera nods. I add, 'And here I am now, yet another new person, talking to you about your personal life! Another person who may appear to be monitoring you!'

I wonder how she felt about coming today, and if she knows anything about our clinic. 'Obviously', she responds with confidence, 'everyone knows about CAMHS'. 'Really', I say, 'what do people say about it?'

Meera tells me: 'Well, if you want to come to CAMHS, they won't give you an appointment. You'll have to wait six months. But then if you don't want to come, they make you come, like me today, so it's a no-win situation.' After a pause, she says that a couple of her friends come to CAMHS too; but then another hasn't managed to get an appointment and got angry at Meera, who got one so quickly.

I say that all this sounds confusing – hard for Meera to know what to think about CAMHS and me as a therapist. I wonder if Meera knows whether she wants to be here or not. Meera smiles uncomfortably and shakes her head, clearly implying, 'No, I don't want to be here'. But then she pauses and looks at me. I voice her ambivalence about her wish for help but her reluctance to accept it.

During this discussion, Meera has become slowly more animated. She tells me about her friends, some of whom also have depression and anxiety: she worries about them. They all find having a pass to get out of class extremely helpful as it gives them a breathing space. She disagrees with the school stopping them from using it. There are all these rules and conditions now, many of them unclear.

'No one understands what's going on', she tells me. 'The teachers keep telling us that we need to take responsibility for ourselves, but then they make all these rules that make no sense, and don't trust us to know what we need'.

In the school's back-and-forth responses and the negotiations with students, the words of Adam Phillips seem relevant, about normal adolescent truancy and how it clashes with adult rules:

> The job of the truant mind is to keep conflict as alive as possible, which means that adolescents are free to be adolescent only if adults are free to be adults. The real problems turn up when one or other side is determined to resolve the conflict: when adolescents are allowed to live in a world of pure impulse, or adults need them to live in a world of incontestable law.
>
> (Phillips, 2009)

Thinking of this material, we can wonder whether Meera – and others at her school – has been allowed to exist at times in school in a 'world of pure impulse', while stricter new rules are an attempt (in vain) to impose 'a world of incontestable law'. A middle ground of more ordinary exchanges, appropriate to adolescents, and understanding what is going on is hard to achieve. This is partly because of the level of presenting risk, but also because of the school's more limited resources currently.

I reflect, in my discussion with Meera, that this sudden change in school life reminds me how things have changed at home as well. Meera goes quiet and looks at the floor. I sense her anger and comment on this. She suddenly bursts out: 'None of this has to do with my family! They can do what they want, for all I care.' I encourage her to let me know how she's feeling at the moment – I can see that talking about her family is not something that feels relevant, and she wants me to know that. Meera says, 'How do I feel? Well, I want to die all the time, and even when I appear happy, when others might think I'm OK, I'm really not'.

I wonder if those around her might be helped to understand how tricky it is: even when it looks like she's doing well, she still needs help, but they seem to not notice that. She agrees, telling me this is a common misconception about depression: people seem to forget it's going on at the first improvement. I encourage her to tell me about her experience and any questions she has about depression. She says she's researched online and knows it's depression – or maybe it's an anxiety disorder. She's not sure which one. I explore what these terms mean to her.

Without settling on a diagnosis, our discussion moves to her self-harm. She tells me that although it's always on her mind, she mostly manages not to hurt herself and has stayed 'clean' for a while. I ask how she achieves this, and she tells me about an online group she is part of where they all encourage each other not to cut. But then she adds, as an afterthought, 'It's also because my parents are on my back about it! I can't stand hearing them go on and on, so I've stopped self-harming even though I'd love to be doing it'. I acknowledge her mixed feelings about self-harm – part of her really wants to engage in it, but another part doesn't as it limits her independence in the end. I add that it sounds like in her friendship group they are really helping each other with 'keeping clean'. Meera enthusiastically agrees to this.

Following this first appointment, we hypothesise that this family may be struggling to recognise the impact of recent events on their daughter, coming at a time that is already developmentally a challenge. It is noted how animated Meera was when we spoke about the problems at school, her friendship group, and her life online, but that this was in sharp contrast to any mention of difficulties at home, which she seemed determined not to acknowledge or explore.

Meeting with parents

The following week, a meeting with both parents takes place.

Meera's father, Syed, tells me, with shame, that Meera has witnessed angry and emotional scenes at home over the past few months, particularly in relation to his employment difficulties. We think about how, now that he has found work, they as adults felt they had started to recover a sense of stability, but for Meera this hasn't happened yet. Katrina comments that Meera had become much less demanding for a while, not noticing, for example, when her dance lessons were forgotten. I wonder whether it had felt hard to talk to Meera about what was happening at the time of the family crisis because they, as adults, didn't yet quite know how to manage it all. It might have partly been a relief that Meera had withdrawn to her room and was asking less of them. Now that they feel stronger, they want to rebuild things, but it is now Meera who doesn't allow that to happen, as they see it. It must be so frustrating for them that Meera – out of nowhere – has all these problems. Even though they can speculate on the causes, it's still hard.

Syed agrees and tells me he doesn't feel he knows his daughter anymore. 'Maybe she became suicidal when I had my eye off the ball?' He talks, in a faint voice, about how awful it is to be thinking about his little girl cutting herself. He doesn't know how to respond.

We talk briefly about the parents' own adolescence, about that stage of life where there is a wish, and a need, for privacy, but also for care and attention. 'Maybe we've let her take the lead too much', Katrina says. 'When she became reluctant to go to her dance lessons, I thought, "Great, you're growing up. This was bound to happen eventually, and it's a pain to always have to drive you there." But now I wish I'd pushed her more – being part of that group was so important to her.'

Meeting with Meera again

In her second individual session, Meera talks more about her life at school and her friendship groups – both online and offline.

We talk again about the various difficulties her friends have and how she feels compelled to support them. I wonder whether it's hard when she gets pulled into supporting friends online and offline with their own mental health issues – that must be so worrying. Initially, she denies this, but then tells me about an instance where she was left feeling extremely worried about a friend. This discussion feels like a chink in Meera's armour and offers us a moment to reflect together on how unfamiliar these online environments can be, despite their promise of friendship and camaraderie; she acknowledges that with all the discussions of mental health, she sometimes feels out of her depth and responsible for her friends' well-being.

When talking about Meera's school friends, I find myself inwardly concerned about their talk of self-harm and suicide, yet I'm conscious that expressing this directly will threaten the alliance Meera and I are building, and so I continue to listen and occasionally question, showing curiosity.

Liaising with the school

As the first appointments take place, there continues to be liaison with the school, via Meera's head of year, Ms Lacey.

We think about ways they can support Meera to stay in school and in class which don't involve only following her lead or requests but which attend to her emotional needs. The head of year acknowledges that although she disagrees with the new rule not to allow pupils to use their pass and access staff support easily, she also doesn't feel that unlimited access was useful or had led to things improving. It still seems to her an impossible situation.

We think about how supporting Meera is about building relationships that she can access when school life becomes a challenge. This feels so demanding when there are so many students who struggle, and I remind Ms Lacey that this isn't just her responsibility and can be achieved even with small amounts of time with students – just letting them know they are remembered and cared for is important.

She then tells me how she feels she's become the 'go-to' member of staff to support struggling pupils; she feels so frustrated about this. She continues that she doesn't have any specific skills or training, but I disagree and tell her she is interested in pupils' emotional lives and knows what is going on with them on a day-to-day basis. This doesn't mean that it should just be her, though, doing this; we consider together whether other school staff could join her in this, and what gets in the way of that happening.

A brief intervention

In our continued work, conversations take place between all parties involved – school, home, Meera, and the therapist. Meera and Katrina have an argument about her giving up dance lessons, and Meera shouts at her mother that she hadn't come to her last recital, anyway. In a parent session, it is acknowledged that although Meera would no longer show excitement at her parents' attendance, we can assume she still had a powerful wish to be admired while dancing: she just won't say so. Meanwhile, Meera tells her therapist that she's started meeting with a mentor in school, who has been helping her think about how she can relax.

> She realises, she says shyly, that she likes drawing, and has started a new Instagram account to share her artwork: it's a space on social media where there is no mention of self-harm and suicide. 'As strange as it sounds – as I do want the support of friends for my mental health – I find it refreshing that no one talks about mental health in "Artstagram"', she confesses. 'No one else knows about my art account, not even my friends online.'

Meera has started to create a space in her life – and progressively, in her mind – where a healthier way of being and thinking can slowly emerge. She talks about how art helps her deal with the suicidal thoughts, through the different focus it offers. Her parents have also stepped back from constantly monitoring the risk, allowing Meera more space, as discussed in the parent sessions. They have been focusing on more ordinary, day-to-day conversations whenever Meera feels able to talk. It's clear that as Meera feels more connected to, and understood by, those around her, she is becoming more confident in expressing thoughts and emotions, sensing her parents' recovered capacity to tolerate and contain them.

A couple of months pass. In between moments of intensity and continued work with parents and the school, a more individual narrative peeks through.

> Meera tells me faintly that others need the help more; she should be managing things on her own by now: 'It's not so bad. I worry I'm faking it', she says. She regrets all the efforts that were made to help her yet keenly notices each time the guard is let down, feeling alone and unheard. By giving up the grip she had on the suicidal thoughts and self-harm, as conduits of expressing how bad she felt, she now feels vulnerable. I suggest that perhaps she had only one way to understand her struggle, and that if the words to describe it change, it appears less valid, but what she feels and thinks is still deeply painful and needs addressing.

She tentatively starts talking about her parents' sense of overwhelm; she secretly wonders whether they'll still move from the UK, which unsettles her, keeping her awake at night. And what if her dad loses his job again? Or a family member dies? She is also unsettled with her changing body and sexuality, which she hadn't had a chance to explore before. I am put keenly in touch with her feelings of shame but then experience her relief as we talk about these.

We try to find, together, a new, tentative language, moving away from action and talk of anxiety. She finds it strange to not use the language shared within her groups, online and offline. If not anxiety, not suicidality, not depression, not self-harm, then what? Her body starts to visibly relax as time passes. She becomes quieter. A more reflective conversation starts.

Gradually, and somewhat sooner than we expect, we come to agree that things have improved. Meera and her family's need for support is not as strong as it once was. Meera has not self-harmed for a while and no longer talks of wanting to die: that language doesn't make sense to her anymore. Work with her parents and her school mean that she now feels more supported and understood in her day-to-day life. Although Meera has made effective use of the sessions, she doesn't feel that longer-term work is necessary, and we tend to agree, as it could reinforce an unhelpful link with being unwell. We agree to bring this work to a close at our service.

In our final session, Meera says that sometimes she still thinks she has depression and anxiety, but not all the time. She has found it refreshing, stepping back from these discussions in her group of friends. We talk about how low mood and anxiety are signals that something isn't right and need to be taken seriously, but they're not necessarily an illness in themselves: they let us know we need to change things or get support.

Meera says that she had an awful day in school last week: she felt worried and sad and didn't want to be there. When she got home, her mum made her toast, and they sat in the garden together. It was a mild summer day, with a breeze. 'We didn't talk about any of it, but I felt better.' Later, she'd shown her mum her sketchbook, and they'd watched a TV show together. I reflected that what sounds like a difficult day had got better, and Meera nodded.

A theoretical framework

Meera is a challenge to us, because she adopts the language and behaviour of a very unwell young person, yet her difficulties fall at the extreme end of what every ordinary adolescent struggles with. She is negotiating the process of separation, working out how to care for herself, what space she needs at home, how to manage school life, how to develop and maintain friendships: how to discover who she is. Her family is under strain, yet in certain ways they cope admirably well.

There is nothing that striking in Meera's developmental history to suggest a pronounced difficulty in early relationships. We could guess that the internal reorganisation brought about by adolescence and emerging sexuality has exposed a level of fragility in her, coupled with a parallel fragility in her parents and wider family. This is also linked to Meera's rigid ego ideal of accomplished student, perfectly in control. The rigidity of this aspect of the ego leads to intolerable feelings of shame, feelings that the therapist was given a taste of in sessions.

Meera's friendship groups, online and offline, spoke the language of mental health and dangerous behaviour. They regularly discussed suicide and self-harm, as she repeatedly told me. When they struggled, they would text and ask each other about their mental health, with concern, with a sense of camaraderie; yet at other times, Meera would describe how guilty she and others would feel about influencing each other down this path.

For Meera, the ordinary omnipotence of early adolescence, which offers fuel to development, had got out of hand and had become anti-developmental, as the expectations of her age had become too much. Despite best intentions, she had been, we think, implicitly encouraged by how adults responded to her, reinforcing the unwell identity to get the help she needed. She unwittingly tested the adults around her with teasingly delinquent acts, leading to splits within the network, some seeing Meera's fragility, others seeing delinquency.

To stand up to Meera's behaviour, encourage boundaries and expectations, and try to engage her in therapeutic support felt hard. But to collude with the quite mad world she had been allowed to create would allow something disturbing to happen, risking the expansion and entrenchment of these behaviours, distorting Meera's ordinary adolescent process.

The passage through narcissism in adolescence

Attempting to create a formulation, we could speculate that Meera's mental health identity, like that of many others, accomplishes the following things: it buffers from reality, it opens access to care and support from adults, and it creates connection with peers.

Adolescents experience a smallness in their move towards the adult world. Margot Waddell (2006) highlights the special consideration we need to give to narcissism during this period. She argues that, during adolescence, narcissistic functioning represents a form of exploration. It is 'much more in the service of development than (it) may appear to be' (p. 22). The narcissistic, omnipotent behaviours of early adolescents thus represent a normal defence against the smallness and fragility felt in the face of the changes happening within their bodies and in their world, protecting them from shame when they don't live up to their elevated ideals. They seek refuge in the intense involvement in group life, and in twinning but also rivalrous relationships with peers. Waddell suggests that this:

> may indicate a healthy capacity to deal with a sense of internal fragility, even fragmentation, thus providing a constructive function, albeit narcissistic in essence.

Thus, for adolescents,

> what looks like a narcissistic disorder may be nearer to a defensive/self-protective, two-stage process of the projection of unfamiliar, unwanted or unmanageable parts of the self, or, indeed, cherished and loving parts, to be followed, in time, and perhaps with help, by a painful re-owning of those projections.
>
> (pp. 23–24)

In early adolescence, the friendship group is where one turns to discover and mirror identities. The peer group, as Dartington (1994) proposes, can become a space of 'temporary outsiders' from the adult-governed world, a transitional space (Winnicott, 1971) on the road to adulthood. When the boundary of the group is fluid – moving comfortably between inside and outside positions – it can be a space that helps teenagers digest experiences and develop an individual identity. Armstrong (2005) shows how containing the peer group can be, when parts of the adolescent personality projected into the group members can be reassembled helpfully.

However, in the poorly functioning group, peer relationships may become primarily narcissistic, with the group becoming rigid in its rules on how to identify and behave. Copley (1993) drew parallels between the adolescent group's function and Esther Bick's (1968, 1986) ideas on early object relating, suggesting that sometimes group relations can acquire an 'adhesive stickiness' and provide 'second skin'–type containment (Copley, 1993, p. 100). In these cases, peers, both online and offline, can become idealised, representing the adolescent's rigid ego ideal.

Adolescent depression

When considering mental health difficulties in adolescence, it has long been acknowledged that relying on adult diagnostic criteria and frameworks is at best limiting, and at worst risks total misunderstanding. Anastasopoulos (2007) believes that narcissistic mechanisms are dominant in most cases of adolescent depression.

While clinicians and researchers (for example, Midgley et al., 2015) have long been aware that depression appears differently in adolescents, the specifics of this developmental context can sometimes be overlooked. Researchers in Norway (Stänicke & Haavind, 2018; Stänicke, 2021) have emphasised the differences between adult and adolescent self-harm – in adolescence, self-harm is linked to confusion around relational needs and identity development.

Loss is a central theme in early adolescence, one which Anastasopoulos suggests is 'structural . . . [and] threatens the whole of the individual's psychic cohesion' (p. 348). The adolescent is perilously dependent upon external affirmation to shore up their constructed image, the primary aim of which is to defend against the 'small' fragile self that exists underneath and their anxieties around sexuality. We see this need for affirmation in their powerful desire to be admired and validated and their uncompromising criticism of others. When these mechanisms fail, it can lead to self-harm, which can relieve anxiety through punishment of the environment that has failed to support their defensive operation.

We think that narcissistic depression is a useful framework when considering young people presenting with this 'unwell identity'. The failure to understand the depression within its developmental stage, coupled with the alarming risky symptoms, has led to a collective misunderstanding of this presentation, encouraged by society's mental health discourse based on adults. It is worth noting that we have both worked in services where, from referral, young people presenting in this way are labelled personality disordered or 'borderline'. This misunderstanding leads to unhelpful management strategies from parents, schools, and mental health teams, robbing the adolescent of the reality touchstone they need to help them move forward developmentally, and risking such relational difficulties becoming entrenched.

The intense friendship groups of young people who identify as unwell can offer containment. But when these mental health identifications take control and the adult world becomes ineffective in its responses, because of fearing suicide, the results can be profoundly serious. The risk is, we think, that narcissistic mechanisms can become ingrained, with self-harming and suicidal behaviours becoming the way to live adolescent life. School engagement can suffer, and the ego can become gradually rigid and uncompromising. That is why early intervention is crucial.

Walking the tightrope

Adam Phillips (2011, p. 191) talks about the paradoxical, tightrope position we need to hold when working with adolescents:

> In treating adolescents we have to be double agents – on the side of the adult world and its values that the adolescent needs to enter, and on the side of the adolescent's protest against this world, on the side of his intelligent protest against it. If we take either side too strongly – become either policemen or fellow delinquents – the adolescent will feel betrayed by us. In other words, in

order to engage with their struggle we have to do the one thing they can't as yet do; remember what it is to be a child and remember what it is to be an adult.

As a society, the more we discuss and take the stigma out of 'mental health', the more we miss everyday conversations about discomfort and unhappiness – the ups and downs of life. The flashing lights of suicide, self-harm, dissociated states, and anorexia cause us to lose sight of what lies beneath. The ordinary smallness and confusion that the adolescent experiences do not flash as brightly, but getting in touch with these experiences can sometimes be more painful than talking about suicide or self-harming.

We are reminded of Anna Freud, who guides us to bypass the 'misleading quality of manifest symptomatology' (1970, p. 19). Indeed, we have noticed that often, when we put aside the external presentation (= the risk) and attend to the latent material (= the meaning), the risky behaviours subside. Anna Freud (1970, pp. 19–20) says:

> Symptoms are no more than symbols, to be taken merely as indications that some mental turmoil is taking place in the lower strata of the mind. Many symptoms, important and unassailable as they seem if untreated, give way fairly easily to many types of therapy.

Our interventions with these young people focus on three areas: first, supporting the development of healthy narcissism; second, addressing the meaning of the risk behaviours, or more widely, the meaning of the existing crisis; and third, encouraging ego growth. Identity is a key element, as we negotiate the move from the grandiose, omnipotent, 'unwell persona' to a more reality-based position, where vulnerability, sexuality, aggression, and loss can be experienced without overwhelming the ego.

Establishing a therapeutic relationship is the first and most crucial step, and we have found it helpful to align ourselves with the narcissistic defence. This means strongly conveying our interest, curiosity, and admiration for the young people. Over time, the ego ideal – a major source of persecutory anxiety for adolescents – becomes clearer in the therapy, and a shared understanding of its defensive function and unhelpful nature can develop. This work can develop in a 'two steps forward, one step backward' way. The question of *who am I* is central. As projections are re-owned, the adolescent can discover creative parts of themselves which develop into pillars of their new identity.

Work with the network (parents and school) is key. We have been helped to develop our thinking by Bronfenbrenner's ecological systems theory (1979), and the work of Ruth Schmidt Neven (2016). Both these authors have underlined that young people exist within 'circles' of connection and care – these circles need to be central to our work, rather than peripheral. Parents and schools often feel confused and powerless in the face of the dramatic behaviour and language of adolescents and can turn to infantilising, placatory measures to keep them safe.

We have found that helping both parents and schools engage with the developmental context in which these difficulties arise can re-awaken curiosity and help decipher the communication behind the symptoms. Rather than use words like 'regression', we can think with parents and schools about 'states of mind' in which adolescents might communicate like younger children. We find that in cases where parents and schools collaborate closely with us and we create a joint formulation, the young person can sometimes recover fairly quickly. However, even in cases where this work is slow, it is striking to us how slight changes in this area can have a profound impact on the young person's capacity to move forward developmentally and beyond the need to be unwell.

We were interested by recent research from Norway on adolescents' pathways into and out of self-harm (Stänicke, 2021). The participants in this study had received therapy, and although they valued their exploration of self-harm through this medium, they also felt ambivalent about the help they had received. They reported that they had found their own way to stop injuring themselves, which, they felt, was unrelated to the therapy. Stänicke (2021) links this to the developmental holding the therapy offered, allowing the self-agency, autonomy, and identity of these young people to progress, forming into a healthy, core narcissism rather than its more malignant version.

This is precisely where we feel the work has been with these young people. We have needed the support of a team that broadly shares our way of thinking, making it possible for us to look beyond the young people's frightening presenting symptoms and to feel able to create a robust therapeutic structure within which the adolescent can feel safe enough to explore their fears around the 'smallness' of their core self.

Notes

1 This chapter is based on an article originally published in the *Journal of Child Psychotherapy*, 49, 1, 2023, pp. 95–119.
2 Diagnostic and Statistical Manual of Mental Disorders.
3 The therapist will be referred to in the first person throughout.

References

Anastasopoulos, D. (2007). The narcissism of depression or the depression of narcissism and adolescence. *Journal of Child Psychotherapy*, 33(3), 345–362. https://doi.org/10.1080/00754170701667197

Armstrong, D. (2005). *Organisation in the mind: Psychoanalysis, group relations and organisational consultancy*. Karnac.

Bick, E. (1968). The experience of the skin in early object-relations. *International Journal of Psychoanalysis*, 49(2), 484–486.

Bick, E. (1986). Further considerations on the function of the skin in early object relations. *British Journal of Psychotherapy*, 2(4), 292–301. https://doi.org/10.1111/j.1752-0118.1986.tb01344.x

Blos, P. (1967). The second individuation process of adolescence. *The Psychoanalytic Study of the Child*, 22(1), 162–186. https://doi.org/10.1080/00797308.1967.11822595

Bollas, C. (2000). *Hysteria*. Routledge.

Bronfenbrenner, U. (1979). *The ecology of human development: Experiments by nature and design*. Harvard University Press.

Caron, C. (2022, October 29). Teens turn to TikTok in search of a mental health diagnosis. *The New York Times*. Retrieved November 1, 2022, from https://www.nytimes.com/2022/10/29/well/mind/tiktok-mental-illness-diagnosis.html

The Children's Society. (2022). *The good childhood report*. https://www.childrenssociety.org.uk/good-childhood

Copley, B. (1993). *The world of adolescence*. Free Association Books.

Dartington, A. (1994). The significance of the outsider in families and other social groups. In: S. Box (Ed.), *Crisis at adolescence* (pp. 91–110). Aronson.

Durlofsky, P. (2020). *Logged in and stressed out: How social media is affecting your mental health and what you can do about it*. Rowman & Littlefield.

Eugenides, J. (1993). *The virgin suicides*. Farrar, Straus & Giroux.

Evans, S., & Evans, M. (2021). *Gender dysphoria: A therapeutic model for working with children, adolescents and young adults*. Phoenix Publishing House.

Ferenczi, S. (1949). Confusion of tongues between the adult and the child. *International Journal of Psychoanalysis*, 30(2), 225–230.

Flanagan, C. (2012, January 28). Hysteria and the teenage girl. *New York Times*. Retrieved May 18, 2022, from https://www.nytimes.com/2012/01/29/opinion/sunday/adolescent-girl-hysteria.html

Foster, J., & Schmidt Neven, R. (2022, May 18). Podcast: #9 *Keeping children and young people safe in the cyber-world* with Jordan Foster. https://ccfdau.podbean.com/e/9how-to-keepchildren-and-young-people-safe-with-jordan-foster/

Freud, A. (1970). The symptomatology of childhood – a preliminary attempt at classification. *The Psychoanalytic Study of the Child*, 25(1), 19–41. https://doi.org/10.1080/00797308.1970.11823274

Freud, S. (1895). Studies on hysteria. *Standard Edition*, 2, 1–355. The Hogarth Press and the Institute of Psycho-Analysis, London.

Green, A. (1995). Has sexuality anything to do with psychoanalysis? *The International Journal of Psycho-Analysis*, 76(Pt 5), 871–883.

Hacking, I. (1998). *Mad travellers: Reflections on the reality of transient mental illnesses*. University Press of Virginia.

Hacking, I. (2006, August 17). Making up people. *London Review of Books*, 28(16). Retrieved November 1, 2022, from https://www.lrb.co.uk/the-paper/v28/n16/ian-hacking/making-uppeople

Hari, J. (2018). *Lost connections: Uncovering the real causes of depression – and the unexpected solutions*. Bloomsbury Publications.

Kammeyer, K. (2013). *A hypersexual society: Sexual discourse, erotica, and pornography in America today*. Palgrave Macmillan.

Kristeva, J. (2007). *Rethinking "normative conscience"*. *Common Knowledge,* 13 (Spring-Fall) (translation altered). Cited in Phillips (2011).

Le Breton, D. (2017). Understanding skin-cutting in adolescence: Sacrificing a part to save the whole. *Body & Society*, 24(1–2), 33–54. https://doi.org/10.1177/1357034X18760175

MacGregor, E. (2022, April 1). What it's really like being a teenage girl in Britain today. *The Times*. https://www.thetimes.co.uk/article/what-its-really-like-being-a-teenage-girl-in-britaintoday-jrh67hkrp

Mahler, M., Pine, F., & Bergman, A. (1975). *The psychological birth of the human infant*. Basic Books.

Masterson, J. E. (1967). *The psychiatric dilemma of adolescence*. Brunner/Mazel Publishers.

McWilliams, N. (2015, November 6). *Nancy McWilliams talks to New Therapist. YouTube video*. Retrieved November 1, 2022, from https://www.youtube.com/watch?v=ptvbUjjdJ8E

Meltzer, D. (1967). Identification and socialization in adolescence. *Contemporary Psychoanalysis*, 3(2), 96–103. Reprinted in *Meltzer, Sexual States of Mind* (1973). https://doi.org/10.1080/00107530.1967.10745117

Midgley, N., Parkinson, S., Holmes, J., Stapley, E., Eatough, V., & Target, M. (2015). Beyond a diagnosis: The experience of depression among clinically-referred adolescents. *Journal of Adolescence*, 44(1), 269–279. https://doi.org/10.1016/j.adolescence.2015.08.007

Miranda-Mendizabal, A., Castellví, P., Parés-Badell, O., Alayo, I., Almenara, J., Alonso, I., Blasco, M. J., Cebrià, A., Gabilondo, A., Gili, M., Lagares, C., Piqueras, J. A., Rodríguez-Jiménez, T., Rodríguez-Marín, J., Roca, M., Soto-Sanz, V., Vilagut, G., & Alonso, J. (2019). Gender differences in suicidal behavior in adolescents and young adults: Systematic review and meta-analysis of longitudinal studies. *International Journal of Public Health*, 64(2), 265–283. https://doi.org/10.1007/s00038-018-1196-1

Papadima, M. (2019). Rethinking self-harm: A psychoanalytic consideration of hysteria and social contagion. *Journal of Child Psychotherapy*, 45(3), 291–307. https://doi.org/10.1080/0075417X.2019.1700297

Papadima, M. (2021). Trauma in child psychotherapy: Some thoughts around a concept. *Journal of Child Psychotherapy*, 47(3), 433–452. https://doi.org/10.1080/0075417X.2021.2021545

Patalay, P., & Gage, S. H. (2019). Changes in millennial adolescent mental health and health related behaviours over ten years: A population cohort comparison study. *International Journal of Epidemiology*, 48(5), 1650–1664. https://doi.org/10.1093/ije/dyz006

Phillips, A. (2009). In praise of difficult children. *London Review of Books*, 31(3).

Phillips, A. (2011). The pleasures of working with adolescents. *Psychodynamic Practice*, 17(2), 187–197. https://doi.org/10.1080/14753634.2011.562698

Schmidt Neven, R. (2016). *Time-limited psychodynamic psychotherapy with children and adolescents: An interactive approach*. Routledge/Taylor & Francis Group.

Stänicke, L. I. (2021). The punished self, the unknown self, and the harmed self – toward a more nuanced understanding of self-harm among adolescent girls. *Frontiers in Psychology*, 12. https://doi.org/10.3389/fpsyg.2021.543303

Stänicke, L. I., & Haavind, H. (2018). How do young people understand their own self-harm? A meta-synthesis of adolescents' subjective experience of self-harm. *Adolescent Research Review*, 3(2), 173–191. https://doi.org/10.1007/s40894-018-0080-9

STEER Education. (2022). *Navigating the road of adolescence: Young people's mental health in the UK*. https://steer.education/wp-content/uploads/2022/02/Young-Peoples-Mental-Health-inthe-UK-STEER-Report-Feb-2022.pdf

Uh, S., Dalmaijer, E. S., Siugzdaite, R., Ford, T. J., & Astle, D. E. (2021). Two pathways to self-harm in adolescence. *Journal of the American Academy of Child and Adolescent Psychiatry*, 60(12), 1491–1500.

Waddell, M. (2006). Narcissism – an adolescent disorder? *Journal of Child Psychotherapy*, 32(1), 21–34. https://doi.org/10.1080/00754170600563703

Winnicott, D. W. (1971). Transitional objects and transitional phenomena. In: D. W. Winnicott (Ed.), *Playing and reality* (pp. 1–25). Tavistock Publications.

Chapter 3

'Too late for me'

The adolescent mental health crisis in time

Jocelyn Catty

Introduction

> The day before Layla, aged 13, was due to meet her psychotherapist for the first time, she took a significant overdose; frightened, she told her mother and was admitted to hospital. She later told her therapist, 'I think this therapy is too late for me'.

What might lead a young person of 13, from a generation popularly described as having 'their whole future ahead of them', to wish to throw that future away? In this chapter, I shall use psychoanalytic conceptions of time, along with the scholarship of an interdisciplinary study of time and waiting, to explore ideas about the adolescent mental health crisis, particularly as expressed in suicidal wishes and acts: acts that threaten to stop time. I shall argue that adolescence itself may be regarded as a crisis of time, and that to highlight its temporal dimensions may illuminate aspects of the adolescent suicidal mental health crisis.

In thinking about adolescence in time, I draw on the Waiting Times project (https://waitingtimes.exeter.ac.uk/), an interdisciplinary psychoanalytic and psychosocial study of time and care which focuses on waiting in and for healthcare and explores 'the value of waiting, even in the face of anxiety, urgency and political pressure' (Catty, 2023). The study foregrounds the waiting that is intrinsic to care and that may increasingly be lost or overshadowed as waiting *for* treatment becomes the defining experience of the modern National Health Service (NHS):

> Waiting is intrinsic to care. It is there in the extended time needed for therapy or therapeutics to work; in the watchful waiting before or after diagnosis; and in the time that stretches through remission, relapse, or palliative care.
>
> (Salisbury et al., 2023)

Temporal models that derive from Greek mythology help shape our understanding of the different functions and meanings of time, particularly in European cultures.

DOI: 10.4324/9781003592778-5

The three Greek gods *Chronos, Kairos*, and *Aion* represent fundamentally different models of time: Chronos, the time that progresses in linear fashion, time that can be counted; Kairos, the events that punctuate time, milestones, life events, or crises, including the opportune moment; and Aion, the epoch, the time of trends and cycles, of the unconscious and dreams. Consideration of Aion may also illuminate the specific pressures that predominate at a particular point – for instance, those exerted on adolescence in the present day.

In considering how today's young people may find themselves in a particular relationship to time, I shall focus on the idea of *too-lateness* encapsulated in the utterance of 'Layla' (who, like other young people described in this chapter, is a composite case derived from a range of clinical experiences) and other young people struggling with their relationship to the world, time, and help. I shall consider whether too-lateness may be seen as a distortion of *afterwardsness* (*Nachträglichkeit*) operating in young people trapped between a traumatic past and the fantasy of a bleak future, and I shall consider different uses of the time of psychoanalytic psychotherapy to help them.

Psychoanalytic time

To understand how adolescence itself might be seen as a crisis of time, it is helpful to consider, albeit briefly, psychoanalytic views of the importance of time in psychic development, along with the foregrounding of time in key psychoanalytic concepts. Understanding the distinctions between Chronos (linear time), Kairos (milestone time), and Aion (cyclic time) is useful here because of the ways in which the psychoanalytic literature interweaves models built on Chronos, linear or developmental time, and those built on Kairos, the time of the milestone, the transformative event, or the crisis. Psychoanalytic theory, in fact, is replete with models of time:

> Development, fixation, regression, repression, the return of the repressed, the timelessness of the unconscious, and Nachträglichkeit are some of the axes that permeate Freud's writings, in his discovery of a temporality that is truly psychoanalytical, and does not follow traditional, linear sequences of chronological time.
>
> (Perelberg, 2007a, p. xiii)

Rosine Josef Perelberg argues that 'dreams enabled Freud to discover a dismembered temporality, . . . and the timelessness of the unconscious' (Perelberg, 2007a, p. xiv). But Freud's discovery of the 'compulsion to repeat' (Freud, 1914) brought a 'paradigmatic shift', emphasising a network of concepts including trauma and infantile sexuality (Perelberg, 2007b, p. 1,475). If the unconscious is timeless, this involves less a suspension of time but, rather, a freedom from linear development that renders the past always present, imbuing conscious experience with powerful fantasies of the past and the future. The unconscious is thus characterised by 'the insistent rhythms of repeating, remembering and working through' (Baraitser, 2022, p. 382), and by a 'temporality that does not temporalize' (Kristeva, 2003, p. 31). In this psychoanalytic conception of time, time cannot simply be smoothly put behind us.

André Green argues that the superego has a particular function as 'an orientator of time' (2007, p. 18). Time becomes 'a logical structure in the human mind' (Kohon, 2007, p. 106) that is an essential prerequisite for the move to the depressive position (Bell, 2007, p. 81) and in which 'memory, though it contains fracture and loss, defines the relationship between past, present, and future' (Bell, 2007, p. 122). Andrea Sabbadini argues that the subjective sense of time is crucially connected to the development and maintenance of identity (1989, p. 475). He suggests that the child 'has to discover time, its presence, its absence, its duration':

> But the child has also to invent time, to construe it in his own peculiar way . . . as he becomes capable of reflecting upon himself as a separate person with his own individual history and his own individual destiny.
>
> (p. 479)

This description illustrates the interplay of Chronos (linear time) and Kairos (milestone time). Sabbadini's child progresses along a developmental axis, a chronology, but in the process, he *invents*, *discovers*, and *construes* time as he starts to experience fantasies of present, past, and future with a non-linear fluidity: fantasies that may be observed clinically and in everyday life in the satisfaction many children take in charts that mark the progress of time and their own activities, orienting them in time.

That developmental time is multiply layered is conveyed in the psychoanalytic child psychotherapy literature. Susanne Maiello has drawn attention to the ability of the foetus to perceive its mother's voice from four months' gestation, and her heartbeat from even earlier (1995, p. 26); against the sustaining rhythm of the maternal heartbeat, the mother's voice, coming and going, provides a 'prenatal precursor' to the breast: a 'sound object' that introduces the foetus to a proto-experience of separation (p. 28). This links with developmental psychology research into 'primary intersubjectivity' and the mutual regulation of feeling between mother and infant through sound (Trevarthen & Aitken, 2001, p. 5), which is regarded as central to the infant developing a sense of duration and 'going on being' (Shulman, 2019). The significance of sound and rhythm in early life has also been emphasised in the literatures on 'communicative musicality' (Malloch & Trevarthen, 2009) and neuroscience (McGilchrist, 2009).

Anne Alvarez (1992) has broadened the understanding of the significance of time and rhythm to consider the ways in which the rhythmic patterns and structures of an infant's life – the 'rhythm of life' (p. 28) – bound by feeding and sleeping, help institute a sense of time. This is consistent with Bion's idea that 'an infant acquires the concept of time from the experience of the primary relationship' (Civitarese, 2019, p. 198). A child's development of a sense of time is thus regarded as central to his or her psychological health, with adopted and 'looked-after' children, and those who have suffered early trauma, found to have a 'confused sense of past, present, and future' (Canham, 1999, p. 160), to the extent that they often find it hard to 'tell the time'.

Cutting across this developmental narrative driven by the 'arrow of time' (Rose, 2007, p. 44), key psychoanalytic concepts bring the layers of time together. The repetition compulsion (Freud, 1914) keeps the past continuously present, as does the transference in both clinical and everyday life. Heinz Weiss (2020) indeed describes the repetition compulsion as 'a hidden, embedded activity, which operates against the acknowledgement of time' (p. 1,179). Baraitser describes how *Nachträglichkeit* emerged in Freud's thinking (Freud, 1895) after the 'time frozen or blocked by fixation and trauma', where 'the ever-presentness of unconscious life is understood as the constant temporality that accompanies waking life and not just dream time or psychopathology' (Baraitser, 2022, p. 382). Later in this chapter, I shall consider whether the adolescent mental health crisis may put a particular inflection on the idea of Nachträglichkeit or afterwardsness: what I am thinking of as too-lateness.

Adolescence as a crisis of time

> I think of [adolescents] as being, essentially, Janus-faced – that is, looking both from the present to the unknown and therefore unsafe future, and also from the present back to the past.
>
> (Waddell, 2018, p. 199)

In considering whether adolescence might ever be experienced as *too late*, it is necessary to consider the pivotal nature of this stage of life, when 'one's past begins to catch up with one' (Laufer, 1995a, p. 72). At this time of bodily and emotional changes, described by Winnicott as the 'long meanwhile' (1962, p. 81) of adolescence, the young person may feel caught between a sense of stuckness and one of being propelled forwards. Moses Laufer argues that adolescence is crucial as a time 'during which a mental picture of oneself with a specific and fixed sexual identity will be established' (1995a, p. 73). Social pressures also compel the young person to try to keep level with the peer group while exacerbating a drive to become independent from parents or carers just when they are most needed; this may bring conflicting feelings of being intruded upon or abandoned. Laufer argues that while the past is a significant determinant, 'there are some critical events within ourselves during adolescence that make a difference not only to present and future life but to present and future mental health' (1995a, p. 73). Its only cure, Winnicott argues, 'belongs to the passage of time' (1962, p. 79). Adolescence is thus a pivotal stage, a *hinge-point*:

> [A] temporal crisis, a crisis in and of developmental time [in which] the pressure on the individual to fall into step with a relentless march forward, while also being in the grip of the conscious and unconscious reworking of earlier traumas, is perhaps unparalleled.
>
> (Catty, 2021, p. 194)

Winnicott argues that alongside the psychological crisis, a different state may emerge in adolescence, which he names 'the doldrums', in which the adolescent feels futile:

> They do not know what they are going to become. They do not know where they are and they are waiting. Because everything is in abeyance, they feel unreal.
>
> (1962, p. 84)

Winnicott argues that this is a crucial developmental phase: a period of waiting from which a more secure identity can emerge.

It is important to be clear here about different definitions of *crisis* and, related to this, *trauma*. The 'Oxford English Dictionary' (OED) defines crisis in three ways: as a 'time of intense difficulty or danger', as a 'time when a difficult or important decision must be made', and as the 'turning point of a disease'. If adolescence is a temporal crisis, this is not to say that it is experienced as traumatic or threatens catastrophic outcomes for all young people. More relevant here is the sense of the crisis being a turning point, although it is also rather ordinary for young people to experience some degree of difficulty during this period. (The difficulty in clinical practice of distinguishing between a mental health crisis in a young person and a 'particularly extreme case of adolescence' is well made by Waddell, 2018, p. 177.)

Analogously, Maria Papadima (2021) has drawn on the distinction between ontological and historical trauma made by historian Dominick LaCapra (2001), where the latter is a shocking or overwhelming event occurring in the real, external world, whereas the former is a 'defining, limiting experience which does not overwhelm the ego and which the child either accepts or rebels against' (Papadima, 2021, p. 437) and is universal. Ontological trauma is thus developmentally necessary and part of normal development. Papadima describes how, in Freud's work, 'this involves the key phantasies that structure our lives – seduction, primal scene, castration . . ., and of course the passage through the Oedipus stage' (2021, p. 437), and advocates holding this kind of trauma in mind alongside historical trauma (p. 450).

I would argue, then, that ordinary adolescence may constitute an ontological trauma owing to the intensely pivotal nature of this stage of life, and the psychological and existential pressures that this entails, which I am calling a *crisis of time*. Yet Laufer argues that in normal development, the adolescent can look forward to the future 'as a time when he can make amends for his own hatreds or his own disappointments, a time to have the inner freedom to allow himself to forgive the parents of the past' (1995a, p. 75). How different pressures may produce a mental health crisis will be the subject of my next section.

First, however, it is important to bring in Aion (cyclic time) and consider factors that belong to a particular era, the time and place of Western European culture in the 21st century. Waddell (2018, p. 236) points out the particular pressures of the external world for today's adolescents, who are known to be adversely affected by exam stress (Steare et al., 2023). Green's emphasis on the superego as an orientator of time (2007, p. 18) is illuminating here: adolescence in Western culture is powerfully constructed as a time of targets and milestones, invoking an urgency about Kairos (milestone time), which leaves many young people with the impression that their opportunities are fleeting. A sense that the pace of ordinary life has sped up hugely in the last decades, driven by technological advances, including the internet and communication via social media (Baraitser, 2017, pp. 6–9), also contributes to a sense that adolescence may be lived out in a bewildering whirlwind of activity – one in which the halting pace of uncertainty in the 'doldrums' (Winnicott, 1962/2016) may no longer be tenable.

Where Steiner posits an awareness of the difference between the generations as an important developmental realisation (2018, p. 1279), Rachel Acheson and Maria Papadima observe that young people seen in Child and Adolescent Mental Health Services (CAMHS) 'often think of their generation as quite separate from the generations that came before' (2023, p. 98). While this may be typical of adolescence, the particular urgency they observe may be linked to a range of external factors: today's young people face the pressures of social media (Zsila & Reyes, 2023), they believe that they will have more difficult lives than their parents (Barnardo's, 2024; Devlin, 2024), and their anxiety about the climate crisis is taking a toll on their mental health (Skopeliti & Gecsoyler, 2023). Indeed, anxiety about the climate crisis today provides an alternative model of intergenerational trauma: one in which trauma is visited upon young people by previous generations. Young people's protests foreground this crisis as a 'cry for help' (Thunberg, 2019, p. 3), the more powerful because uttered by teenagers (cf. Baraitser, 2020).

The adolescent mental health crisis

A substantial increase in adolescent mental health presentations in recent years (23% in a single year in the UK: Gregory, 2023), including for anxiety (Gregory, 2024) and self-harm (Fillis et al., 2023), has also been linked to the impact of social media (Karim et al., 2020), along with the impact of ongoing structural racism (Simon, 2023) and discrimination, including that experienced by LGBTQ+ young people (Mustanski et al., 2016). Moreover, it is already clear that the multiple lockdowns of the Covid-19 pandemic have had an adverse effect on young people's mental health, particularly for those groups who were already suffering (Branje & Morris, 2021; Kiss et al., 2022; Li et al., 2022; Luijten et al., 2021) (see also Baraitser et al., 2024). Indeed, lockdown strategies may have invoked a fantasy that time could be suspended: a fantasy called out by the insistent rhythms of adolescent life (Catty, 2020).

If adolescence, even for the psychologically healthy individual, is inherently a temporal crisis, this lays the ground for the adolescent suffering a mental health crisis, in the primary sense of 'a time of intense difficulty or danger' (OED). If adolescents find themselves at a hinge-point, looking forwards and back, where there is trauma in the picture, this hinge-point becomes invested with both grief and dread. The shift from a developmentally 'normal' crisis to the crisis of mental breakdown is apparent in Peter Fonagy and Mary Target's description of the conflict between separateness and dependency:

> Developmentally, a crisis arises when the external demand for separateness becomes irresistible, in late adolescence and early adulthood. At this time, self-destructive and (in the extreme) suicidal behaviour is perceived as the only feasible solution to an insoluble dilemma: the freeing of the self from the other through the destruction of the other within the self.
>
> (1999, pp. 53–54)

Similarly, Laufer identifies as a warning sign of psychological disturbance the question of whether 'the pull back to childhood forms of behaviour [is] so strong that there is the danger of giving up the effort or the wish to move forward to more adult behaviour' (1995b, p. 14), as well as whether the young person sees the future as 'something to look forward to or as something dreadful' (p. 19).

Past traumas endlessly play out in new contexts; 'the combination of the past with the more immediate fantasies of adolescence . . . ultimately establishes the pathologies we see later' (Laufer, 1995a, p. 74). Developmental and relational traumas, along with intergenerational ones, are known to figure largely in the aetiology of adolescent depression (Cregeen et al., 2017; Rhode, 2011). Models of relational trauma deriving from work with 'looked-after' children – the idea of having 'multiple families in mind' (Rustin, 2008) or inhabiting 'two worlds' (Fagan, 2011, pp. 136 ff) – emphasise a split in consciousness that is both spatial and temporal. Children removed from their birth families can thus 'struggle to know which is the true reality . . . – the traumatising relationships of the past or the new relationships of the present' (Fagan, 2011, p. 130), while family and intergenerational traumas can cast shadows when they converge with developmental pressures and anxieties (Rustin, 2008, p. 88).

The impact of intergenerational trauma has been increasingly emphasised in psychoanalytic child psychotherapy theory and practice (Fraiberg et al., 1975), as well as in psychoanalysis (Abraham & Torok, 1994; Harris et al., 2016; Kimbles, 2021); it chimes with a burgeoning field of empirical research into the intergenerational transmission of attachment difficulties (Main et al., 1985; Ricks, 1985), as well as neuroscientific research focusing on epigenetic factors (Bale, 2015; Skinner, 2014). The future thus becomes unsafe, as Waddell puts it, not just because it is unknown, but because it is invested with dread that a traumatic past – one's own or intergenerational – may be repeated.

In their work on *depressing time*, a concept conveying the stasis and suspended time of depression, Laura Salisbury and Lisa Baraitser (2020) describe the development of conceptions of melancholia and depression in the first half of the 20th century. They note that 'waiting uncoupled from a future into which one might step came to be understood as a key feature of the affective condition termed "melancholia", or . . . "depression"' (pp 104–105). They also note that 'one of [the] key insights [of 20th century phenomenological psychiatry] was that chronic mental distress can be understood as a disturbance of a sense of lived time' (p. 106). Yet as I have argued elsewhere (Catty, 2021), models of depression that link it to suspended time and impeded movement may need to be modified when applied to adolescents, as they may fail to do justice 'to the drama of adolescent life, to the whirlwind of peer or family conflict or self-harm – and to adolescent rage' (p. 193).

Salisbury argues that anxiety, which derives from the Latin *anxietas* (worry, solicitude, extreme care), took on particular associations in modern English with worrying about the future (2022, p. 3): associations which endure into both cognitive and psychoanalytic conceptions of anxiety as 'taking a certain care of the self by producing a particular sense of time' (p. 5). Salisbury and Baraitser also utilise Paul Saint-Amour's argument that 'violence anticipated is already violence unleashed' (2015, p. 13). His conceptualisation of '*pre* traumatic stress syndrome' arises 'not in the wake of a past event, but in the shadow of a future one' (pp 7–8). Salisbury argues that in this model of *pre-traumatic stress syndrome* (https://dictionary.apa.org/pretraumatic-stress-disorder; Kaplan, 2020), tolerance of this anxious orientation towards the future is always 'determined by one's expectations of what it might bring' (Salisbury, 2020, p. 97).

Young people in crisis, then, may be caught between the past of intergenerational trauma or personal relational trauma and dread of the future, mediated by pre-traumatic stress. The states of depression, slowed time, or anxiety generate a particular intensity when experienced by the adolescent, for whom societal, biological, and developmental clocks are ticking, so that the future bears down on them in a particularly alarming way. A crisis event signals both the deathly but also the dramatic nature of this mental state.

The following vignette highlights the impact of multiple losses on a young man's sense of the future:

Mark, 16, had experienced the deaths of two grandparents in rapid succession during his teens and remembered the loss of another in his early years and its impact on his mother. His mother had also lost a sibling in her own childhood. He came to the attention of CAMHS after taking a serious overdose of painkillers washed down with alcohol, after which he was found by his father and taken to the Accident and Emergency (A&E) Department of the local hospital. His future therapist met him there while on 'duty' and tried to explore what had led him to this act; while the bereavements took longer to be disclosed, he was eloquent about his sense that the future was bleak and that adult life had nothing to offer him. Nevertheless, he seemed to engage reasonably well with the initial contacts in the emergency setting, and he accepted the offer of working with the clinician. It was arranged that they would meet for an assessment for psychotherapy after his discharge from hospital, which was supported by other multidisciplinary clinicians. The psychotherapist came to work after a weekend, expecting to see Mark for his first session, but learned that he had taken an overdose during that weekend and been re-admitted to the hospital.

Mark may be seen as caught between a traumatic past which includes his parents' own 'ghosts' (Fraiberg et al., 1975) and a future which seems destined to be bleak: a seemingly endless repetition of his parents' mourning and his own. He does not alert an adult when he takes the overdose and is lucky to receive such prompt medical attention. His overdose after the initial encouraging contacts with professionals seems to function as a demonstration that help is being offered 'too late': a phenomenon to which I shall return in due course.

The suicidal adolescent may be seen as one who attempts to call a halt to time, and to stop its intergenerational flow. While the wish to 'kill time' has been linked to the pathological retreat into a timeless state (Williams, 2007; Steiner, 2018), some adolescents, like Mark, take time into their own hands in acts of dangerous self-harm. Mark's act seems to be an attempt to resist the onward temporal pull towards both the future and the adult world of sexuality and a changed body. This may be linked to the perception of Moses and Eglé Laufer that a suicide attempt may allow the adolescent to feel more in control of his or her body (Laufer & Laufer, 1989; Laufer, 1995c). The suicidal act, in Perelberg's words, is

> thus ultimately seen as these adolescents' attempts to regulate their distance in relation to their internal objects (which they identify with their bodies) and achieve separateness (either by abandoning their objects as they themselves had been abandoned or by attacking them as they felt they had been attacked).
>
> (Perelberg, 1999, p. 24)

Yet this quest for separateness also puts them outside of time, in a phantasy of suspension between childhood and adulthood, the future indefinitely postponed – and running the risk of the future being cancelled entirely.

The impact of the increase of presentations of young people in acute crisis has a corresponding effect on the services designed to support them, as well as the individual professionals within them. I have argued elsewhere that CAMHS services are often structured around time and urgency and a 'temporal hierarchy of risk' (Catty, 2021, p. 196). A significant revision to the NICE Guideline on managing self-harm, in the UK, has, however, recently privileged an understanding of the meaning of a suicidal act over any simplistic assessment of the riskiness of the act. The guideline advocates paying careful attention to the meaning of the suicidal presentation in the context of a holistic assessment, positioning the clinician as one who searches for meaning, and warns against providing services based on a stratification of risk (NICE, 2022). Nevertheless, the urgency of the self-harming or suicidal presentation is difficult to mitigate, with the possibility of suicide casting a shadow over mental health practice (Catty, 2021).

The emphasis on time and waiting in psychoanalytic practice also exists in tension with the values of mental health treatment in the NHS (Bent-Hazelwood, 2020): an extreme version of Winnicott's juxtaposition of the questions 'How much can one be allowed to do?' and 'How little need be done?' (1965, p. 166; cf. Bent-Hazelwood, 2020). Long waits for assessment or treatment may compound the sense of some young people that what they are offered is 'too little too late'. This may be particularly concrete for a young person approaching 18, who is to be discharged or transitioned to another service by this significant birthday, whereas for children in the care system, dealing with the impact of early trauma, intervention may feel as though it is always already too late (Rebecca Bolam, personal communication). Like the young people they work with, professionals may thus have reason to fear being *too late*.

'Too late for me': *too-lateness* and despair

The following vignette conveys the sense of hopelessness of a young girl caught between past trauma and her sense of the absence of the future:

'Layla' was referred to her local CAMHS at the age of 12 because of her increasingly low mood and anxiety, which seemed to have gotten worse when she started secondary school. By the time she was seen for an initial appointment, she had been waiting for over a year and had started self-harming by cutting herself on a regular basis: a situation that her school and parents could barely contain. Clinicians elicited from her concerned mother and stepfather a history of domestic violence perpetrated by her birth father, much earlier in her life, and a sense that she was an unofficial 'young carer' for her significantly depressed mother. Layla herself engaged in a rather perfunctory way with a series of appointments with CAMHS clinicians, who felt they could not elicit any sense of optimism from her about the future, nor any authentic account of why she was self-harming. The appointments had no apparent effect on her mood or self-harm. She was then referred to the team's psychotherapist. The day before she was due to meet the psychotherapist, however, Layla took a significant overdose of painkilling medication; frightened, she told her mother and was admitted to hospital.

When Layla was discharged and the sessions with her psychotherapist commenced, the therapist was able, gradually, to talk with Layla about the timing of this overdose, picking up on a sense of 'too-lateness': that a space for care and attention was being provided, but too late to be of use. When the psychotherapist named this feeling, Layla for the first time brightened. She admitted, 'I think this therapy is too late for me'.

(adapted from Baraitser et al., 2024)

Too-lateness is a concept coined to capture a disjunction in time that leaves some distressed young people unable to take the help offered to them or access any sense of hopefulness. It points to the overwhelming affect that attempts to shut the young person down even in the face of evidence of change to come. Struggling with the pressure of developmental and intergenerational trauma, Layla may feel that she is doomed to replay her own and her mother's past through the compulsion to repeat, or that the future holds nothing for her. This is, of course, related to the phenomenon that a young person in the grip of suicidal or self-destructive thoughts is likely to reject help, sometimes with 'a paradoxical triumphant determination to prove himself to be beyond help' (Joffe, 1995, p. 56). Rosalie Joffe relates this to the young person's simultaneous desire for and fear of dependency, which leads to self-punishment (p. 58). She also argues that the suicidal young person has repudiated their guilt about parental concern (p. 56). Yet Layla, like Mark, seems to be conveying something about timing, along with the rejection of help per se.

Where many young people who self-harm or express suicidal ideation use ideas about time (such as the need to die before a significant date) as a way of communicating urgency (Catty, 2021), Layla here communicates the idea of being too late, articulating it only in action, by overdosing on tablets designed to 'kill' pain. In her pre-transference to the psychotherapist she has not yet met, it seems likely that she believes that the new professional has nothing to offer her: perhaps a projection of her sense of a depleted maternal object, perhaps exacerbated because she has already projected this sense of uselessness onto the other CAMHS professionals she has met, giving her multiple, apparently confirmatory, negative experiences. As Joffe observes, young people with suicidal intentions 'seem to want us to prove to them that we, too, like the parents, have nothing of value for them and/ or are uncaring' (1995, p. 55). Layla has no reason to think that the new professional promises her anything different. Whether her overdose is an unconscious attempt to elicit help – it does, at least, frighten her into alerting her mother – or a more determined attempt to end her life is something that may come to be understood in her psychotherapy, in time. Meanwhile, her therapist is left trying to digest the impact of the communication ('You are not worth waiting for'), so that she can metabolise it into a better understanding of Layla's internal world and self-belief: Layla is not worth anyone's while to wait for; she can no longer be helped; she is somewhere in time between her childhood and a future that seems unimaginable.

How might too-lateness differ from Nachträglichkeit or afterwardsness? Afterwardsness is defined as the way in which 'experiences, impressions and memory-traces may be revised at a later date to fit in with fresh experiences or with the attainment of a new stage of development' (Laplanche & Pontalis, 1967, p. 111). Gregorio Kohon (2007) argues that this 'makes it impossible to merely explain the present through the events of the past' as the past becomes a 'historicization' of the present (p. 106). He emphasises how Nachträglichkeit also helps illuminate how a stuck temporality can hold us in the past (p. 115). If Nachträglichkeit describes the situation where 'something is perceived but only takes on meaning retrospectively' (Birksted-Breen, 2003, p. 1,501), I would argue that too-lateness incorporates that perception and infuses it with bleakness about the future. While the paradigmatic experience in Freud's account is the child's retroactive understanding of sexuality (Perelberg, 2007a, p. xiv; Baraitser,

2022, p. 382), for young people managing loss or the developmental traumas of domestic violence or parental ill health, afterwardsness may play out in a memory of loss or violence infused with a more adult understanding ('My father hits my mother' becomes 'Adult life holds only pain and violence'). The second event that re-activates the first, in this model, may be any of the pressures on adolescent life that bring to the fore and re-shape the internal situation of trauma and loss. For Layla, transfer to secondary school may have brought a sense of being more 'grown-up', reactivating an internal sense of powerlessness in the face of relational trauma and parental ill health, while puberty may have intensified her sense of being pulled into a terrifying adult identity. The long wait for treatment or attention she experienced may, of course, have compounded these factors, re-constellating a sense of being overlooked in favour of another's distress.

Caught in the pivotal position of adolescence and faced with the afterwardsness of post-traumatic and pre-traumatic stress about a future of traumatic repetition or emptiness, the adolescent may thus feel too late not just for help but existentially: too late to shape life in a different way. The concept is thus not simply relational, as Layla's example might suggest ('I am too late to be helped by therapy, by parents or teachers or you'), but also existential ('I find myself too late in time, too late to change my destiny, propelled from a past that traumatised me towards a future that must be avoided at all costs').

Layla and Mark recovered from their overdoses; indeed, the thoughtful responses of their families and mental health teams enabled these young people to make progress, once their suicidal gestures had been understood. An act of self-injury, while always dangerous, may come 'in time' to generate help. It cannot be assumed that this is the intention, unconscious or otherwise; indeed, Acheson and Papadima (2023) emphasise the range of meanings that a suicidal act may have, and the importance of attending to its underlying meaning (p. 97). That in each case, however, it took an overdose requiring hospital admission to reach a turning-point may help to illuminate something about the nature of crisis, bearing out the suggestion of Anna Motz (2010) that self-harm may, in its communicative function, contain hope.

For the adolescent, already, perhaps, experiencing adolescence as an ontological crisis in which they feel propelled forwards but also drawn back, the act of self-harm or the suicide attempt might be seen as involving not only a 'time of intense difficulty or danger' but also a turning-point at which a decision must be made, or something done differently. Terrifyingly, the wrong decision might be made, including the potential for the young person to decide not to carry on at all. But this definition also implies a pausing: a suspension, even if brief, between paths, where crisis may 'paradoxically, call for the suspension of judgement' in an offer of care that simply offers 'more time' (Baraitser & Brook, 2020, p. 237). The crisis thus parallels and reflects the pivotal nature of adolescence itself. Waddell's 'Janus-faced adolescent' finds him- or herself at a hinge-point where there are conflicting pressures to move rapidly forward or to turn back; where this precipitates a mental health crisis, there may be conflicting urges to either slow time down (by withdrawing) or speed it up (in frenetic and dangerous activity), or an urge to stop time altogether.

While it is not the only way to slow time down, psychoanalytic psychotherapy has a particular role in helping young people and their networks to pause for thought and to add time to a situation.

Treating young people with time

Psychoanalytic practice has been conceptualised as a 'treatment *of* or *with* time' or a *waiting with* (Salisbury & Baraitser, 2020, pp. 114, 115), which takes time, and is structured into the rhythm of treatment. The containment it provides is both durational and rhythmic, the process in time being central (Birksted-Breen, 2003, p. 1,512) and the rhythm of sessions evoking 'the most primal level of post-natal infant biorhythmic-embodied experience' (Shulman, 2019, p. 330). Psychoanalytic practice requires a balancing of temporal models: Chronos (linear time) underpinning the psychoanalytic frame, Kairos (milestone time) enabling the opportune moment, and both bringing in an awareness of the unconscious Aion (cyclic time) (Bent-Hazelwood, 2020, p. 7). Psychoanalysis thus offers 'a specifically chronic cure – the offer of time *as* care' (Salisbury & Baraitser, 2020, p. 106). It also uses the interpretation to reinstate a sense of time where that has been lost, bringing the patient a sense of their location in intergenerational history and allowing them to work through the Oedipus complex (Rose, 2007, pp. 39–40).

What, then, does the temporal nature of psychoanalytic treatment offer to adolescents in crisis? Layla's story, as described earlier, entailed a durable transference relationship, building from the moment of contact previously described:

> From this moment of contact between patient and therapist, a genuine therapeutic relationship was able to grow. Layla started to talk more freely to the therapist, and to speak not just about feeling low, but about things that annoyed her: at school, sometimes, or even at home. Gradually, she dared to voice resentment at her mother for being unwell, risking the shame of admitting her mixed feelings about the burden and the worry of being regarded as her mother's 'carer'. Gradually, her self-harming seemed to have stopped; much later, she was able to tell her therapist that she felt a sense of pride in having ceased to resort to this way of signalling her distress.
>
> (Baraitser et al., 2024)

Layla was treated with open-ended psychoanalytic psychotherapy. Yet offering psychoanalytic work to young people in crisis may take other forms.

Acheson and Papadima (2023) argue that longer-term psychotherapy is not always indicated, particularly for a specific group 'whose behaviour and feelings, even though needing close care and attention as signs of great distress, [are] not expressions of enduring mental health disturbance' (p. 96). Indeed, the child psychoanalytic psychotherapy profession has been exploring different uses of time with young people, including Short-Term Psychoanalytic Psychotherapy (STPP), the 28-week model arising from the IMPACT research study of depressed adolescents

(Improving Mood with Psychoanalytic and Cognitive Therapies; Goodyer et al., 2011), many of whom had significant risk histories and suicidal ideation. It has been suggested that the time-limited framework of STPP, building the anticipation of loss into the treatment, may be particularly helpful for young people suffering multiple losses and intergenerational trauma (Cregeen et al., 2017, p. 2) and may also introduce the idea of *new* development: 'not just an ending, but also a new beginning' (p. 119). The future can thus be conceived of as something that is possible to contemplate.

Mark, the 16-year-old boy described earlier, who took a second overdose just before starting to meet his psychotherapist for an assessment, was offered STPP:

> Mark attended his STPP sessions religiously. He told the psychotherapist angrily how bleak adult life was: it apparently held nothing for him. Gradually, he started to talk about the deaths that had blighted both his recent years and his mother's life. In the last stretch of the therapy, he started to refer to the future, first tangentially, and then with greater confidence, to make plans, and to suggest that he might be able to find his way.

Young people may, however, need us to be flexible and accommodate to their use of time (Bent-Hazelwood, 2020, p. 8) or take control of time in ways that we fail to anticipate. The participants in the IMPACT study took control of the time offered in the time-limited interventions in the study, including STPP, where the average number of sessions attended was 11 rather than the 28 of the model (Goodyer et al., 2016). A sub-study looking at a representative group of 32 young people who had dropped out of treatment found that they could be grouped into three categories based on their own descriptions: 'got-what-they-needed', 'dissatisfied', and 'troubled' (O'Keeffe et al., 2019), the latter lacking the external-world stability to engage. While both the 'dissatisfied' and the 'got-what-they-needed' groups were taking control of time by leaving therapy rather than settling for an adult's model, the existence of the latter group in particular suggests that some young people can benefit from a much shorter treatment and may prefer exercising their autonomy by choosing when to end. One participant, 'Conor', reported: 'I just wanted to kind of, get that kind of phase of my life over with' (O'Keeffe et al., 2019, p. 7).

The case of a young man I shall call 'Peter', while somewhat unconventional, shows the need of an adolescent to take control of the treatment in order to make use of it in his own way.

> 'Peter', 16, was well known to the CAMHS team responsible for dealing with mental health crises. In his early years, he had been repeatedly removed from, and then returned to, first, his birth parents and, later, a succession of foster carers. Subsequent attention from a stable and

kind caregiver was not enough to address this early containment failure. He first became known to the team after an overdose; subsequently, his presentation was to engage minimally with staff when they reached out to him after such a crisis (of which there were many), but then to drop out of any therapeutic relationship offered. Another emergency presentation would follow within a few months or so. At age 16, by which time he had been NEET (Not in Employment, Education or Training) for some time, it was suggested that he be offered psychotherapy, and the therapist, following an assessment, suggested STPP.

It was not clear whether Peter took on board the offer of this 28-week treatment model, with its weekly rhythm punctuated by planned holiday breaks. Nobody in the team thought he would engage with it. For a stretch of six weeks, he attended reliably, however. He spoke intermittently about various matters that concerned him, with a sense of puzzlement as to why the therapist might be interested in such things, lapsing often into silence. In such silences, the ticking of the therapy room clock seemed to become louder. Peter seemed amused and intrigued by this, and comments on the ticking of the clock became a regular feature of this short stretch of sessions. In one such session, the psychotherapist found herself thinking about what she had been told about Peter's grandfather, a somewhat more stable presence in his life. She was amused to consider inwardly whether the association had come to her via the idea of the 'grandfather clock'.

One day, Peter's carer got in touch to say that Peter had secured a job and would no longer be able to attend. In a later call, the carer marvelled at Peter's commitment to the new job, telling the therapist, 'He's a totally different person!'. Peter never contacted the team again, and there were no further emergency presentations.

Many adolescents regard the 28-week model of STPP as rather a long time (Cregeen et al., 2017, p. 54). Yet it seems there was more than this to Peter's brief engagement with STPP. We might wonder what it was about the offer of psychotherapeutic time that had this unusual but, it seems, helpful, effect on him. For a young person who had had no experience of dependability, it seems that the regular commitment to a particular time and place every week, in which the therapist would give him her uninterrupted attention, was paramount. Peter had, after all, previously replicated with the mental health team a painful pattern of abandonment from his earlier years. In hindsight, his overdoses and other suicidal gestures could be seen as frantic attempts to call a halt to this vicious circle, which replicated the patterns of care and abandonment in the relationship with the team but was unsuccessful as an attempt to elicit solid help. Peter could not sustain the relationships being offered by the team, which might be seen as comprising a model of irregular contacts responsive to perceived urgency. By contrast, he metabolised something about the time being offered by psychotherapy, with its 'ticking' regularity or *chronicity*, which gave him a chance to step away from the vicious circle of crisis, recovery, and more crisis, for a regular period each week.

Rose argues that the offer of psychoanalysis, with its particular timing and duration, 'emphasizes something finitely limiting that may threaten various internal structures that are built upon a denial of time' (2007, p. 23). Peter had, indeed, been denying time in the years when he was NEET, as though his failure to engage in life did not signify; yet he was living out the significance of the temporal rhythm of presence and abandonment through the repetition compulsion. Following Rose's (2007) advocacy of attending to distortions of time in the transference, one might ask whether Peter experienced his therapist as representing *Time*: perhaps Chronos or *Old Father Time*, represented in the ticking (grandfather) clock. This may have coexisted with a maternal transference never worked through, in which he needed to abandon her as revenge on the abandoning mother. Yet had this latter transference predominated, one would imagine that the vicious circle of abandoning CAMHS and then returning via a crisis hospital admission would have continued. Instead, the (grandfather) clock transference seems to have had greater weight and enabled Peter to take some control of time by re-engaging with the external world of work and choosing to leave the stuck world of CAMHS – perhaps, thus, acquiring more of a sense of a past and a future.

Conclusion

In conclusion, then, I have been suggesting that adolescence may be regarded as an ontological temporal crisis, owing to its position as a pivotal stage or *hinge-point* that pulls the young person both forwards and back, with their lived sense of Chronos (linear time) putting them under unbearable pressure. For young people today, the pressures particular to our current times, illuminated by considering Aion (cyclic time), exacerbate this sense of a critical hinge-point, as difficulties in the present combine with an increasing bleakness about the future, and the opportune moment of Kairos (milestone time) seems ungraspable. While the majority pass through this stage unscathed, an increasing number find themselves in a mental health crisis as they become caught between the past of developmental and intergenerational trauma and fear of its repetition in an uncertain future. The adolescent mental health crisis, when it plays out in self-harm or suicide attempts, may be seen as threatening to stop time, although, crucially, for many, it may also provide an opportunity: to pause, to consider, and to bring in others alongside to offer careful attention. The time that may be provided for young people through psychoanalytic psychotherapy, I have argued, may play out in diverse ways but aims both to enliven the stuck time of depression and to slow down the adolescent whirlwind. I have also suggested that a sense of too-lateness, perhaps usefully seen as a distortion of Nachträglichkeit in adolescents in crisis, may be part of the experience of such adolescents, indicating both an existential sense of being too late and a relational one (being too late for help) that can helpfully be worked through in psychoanalytic psychotherapy.

Acknowledgements

This chapter was developed and written as part of the project Waiting Times, supported by the Wellcome Trust [205400/A/16/Z] (see https://waitingtimes. exeter.ac.uk). I am grateful to Laura Salisbury for the conception of adolescence as a temporal *hinge-point*. I am indebted to Lisa Baraitser and Laura Salisbury for helpful comments on this chapter, and to our colleagues on the Waiting Times project for their insight and inspiration, in particular Kelechi Anucha, Stephanie Davies, Michael J. Flexer, Martin D. Moore, and Jordan Osserman. I have also benefited greatly from the advice of the book's editors, Rachel Acheson and Maria Papadima; from insightful feedback from Rebecca Bolam; and from wise clinical supervision over the years from Martin Daltrop, Margaret Rustin, and Margot Waddell.

References

Abraham, N., & Torok, M. (1994). *The shell and the kernel*. London & Chicago: University of Chicago Press.
Acheson, R., & Papadima, M. (2023). The search for identity: Working therapeutically with adolescents in crisis. *Journal of Child Psychotherapy*, 49(1), 95–119. https://doi.org/10.1 080/0075417X.2022.2160478
Alvarez, A. (1992). *Live company*. London: Routledge.
Bale, T. (2015). Epigenetic and transgenerational reprogramming of brain development. *Nature Reviews Neuroscience*, 16, 332–344. https://doi.org/10.1038/nrn3818
Baraitser, L. (2017). *Enduring time*. London: Bloomsbury.
Baraitser, L. (2020). The maternal death drive: Greta Thunberg and the question of the future. *Psychoanalysis, Culture & Society*, 25(4), 499–517. https://doi.org/10.1057/ s41282-020-00197-y
Baraitser, L. (2022). 'Time' for 'the People': Reflections on 'Psychoanalysis for the People: Free Clinics and the Social Mission of Psychoanalysis'. *Psychoanalysis and History*, 24(3), 375–392. https://doi.org/10.3366/pah.2022.0445
Baraitser, L., Anucha, K., Catty, J., Davies, S., Osserman, J., Salisbury, L., Flexer, M. J., & Moore, M. D. (2024). (Un)timely care: Findings from the Waiting Times Project. *Wellcome Open Research*. https://wellcomeopenresearch.org/articles/9-490/v
Baraitser, L., & Brook, W. (2020). Watchful waiting: Crisis, vulnerability, care. In: V. Browne, J. Danely, T. Managhan, & D. Rosenow (eds.), *Vulnerability and the politics of care. Proceedings of the British Academy* (Vol. 235, pp. 230–247). Oxford: Oxford University Press.
Barnardo's. (2024). *Changing childhoods, changing lives*. Report. Retrieved April 14, 2024, from https://www.barnardos.org.uk/research/changing-childhoods-changing-lives
Bell, D. (2007). Existence in time: Development or catastrophe? In: R. J. Perelberg (ed.), *Time and memory* (pp. 65–84). Reprinted 2018: London & New York: Routledge.
Bent-Hazelwood, J. (2020). How much time do we need? Time and psychoanalytic psychotherapy in CAMHS. *British Journal of Psychotherapy*. https://doi.org/10.1111/ bjp.12561

Birksted-Breen, D. (2003). Time and the après-coup. *International Journal of Psychoanalysis*, 84(6), 1501–1515. https://doi.org/10.1516/1DM9-6X63-248B-U5F6

Branje, S., & Morris, A. S. (2021). The impact of the COVID-19 pandemic on adolescent emotional, social, and academic adjustment. *Journal of Research on Adolescence*, 31(3), 486–499. https://doi.org/10.1111/jora.12668

Canham, H. (1999). The development of the concept of time in fostered and adopted children. *Psychoanalytic Inquiry*, 19(2), 160–171. https://doi.org/10.1080/07351699909534239

Catty, J. (2020). Lockdown and adolescent mental health: Reflections from a child and adolescent psychotherapist. *Wellcome Open Research*, 5(132). https://wellcomeopenresearch.org/articles/5-132

Catty, J. (2021). Out of time: Adolescents and those who wait for them. *Journal of Child Psychotherapy*, 47(2), 188–204. https://doi.org/10.1080/0075417X.2021.1954977

Catty, J. (2023). The time of care: A Waiting Times conference. *New Associations*, 40, 12. https://www.bpc.org.uk/download/9537/NA-Summer-2023_LO_RES_v2.pdf

Civitarese, G. (2019). The concept of time in Bion's 'A Theory of Thinking'. *International Journal of Psychoanalysis*, 100(2), 182–205. https://doi.org/10.1080/00207578.2019.1570216

Cregeen, S., Hughes, C., Midgley, N., Rhode, M., & Rustin, M. (2017). *Short-term psychoanalytic psychotherapy for adolescents with depression: A treatment manual*. J. Catty (Eds.). London: Karnac.

Devlin, H. (2024, March 4). UK teens believe they will have harder lives than their parents, research finds. *The Guardian*. Retrieved April 14, 2024, from https://www.theguardian.com/society/2024/mar/04/uk-teenagers-parents-standard-of-living-research

Fagan, M. (2011). Relational trauma and its impact on late-adopted children. *Journal of Child Psychotherapy*, 37(2), 129–146. https://doi.org/10.1080/0075417X.2011.581467

Fillis, V., Fagg, J., & Unia, E. (2023, March 23). Self-harm hospital admissions up 22% for children aged eight to 17. *BBC News*. Retrieved September 1, 2024, from https://www.bbc.co.uk/news/uk-england-64874355

Fonagy, P., & Target, M. (1999). Towards understanding violence: The use of the body and the role of the father. In: R. J. Perelberg (ed.), *Psychoanalytic understanding of violence and suicide* (pp. 44–61). London & New York: Routledge.

Fraiberg, S. H., Adelson, E., & Shapiro, V. (1975). Ghosts in the nursery: A psychoanalytic approach to the problems of impaired mother-infant relationships. *Journal of the American Academy of Child Psychology*, 14, 387–422. https://doi.org/10.1016/s0002-7138(09)61442-4

Freud, S. (1895). Project for a scientific psychology. In: S. Freud (ed.), *The Standard Edition of the Complete Psychological Works of Sigmund Freud* (Vol. 1, pp. 281–391). Trans. J. Strachey. London: Hogarth Press and the Institute of Psycho-Analysis.

Freud, S. (1914). Remembering, repeating, and working through. In: *Standard Edition* (Vol. 12, pp. 145–156). London: Vintage (2001 reprint).

Goodyer, I., et al. (2011). Improving mood with psychoanalytic and cognitive therapies (IMPACT): A pragmatic effectiveness superiority trial to investigate whether specialized psychological treatment reduces the risk for relapse in adolescents with moderate to severe unipolar depression: Study protocol for a randomized controlled trial. *Trials*, 12, 175. http://www.trialsjournal.com/content/12/1/175

Goodyer, I., et al. (2016, November 30). Cognitive behavioural therapy and short-term psychoanalytical psychotherapy versus a brief psychosocial intervention for adolescents with unipolar major depressive disorder (IMPACT): A multi-centre, pragmatic, observer-blind randomised controlled trial. *Lancet Psychiatry*. https://doi.org/10.1016/S2215-0366(16)30378-9

Green, A. (2007). The construction of heterochrony. In: R. J. Perelberg (ed.), *Time and memory* (pp. 1–22). Reprinted 2018: London & New York: Routledge.

Gregory, A. (2023, January 3). Child referrals for mental healthcare in England up 39% in a year. *The Guardian*. Retrieved September 1, 2024, from https://www.theguardian.com/society/2023/jan/03/child-referrals-for-mental-health-care-in-england-up-39-in-a-year

Gregory, A. (2024, August 27). NHS referrals for anxiety in children more than double since pre-Covid levels. *The Guardian*. Retrieved September 1, 2024, from https://www.theguardian.com/society/article/2024/aug/27/nhs-referrals-for-anxiety-in-children-more-than-double-pre-covid-levels-england

Harris, A., Kalb, M., & Klebanoff, S. (2016). *Ghosts in the consulting room: Echoes of trauma in psychoanalysis*. London & New York: Routledge.

Joffe, R. (1995). Don't help me! – The suicidal adolescent. In: M. Laufer (ed.), *The suicidal adolescent* (pp. 53–65). London: Karnac Books.

Kaplan, E. A. (2020). Is climate-related pre-traumatic stress syndrome a real condition? *American Imago*, 77(1), 81–104. https://doi.org/10.1353/aim.2020.0004

Karim, F., Oyewande, A., Abdalla, L. F., et al. (2020). Social media use and its connection to mental health: A systematic review. *Cureus*, 12(6), e8627. https://doi.org/10.7759/cureus.8627

Kimbles, S. L. (2021). *Intergenerational complexes in analytical psychology: The suffering of ghosts*. London & New York: Routledge.

Kiss, O., Alzueta, E., Yuksel, D., et al. (2022). The pandemic's toll on young adolescents: Prevention and intervention targets to preserve their mental health. *Journal of Adolescent Health*, 70(3), 387–395. https://doi.org/10.1016/j.jadohealth.2021.11.023

Kohon, G. (2007). The Aztecs, Masada, and the compulsion to repeat. In: R. J. Perelberg (ed.), *Time and memory* (pp. 103–128). Reprinted 2018: London & New York: Routledge.

Kristeva, J. (2003). *Intimate revolt: The powers and limits of psychoanalysis*. Trans. J. Herman. New York: Columbia University Press.

LaCapra, D. (2001). Trauma, absence, loss. In: *Writing history, writing trauma* (pp. 43–85). Baltimore, MD: Johns Hopkins University Press.

Laplanche, J., & Pontalis, J.-B. (1967). *The language of psychoanalysis*. London: Hogarth.

Laufer, M. (1995a). Understanding suicide: Does it have a special meaning in adolescence? In: M. Laufer (ed.), *The suicidal adolescent* (pp. 69–82). London: Karnac Books.

Laufer, M. (1995b). Psychological development in adolescence. In: M. Laufer (ed.), *The suicidal adolescent* (pp. 3–20). London: Karnac Books.

Laufer, M. (ed.) (1995c). *The suicidal adolescent*. London: Karnac Books.

Laufer, M., & Laufer, M. E. (1989). *Developmental breakdown and psychoanalytic treatment in adolescence: Clinical studies*. New Haven & London: Yale University Press.

Li, S. H., Beames, J. R., Newby, J. M., Maston, K., Christensen, H., & Werner-Seidler, A. (2022). The impact of COVID-19 on the lives and mental health of Australian adolescents. *European Child & Adolescent Psychiatry*, 31(9), 1465–1477. https://doi.org/10.1007/s00787-021-01790-x

Luijten, M. A., van Muilekom, M. M., Teela, L., Polderman, T. J., Terwee, C. B., Zijlmans, Klaufus, L., Popma, A., Oostrom, K. J., van Oers, H. E., & Haverman, L. (2021). The impact of lockdown during the COVID-19 pandemic on mental and social health of children and adolescents. *Quality of Life Research*, 30(10), 2795–2804. https://doi.org/10.1007/s11136-021-02861-x

Maiello, S. (1995). The sound-object: A hypothesis about prenatal auditory experience and memory. *Journal of Child Psychotherapy*, 21(1), 23–41. https://doi.org/10.1080/00754179508254905

Main, M., Kaplan, N., & Cassidy, J. (1985). Security in infancy, childhood, and adulthood: A move to the level of representation. In: I. Bretherton, & E. Waters (eds.), *Growing points of attachment theory and research: Monographs of the Society for Research in Child Development*, 50(1–2), 66–104. https://doi.org/10.2307/3333827

Malloch, S., & Trevarthen, C. (Eds.). (2009). *Communicative musicality: Exploring the basis of human companionship*. Oxford: Oxford University Press.

McGilchrist, I. (2009). *The master and his emissary: The divided brain and the making of the Western world*. New Haven and London: Yale University Press.

Motz, A. (2010). Self-harm as a sign of hope. *Psychoanalytic Psychotherapy*, 24(2), 81–92. https://doi.org/10.1080/02668731003707527

Mustanski, B., Andrews, R., & Puckett, J. A. (2016). The effects of cumulative victimization on mental health among lesbian, gay, bisexual, and transgender adolescents and young adults. *American Journal of Public Health*, 106(3), 527–533. https://doi.org/10.2105/ajph.2015.302976

NICE. (2022). *Self-harm: Assessment, management and preventing recurrence*. National Institute for Health and Care Excellence Guideline NG 225. Retrieved September 1, 2024, from https://www.nice.org.uk/guidance/ng225

O'Keeffe, S., Martin, P., Target, M., & Midgley, N. (2019). 'I Just Stopped Going': A mixed methods investigation into types of therapy dropout in adolescents with depression. *Frontiers in Psychology*, 10(75), 1–14. https://doi.org/10.3389/fpsyg.2019.00075

Papadima, M. (2021). Trauma in child psychotherapy: Some thoughts around a concept. *Journal of Child Psychotherapy*, 47(3), 433–452. https://doi.org/10.1080/00754 17X.2021.2021545

Perelberg, R. J. (1999). Psychoanalytic understanding of violence and suicide: A review of the literature and some new formulations. In: R. J. Perelberg (ed.), *Psychoanalytic understanding of violence and suicide* (pp. 15–43). London & New York: Routledge.

Perelberg, R. J. (2007a). Introduction. In: R. J. Perelberg (Ed.), *Time and memory* (pp. xiii–xxi). Reprinted 2018: London & New York: Routledge.

Perelberg, R. J. (2007b). Space and time in psychoanalytic listening. *International Journal of Psychoanalysis*, 88(6), 1473–1490. https://doi.org/10.1516/VG65-8L74-2317-8492

Rhode, M. (2011). Some reflections on the individual therapy: Themes and interventions. In: J. Trowell, & G. Miles (Eds.), *Childhood depression: A place for psychotherapy* (pp. 125–136). London: Karnac.

Ricks, M. H. (1985). The social transmission of parental behavior: Attachment across generations. In: I. Bretherton, & E. Waters (eds.), *Growing points of attachment theory and research: Monographs of the Society for Research in Child Development*, 50(1–2), 211–227. https://doi.org/10.2307/3333834

Rose, J. (2007). Distortions of time in the transference: Some theoretical and clinical implications. In: R. J. Perelberg (ed.), *Time and memory* (pp. 23–46). Reprinted 2018: London & New York: Routledge.

Rustin, M. (2008). Multiple families in mind. In: D. Hindle, & G. Shulman (eds.), *The emotional experience of adoption: A psychoanalytic perspective* (pp. 77–89). London: Routledge.

Sabbadini, A. (1989). How the infant develops a sense of time. *British Journal of Psychotherapy*, 5(4), 475–484. https://doi.org/10.1111/j.1752-0118.1989.tb01107.x

Saint-Amour, P. (2015). *Tense future: Modernism, total war, encyclopedic form*. Oxford: Oxford University Press.

Salisbury, L. (2020). 'Between-time stories': Waiting, war and the temporalities of care. *Medical Humanities*, 46, 96–106. https://doi.org/10.1136/medhum-2019-011810

Salisbury, L. (2022). On not being able to read: Doomscrolling and anxiety in pandemic times. *Textual Practice*. https://doi.org/10.1080/0950236X.2022.2056767

Salisbury, L., & Baraitser, L. (2020). Depressing time: Waiting, melancholia, and the psychoanalytic practice of care. In: E. Kirtsoglou, & B. Simpson (eds.), *The time of anthropology: Studies of contemporary chronopolitics* (pp. 103–122). London & New York: Routledge. https://library.oapen.org/handle/20.500.12657/43315

Salisbury, L., Baraitser, L., Catty, J., Anucha, K., Davies, S., Flexer, M. J., Moore, M. D., & Osserman, J. (2023). A Waiting Crisis? *The Lancet*, 401, 408–409. https://doi.org/10.1016/S0140-6736(23)00238-6

Shulman, G. (2019). Time past, time present, time future: Reflections on the development of the sense of duration as a foundation for a durable object, going on being and sense of self. *Journal of Child Psychotherapy*, 45(3), 323–339. https://doi.org/10.1080/00754 17X.2019.1690027

Simon, K. (2023). Mitigating the negative mental health impact of racism on Black adolescents – A preventive perspective. *JAMA Network Open*, 6(11): e2340577. https://doi.org/10.1001/jamanetworkopen.2023.40577

Skinner, M. K. (2014). Environmental stress and epigenetic transgenerational inheritance. *BMC Medicine*, 12(153), 1–5. https://doi.org/10.1186/s12916-014-0153-y

Skopeliti, C., & Gecsoyler, S. (2023, March 30). 'Terrified for my future': Climate crisis takes heavy toll on young people's mental health. *The Guardian*. Retrieved April 15, 2024, from https://www.theguardian.com/environment/2023/mar/30/terrified-for-my-future-climate-crisis-takes-heavy-toll-on-young-peoples-mental-health

Steare, T., Gutiérrez Munoz, C., Sullivan, A., & Lewis, G. (2023, October 15). The association between academic pressure and adolescent mental health problems: A systematic review. *Journal of Affective Disorders*, 339, 302–317.

Steiner, J. (2018). Time and the Garden of Eden illusion. *International Journal of Psychoanalysis*, 99(6), 1274–1287. https://doi.org/10.1080/00207578.2018.1556072

Thunberg, G. (2019). *No one is too small to make a difference*. London: Penguin Random House.

Trevarthen, C., & Aitken, K. J. (2001). Infant intersubjectivity: Research, theory, and clinical applications. *Journal of Child Psychology and Psychiatry*, 42(1), 3–48.

Waddell, M. (2018). *On adolescence: Inside stories*. London: Routledge.

Weiss, H. (2020). A river with several different tributary streams: Reflections on the repetition compulsion. *International Journal of Psychoanalysis*, 101(6), 1172–1187. https://doi.org/10.1080/00207578.2020.1809155

Williams, P. (2007). Making time, killing time. In: R. J. Perelberg (ed.), *Time and memory* (pp. 47–63). Reprinted 2018: London & New York: Routledge.

Winnicott, D. W. (1962/2016). Adolescence: Struggling through the doldrums. In: L. Caldwell, & H. T. Robinson (eds.), *The collected works of D. W. Winnicott: Volume 6, 1960–1963* (pp. 187–196). Oxford: Oxford University Press.

Winnicott, D. W. (1965). *The maturational processes and the facilitating environment*. The International Psycho-Analytical Library (Vol. 64). London: The Hogarth Press and the Institute of Psycho-Analysis.

Zsila, A., & Reyes, M. E. S. (2023). Pros & cons: Impacts of social media on mental health. *BMC Psychology*, 11, 201. https://doi.org/10.1186/s40359-023-01243-x

Part 2

Chapter 4

Considering crisis and risk in psychoanalytic work with adolescents

Maria Papadima

Introduction: central questions

I want to discuss some broad questions that arise in our work with adolescents, even when our intended focus may be solely on the here and now between two people – therapist and patient. The cultural beliefs about risk and crisis that I'll discuss here inevitably affect our understanding of the issues faced by the adolescents we care for. A central question I wonder about is: how can we approach and address young people's emotional struggles within a society that increasingly characterises adolescent mental health using terminology saturated with risk and crisis? These societal discussions include the assumptions held by adolescents about their difficulties, those of their parents, and our own assumptions as therapists.

A search for academic articles on adolescent mental health generates a dizzying number of studies highlighting the idea of a crisis happening in this age group. Examples of academic articles referencing a crisis include, amongst many others 'Addressing the global crisis of child and adolescent mental health' (Benton et al., 2021), 'The escalating crisis in adolescent mental health' (Wiederhold, 2022), and 'Uncertainty as a driver of the youth mental health crisis' (Schweizer et al., 2023). News stories and online commentary add to this picture (e.g. Caron, 2024; Barry, 2024). This trend is backed by hard numbers – in the alarming rise of suicide rates among young men, one of the most vulnerable demographics (Sher, 2020; Labuhn et al., 2021) – and the worsening mental health among adolescent girls too, which manifests differently from boys but is no less serious. Emergency department visits in the UK and the United States are increasing too, both for severe mental illness, such as emerging psychosis and overdoses, but also for adolescents who see the ED as their last resort to seek help.

This shared cultural discourse of adolescent mental health as being 'in crisis' has evolved into a societal reality, profoundly affecting adolescents and their families, with serious implications at various levels. This issue captured public attention during the Covid years, sparking heated discussions about the impact of lockdowns on isolation, uncertainty, and anxiety among adolescents (Benton et al., 2021; Guessoum et al., 2020; Panchal et al., 2023; Hoekstra, 2020). Yet this narrative of crisis for this age group has persisted even after the pandemic.

DOI: 10.4324/9781003592778-7

As an example, during one single week in August 2024, while writing about these ideas, I noticed two successive headlines in The Guardian on the crisis in youth mental health: On 28 August 2024, I read: 'NHS referrals for anxiety in children more than double pre-Covid levels' (Gregory, 2024). The very next day: '"Happiness recession": UK 15-year-olds at bottom of European satisfaction league' (Booth, 2024).

This gloomy picture extends beyond adolescence. After years of efforts to think about and protect workers' health and safety, improve working conditions for both children and adults, and regulate standards to ensure staff competence (such as in the NHS in the UK), the pendulum has now swung towards an ethos of risk minimisation. This has led to increased public and professional expectations of risk elimination and safety *wherever possible*. Despite these efforts towards greater safety, there is a parallel increase in dissatisfaction and rising mental health problems. The Zero Suicide Alliance is one example of a well-intended initiative that falls flat against the backdrop of growing mental illness numbers and limited public sector support.[1] So the general trend appears to focus on risk aversion and safety over other values (Beck, 1992), with various areas of life framed around these principles, while at the same time resources for support are diminishing and mental health problems continue to rise in number.

More broadly, the shift towards risk aversion and safety reflects a quasi-magical belief in the possibility of reducing *all danger*. Psychoanalytically, this could be seen as an effort to rewrite history or offer a complete 'corrective emotional experience' (Abend, 1979) in the face of intolerable realities – aiming for a risk-free existence and reflecting the 'fantasy of an alternative, better, parent' (Abend, 1979). Elements of defensive practice within the NHS and social care come into play here too, given the increasing real-world risks, including institutional crises, waiting lists, growing poverty, inequality, and fewer resources overall. This set of conditions often leads to a focus on eliminating risks through checklists and questions designed to cover workers' backs in case something goes wrong. In the British NHS, all this results in crisis management largely displacing preventative, long-term, and relational approaches.

This crisis-driven model inevitably also shapes adolescents' self-perceptions, including how they're perceived by others and how help is sought. When adolescent struggles are increasingly assumed to be *mental health crises*, young people can't help but internalise a sense of vulnerability, hopelessness, and despair, which can erode their resilience and hope and their sense that there is good, appropriate, measured help available 'out there'.

My goal here is not to comprehensively critique risk- and crisis-centred framings or to investigate the origins of this cultural storyline in depth. Clearly, it has a number of complex historical reasons for existing. I'm sure there are, as mentioned earlier, both positive and fought-for, as well as negative, aspects to this framing. What I'm looking at here is how we, as therapists, position ourselves within these crisis-focused frameworks that so often dominate our work, without being swept away by them. When risk is perceived as the enemy, what risks are we willing to tolerate, and what is our own definition of a *crisis*? And – thinking about the teenagers we see – how does continuously hearing that their generation *is in crisis* affect their belief in a viable future? And how does it affect their self-perception?

To start with, a key question is whether, in the first place, we *should* make time to explore these issues in our day-to-day work as therapists. My quick answer is definitely yes. More details in what follows.

Interweaving the internal and the external

Psychoanalytic child psychotherapists focus on areas that others often overlook: the internal world of children and adolescents, populated by fantasies, dreams, and defensive patterns. There is great value in this focus – it's the basis of our training and captures the unique contribution we make to child and adolescent mental health teams, especially today, when other disciplines prioritise external or biological factors over subjectivity.

The world around us, however, is woven into the fabric of our daily life, and also into the content of our unconscious experiences. Placing this close interaction of external and internal at the centre of our thinking aligns with Freud's view that inner and outer – what some now call *nurture* and *nature* – cannot be fully separated. Freud's concept of *the drive* illustrates this connection: the drive is imagined as existing at the border (Jaffe et al., 2024; citing Freud, 1912), highlighting the interconnection between brain, consciousness, and unconscious forces (Compton, 1981).

Modern neuroscience, using its own language, has also pointed to this connection, showing us how the brain, particularly during early development, is built through emotional interactions with others (Clark et al., 2021). For instance, we know that severe neglect and abuse can have lasting effects on children and adolescents, leading to a variety of mental and bodily symptoms and responses (Vela, 2014; Twardosz & Lutzker, 2010). Psychological causes can lead to somatic symptoms, and traumatic experiences or intense anxiety can impact brain structures (Neumeister et al., 2007; Fonzo et al., 2016; Bremner, 2004). Modern psychoanalytic thinkers have expanded on these findings (e.g. Kaplan-Solms & Solms, 2018; Mills, 2022), returning us to the foundational Freudian idea of the body–mind interconnection.

Additionally, there has been a continuous line of thinking from Freud to contemporary psychoanalysts that explores the ways in which sociocultural narratives shape psychology (e.g. Meissner, 2009; Fonagy & Target, 2007; Chodorow, 2019; Frie, 2014; Golding, 1982; Smadja, 2018). Psychoanalysis interprets these connections differently from the biopsychosocial approach, which also makes similar links (Engel, 1977). While the biopsychosocial model attributes symptoms to separate domains – neurodiversity, trauma, biology, and culture – as if these could be weighed separately, psychoanalysis views these factors as mutually constitutive, co-shaping each other in a dense, interwoven amalgam. The idea is that biology, subjectivity, and environment *all together shape* experience, creating the unique experience of each person – transformed again through fantasies and defensive structures.

The goal, then, is not to list factors causing a symptom but to interpret the meanings behind symptoms and behaviours holistically, bypassing the discrete domains in which we might imagine them to belong. These factors together culminate in the one-of-a-kind person in front of us (Bell, 2018; Cohen, 1989). This can be visualised as a Möbius strip, showing us in a picture how inner and outer realities are *seamlessly connected* (Wachtel, 2017; see Figure 4.1), fantasies, thoughts, and experiences continuously interacting with reality and modifying each other (Abrams, 1984; Josephs, 1987). Similarly, memories evolve each time we retell them (Marsh, 2007; Schacter, 2002), coloured by our desires, perceptions, and what's happening around us. Inner life is therefore *profoundly shaped* by the world we inhabit.

Josh Cohen's perspective illustrates what a psychoanalytic approach brings here. He says:

> Psychoanalysis does not allow us to think of the body as a raw biological entity, in isolation from the psyche which processes its experiences. . . . Freud's conception of the body was transformed when he cut off the bodily symptoms of hysteria from the 'neuroanatomical' sources in which psychiatry had previously located them, and demonstrated their 'ideogenic' (or psychic) derivation. Physiological symptoms become, from this perspective, one form among many (including, most famously, dreams and 'slips') through which the unconscious mind reveals and disguises itself.
>
> (Cohen, 2015, p. 214)

Figure 4.1 a Möbius strip[2]

I will now look at the main concepts of crisis, risk, and breakdown, especially in the context of clinical work with adolescents.

Definitions: crisis, risk, and breakdown

The terms crisis, risk, and breakdown offer distinct yet connected viewpoints for understanding developmental and mental health issues in young people. These terms, of course, go beyond adolescence. Whether discussing the shocking acuteness of a *crisis,* the disquieting thought that *someone is at risk,* or the rupture implied in the word *breakdown,* these terms indicate disorder – which, however, can also lead to growth and transformation. I'll start with the term crisis.

Crisis

This book primarily addresses a specific type of adolescent crisis, characterised by suicidal thoughts, suicide attempts, or moderate to severe self-harm. However, this is only one form of crisis. Here, I want to expand the definition of the concept to encompass its wider cultural use in relation to adolescents, serving as a shorthand for a general decline in adolescent mental health, of which suicidal and self-harm crises are only components.

This refers to the widely perceived adolescent mental health crisis, reinforced by a wealth of academic and media reports that describe it and propose solutions (e.g. Davey, 2024; Richtel & Flanagan, 2022; Haidt, 2024; Twenge, 2024). As we describe in more detail elsewhere in this book,[3] the dictionary definition of crisis, in this broader sense, refers to 'an extremely difficult or dangerous point in a situation' or 'a time of great disagreement, confusion, or suffering'.[4]

A crisis presents both risks and dangers but also carries the potential for significant change, as it can lead to internal and external reorganisation. Successfully navigating – and surviving – a crisis requires tolerance, curiosity, and a degree of openness to its implications. Unlike the medical model (in its more rigid applications) that focuses on fixing symptoms, a developmental perspective sees life as a process of gradual, imperceptible growth punctuated by periods of accelerated, visible change. These transformative periods are crises, as they lead to radical reorganisation. We can think more generally of a crisis as an urgent signal requiring attention, indicating that something significant, whether positive or negative (or both), must be addressed right now.

But to allow any space for the opportunities in a crisis, we must, to some degree, accept its inherent risks. This is challenging in a risk-averse culture, bringing me to the next central concept: risk.

Risk

In a psychodynamic context, *risk* encompasses both predictive outcomes – measuring, assessing, and managing – and developmental possibilities. Risk is integral to any crisis, potentially leading to either growth or harm, or to both growth and harm. Even seemingly irrational or destructive behaviours may reveal underlying issues if we look deeper. Risk signifies tension points – felt by the child or perceived in the object/environment – within larger crises. Recognising that any change involves risk and loss as well as gain is at the heart of this idea.

It's important to think carefully about what we mean by *risk* in the first place. The term varies significantly between communities, families, and societies. One clear example, when it comes to families, is a young child stepping outside their home and gaining some independence in doing so. Society's tolerance for this type of ordinary risk has changed markedly in recent decades (see Alparone & Pacilli, 2012; Clements, 2004; Gray, 2011).

A recent podcast with Marion Nestle and Mark Bittman[5] illustrated how children in the past mostly spent their afternoons. Nestle and Bittman recalled being sent outside after school to play and roam freely, told not to return until dinner – something then taken for granted as completely safe. My father shared similar memories with me years ago, of roaming the neighbourhoods of his city in Northern Greece with friends from a young age. All this was seen as ordinary, part of everyday life. Today's children, though, spend far more time indoors or (at best) at each other's homes, only going out independently when much older – a dramatic change in just a few decades.

Another example is found in the 1980 movie 'Fame', directed by Alan Parker, which I watched as a child. Watching it again recently after 30 years, I was struck by the level of resilience and *toughness* expected then from both teachers and students in the film's performing arts school. During this second viewing, the famous line 'You've got big dreams? You want fame? Well, fame costs. And right here is where you start paying . . . in sweat' struck me. It reflects an approach focused on hard work, competition, and toughness, a mentality that has largely faded, replaced by an emphasis instead on self-care, safety, and acceptance. Many interactions in the movie would now be decried, I think rightly, as instances of bullying or racism. But there is also something we lose as well as gain with this reframing.

Today's excessive focus on risk aversion and safety has other drawbacks. It can fail to address structural inequalities, such as financial, race, and class disparities, which make the centrality of safety and avoidance of risk a glib, surface-level pronouncement with no substance. After all, access to quality, timely mental health care remains uneven across different classes and societal groups (Cook et al., 2017; Henderson et al., 1998) despite the existence of the UK's universal care system, and these inequalities may be, in fact, more pronounced now than in the 'Fame'-depicted teenage life of the 1980s United States.

The Covid-19 pandemic further highlighted these inequalities in resource allocation (Loeb et al., 2021). The result today is that, while there is a societal expectation that help should be readily available and should be sought without shame – and that risks should be mitigated – the reality makes this a moot point. This is a bitter pill to swallow for young people who grow in this confusing environment. In a society focused on spotting and avoiding risks – amid stark inequalities, individualistic materialism, and political polarisation – sounding alarms without available solutions leaves us with the worst of both worlds: in such an environment, risks are heightened and solutions become elusive and tantalisingly out of reach.

This brings us to the concept of breakdown, which can occur when crises aren't addressed and when risks are either ignored or managed superficially.

Breakdown

In psychoanalysis, particularly in the contemporary Freudian and Independent traditions, a breakdown is different from crisis and risk, though related. Breakdown signifies severe difficulty and rupture yet can also offer hope – akin to Leonard Cohen's line in 'Anthem': 'There is a crack in everything, that's how the light gets in'.

Moses and Eglé Laufer (Laufer, 1995; Laufer & Laufer, 1984) described adolescent breakdown as a sudden stop in ordinary development, leading to various outcomes, some more severe than others. It disrupts both developmental progress and psychic continuity, in extreme cases resulting in psychosis (Bollas, 2012; Kennedy, 2018). Breakdown thus signifies a larger disruption than a crisis (which can be momentary), often indicating past unresolved issues coming to the surface again.

A useful related concept is Donald Winnicott's 'fear of breakdown' (1974). In that paper, he describes a paradox where a person lives in constant fear of a breakdown that has already occurred *but was not experienced at that time*, as it happened before the formation of the ego. As Claire Winnicott suggested, the early ego is dependent and unable to handle environmental failure (1980); hence, a breakdown starting at that time can be much harder to overcome. Adolescents, years later, may act out, seeking in desperation to identify the unknown source of their terror – a terror they faced in their past unknowingly to them. Thomas Ogden (2014) has expanded on this idea, describing the strange feeling of living 'mostly an unlived life'. An adolescent's self-destructive behaviour today can therefore sometimes be an unconscious response to a past, forgotten breakdown rather than a sign of a current one.

A breakdown is far more likely when crises and their associated risks are ignored or managed superficially. Just as restricting a child from exploring their surroundings – not allowing them reasonable risks – can hinder development, a breakdown may occur if a crisis within a family or friendship isn't acknowledged and addressed.

In summary, the concepts of crisis, risk, and breakdown remind us that adolescence is a time of both growth and fragility. Each crisis carries risks within it, and a breakdown may follow from an unresolved crisis or from warding off risks prematurely, without allowing space for thought. Adolescence is a time of change, self-confrontation, and the revisiting of childhood themes. Rather than avoiding the risky moments and crises it contains, these can be accepted as inevitable – and more than that, as drivers of growth and identify formation.

I will now turn in more detail to the societal shift toward risk avoidance and a crisis-centred view of events, a clear trend in many settings over recent decades.

A risk-averse and crisis-prone society

As discussed so far, in recent decades, society has shifted from accepting risks as part of life to viewing them as avoidable and dreaded. I think that this change is linked to the current adolescent mental health crisis. In what I discuss here, I draw primarily from trends in the United Kingdom, where I have lived and worked for years. However, this anti-risk focus extends far beyond the UK, reflecting broader global shifts in the Western world.

Anne Dufourmantelle's 'In praise of risk' (2011) traces modern society's widespread 'principle of precaution', arguing that it 'has become the norm, an unquestioned value', and the axis around which individuals, groups, and institutions orient themselves and make decisions. Dufourmantelle urges us, instead, to see the opportunities risk can bring: each 'risk – its object still indeterminate for now – opens an unknown space' (chapter 1), she writes, inviting us to imagine risk as belonging to the side of life rather than to the side of death and destruction.

Ulrich Beck's 'Risk society' (1992) was one of the earliest works examining how preoccupied modern society is with avoiding future risks. The version of this phenomenon in younger populations was some years ago termed 'safetyism' by Lukianoff and Haidt (2018). Although focusing on risk avoidance is well-intentioned, if taken too far, it hinders natural developmental processes. This is the case throughout life, not only in adolescence.

Media sensationalism often distorts the perception of risk and exacerbates societal anxieties. Barry Glassner's 'The culture of fear' (1999) explores how media and political rhetoric amplify fears beyond actual risks, leading to societal anxiety that pathologises normal adolescent behaviours, framing them within a crisis discourse rather than viewing them as part of the natural spectrum of human development.

There are various views and nuances within the debates in this area (e.g. Kitzinger, 1999; Barker & Petley, 2002). But one interesting idea is that the widespread account of adolescent vulnerability and perpetual crisis may be reinforced through continuous references to it, resulting in a looping effect (Hacking, 1995). In addition, topics such as cyberbullying, sexting, and self-harm – while real and sometimes serious concerns – can also be sensationalised, creating a feedback loop that heightens anxiety for both adolescents and the adults who care for them. This cycle erodes perspective, with dissenting views often shut down by reminders of the threats facing young people.

Mary Douglas (1990, 1992) has explored how societies use risk to reinforce social norms and power structures, suggesting that the framing of risk can serve to maintain control and often makes certain groups, such as adolescents, receptacles for wider social anxieties. She says that in the Global North, risk has replaced other feared phenomena, such as witchcraft or sin, and is often proposed as 'the [most likely] explanation for misfortune' (1990). Believing this then promotes increased surveillance and self-surveillance among young people.

Another characteristic of the focus on risk is the responsibility it places on human actions and mistakes, making risk avoidance not just something to aspire to but *a moral imperative*. The implicit belief here is that all risks can be controlled and predicted *if only we try hard enough*.

Judith Green (1999) argues that part of the reason for all this is that we struggle to accept the inevitability of risk, which we can often observe in the case of high-profile disasters. One example is that of Sharon Shoesmith, former Haringey Director of Education and Children's Social Care, who was blamed as an individual and eventually lost her job following the death of 'Baby P'. Green presents this case as emblematic of the demand for specific and personal accountability in the aftermath of a tragic case like this.

Nassim Nicholas Taleb's 'The black swan' (2007) argues, however, that there is a degree of unpredictability in rare, high-impact events that, despite efforts, we can never fully overcome. In a society that wants to minimise risk as much as possible, the concern about these 'black swan' events – always after the fact – can lead to overreactions and too stringent measures that will sadly fail to prevent the next, equally unpredictable, 'black swan' event. These measures not only fail to control future events (simply because of their rarity) but can also squander resources in the excessive efforts of prevention, a point also made by Glassner (1999).

These societal attitudes towards risk and crisis, of course, influence how adolescents experience their world. For therapists, parents, and educators, understanding these wider societal ideas towards risk avoidance helps contextualise and evaluate the challenges young people face. This understanding is crucial for balancing exploration and growth with safety and protection.

I now turn to the evolving concept of crisis in adolescent mental health and some of the ways the societal attitudes I've mentioned enter our therapeutic space with adolescents.

Adolescence in crisis: societal risks and mental health in the post-pandemic era

The idea that adolescence is a distinct stage characterised by unique risks is fairly recent. Our current understanding of adolescent mental fragility and the risks this stage involves (e.g. from cyberbullying, sexual assault, climate anxiety, the risks of AI, etc.) is also relatively recent. What has remained constant across cultures and historical periods is the idea of adolescence as a time of change, marked by transformative rituals, all contributing to growth (Foulkes, 2024), signifying the transition from childhood to adulthood. Adolescents typically engage in boundary-testing and exploration as part of developing independence and confidence during this phase, but the way these risks and boundary-pushing are conceptualised varies across contexts and cultures. Likewise, the concept of *adulthood* (like that of adolescence) varies across cultures, influenced by factors such as class, race, and family structures.

In the current framework, adults – parents, teachers, clinicians – have roles that are close to impossible. Instead of guiding and supporting young people through natural developmental challenges, they end up becoming risk mitigators. Economic and social factors also come into this, in terms of what adults are supposed to offer young people. For example, parents today are expected to provide a high level of practical and financial support, which can affect their emotional and time-based availability to adolescents. The impossibly high expectations of what a parent has to be and do undermine the ability to parent with confidence. The commonplace lack of family and societal supports worsens this picture, as families more and more live far from their relatives and communities.

The government's actions, such as undermining carriers of expertise and support – for example, undermining the probation service (Newburn, 2013); attacking the youth justice service, leaving few youth workers employed by underfunded local authorities; and creaming off education funding to academies whose results are no better than their local authority counterparts (Weale, 2022) – reduce the number of trustworthy adults outside the family for adolescents to turn to. The context is complex. But the bottom line is that, at the same time that we expect so much of parents, there is less and less societal and family support to make it all possible. The result is that, with all this pressure for 'ideal' parenting, coupled with reduced community support and emphasis on avoiding adolescent challenges and risks, natural developmental behaviours become *skills to obtain*, or *abnormalities to diagnose and manage*.

In a nutshell, with all this focus on adolescent mental health crisis, adolescence has come to represent – through a projective process – some of the issues we wish to avoid, such as sexuality, adventure, unpredictability, as well as the power of youth (which, of course, has always evoked envy). The result is the widespread pathologising of adolescence's core traits. Surprisingly, adolescents have not resisted but have instead embraced and internalised this narrative (Acheson & Papadima, 2023).

Assessing risk

All this doesn't mean we shouldn't assess risk. Assessing the level of risk is, of course, vital in our work as therapists. But in doing so, we must hold in mind all the different sides of one and the same child: the child who acts, the child who is a risk to himself/herself or others, and the troubled child underneath, whose history informs our thinking. Ignoring any one of these sides – which often happens – leads either to systems being centred on risk avoidance or, on the other side, to systems focusing too much on protection, which turns into overprotection. The result is that the actual risks facing children and adolescents are not meaningfully addressed. Paradoxically, the idealistic and unachievable emphasis on either predicting and avoiding all risks or on fully protecting the young person means resources are spent on firefighting and complex tools and risk-elimination strategies, often duplicating efforts meaninglessly and missing the real issues.

At the heart of this lies the impossible hope that all risks can be kept at bay – a hope that, in practice, may paradoxically mean that the actual dangers adolescents face are overlooked. When the child's whole story and current context are held in mind, risk can instead be addressed within the therapeutic relationship. This approach may not, on the surface, look as if it's 'fighting' the risk in an obvious way, but bit by bit, it allows for gradual mitigation of risks, once they're articulated in therapy and thought about, if allowed to be opened up and borne by the therapist.

Adolescents in Western cultures have been changing how they live; because of this, there are also changes in the risks they're willing to take. Historically, adolescent issues often manifested as externalising behaviours – actions directed outward. Today's adolescents, in contrast, have been described as 'generation sensible' (Burgess et al., 2022), noted for their increased 'focus on social issues, healthy living and drinking less alcohol' (Batty, 2022; see also Guardian Today in Focus Podcast, 2025: Is the gym gen Z's pub?).[6] While many UK adolescents fit these generalisations, some, of course, don't: their economic and other pressures lead them to different trajectories. Nevertheless, these wider societal trends are there, without implying they apply to all adolescents.

Through these societal changes, the natural developmental crisis of adolescence has subtly been reframed into a broader story of *adolescent mental health in crisis.* This extends to the belief that *young people – and their future – are in a deadly crisis.* Before responding reflexively – 'But it's true, their future is in crisis!' – it's worth pausing to think about the implications of this claim, especially from our perspective as psychoanalytic child psychotherapists. Blissfully ignoring societal problems – sometimes catastrophes – occurring around us is irresponsible, but there is an equally serious cost in abandoning all hope for a viable future. I prefer to believe that this young generation might show us possibilities we can't yet imagine.

Research and statistics do support a narrative of adolescent crisis. Young people increasingly perceive their lives negatively, with declining happiness and increasing pessimism (Duckworth & Maughan, 2024). Mental health indicators are also worsening (Benton et al., 2021; The Lancet Psychiatry Commission on Youth Mental Health, 2024; Piao et al., 2022). These trends have many different causes and have sparked intense debates in academia and popular media. One convincing explanation for the rising levels of unhappiness among young people is the societal shift toward individualism, over the last decades, which emphasises self-identity over a sense of communal belonging, with a self-centric narrative on life's meaning (Brooks, 2024). This shift, amongst the other problems it brings, limits the availability of the adolescent group as a venue for exploration, identity experimentation, and mild – but necessary! – antisocial and risky behaviour.

This cultural shift, first noticed in the 1950s and 1960s (Keniston, 1981), has widened with social media and digital culture, fostering isolation, amplifying performance pressures and competition, as well as body image concerns. David Brooks (2024) calls this 'expressive individualism', noting that it transcends political fault lines:

The right-wing version of this individualism (which emphasized economic freedom) and the left-wing version (which emphasized lifestyle freedom) were different, but it was individual freedom all the way down.

Other reasons for the increased unhappiness and pessimism among young people (Twenge, 2023) include the climate crisis, long-term impacts of the Covid-19 pandemic, the global rise of authoritarianism, the rise in inequality and perceived injustice in Western countries, social media and smartphone use (Haidt, 2024), and finally, the growing *'expertisation' and 'psychologisation'* of daily life, together with the broadening definitions of mental health and mental illness (Foulkes, 2022; Acheson & Papadima, 2023).

Despite differences in gender, class, and political beliefs, the younger generation does consistently show a decline in quality of life and satisfaction. This results in many young people today feeling hesitant about parenthood (Cohen Booth, 2023), engaging less in sexual activity when compared to previous generations, and often adopting apocalyptic framings of life (Winter, 2023) matter-of-factly. These trends resemble previous historical anxieties about 'end times', but they stand out for the near-total absence of hope or potential for change. Another reason for this, adding to all those already mentioned, may be the continuous, overwhelming influx of information and news coverage, which can lead any of us to despair and catastrophic thinking. This can be worse in young people, though, as they've had limited experience of how events can turn out, including all their possible outcomes, both negative and positive.

Having all this in mind when meeting and working with young people offers us the opportunity for more clarity and nuance in our work. Without this perspective, our responses risk falling into two extremes: first, uncritical identification with societal risk framing or, second, an over-focus on the adolescent's internal world, ignoring the context within which a young person's story is borne.

Can we ever fully predict and prevent risk?

In the context of suicide and self-harm – two of the most prominent risks faced by adolescents – both one-to-one interventions and public health efforts can reduce risk, *but only to an extent*. Research on this underscores the limits of predictability at the individual level (Gibbons, 2024). While public health measures hold promise, especially in areas like suicide prevention, the attempt to eliminate all risk – epitomised by the Zero Suicide goal – is neither realistic nor beneficial in the long term, for adolescents or for clinicians. Supportive interventions and fostering meaningful connections can undoubtedly make a positive difference for adolescents and their families. However, the aspiration to *eradicate risk* inadvertently creates a stifling atmosphere, burdening both young people and those who care for them with unattainable expectations.

One longstanding, well-known truth – though recently somewhat overshadowed by the crisis focus – is that adolescents take more risks than both adults and children, a pattern found globally and historically. Risk-taking is described as 'peaking in the late teens and early twenties, and then declining again' (Foulkes, 2024 p. 62; citing DiClemente et al., 2009; Wang et al., 2024).

Research has identified several reasons for this phenomenon. Lucy Foulkes outlines some, including perceived invulnerability (Foulkes, 2024, pp. 64–65; Millstein & Halpern, 2002), sensation-seeking (Siraj et al., 2021), and the evolutionary utility of risk-taking, which allows teenagers to learn about safety through exploration and novelty (Foulkes, 2024, pp. 66–68). Other theories, like the dual systems model (Steinberg, 2010), suggest that during adolescence, the 'cognitive control system' in the brain isn't fully developed, while the emotional system is more powerful, though evidence supporting this is mixed (Foulkes, 2024, pp. 68–69). Additionally, peer influence and the signalling of pseudo-mature behaviour – essentially demonstrating independence through risk-taking – play a crucial role (Foulkes, 2024, pp. 69–71).

Jonathan Haidt (2024) highlights how this societal attitude toward risk avoidance has profound implications for how adolescents live their lives. Adolescents, while biologically and evolutionarily predisposed to risk-taking, are also deeply influenced by the desire to fit in with their peers. When the prevailing peer standard leans towards safety and risk avoidance, adolescents often align with this standard to be accepted. As Foulkes (2024, p. 71) observes, the 'social risk of being rejected by peers outweighs other potentially negative outcomes of decisions, such as threats to one's health or the prospect of getting caught'.

Given the historical and cross-cultural necessity of risk-taking and exploration during adolescence, it's possible that young people today are finding alternative ways to engage with risk and to destabilise safety and are not as risk-avoiding as we think. One such avenue may be through their mental health crises, where they inadvertently destabilise both their environment and themselves. Another is through their extensive online explorations, which bring their own set of risks and challenges.

Thus, how do our contemporary notions of risk and crisis, alongside the demands of a safety-first society, align – or fail to align – with adolescents' natural tendency toward exploration and risk-taking? What unconscious societal needs might this prevailing narrative serve?

One perspective, drawing from psychoanalytic thinking, suggests that the crisis narrative could function as a scapegoat mechanism. Adolescents may be burdened with the task of embodying and expressing the anxieties and contradictions of the adult world, which manifests in an exaggerated societal focus on avoiding risks at all costs. After all, adolescents often act out most 'loudly' the unspoken or repressed fears of broader society (Acheson & Papadima, 2023).

By critically examining the underlying assumptions of the crisis storyline – or, at least, keeping them in mind – we can better understand its far-reaching implications on both adolescents and the clinicians who work with them.

We could conclude that the continuous headlines and widely accepted pronouncements about adolescents 'in crisis' imply certain things: an urgent need to address their challenges, often within a mental health context. But also, they imply that these issues are largely unaddressed or inadequately managed and that today's adolescent struggles are unique compared to those of past generations. Ultimately, labelling all these multifactorial struggles as a crisis implies *a need for drastic interventions*. This framing stresses the necessity for ever more resources and responses. In reality, though, as I've discussed, the support that's on offer often amounts to a hotline or text line – well intentioned but lacking the depth and continuity adolescents require and, in the end, perhaps making things worse. In the end, despite all the campaigns to destigmatise mental illness and promote support – such as high-profile efforts by the UK royals – the problems continue to grow (Armitage et al., 2024).

The adolescent mental health crisis entering the therapy room

Communicating effectively and meaningfully with adolescents in crisis is inherently challenging. Facilitating a sense of hope becomes increasingly hard when they view their external surroundings (rather than only their internal world) as fraught with dangers and pitfalls. In the face of this, as a psychotherapist working with adolescents, I've thought a lot about my responses; my decision is to hold on quite stubbornly to the crucial importance of *fostering and sustaining hope*. Adolescents need this from us, especially those grappling with suicidal thoughts or severe depression, but not just them. If we find ourselves succumbing to pessimism, or even despair, about the current state of the world and fully aligning with an apocalyptic narrative, how can we help adolescents distance themselves from it? The question becomes: How can we help them out of their despair, towards optimism and a sense of agency within the society they find themselves in, when we have our own doubts about this society?

As therapists working with adolescents, I see our role as managing the delicate balance between actual and perceived risks despite the challenges involved. One of these challenges is that we're not separate from the overwhelming crisis narratives; we are participants in the same world that adolescents navigate, and we can get caught up in alarming narratives too.

This is not about disputing – or validating – the crisis discourse outright, as framed by either the political left or right; the question for us is how it permeates psychoanalytic work with adolescents and shapes our understanding of and response to risk and crisis as therapists. We respond to climate change (e.g. Weintrobe, 2013) or income inequality as citizens as well as therapists; yet in therapy, the overarching crisis framing, in the way it gets frenetically reproduced through media and social media, can paralyse rather than mobilise toward shared goals. I have observed repeatedly how this narrative paralyses adolescents on an individual level, amplifying their struggles rather than empowering them.

A few examples drawn from my work in an adolescent crisis team illustrate what I mean:

A young adolescent boy who has taken a small overdose after an argument with their parents reveals during the hospital assessment that he recently participated in a school-wide Mental Health Awareness Week event. His classmates sharing their struggles – including self-harm behaviours – becomes part of his own story, due to a confused new belief that self-harming behaviours can help him cope with difficult feelings.

Or . . .

A 13-year-old girl is found crying and self-harming in school, for the first time. She discloses during the assessment that her best friend recently overdosed and was hospitalised. The event sparks group discussions about trauma and mental health among her peers, leading to a school assembly on the topic and eventually prompting the school to hire additional counsellors, given the rising number of anxious young people in the school.

How can we respond to such stories? We might assume that these cases are isolated examples and not generalisable; or we might conclude that similar situations always existed in adolescent groups and there's nothing new here; or we might assume that these stories tell us nothing about the suffering of the person in front of us and the way we listen to them: only a purely individual focus can do that. But as both examples show (and similar examples abound in adolescent crisis teams), societal discourses on mental health and crisis have a distinct 'flavour' today that we need to recognise, as this has become *integral* to understanding the adolescent's experience, both in their external behaviour and in the way they see themselves.

In therapy, adolescents often articulate this sense of societal crisis through their descriptions of dreams and hopes for the future. For instance, a 19-year-old once shared with me: *I have this gut feeling that a world war will lead society to crumble within the next five years. I feel as if I'm circled by this thought.* Responding, and connecting his perception of looming societal collapse to the field of his personal self-destructiveness, I said: *The world may not be crumbling, but you also, before that, feel like you're crumbling inside.*

Many psychotherapists might have interpreted, I'm guessing, in a similar way. Yet our exchange with this young man lingered with me, leading me to two reflections: first, I kept returning to the frequency with which I now hear versions of this dystopian narrative from adolescents across diverse backgrounds. Even 'well-adjusted' or 'ordinarily happy' adolescents refer casually to the end of the world as a given truth, no questions asked, and it's not always easy to know how to respond.

Winnicott's transitional phenomena and the concepts of risk and crisis

I now shift to Winnicott's ideas and how they might be applied to understanding risk and crisis, especially in relation to identity formation.

Winnicott's concept of transitional phenomena – that zone at the overlap between fantasy and reality (1971) – is highly relevant when considering adolescent risk-taking within the Möbius strip interplay of internal and external. We can read adolescents' attraction to risk, whether minor or extreme, as their attempt to negotiate the shifting space between childhood and adulthood, and between closeness to parents and separation from them.

Teenagers, as discussed already, often test boundaries through risk-taking, exploring where their internal experiences end and the external world starts. Extending this idea, we can think of risk-taking as a thrilling, playful, and *necessary* aspect of exploring identity during this transitional time – a way for adolescents to engage with the world while experimenting with different facets of their emerging, though still unformed, identities. Professor Cynthia Lightfoot, in her book 'The culture of adolescent risk taking' (1997), develops similar ideas, stating:

> Adolescents are makers of new talismans. The clothes they wear, their music and media choices, their language and slang, their hangouts: all these express who they are, and who they would like to be. Borrowing a term from Winnicott (1971), these talismans are the 'transitional objects' of adolescence; risk-taking can be included among them.

(Lightfoot, 1997, p. 9)

Final thoughts

I have been discussing the widely accepted narrative of an adolescent mental health crisis, and I've tried to show its complexities and limitations. I've questioned the assumptions within the term 'crisis' itself, including the consequences of a crisis-centred framing in how adults relate to young people. Does this assumption of constant crisis lead to adults losing their confidence and authority out of fear, or does it reinforce a particular type of authority – too much monitoring, too much protecting – that ultimately doesn't benefit young people?

My main point has been that while crises and risks are inevitable difficulties faced in adolescence, they also represent important and necessary routes towards growth, transformation, and deeper understanding, both for adolescents and for those who support them. By adopting a psychoanalytic lens that integrates inner and outer worlds, we can hopefully navigate the complexities of risk and crisis with more clarity and balance, fostering resilience and agency in the adolescents we work with.

Notes

1 https://www.zerosuicidealliance.com/.
2 https://en.wikipedia.org/wiki/M%C3%B6bius_strip.
3 See chapter 13 in this book.

4 https://dictionary.cambridge.org/dictionary/english/crisis.
5 https://podcasts.apple.com/gb/podcast/the-inspiring-persistence-of-marion-nestle/id1567
   511802?i=1000591483824.
6 https://www.theguardian.com/news/audio/2025/apr/18/is-the-gym-gen-zs-pub-podcast.

References

Abend, S. M. (1979). Unconscious fantasy and theories of cure. *Journal of the American Psychoanalytic Association*, 27, 579–596.

Abrams, S. (1984). Fantasy and reality in the Oedipal phase: A conceptual overview. *The Psychoanalytic Study of the Child*, 39(1), 83–100.

Acheson, R., & Papadima, M. (2023). The search for identity: Working therapeutically with adolescents in crisis. *Journal of Child Psychotherapy*, 49(1), 95–119.

Alparone, F. R., & Pacilli, M. G. (2012). On children's independent mobility: The interplay of demographic, environmental, and psychosocial factors. *Children's Geographies*, 10(1), 109–122.

Armitage, J. M., Collishaw, S., & Sellers, R. (2024). Explaining long-term trends in adolescent emotional problems: What we know from population-based studies. *Discover Social Science and Health*, 4(14). https://doi.org/10.1007/s44155-024-00076-2

Barker, M., & Petley, J. (2002). *Ill effects: The media violence debate*. Routledge.

Barry, D. (2024, August 8). The worsening trends in youth mental health. *The New York Times*. https://www.nytimes.com/2024/08/08/briefing/mental-health-anxiety-depression.html

Batty, D. (2022, August 19). 'Generation sensible' risk missing out on life experiences, therapists warn. The Guardian. Retrieved October 12, 2025. https://www.theguardian.com/society/2022/aug/19/generation-sensible-risk-missing-out-life-experiences-therapists

Beck, U. (1992). *Risk society: Towards a new modernity*. SAGE Publications.

Bell, D. (2018). External injury and the internal world. In: *Understanding trauma* (pp. 167–180). Routledge.

Benton, T. D., Boyd, R. C., & Njoroge, W. F. (2021). Addressing the global crisis of child and adolescent mental health. *JAMA Pediatrics*, 175(11), 1108–1110.

Bollas, C. (2012). *Catch them before they fall: The psychoanalysis of breakdown*. Routledge.

Booth, R. (2024, August 29). 'Happiness recession': UK 15-year-olds at bottom of European satisfaction league. *The Guardian*. https://www.theguardian.com/society/article/2024/aug/29/uk-teenagers-low-life-satisfaction-europe?utm_source=pocket_shared

Bremner, J. D. (2004). Brain imaging in anxiety disorders. *Expert Review of Neurotherapeutics*, 4(2), 275–284.

Brooks, D. (2024, January 31). Chicken littles are ruining America: Doomsaying can become a self-fulfilling prophecy. *The Atlantic*. Retrieved October 12, 2025, https://www.theatlantic.com/ideas/archive/2024/01/cultural-pessimism-america-self-fulfilling-effects/677261/

Burgess, A., Yeomans, H., & Fenton, L. (2022). 'More options . . . less time' in the 'hustle culture' of 'generation sensible': Individualization and drinking decline among twenty-first century young adults. *The British Journal of Sociology*, 73(4), 903–918.

Caron, C. (2024, August 13). Trends in young adults' mental health. *The New York Times*. https://www.nytimes.com/2024/08/13/well/mind/mental-health-young-adults-trends.html

Chodorow, N. (2019). *The psychoanalytic ear and the sociological eye: Toward an American independent tradition*. Routledge.

Clark, E. L., Jiao, Y., Sandoval, K., & Biringen, Z. (2021). Neurobiological implications of parent-child emotional availability: A review. *Brain Sciences*, 11(8), 1016.

Clements, R. (2004). An investigation of the status of outdoor play. *Contemporary Issues in Early Childhood*, 5(1), 68–80.

Cohen Booth, R. (2023, December 4). How millennials learned to dread motherhood. *Vox*. Retrieved October 12, 2025. https://www.vox.com/features/23979357/millennials-motherhood-dread-parenting-birthrate-women-policy

Cohen, J. (2015). Psychoanalytic bodies. In: *The Cambridge Companion to the Body in Literature* (pp. 214–229). Cambridge University Press.

Cohen, S. (1989). The reality in fantasy-making. *The Psychoanalytic Study of the Child*, 44(1), 57–72.

Compton, A. (1981). On the psychoanalytic theory of instinctual drives: I: The beginnings of Freud's drive theory. *The Psychoanalytic Quarterly*, 50(2), 190–218.

Cook, B. L., Trinh, N. H., Li, Z., Hou, S. S. Y., & Progovac, A. M. (2017). Trends in racial-ethnic disparities in access to mental health care, 2004–2012. *Psychiatric Services*, 68(1), 9–16.

Davey, M. (2024, August 14). Alarming surge in mental ill-health among young people in face of unprecedented challenges, experts warn. *The Guardian*. https://www.theguardian.com/society/article/2024/aug/14/alarming-surge-in-mental-ill-health-among-young-people-in-face-of-unprecedented-challenges-experts-warn

DiClemente, R. J., Santelli, J. S., & Crosby, R. (Eds.). (2009). *Adolescent health: Understanding and preventing risk behaviors*. John Wiley & Sons.

Douglas, M. (1990). Risk as a forensic resource. *Daedalus*, 119(4), 1–16.

Douglas, M. (1992). *Risk and blame: Essays in cultural theory*. Routledge.

Duckworth & Maughan. (2024). Why are we so pessimistic? (Podcast). Freakonomics Radio. https://freakonomics.com/podcast/why-are-we-so-pessimistic/

Dufourmantelle, A. (2019). *In praise of risk*. Trans. S. Miller. Fordham University Press, New York (original 2011).

Engel, G. L. (1977). The need for a new medical model: A challenge for biomedicine. *Science*, 196(4286), 129–136.

Fonagy, P., & Target, M. (2007). The rooting of the mind in the body: New links between attachment theory and psychoanalytic thought. *Journal of the American Psychoanalytic Association*, 55(2), 411–456.

Fonzo, G. A., Ramsawh, H. J., Flagan, T. M., Simmons, A. N., Sullivan, S. G., Allard, C. B., . . . & Stein, M. B. (2016). Early life stress and the anxious brain: Evidence for a neural mechanism linking childhood emotional maltreatment to anxiety in adulthood. *Psychological Medicine*, 46(5), 1037–1054.

Foulkes, L. (2022). *What Mental Illness Really Is . . . (and what it isn't)*. Random House.

Foulkes, L. (2024). *Coming of Age: How Adolescence Shapes Us*. Random House.

Freud, S. (1912). The dynamics of transference. In: J. Strachey (ed.), *The Standard Edition of the Complete Psychological Works of Sigmund Freud: Vol. 12 (1911–1913)*. The Case of Schreber, Papers on Technique and Other Works. London: Hogarth, 1953, pp. 97–108.

Frie, R. (2014). What is cultural psychoanalysis? Psychoanalytic anthropology and the interpersonal tradition. *Contemporary Psychoanalysis*, 50(3), 371–394.

Gibbons, R. (2024). Eight 'truths' about suicide. *BJPsych bulletin*, 48(6), 350-354.

Glassner, B. (1999). *The culture of fear: Why Americans are afraid of the wrong things*. Basic Books.

Golding, R. (1982). Freud, psychoanalysis, and sociology: Some observations on the sociological analysis of the individual. *British Journal of Sociology*, 545–562.

Gray, P. (2011). The decline of play and the rise of psychopathology in children and adolescents. *American Journal of Play*, 3(4), 443–463.

Green, J. (1999). From accidents to risk: Public health and preventable injury. *Health, Risk & Society*, 1(1), 25–39.

Gregory, A. (2024, August 28). NHS referrals for anxiety in children more than double pre-COVID levels. *The Guardian*. https://www.theguardian.com/society/article/2024/aug/27/nhs-referrals-for-anxiety-in-children-more-than-double-pre-covid-levels-england?utm_source=pocket_shared

Guardian Today in Focus podcast. (2025, April 18). Retrieved April 18, 2025, from https://www.theguardian.com/news/audio/2025/apr/18/is-the-gym-gen-zs-pub-podcast

Guessoum, S. B., Lachal, J., Radjack, R., Carretier, E., Minassian, S., Benoit, L., & Moro, M. R. (2020). Adolescent psychiatric disorders during the COVID-19 pandemic and lockdown. *Psychiatry Research*, 291, 113264.

Hacking, I. (1995). The looping effects of human kinds. In: D. Sperber, D. Premack, & A. J. Premack (eds.), *Causal cognition: A multidisciplinary debate* (pp. 351–394). Clarendon Press/Oxford University Press.

Haidt, J. (2024). *The anxious generation: How the great rewiring of childhood is causing an epidemic of mental illness*. Penguin.

Henderson, C., Thornicroft, G., & Glover, G. (1998). Inequalities in mental health. *The British Journal of Psychiatry*, 173(2), 105–109.

Hoekstra, P. J. (2020). Suicidality in children and adolescents: Lessons to be learned from the COVID-19 crisis. *European Child & Adolescent Psychiatry*, 29, 737–738.

https://en.wikipedia.org/wiki/M%C3%B6bius_strip

Jaffe, C. M., Bucci, W., Maskit, B., & Murphy, S. (2024). Clinical and Research Perspectives on the Therapeutic Conversation: The Case of MS. M. *Journal of the American Psychoanalytic Association*, 00030651241256650.

Josephs, L. (1987). The paradoxical relationship between fantasy and reality in Freudian theory. *Psychoanalytic Review*, 74(2), 161.

Kaplan-Solms, K., & Solms, M. (2018). *Clinical studies in neuro-psychoanalysis: Introduction to a depth neuropsychology*. Routledge.

Keniston, K. (1981, November 8). The mood of Americans today. *The New York Times*. Retrieved October 12, 2025. https://www.nytimes.com/1981/11/08/books/the-mood-of-americans-today.html

Kennedy, R. (2018). A severe form of breakdown in communication in the psychoanalysis of an ill adolescent. In: *Independent Psychoanalysis Today* (pp. 407–425). Routledge.

Kitzinger, J. (1999). Researching risk and the media. *Health, Risk & Society*, 1(1), 55–69.

Labuhn, M., LaBore, K., Ahmed, T., & Ahmed, R. (2021). Trends and instigators among young adolescent suicide in the United States. *Public Health*, 199, 51–56. https://www.sciencedirect.com/science/article/abs/pii/S0033350621003292

The Lancet Psychiatry Commission on Youth Mental Health. https://www.thelancet.com/commissions/youth-mental-health

Laufer, M. (1995). Adolescent breakdown and beyond: Detecting and responding to present and future risk. *Brent Adolescent Centre Conference*, London, 28 October.

Laufer, M., & Laufer, M. E. (1984). *Adolescence and developmental breakdown*. Yale University Press.

Lightfoot, C. (1997). *The culture of adolescent risk-taking*. Guilford Press.

Loeb, T. B., Ebor, M. T., Smith, A. M., Chin, D., Novacek, D. M., Hampton-Anderson, J. N., Norwood-Scott, E., Hamilton, A. B., Brown, A. F., & Wyatt, G. E. (2021). How mental health professionals can address disparities in the context of the COVID-19 pandemic. *Traumatology*, 27(1), 60.

Lukianoff, G., & Haidt, J. (2018). *The coddling of the American mind: How good intentions and bad ideas are setting up a generation for failure*. Penguin Press.

Marsh, E. J. (2007). Retelling is not the same as recalling: Implications for memory. *Current Directions in Psychological Science*, 16(1), 16–20.

Meissner, W. W. (2009). Mind-brain and body in the self: Psychoanalytic perspectives. *The Psychoanalytic Review*, 96(2), 369–402.

Mills, J. (Ed.). (2022). *Psychoanalysis and the Mind-Body Problem*. Routledge.

Millstein, S. G., & Halpern-Felsher, B. L. (2002). Judgments about risk and perceived invulnerability in adolescents and young adults. *Journal of Research on Adolescence*, 12(4), 399–422.

Neumeister, A., Henry, S., & Krystal, J. H. (2007). Neurocircuitry and neuroplasticity in PTSD. In: *Handbook of PTSD: Science and Practice* (pp. 165–182). Guilford Press.

Newburn, T. (2013, January 10). *This is not quite the death knell for the probation service, but it is certainly the most radical change it has ever seen*. Retrieved 12 October 2025. https://blogs.lse.ac.uk/politicsandpolicy/this-is-not-quite-the-death-knell-for-the-probation-service-but-it-is-certainly-the-most-radical-change-it-has-ever-seen/

Ogden, T. H. (2014). Fear of breakdown and the unlived life. *The International Journal of Psychoanalysis*, 95(2), 205–223.

Panchal, U., Salazar de Pablo, G., Franco, M., Moreno, C., Parellada, M., Arango, C., & Fusar-Poli, P. (2023). The impact of COVID-19 lockdown on child and adolescent mental health: Systematic review. *European Child & Adolescent Psychiatry*, 32(7), 1151–1177.

Piao, J., Huang, Y., Han, C., Li, Y., Xu, Y., Liu, Y., & He, X. (2022). Alarming changes in the global burden of mental disorders in children and adolescents from 1990 to 2019: A systematic analysis for the Global Burden of Disease study. *European Child & Adolescent Psychiatry*, 31(11), 1827–1845.

Richtel, M., & Flanagan, A. (2022, April 23). It's life or death': The mental health crisis among US teens. *The New York Times*. Retrieved October 12, 2025. https://www.nytimes.com/2022/04/23/health/mental-health-crisis-teens.html

Schacter, D. L. (2002). *The seven sins of memory: How the mind forgets and remembers*. Houghton Mifflin Company.

Schweizer, S., Lawson, R. P., & Blakemore, S. J. (2023). Uncertainty as a driver of the youth mental health crisis. *Current Opinion in Psychology*, 53, 101657.

Sher, L. (2020). Suicide in men: An underappreciated public health challenge. *European Archives of Psychiatry and Clinical Neuroscience*, 270(2), 277–278. https://link.springer.com/article/10.1007/s00406-019-01041-w

Siraj, R., Najam, B., & Ghazal, S. (2021). Sensation seeking, peer influence, and risk-taking behavior in adolescents. *Education Research International*, 2021(1), 8403024.

Smadja, E. (2018). *Freud and culture*. Routledge.

Steinberg, L. (2010). A dual systems model of adolescent risk-taking. *Developmental Psychobiology: The Journal of the International Society for Developmental Psychobiology*, 52(3), 216–224.

Taleb, N. N. (2007). *The black swan: The impact of the highly improbable*. Random House.

Twardosz, S., & Lutzker, J. R. (2010). Child maltreatment and the developing brain: A review of neuroscience perspectives. *Aggression and Violent Behavior*, 15(1), 59–68.

Twenge, J. M. (2023). *Generations: The real differences between Gen Z, Millennials, Gen X, Boomers, and Silents – and what they mean for America's future*. Simon and Schuster.

Twenge, J. M. (2024, April 22). Suicide rates are now higher among young adults than the middle-aged. *Generation Tech Blog*. https://www.generationtechblog.com/p/suicide-rates-are-now-higher-among?isFreemail=true&post_id=143813969&publication_id=1494698&r=3bplh4&triedRedirect=true&utm_source=pocket_saves

Vela, R. M. (2014). The effect of severe stress on early brain development, attachment, and emotions: A psychoanalytical formulation. *Psychiatric Clinics*, 37(4), 519–534.

Wachtel, P. L. (2017). Psychoanalysis and the Moebius strip: Reexamining the relation between the internal world and the world of daily experience. *Psychoanalytic Psychology*, 34(1), 58–68. https://doi.org/10.1037/pap0000101

Wang, M., Deng, Y., Liu, Y., Suo, T., Guo, B., Eickhoff, S. B., & Rao, H. (2024). The common and distinct brain basis associated with adult and adolescent risk-taking behavior: Evidence from the neuroimaging meta-analysis. *Neuroscience & Biobehavioral Reviews*, 105607.

Weale, S. (2022, May 22). *Council-maintained schools outperform academies in England, study shows*. The Guardian. https://www.theguardian.com/education/2022/may/10/council-run-schools-outperform-academies-england-analysis-shows

Weintrobe, S. (Ed.). (2013). *Engaging with climate change: Psychoanalytic and interdisciplinary perspectives*. Routledge.

Wiederhold, B. K. (2022). The escalating crisis in adolescent mental health. *Cyberpsychology, Behavior, and Social Networking*, 25(2), 81–82.

Winnicott, C. (1980). Fear of breakdown: A clinical example. *The International Journal of Psycho-Analysis*, 61, 351.

Winnicott, D. W. (1971). Transitional objects and transitional phenomena. In: *Playing and Reality* (pp. 1–25). Routledge.

Winnicott, D. W. (1974). Fear of breakdown. *International Review of Psycho-Analysis*, 1(1–2), 103–107.

Winter. J. (2023, November 20). The morality of having kids in a burning, drowning world. *The New Yorker*. Retrieved October 12, 2025. https://www.newyorker.com/magazine/2023/11/27/the-quickening-elizabeth-rush-book-review-the-parenthood-dilemma-gina-rushton

Chapter 5

Meanings of adolescent overdose

Hillel Mirvis

I am encountering in recent years what can feel, at times, like an overdose of overdoses amongst my adolescent patients. I am struck by its overwhelming prevalence, and I, in turn, at times feel overwhelmed. I am cumulatively left with something that I have been struggling to swallow and digest.

I seem not to be alone in this experience (Rausch & Haidt, 2023). The rise in intentional overdose has been steadily increasing in the UK, particularly among adolescent girls (10–24), since 2010 (Rausch & Haidt, 2023, citing the UK Office of National Statistics from 2022), with reporting consistently showing higher suicide attempts among girls when compared to boys (Rausch & Haidt, 2023). This has been called the 'gender paradox in suicide' (Canetto & Sakinofsky, 1998).

My interest in writing about overdose (Mirvis, 2018) initially arose out of what felt to me to be a pressing need to forge a thinking space for this 'overdose of overdoses' among adolescents in crisis, as part of the widely reported adolescent mental health crisis which began before the Covid-19 pandemic. I have come to believe that it is worth considering possible unconscious reasons for why specific adolescents are driven towards overdosing, as opposed to other methods of self-harm, as a means of communicating their internal distress.

Overdose per se (and I am referring specifically to overdose on legal drugs, such as painkillers) is surprisingly 'underdosed' – or under-represented – in the psychoanalytic literature. There is a wealth of psychoanalytic literature about self-harm as an overarching 'umbrella' category (e.g. Briggs et al., 2009; Persano, 2022; Yakeley & Burbridge-James, 2018), but there is little written about the psychodynamics of adolescent overdose *specifically*. It is often assumed that whatever psychoanalytic theory has to say about self-harm can de facto be applied to our understanding of overdose, but we can question whether that is the case.

Self-cutting, as another subcategory of the wider group of self-harming behaviours, has, by contrast to overdose as a form of self-harm (rather than only as a form of suicidal action), been a focus of psychoanalytic theory in its own right (e.g. Brady, 2014; Nicolò, 2024; Nathan, 2004). I wonder whether self-cutting as an act naturally lends itself metaphorically to theories that underpin its psychological function, in contrast to overdose. For example, Mary Brady (2014) has written about self-cutting being a way of 'cutting through the silence' with respect

DOI: 10.4324/9781003592778-8

to family complexity – or, indeed, with respect to the adolescent's own internal distress – that has yet to be acknowledged or articulated.

And yet there is little, if anything, written about overdose as a symptom or phenomenon in its own right, and I wonder why this is the case. Is overdose more difficult to think about than self-cutting? This seems unlikely, as we could argue that self-cutting is all the more visceral and gorier to contemplate. However, my clinical experience of adolescents who habitually overdose suggests to me that there is a particular difficulty that's worth reflecting on when thinking about the particular meanings of overdose.

In my experience of hearing about adolescents' acts of overdose, which may be disclosed directly to me by the patient or indirectly through hearing about the context of their admission to a hospital, I have noticed that there often exists, projected into me, a virtual incapacity to swallow, process, and digest what I am receiving – an incapacity experienced by me as a therapist. This, I believe, runs in parallel with the effect that the overdose has on the patient's body: that is, overwhelming oneself with *far too much* for one's body to safely or easily digest and process. In this sense, perhaps there is indeed something difficult to think about that is peculiar to overdose and that tends to be avoided.

Some observations about overdose, as compared to self-cutting

In my experience of responding to adolescents in crisis who have self-harmed, in the majority of cases, they will have either cut themselves or overdosed. Generally, as mentioned earlier, these adolescents are thought about clinically within a broad category as having 'self-harmed'. Indeed, there may well be similarities in the ways adolescents who either self-cut or overdose present. Such similarities may have to do, for example, with the complexity of the adolescent's environment, or may involve their underdeveloped capacity to process their more unbearable thoughts and feelings when in distress (Gibbons, 2021). However, there are some general observations about overdose that may strike us, on the surface, as distinguishing this phenomenon from self-cutting. Of course, this set of thoughts is by no means exhaustive.

In my view, one aspect of overdose that distinguishes it from self-cutting involves its (typically) *oral component*. In this sense, it bears a more obvious connection to psychoanalytic ideas about the process of internalisation. For a very young child, internalisation quite literally involves the process of eating and digesting. Subsequently, internalisation may refer to the process of psychologically 'taking in' (or indeed, refusing), the care that is offered.

A second aspect that I think is peculiar to overdose, not necessarily mutually exclusive to the first aspect, is that overdose, by its very definition, connotes that the patient has taken in *too much of a good thing.* Taken at the right time, with the right dose, painkillers are necessary and helpful. If far too many painkillers are ingested, though, the consequences can be catastrophic. In contrast, is any amount of self-cutting, no matter how negligible, ever useful to the body? There may well be any number of functions for self-cutting (such as eliciting care and concern), but at face value, no amount of self-cutting can be thought of as helpful in any quantity.

We might therefore hypothesise that some adolescents who overdose really do have a (heavily disguised) wish to be helped, to receive, as it were, a 'good feed', as represented orally through the act of overdose, and symbolically in wishing to 'take in' something nurturing and nourishing. Masked beneath the overdose, therefore, may be a wish to take in something good. But then something about the process goes awry and becomes toxic. In any case, there is a difficulty in consciously acknowledging, in the act of overdose, this underlying wish: that is, acknowledging the wish to take in something good is experienced as potentially dangerous.

Unconscious underpinnings of adolescent overdose

In an earlier paper I wrote about adolescent overdose (Mirvis, 2018), I suggested four different hypotheses for possible unconscious underpinnings as to why specific adolescents principally use overdose as a means of self-harm. For the purposes of this chapter, I will briefly share the story of 'Sarah' as a composite case, combining ideas and thoughts about many adolescents I have treated. All four hypotheses that I outlined in the earlier paper, I will suggest, are illustrated within this case example, which I will subsequently explore in more depth.

Some years ago, I had just returned from a period of leave and was abruptly and shockingly informed that an adolescent girl patient of mine, whom I had been seeing in long-term psychotherapy, had just been admitted to hospital after having swallowed half a bottle of bleach, in addition to overdosing on painkillers. Just before ingesting the bleach and painkillers, Sarah had gorged herself on packets of sweets and chocolate that she had been hoarding, and specifically packets of 'M&M's'.

In terms of her background, Sarah had gone into care following a period of severe neglect. Sarah's carers had previously been explicitly and persistently open with her and with professionals about their regret in, and resentment at, having taken her into their care, and generally about how abhorrent they found her.

I learned that Sarah had been found by her carers on the floor in the bathroom in a near-unconscious state. Next to her, there was a suicide note saying goodbye to her carers, apologising for having been such a 'burden' to them.

When hearing this, I felt utterly overwhelmed, struggling myself to 'swallow' and process what I was hearing. Sarah, up to this point, had not demonstrably presented as being at such a high level of risk to herself.

> I initially considered that I would meet with Sarah again in the clinic, if and when she was discharged, following assessment by another colleague who was on the duty rota that day, dealing with hospital assessments. I then considered that in 'handing this over' to my colleague, I could be avoiding facing the seriousness of what I was hearing. Eventually, I realised that it felt clinically more appropriate to assess her myself, as her known clinician, at the hospital.

I will now discuss, connected to this clinical material, my first hypothesis about the possible unconscious underpinnings of adolescent overdose.

Overdose as unconscious communication of internalised 'self-poisoning'

In their book 'Working in the dark' (2017), Donald Campbell and Robert Hale discuss some of the unconscious underpinnings of the pre-suicidal state of mind. The authors emphasise the importance of acknowledging and trying to understand the origins of self-destructive impulses and wishes, which are always behind self-destructive action. What I wish to focus on in this section, based on my experience of adolescents who have overdosed, are certain possible unconscious underpinnings for adolescents using overdose, per se, as a means of communicating self-destructive impulses.

Overdose is often referred to as 'self-poisoning' because of the specifically harmful, toxic physical effects that it can have (e.g. Finkelstein et al., 2015). What I am arguing here is that perhaps adolescent overdose can also represent psychological projections into the child – both past and present – that have been experienced as exclusively bad, even 'poisonous'.

Dowling writes about her work with a latency girl whose mother had Munchausen syndrome by proxy, now called most often fabricated or induced illness (a psychological condition in which a parent elicits care for themselves vicariously, through falsely pathologising their child). In addition to the psychological effects of her actions and emotional state, this mother, as described by Dowling, had also *actually* poisoned her daughter with an overdose of medication. It seems that she seriously struggled with psychologically separating her daughter from herself and her own illness, to the point that she eventually made her daughter physically ill, and even to some extent psychologically unstable – through locating her own physical and psychological illness into her daughter – in order to ensure that they would remain inseparable (Dowling, 1998).

Dowling's case is an unusual and extreme example of the sort of dynamic that I'm referring to. Nonetheless, I believe that 'poisoning' can naturally be viewed as symbolic of psychologically harmful projections into the child, which can inhibit their development. In my clinical experience, it is not uncommon to see this dynamic in parent–child dyads, where there is great difficulty in the process of separation.

The female patient Dowling describes was not self-harming. But of course, with any suicide attempt by any method, there may also be an underlying internalised death wish, originating in the hostility the parents may at times feel towards the child. It is then this internalised death wish that is enacted. The phrase 'self-poisoning' is, however, peculiar to overdose as a means of self-harm. I would suggest that there can sometimes be links between 'poisonous' psychological projections into the child and the child's subsequent physical enactment of this through 'self-poisoning'.

In my own vignette earlier, it was not difficult to surmise how Sarah may have internalised an extreme, even 'poisonous' idea of herself as a 'burden'. Originally, Sarah may have internalised this idea from her biological parents, who may have projected into her over time a message of her being too much of a burden for them to look after, even in terms of her basic needs. Subsequently, openly disappointed at the realisation of having taken in a child with such complexity into their care (as children in care may at times be), Sarah's carers had repeatedly expressed their disappointment and hostility towards her in an untrammelled way, which had been experienced by Sarah as overwhelming and impossible to 'swallow' (linked with hypothesis two presented later). These internalised death wishes, and, I suggest, specifically the psychologically 'poisonous' aspects of what was projected into her, were subsequently communicated through my patient herself ingesting substances that were *actually* poisonous (bleach and an overdose of painkillers) with potentially devastating effects.

Thinking in this way about Sarah's ingestion of bleach and painkillers enabled me to consider the ways in which the specific method of self-harm she used might have been unconsciously linked with messages about herself that Sarah had powerfully, over time, internalised, both past and present. This, in turn, helped me see how Sarah may have expected me to also view her as a 'burden', as someone obnoxious, unwanted, and not worth keeping within my care. My extended absence from the clinic, it felt to me, might have, to Sarah's mind, confirmed her internal beliefs in adults that wished to abandon her from their care as she was so 'poisonous'.

Upon Sarah's eventual return to therapy within the clinic, I was able to think with her about these beliefs: how hard it seemed to be for her to feel able to hope that adults could see her and her difficulties more holistically, could tolerate her and want to see her, would not be 'poisoned' by her and abandon her, nor would they 'poison' her with their own projections, involving unbearable shame at unpalatable aspects of themselves.

Overdose as a physical enactment of the way the patient's mind is overwhelmed by thoughts, feelings, and experiences that cannot be processed

I remember well how overwhelmed with shock and anxiety I felt when I was informed of the nature and seriousness of Sarah's suicide attempt. I came to realise that I was struggling in that moment to wholly 'swallow', process, and digest what I was receiving in this information. Initially, I had considered 'parking' my anxiety about having to face Sarah's suicidality and self-destructiveness for a while, while waiting for her to be eventually discharged from the hospital before meeting her. Perhaps I was also seeking, through this avoidance, to 'park' my own curiosity about the meaning of Sarah's suicide attempt as a communication within our therapeutic relationship. But then I realised that in doing this I could be evading having to face Sarah during the time that she was in this state of mind and, indeed, at the moment when she was most in need of my support.

My own emotional responses (or countertransference) in such circumstances, while receiving the news and eventually understanding the seriousness of an adolescent having overdosed, have led me to believe that there is a chain of psychological precursors leading up to my virtual incapacity in the case of Sarah, in the moment, to think clearly (for example, in my initial reluctance to assess Sarah at the hospital myself), which runs as follows:

1. The adolescent finds it difficult to process their complex thoughts and feelings, especially when in distress (this may be, in part, due to experiences that have left them ill-equipped to process psychological complexity).
2. In moments leading up to an overdose, the adolescent's mind becomes overwhelmed by thoughts and feelings that he/she cannot 'swallow', process, and digest (see hypothesis three, where I expand on what, more precisely, might be so overwhelming).
3. This emotional state of feeling overwhelmed is then enacted symbolically through the act of overdose – a physical communication of overwhelming one's body with far more than can be safely swallowed, processed, and digested.
4. The impact on me, as a clinician, is that I, in turn, feel overwhelmed, unable in the moment to wholly 'swallow' what I am receiving.

Fortunately, with Sarah, I soon became sufficiently alert to my own fluctuating capacity to stay with the serious implications of what I was hearing, so that I could make more clinically sound and humane decisions about how to try to help her during this time of crisis.

After Sarah was eventually discharged from the hospital, this way of thinking about the unconscious function of her overdose enabled discussion between us around how important it was for Sarah to see that I could tolerate and survive the communication of her more complex thoughts and feelings – the hope being that this would eventually be internalised by Sarah and form part of her own capacity to swallow and process these thoughts and feelings in future times of distress, without recourse to self-harm.

The emotional impact of being on the receiving end of this 'overdose of overdoses' as a clinician underlines the importance of clinical thinking spaces as a way to understand what is being communicated and what is so difficult for us as clinicians to receive. This could involve both formal and peer supervision, within which the process of 'swallowing' and processing these communications for clinicians can be enabled. That way, we can be clinically better able to receive the difficult communications in these acts and thus be able to help the adolescents in crisis whom we treat.

In this section, I have focused specifically on the idea of adolescent overdose as a possible communication of internalised 'self-poisoning'. Regardless of the potential meaning behind an overdose, I would suggest that the cumulative psychological strain and anxiety induced by working with so many adolescents in crisis presenting with such elevated levels of risk further underline the importance of spaces for clinicians within which the emotional strain of this experience can be shared, thought about, and processed. Otherwise, we may run the risk of feeling ourselves as though 'poisoned' or generally overwhelmed by what we are cumulatively receiving from adolescents in crisis, leading to an urge to evacuate what has been overdosed psychologically into us, without being able to face and sit with what our adolescent patients are communicating.

Overdose as enactment of force-feeding, either literally or figuratively, from parents/carers

Winnicott writes about the importance of a 'moment of hesitation' before the infant is presented with the breast. In that moment, the infant comes to associate feelings of hunger and need with subsequent feeding and the satisfaction of need (Winnicott, 1941). If the moment of hesitation is absent, a kind of force-feeding can develop, with two possible outcomes. Either the infant will comply with the force-feeding, which may entail in the long run the development of a 'false self', potentially stunting future development, or they may, in a healthier way, protest against the force-feeding and thus force the precocious development of their own independence. Casement (2002) has written about this second possibility, wondering about contexts in which perhaps interpretations in therapy are forcefully given or offered for the patient to play with and to either deny or accept to some degree.

I find the idea of the 'moment of hesitation' particularly useful in the context of the many transitions and changes that looked-after and adopted children have to go through in their early life. Despite their good intentions, it is not uncommon for adoptive parents or foster carers to harbour fantasies of wishing to save or rescue these children when they are brought into their care. Such wishes can also be held, more or less consciously, within the child's professional network that is responsible for these transitions. This can, at times, contribute to abrupt transitions for children going into care, in which the new reality of leaving their biological parents and transitioning to a new family can, unwittingly, be experienced as being 'force-fed', without a 'moment of hesitation' existing before this big change. This may be because there is not enough of a 'moment of hesitation' on the part of the prospective carers, whose natural ambivalence about taking a child into their care may be temporarily denied. In turn, there may then be no 'moment of hesitation' for the child transitioning into their care, in which the child's natural ambivalence about this momentous change could crucially be thought about. The new reality is thus, inadvertently, 'force-fed'.

For Sarah, this experience may have had serious ramifications, as the viability of her foster placement came into question soon after it started. One was left to wonder if there had been a 'moment of hesitation' on the part of the local authority in matching them with Sarah, and if there had been enough time for thought and preparation. Sarah's overall experience in care, I think, contributed in a number of ways towards the dramatic escalation in her risk during her adolescence.

I came to believe that Sarah's significant overdose could also, therefore, have become a physical 'force-feeding' on her part, representing the way these new realities may have been 'force-fed' into her. The only advantage to Sarah overdosing in these circumstances was that at least she could feel in control of the force-feeding herself, having an experience of active mastery over this experience, rather than staying with an utterly passive experience of her new realities being 'force-fed' into her.

This idea of the lack of a 'moment of hesitation' has felt particularly helpful in the context of the experience of looked-after and adopted children, as I have said. However, going beyond that, any adolescent may go through abrupt transitions or traumatic events within which there is sometimes limited space available to process their experience.

Moreover, we have to keep in mind that there are some transitions that all adolescents have to make. These are universal, but that does not mean they are easy to go through for adolescents, and they can vary in their potential complexity. There are differences in the way adolescents succeed or struggle in making these changes and going through these transitions, with varying outcomes in terms of their psychological development. I am struck, in this context, by Acheson and Papadima's (2023) reminder that adolescence itself is a crisis, something which we have to keep in mind when we consider wider discourses about 'adolescents in crisis'. This idea of adolescence as a crisis, which Winnicott eloquently described many years ago (1971), has led me to revisit my own ideas about adolescent overdose as a physical enactment of psychological or physical 'force-feeding'. Many adolescents I have treated, on reflection, have experienced puberty and adolescence *in themselves* as a kind of overwhelmingly sudden physical and psychological maelstrom, which felt to them to be 'force-fed' and which they felt ill-equipped at the time to manage.

It goes without saying that not all adolescents experiencing puberty in this way take recourse to overdose. However, this line of thinking has helped me to further understand the dynamics underlying some of the adolescents who have overdosed while in my care. I have considered, on reflection, that for some adolescents presenting with overdose, the realities of puberty and adolescence may be experienced by them as forcing them to revisit, psychologically, their early and often persistent experience of transitions. Thus, the experience may be one of new realities being 'force-fed' into them – often accompanied by an abrupt experience of loss (be it through the actual loss of carers or through too-early, rushed, and 'forced' development).

Puberty and adolescence, therefore, can be experienced by certain adolescents as potentially catastrophic. This, at times, can be enacted, in turn, by an internalised 'force-feeding' of these new realities, which feel utterly overwhelming. Sometimes this can be enacted by being turned into a literal overdose, followed by an expulsion of the experience through the vomiting out of the pills that follows, or the cleansing that the hospital offers.

Overdose as a communication of a wish to take in something good

There is something important to clarify here. Having suggested that overdose could represent psychological 'poisoning', or that it can be thought of as an experience of 'force-feeding' – an ingestion of overwhelming thoughts and feelings that cannot be processed – it might seem as though one is avoiding the more disturbing aspects of adolescent overdose (including genuine suicidal intent) by suggesting that it could, at times, also be a communication of a wish to take in *something good.*

I first considered the importance of this line of thinking when I met an adolescent patient who told me, apparently without concern, that he had taken 19 pills of paracetamol the previous night. He added, '*The first few didn't help with my headache, so I ended up taking more and more'.* I was struck by how my adolescent patient had been explicit about his initial conscious wish to feel better in a physical way. Given that this had not worked, he ended up, in a destructive and risky way, taking in more and more.

While the alarming aspects of what my patient had done were immediately clear in my mind, I was also left feeling curious about the idea that, masked beneath the overtly destructive intent communicated through overdose, there could also be a wish to *take in something good or to 'fix' something.* Similarly, I also more recently heard of a colleague's adolescent patient who had taken 14 pills of folic acid *'in order to feel* better'. This links with my point in the introduction to this chapter about overdose as something enacted orally, and therefore with the potential, unconsciously, of trying to compensate for early experiences of feeding, either physically or figuratively in the form of care.

It was notable with Sarah (my own patient mentioned earlier) that she had initially gorged herself on chocolate she had been hoarding, in particular a number of packets of M&M's. In the context of a background of severe neglect, unwittingly recapitulated through the care she was now eliciting from her carers, I was left to imagine that M&M's were hoarded and gorged on in order to compensate for a lifetime's lack of 'Mummies & Mummies' (and perhaps also of 'Daddies'). When all this chocolate had failed to meaningfully fill the gap for Sarah, she then resorted to far more destructive means to fill this void, with the process becoming toxic and dangerous (linking more closely with the other three hypotheses for the unconscious meaning of overdose discussed earlier).

I have come to believe that it is clinically important to be alive to the various possibilities of this kind in what overdosing adolescents may be communicating – in addition to other disturbing aspects already outlined. This openness to possibilities offers us as therapists a more hopeful view, along with allowing for a more complex and nuanced understanding of what is being communicated. Sometimes what is being conveyed, despite its bleak implications when self-harm is involved, may in fact not be able to be expressed clearly through other means. With Sarah, for example, I was left to wonder whether she had altogether lost hope of taking in something good – from her therapist and in general.

Implications for clinical practice

It has not been my intention to 'force-feed' the reader with answers here but, rather, to share some of my thoughts about processes involved in overdose, which may or may not pertain to other patients. It is also a truism that some adolescents who overdose may, at times, self-cut or self-harm in other ways and may vacillate between all these different methods of self-harm at different times. Further, any act of overdose must be considered within all that we know about the patient, which needs to be our main guidance and, secondarily, within all that we know through our theoretical knowledge about self-harm and suicide as overarching categories.

I hope that I have conveyed that thinking about the possible unconscious communications arising from overdose *per se* may be as important as thinking in an analogous way about self-cutting. Through such a process of attributing meaning to the experience rather than assuming we know in advance what it's about, we may be led to greater therapeutic insight when it comes to understanding whatever the act of overdose communicates.

I think that the different ways in which overdose is used to communicate unconscious dynamics call upon a variety of responses from the therapist. It is also important to remember that an overdose may be overdetermined. More than one of these meanings – and perhaps others too – may apply for one given patient. I will now offer some suggestions regarding implications for clinical technique in response to various potential meanings discerned underlying the act of adolescent overdose.

Overdose as a communication of a wish to take in something good

In circumstances where overdose conveys a wish to take in something good, beneath its more obviously destructive aspects, it is important for the therapist to be receptive to the more hopeful aspects of what is being communicated, as well as interpreting the patient's need to elicit care and concern where this is appropriate.

Overdose as a physical enactment of the way the patient's mind is overwhelmed by thoughts, feelings, and experiences which he/she cannot process

In these circumstances, from a technical point of view, it is especially important to resist a pull to cut off from thinking in a way that mirrors the patient's dissociated state of mind, and to demonstrate that the overdose can be acknowledged, tolerated, and processed in spite of how unbearable this may seem. Interpretations along the lines of it being important for the patient to see that the therapist can tolerate this may feel appropriate, as well as reflecting to the patient what a desperate state they may have reached.

Overdose as an enactment of force-feeding, either literally or figuratively, from parents/carers

Interpreting the negative transference in these circumstances is important, as adolescents in this context may be more or less consciously experiencing the therapy as yet another 'force-feeding' of thoughts, feelings, and memories that tend to be denied.

Within the transference relationship, the therapist may, for example, be experienced as *pushing things down the patient's throat*, regardless of their best intentions not to do this. Therapy aims to be a process shared by patient and therapist, in which ideas can be suggested, played with, and thought about together, and an ongoing dialogue about this can be helpful. Casement's ideas (2002) are helpful here for how the therapist can present ideas to the patient for them to consider and 'play with', rather than interpretations that are insisted upon and 'force-fed'.

Overdose as representing the internalised death wishes of parents/carers who have projected something 'poisonous' into the patient

In these circumstances, the therapist may be perceived in the transference as pushing something harmful into the patient. Or the patient may feel that the therapist experiences them as 'poisonous', hating the patient or wishing him/her dead. When adolescents find out, over time, that their therapists, in reality, don't fulfil these negative expectations, they can find that potentially mutative. In these circumstances, beginning to experience the other as indeed *other*, separate and tolerant of separateness, can be particularly important.

During the times in therapy where these issues come up, the therapist may make interpretations focused on the patient's beliefs that they are poisonous or harmful, or too much for anyone to 'swallow'. For example, upon my own patient Sarah's eventual return to therapy in the clinic after her overdose, I was able to think with her about her deeply internalised beliefs about herself as 'poisonous' and too much of a burden – how hard it seemed for her to feel able to hope that adults could see her and her difficulties more holistically, could tolerate her and want to see her, would not be 'poisoned' by her and abandon her. Nor would they 'poison' her with their own projections, involving unbearable shame at unpalatable aspects of themselves.

Further reflections on an 'overdose of overdoses'

When I wrote about adolescent overdose originally (Mirvis, 2018), I chose to use the phrase *'an overdose of overdoses'*. For me, this term aimed at that time to convey something of the overwhelming numbers of adolescents I was (and am still) treating who have overdosed. Moreover, I felt it conveyed something about the impact that all these overdoses were having on me, as though I was being overdosed myself with something I was struggling to swallow and process.

My use of the phrase *overdose of overdoses* also captured, more broadly, my overall experience in recent years as a mental health clinician within the British National Health Service, overwhelmed by referrals of young people with all kinds of complex presentations. Even before the Covid-19 pandemic, which began in late 2019, services in the UK had already been under-resourced and overstretched for years. Since then, the number of referrals for under-18s to CAMHS has increased further. This, of course, has to do with multiple factors (especially, more recently, the legacy of the Covid-19 pandemic on child and adolescent mental health). However, I will briefly mention two specific ideas here that I believe are germane to understanding the unconscious meaning of overdose and which may or may not link with the increase in referrals in general to Child and Adolescent Mental Health Services (CAMHS) in the UK.

Firstly, with the ongoing and ever-changing advances in technology, the environment around us has *sped up*, with the ubiquity and availability of the internet and social media offering information and data that can feel 'too much', 'too quick', too overstimulating. This may be particularly the case for adolescents who have grown up in this environment and have had no other experience. Overdoses, when thinking about them this way, can then be seen as one of the ways for adolescents to represent the 'too muchness' of their environment through their actions. This 'too muchness', represented by the overdose, may, in some cases – considering the wider societal picture – represent what is persistently overdosed into adolescents from the outside world.

It may be that these experiences of 'too muchness' exacerbate, in some cases, already-existing mental health difficulties in adolescents. This may be particularly true for those adolescents who are already vulnerable to distress, those who may thus be already ill-equipped to swallow and process their more complex thoughts and feelings.

Secondly, I am struck by the thought that the first lockdown during the Covid-19 pandemic, which began in the UK in March 2020, was perhaps experienced by the adolescents in my care (and, indeed, by everybody else) as an abrupt 'force-feeding' of a new reality. In this reality, physical freedom and peer interaction were suddenly severely restricted, with no 'moment of hesitation' in which to play with or process the ambivalence about this new idea and reality, as it all happened so quickly.

This may seem paradoxical, but for some adolescents, lockdown may have functioned as reinforcement of an already-existing impasse. This may have been particularly the case for those adolescents already inclined towards an 'anti-development state', for example, those with school attendance difficulties. We can also think of overdose (and self-harming in general) in this wider way as part of the adolescent's general inclination to halt the progress of time (as Catty, 2021, suggests). Lockdown in some respects may have therefore suited some adolescents in their wish to halt time. However, I think, less consciously, it may well have been experienced either way, as, for example, an abrupt and traumatic transition that adolescents were not ready for.

As discussed earlier, all this also has to be understood in the context of adolescence, which itself can be experienced by some young people as a 'force-feeding' of a new reality in their physical and psychological development. Perhaps this at least partly contributes to our understanding of the massive surge in referrals for young people for support with their mental health.

Nonetheless, even with the irrepressible advances in technology that adolescents are in contact with, contemporaneous with the legacy of Covid-19, it remains important to be alive to, and curious about, adolescents' wish, however subtly communicated, to 'take in something good'.

During the time of the lockdowns, that 'something good' may have simply involved the wish for face-to-face contact. The deprivation of face-to-face contact imposed on adolescents during the Covid-19 pandemic was experienced universally. However, for some adolescents, this deprivation may have been redolent of deeper and earlier deprivations from the beginning of life – as, for example, with some adolescents who had originally experienced their carers at times as somewhat remote. One legacy of Covid-19 is that online meetings may at times now be resorted to as a means of maintaining contact with adolescents within certain circumstances. It remains important, however, for us as clinicians to remain curious about how adolescents experience this, whether it represents a 'good feed', and whether it is enough for some adolescents to 'swallow'.

References

Acheson, R., & Papadima, M. (2023). The search for identity: Working therapeutically with adolescents in crisis. *Journal of Child Psychotherapy*, *49*(1), 95–119.

Brady, M. T. (2014). Cutting the silence: Initial, impulsive self-cutting in adolescence. *Journal of Child Psychotherapy*, *40*(3), 287–301.

Briggs, S., Lemma, A., & Crouch, W. (Eds.). (2009). *Relating to self-harm and suicide: Psychoanalytic perspectives on practice, theory and prevention*. Routledge.

Campbell, D., & Hale, R. (2017). *Working in the dark: Understanding the pre-suicide state of mind*. Routledge.

Canetto, S. S., & Sakinofsky, I. (1998, Spring). The gender paradox in suicide. *Suicide Life Threat Behaviour*, *28*(1), 1–23. PMID: 9560163.

Casement, P. (2002). *Learning from our mistakes: Beyond dogma in psychoanalysis and psychotherapy*. New York: Guilford Press.

Catty, J. (2021). Out of time: Adolescents and those who wait for them. *Journal of Child Psychotherapy*, *47*(2), 188–204. https://doi.org/10.1080/0075417X.2021.1954977

Dowling, D. (1998). The child's experience of Munchausen syndrome by proxy. *Journal of Child Psychotherapy*, *24*(2), 307–326.

Finkelstein, Y., Macdonald, E. M., Hollands, S., Hutson, J. R., Sivilotti, M. L., Mamdani, M. M., K. Gideon, & Juurlink, D. N. (2015). Long-term outcomes following self-poisoning in adolescents: A population-based cohort study. *The Lancet Psychiatry*, *2*(6), 532–539.

Gibbons, R. (2021, June). The psychodynamics of self-harm. In: *Seminars in the psychotherapies* (p. 234). Cambridge University Press.

Mirvis, H. (2018). Too much to swallow? Some reflections on adolescent overdose. *Journal of Child Psychotherapy*, *44*, 189–201.

Nathan, J. (2004). In-depth work with patients who self-harm: Doing the impossible? *Psychoanalytic Psychotherapy*, *18*(2), 167–181.

Nicolò, A. M. (2024). Self-harm and cutting. In: *Developmental ruptures* (pp. 255–271). Routledge.

Persano, H. L. (2022). Self-harm. *The International Journal of Psychoanalysis*, 103(6), 1089–1103.

Rausch, Z., & Haidt, J. (2023). *Suicide rates are up for Gen Z across the Anglosphere, especially for girls*. After Babel.

Winnicott, D. W. (1941). The observation of infants in a set situation. *The International Journal of Psycho-Analysis*, 22, 229–249.

Winnicott, D. W. (1971). Contemporary concepts of adolescent development and their implications for higher education. *Playing and Reality*, 138–150.

Yakeley, J., & Burbridge-James, W. (2018). Psychodynamic approaches to suicide and self-harm. *BJPsych Advances*, 24(1), 37–45.

Chapter 6

The multifaceted meanings of a symptom

A psychoanalytic exploration of self-harm in contemporary culture

Maria Papadima

Introduction: self-harm now and then

With the alarming increase in adolescent self-harm since the 1990s (Gillies et al., 2018), especially self-harm through cutting, recent decades have seen this issue described as an 'epidemic' among young people (Dutta, 2015; Papadima, 2019; Ougrin et al., 2021). Gathering meaningful research on the exact prevalence of self-harm isn't straightforward, as with other mental health difficulties, due to variations in definitions and measurement approaches. The relevant statistics may appear conflicting and at times confusing, as noted by Farkas et al. (2024; see also Gillies et al., 2018).

Nonetheless, most recent studies globally agree on the rising trends of self-harm among adolescents. Some statistics that illustrate this, amongst many: UK data indicates that by 2015, up to one in five 15-year-olds reported engaging in self-harming behaviours (Stupples, 2015). A meta-analysis published in 2024 reported the prevalence of self-harm in adolescents as 16% 'in studies published between 2015 and 2020' (Farkas et al., 2024), while another study cites similar figures: 'a lifetime prevalence of self-harm of around 3% in adults and 14% in children and adolescents' (Moran et al., 2024). Some studies report even higher numbers, such as one in four 14-year-old girls self-harming (Therrien, 2018; see also Cybulski et al., 2021).

All this can be contextualised within a broader mental health crisis in this age group, particularly involving internalising conditions (Patalay & Gage, 2019; Keyes & Platt, 2024). What is clear, regardless of specific figures, is that self-harm remains a prevalent manifestation of distress among adolescents, especially among young women (Farkas et al., 2024; Hartas, 2024), and that cutting is a common and, in some respects, increasingly normalised behaviour in this age group, something adolescents both do and discuss frequently.

In this chapter, my focus is specifically on self-harm through cutting, as this behaviour is widely recognised as the most frequently understood form of self-harm (Andover et al., 2010; Bresin & Schoenleber, 2015). It goes without saying that the definition of *self-harm* encompasses a wide range of other behaviours too, such as burning, head-banging, intentional drug overdosing, misuse or avoidance of illness medications (e.g. among diabetic teenagers), restrictive eating, and engaging in high-risk activities. But it's cutting that has become 'the paradigm

DOI: 10.4324/9781003592778-9

of self-harm' in contemporary discourse (Chaney, 2017, p. 15). So when people reference 'self-harm' today, we can assume that in most cases they're referring to self-cutting (Lilley et al., 2008; Brausch et al., 2016).

Why cutting?

Why have cutting and scratching emerged as the predominant methods of self-harm today? A range of theoretical frameworks – outside the field of psychoanalysis – have attempted to explain this. Psychological frameworks offer some insights, such as cutting being a way to externalise emotional pain onto the body or as a way to exert control when all feels overwhelming. Alternatively, cutting can symbolically represent self-punishment (e.g. Laye-Gindhu & Schonert-Reichl, 2005; Lloyd-Richardson et al., 2007), or it may be experienced as a ritualistic act of self-soothing (Motz & Jones, 2009). Cutting has also been interpreted as a form of purification or cleansing (e.g. Hodge & Baker, 2021).

Other frameworks offer sociocultural explanations for the visibility and spread of cutting within communities, underlining the impact of social contagion through online social media, where self-harm behaviours and cutting are now fairly normalised (e.g. Arendt et al., 2019; Papadima, 2019; Miguel et al., 2017; Richardson et al., 2012). Society's emphasis on physical appearance and bodily self-expression further contributes to this phenomenon, with the body increasingly being perceived as a 'canvas' for self-expression, or even in some instances, as a form of 'art' – its scars becoming symbolic markings (Favazza, 2011; Hodge & Baker, 2021; Lemma, 2010).

Neurobiological perspectives also attempt to explain how cutting functions (e.g. Chung, 2009; Osuch & Payne, 2008), including its role in sensory stabilisation, pain perception, and immediate feedback mechanisms (Cummins et al., 2021). Cutting, it has been argued, can function to regulate overwhelming emotions through the release of endorphins and dopamine, potentially providing relief or numbing sensations (e.g. Horne & Csipke, 2009). Finally, some theoretical perspectives have focused on practical considerations – such as the ease of access to objects used for cutting or scratching (knives, razors, pencil sharpeners) – framing these within a public-health model similar to suicide-prevention efforts (e.g. Sarchiapone et al., 2011; Hawton et al., 2024).

The individual who self-harms

Putting aside the validity of these ideas, all of which, in one way or another, may reflect elements of truth, a question remains: what are the dynamic, interpersonal, and psychic reasons behind this behaviour, and how does the individual who cuts perceive and relate to their self-harm? For example, McKenzie and Gross (2014) accept the idea of emotion regulation that self-harm offers but wonder about the various possible underlying meanings. They say:

> Simply labeling NSSI as 'emotion regulatory' does not tell us precisely what is going on. This is because at any given moment, NSSI can serve to

regulate emotions in many different ways. One key challenge is to clarify the precise functions NSSI may be serving *for a given individual in a particular context.*

(*italics mine*)

Armando Favazza (2011) and Sarah Chaney (2017), who have both written cultural histories of self-harm, stress that we shouldn't universalise self-harm as a psychiatric condition and caution against imposing a single 'cultural model of harm across entire populations' (Chaney, 2017, p. 9; see also Gilman, 2013). They see self-harm as a complex behaviour with meanings that change across historical and cultural contexts and vary from person to person.

This – the difference from person to person despite the same manifest behaviour – is the area where we, as psychoanalytic child psychotherapists, tend to focus, and thus, this is what I mainly cover in this chapter. To work effectively with adolescents who self-harm and who wish to understand their actions – recognising, too, that some may prefer only to manage rather than deeply explore the meaning of their cutting – we must hold in mind multiple dimensions: psychoanalytic concepts (intrapersonal), sociocultural factors (familial and environmental), and biological or neurodevelopmental (embodied) factors that may interact in shaping the behaviour.

Challenges in working with self-harm

As psychoanalytic therapists, we tend to prioritise exploration over certainties, trying to avoid assumptions and to remain curious about a behaviour's underlying meanings. But in our risk-averse culture, self-harming behaviours generate such fear in families and schools – and sometimes in us as therapists too – that it's hard not to jump to conclusions and to maintain an attitude of curiosity. This is because we may fear repercussions if we don't have a safety plan that appears robust enough, or we may worry that pausing to think before 'managing risk' (however idealised that goal may be, anyway) will be frowned upon in the bureaucratic systems where we work, particularly the NHS.

Currently, external, active behaviours like self-harm often lead to reactive approaches that can paralyse critical thinking and push networks to act quickly to manage or extinguish these actions. Whether we work privately or in the public sector, certainty tends to be highly valued as a goal, above exploration, and services are increasingly organised into fragmented symptom-based pathways that follow this way of thinking (Norris, 2025). The emphasis on safety above all else can unfortunately align with rigid tendencies in those who come to see us, either the self-harming adolescents or their parents, who push us, similarly to the institutions we work in, to 'solve the problem' before pausing to wonder how it emerged in the first place. All this together makes it increasingly hard, in all therapeutic settings, to protect the necessary space for exploring the emotional landscape represented by the self-harm.

Working within networks

In our work, we collaborate with parents, schools, social workers, and other agencies. The rigidity, fragmentation, and reactivity described earlier, which are often associated with self-harm, also affect these networks, making it challenging to think together clearly and practically. Typical unhelpful responses include an insistence on standardised safety plans before even talking to each other; fear-based reactions; an idealisation of what we, as therapists, can do; or a dismissal of the self-harm as 'just for attention'. Another common response is when professionals, operating usually under tight deadlines and high caseloads, shift the responsibility to another agency by categorising the issue in specific ways – for example, labelling the self-harm as a 'mental health issue' instead of a 'safeguarding issue' or referring to it as 'behavioural' rather than 'mental health', as if the two were completely unrelated.

Parents may also pass on responsibility to professionals due to their anxiety and feelings of being unskilled in addressing the cutting, sometimes withdrawing from even basic parenting tasks for fear of exacerbating the issue. This is a form of freezing from the stress experienced. Occasionally, there can be a subtly passive-aggressive quality to these reactions, which may be a projected response to the adolescent's defiance. Parents, for example, might tell us, 'If this is a mental health problem that you want us to respect and attend to, then you, as mental health experts, can handle it, and we will step back'.

In addition, parenting styles, beliefs, cultural background, and individual or couple stressors all influence how the cutting is understood. There may be mental health taboos or fears that self-harm equates to suicidal behaviour – for instance, seeing self-harm as the same to slitting one's wrists – or there may be anger towards a child perceived as disrespectful when self-harming, leading to dismissiveness or fury at their misbehaviour. I've noticed that this latter tendency often arises in families with a history of immigration or other difficult transitions. They can (understandably) struggle to understand the adolescent's suffering within a mental health framework given their own experiences with more collective and, as they see them, much harder struggles.

Our task – never an easy one – is to stay in conversation with parents, engaging with their fears and assumptions rather than questioning them. From there, we can start to think together about what the adolescent's behaviour may be saying – what kind of attention or help they might be seeking, why now, and what it could mean for the parents to offer the very 'attention' they so resist or decry.

Therapeutic prejudices

As therapists, we, too, aren't immune to falling into certainties and drawing quick conclusions. Our training and professional beliefs come into play in how we think about a symptom, as they would do for all professionals, potentially overshadowing relevant factors specific to the case in front of us. Different training backgrounds lead some to respond to self-harm with strict safety protocols (Berk & Clarke,

2019), while others may rigidly classify it under the broad umbrella of 'therapy interfering behaviours' (Chapman et al., 2016) and seek to manage it by suspending therapeutic support for a while.

As to our own prejudices, as psychoanalytic therapists we might assume that a young person's self-harm indicates a deep-seated pathology. Or we might assume it represents aggression directed against the self or others. Conversely, some may adopt an excessively nurturing, validating, and non-challenging approach. What is fascinating is that often a range of these opposing approaches may be applied to the same person within a single network of professionals and relatives, leading to angry splits. These splits, in turn, may reflect the internal conflicts experienced by the young person, creating a vicious cycle where things can escalate and the self-harm may become entrenched.

Although the reactions by parents and professionals will vary in detail, they often all lead to the same outcome: shutting down deeper thought about the self-harming adolescent and the specific messages conveyed through their behaviour. The seemingly straightforward question 'What does this mean?' can be overlooked in the frantic efforts to stop the adolescent from cutting and in the fear of future incidents. Sometimes, questions about the meaning of the cutting abruptly stop after the very first explanation given – the immediate trigger of the act – taking it at face value and not going any further. I have often seen events like a recent breakup or a conflict with parents documented as *the cause of* the self-harm or even of suicide attempts, with nothing further added and prolonged notes afterwards about 'managing' it, taking it for granted that that is what the adolescent wants.

Engaging with adolescents who self-harm, or supporting a self-harming adolescent's parent, is thus a minefield with many traps. The crucial point is that unravelling the causes of self-harm requires identifying various factors within the adolescent's psychological state, biological makeup, and environment. All this often needs to be done quickly, as crises can unfold from one moment to the next. But what is hopeful in this picture is that asking the simple question *'What does this mean?'*, if done without panic and with some time to think, can reveal answers that are closer to the surface and lead to faster solutions than we might expect.

Terminology

The terminology around cutting can become confusing. There is a variety of terms describing the behaviour, such as 'deliberate self-harm' (Liu et al., 2020), 'self-injury' (Nock, 2010), and 'self-mutilation'. The latter, according to Favazza (2011, p. 10), refers to 'major acts of self-injury, such as eye enucleation and amputation'. The term 'non-suicidal self-injury' (NSSI) (Angelotta, 2015) has become increasingly common and refers to 'moderate/superficial acts, such as skin-cutting and burning' (Favazza, 2011, p. 10). The DSM-5 (American Psychiatric Association, 2013) has adopted the term NSSI to describe a syndrome separate from suicidal behaviour, delineating it as a 'distinct clinical phenomenon' (Zetterqvist, 2015) rather than as a symptom of underlying difficulties. This approach fits within the DSM's descriptive, symptom-based methodology for grouping mental health conditions (Demazeux & Singy, 2015; Kernberg, 2012).

Taking a different view, which to me makes more sense, Favazza says that self-harm is 'an associated feature of many mental disorders' (2011, p. 13). He (2011, p. XVIII) defines self-harm as 'the deliberate destruction or alteration of one's body tissue without conscious suicidal intent' (2011, p. XVIII). Within his broad description, I want to note the stark difference between the words *destruction* and *alteration*. Someone who 'destroys' is not someone who 'alters'! The main thing here is to do with the variations in self-harm via cutting, which means different things from person to person and group to group.

And we could add, it can result from various underlying circumstances that may not necessarily amount to a disorder, meaning that in each case the cutting *needs interpretation*. One area for this type of interpretation is the adolescent's sociocultural environment, including the online environment, within which the self-harm occurs. We can think of the body, on which the self-harm occurs, as the intermediate meeting point between internal conflicts and external experiences. At the same time, we can think of online existence as an external space that impacts self-harm by creating connections through texts, likes, follows, and online communities, while also creating distance due to the solitary nature of the medium. I mention online spaces because self-harm often happens within internet communities or is shared on social media (e.g. Biernesser et al., 2020).[1]

Self-harm, hysteria, and links with sexuality

Seen through a cultural and historical lens, modern self-harm inevitably recalls the concept of hysteria. Though the term is often regarded as outdated, burdened by its negative associations to the female body, its long history of giving form to bodily expressed symptoms remains relevant. It is also a foundational concept within psychoanalysis. In addition, ideas surrounding hysteria and hysterical epidemics, irrespective of the terminology used, are significant in understanding how symptoms and syndromes can 'spread' within populations (Showalter, 1997), something that occurs through ordinary sociocultural processes (Christakis & Fowler, 2009; Gould et al., 2003). Today, self-harm via cutting appears to function as one of these socially shared expressions of psychological distress.

Freud, hysteria, and the stigmatisation of terms

Freud's original conceptualisation of hysteria, developed in the late 19th century, led him to propose that sexual traumas were the root cause of the dramatic, externalised behaviours observed in women attending his clinic. At the time Freud arrived at these ideas, there was significant wider interest in hysteria, with notable research undertaken by Charcot and Janet, among others. Their studies focused on how certain individuals, particularly women, expressed psychological pain through somatic symptoms, unconsciously imitating physical disorders (Bogousslavsky, 2020).

Freud's key contribution was the introduction of the 'talking cure' – carefully listening to patients' narratives – which, he argued, helped alleviate symptoms and revealed underlying unconscious causes. Freud, at first, attributed these causes to concrete sexual traumas (Freud & Breuer, 1895; Freud, 1896), but he later expanded his theory to include unconscious fantasies, desires, and conflicts as contributors to suffering, thus incorporating elements of fantasy alongside factual reality (e.g. Borsch Jacobsen & Brick, 1996; Lothane, 2001).

Historically, the specific forms of mental distress expressed across populations – often referred to as psychogenic epidemics – have elicited dismissive reactions, as they frequently incorporate heavily gendered language (Chaney, p. 112–118, 133, 142), with accusations of 'attention seeking', 'manipulation', or 'malingering'. This pattern continues in contemporary responses to women, for example those diagnosed with borderline personality disorder (BPD), a diagnosis that Christopher Bollas (2000) identifies as a modern manifestation of what he terms 'the return of the repressed' hysteria.

In current diagnostic frameworks like the DSM, hysteria no longer exists as a distinct diagnosis; it has been divided into dissociative identity disorder, somatic symptom disorder (formerly psychosomatic disease), and histrionic personality disorder. (I wonder how often this latter diagnosis is used nowadays.) It has also been suggested that borderline personality disorder encompasses traits previously seen as part of the hysteria spectrum. Despite these changes and efforts at destigmatisation, cultural reactions to phenomena historically labelled as 'hysteria' persist, often framing them as female manipulation or expressions of concealed aggression (Chaney, pp. 142, 144).

We can wonder about the continuing dismissal of the social transmission of mental health disorders across populations, which is what the umbrella term hysteria used to cover. We are social beings who learn and grow within relationships and groups. This, naturally, involves observing and emulating what we see around us, whether consciously or unconsciously. Why should this be seen as a problem? This behaviour is intrinsic to human nature, especially during adolescence, when group identifications significantly influence identity formation (Foulkes, 2024, chapters 1 and 2).

But the concept of socially 'picking up' a symptom is frequently criticised for seemingly undermining the legitimacy of someone's suffering. Psychosomatic presentations are, in this way, routinely subjected to heavy disparagement in various contexts. Suzanne O'Sullivan (2016), a neurologist, has written about the strong reactions that psychosomatic symptoms and socially transmissible behaviours provoke. She argues that such symptoms are no 'less "real" than those associated with other diseases' (O'Sullivan, 2016, p. 311) and draws attention to the visceral discomfort they evoke, often expressed in dismissive comments, such as, 'They are being hysterical!', 'She's a drama queen', or 'They're just doing it for attention'. There are, of course, strong elements of misogyny at play here. But I have often wondered whether the rejection of hysteria may also be connected to our cultural emphasis on individuality and the fantasy of the 'self-made' person, ostensibly unaffected by anyone apart from ourselves.

Regarding the link to misogyny, we need to remember the persistent historical misunderstandings and neglect of women's physical and mental pain, as well as the ongoing attacks on women for their particular ways of suffering (Chesler, 2018; Showalter, 1985; Stotland, 2004). The long clinical and sociological history of how distress moves through groups – and of its expression through excessive emotion or action – offers valuable insight, regardless of whether such behaviours are labelled 'borderline', 'histrionic', or 'emotionally unregulated'.

From a psychoanalytic perspective on working with these intense emotional states, American psychoanalyst Nancy McWilliams defends the use of the concept of hysteria to understand certain emotional expressions. She adds that, due to their heightened anxiety and tendency to move from crisis to crisis, certain young people's emotions may, at first glance, appear 'superficial, artificial, and exaggerated' (McWilliams, 1999, p. 312), leading to misunderstandings. Her main point is that despite the intensity and seeming drama of an emotion, its kernel is true and has to be attended to carefully. She says:

> This does not mean that they do not 'really' have the emotions to which they are giving voice. Their superficiality and apparent playacting derive from their having extreme anxiety over what will happen if they have the temerity to express themselves to someone they see as powerful. Having been infantilized and devalued, they do not anticipate respectful attention to their feelings. They magnify them to get past their anxiety and convince themselves and others of their right to self expression.
>
> (McWilliams, p. 322)

McWilliams reminds us, also, that the fate of all mental health concepts is to become stigmatised over time, leading to their replacement by modern equivalents in efforts to reduce stigma. Each new term, however, tends to encounter similar difficulties over time. Phenomena once described as hysteria were reclassified under borderline personality disorder (BPD), a diagnosis that adolescents now often seek for self-diagnosis (while none would consider hysteria as a self-diagnosis). Yet BPD, too, is now increasingly questioned for its potential to stigmatise people, and particularly women, with some proposing the term 'complex trauma' instead. As McWilliams points out, however, it is likely that this new category will also attract similar projections and stigmatisation in the future, just as its predecessors did.

The interpretation of bodily expressions of suffering

Despite later revisions and critiques, hysteria remains a foundational concept in psychoanalysis, alongside trauma, repression, the unconscious, and the Oedipal configuration. These concepts collectively form a framework for interpreting bodily expressions of psychic pain, such as those seen in certain types of self-harm. This framework suggests that understanding a symptom requires considering unconscious motivations, including the dynamic between 'patient' and 'healer' (in the broadest sense), and determining the intended target and purpose of a symptom. During Freud's time, hysteria reflected the rigid sexual and gender roles and cultural anxieties prevalent in Viennese society. Today, we can also assume that the symptoms we see around us mirror current cultural anxieties.

Hysteria, often referred to as 'the elusive neurosis' (Krohn, 1978), has a constantly shifting nature. Historian Ilse Veith (1965, p. viii) noted that while hysteria remains imprecise as a term, its fundamental attributes have remained relatively unchanged over time. What changes is the outward manifestation, which follows 'the ideas and mores current in each society' (Veith, 1965, p. viii). Key features that remain constant include somatisation, altered states of consciousness, emotional instability, intensity, suggestibility, susceptibility to sociocultural influence, relational difficulties, and symbolic expression of internal conflicts. All these characteristics are easily recognisable in the modern syndromes that have replaced hysteria, such as BPD.

The takeaway from this is that none of us can avoid unconsciously adopting culturally available forms of expressing distress. This shouldn't be seen as a problem or weakness. It simply shows that a symptom – mild or severe – is not an endpoint but the beginning of a story: its first, external, 'publication'.

The trajectory of self-harm in culture

Historically, cutting the body (what we now refer to as self-harm) has been associated at different times with various cultural practices that have evolved across contexts. Favazza and Chaney repeatedly point out that cutting hasn't always been considered self-harm as it is today, nor has it consistently been viewed through a psychiatric lens. In earlier times, cutting the skin was sometimes part of medicinal bloodletting, religious castration, or self-flagellation. The modern psychiatric understanding of self-harm, in fact, emerged relatively recently, coinciding with the time psychiatric asylums expanded (Chaney, 2017, p. 51).

The current emphasis, driven by the DSM framework, is to classify NSSI as a 'disorder', with the certainty and finality such classifications imply. However, history gives us many examples of how mental health understandings evolve over time; it's reasonable to assume that the present interpretation of cutting as self-harm will follow the same route as previous iterations and will change again in the future.

Historical shifts of cutting over time

Armando Favazza (2011) and Sarah Chaney (2017), in their respective books, explore in detail how self-harm has evolved over time and across different cultures, situating it within a broader framework that includes all forms of bodily expression. Psychoanalytic theorists distinguish between symbolised (conversion) and unsymbolised (psychosomatic) expressions of meaning. But when it comes to self-harm, particularly among young people, we need to understand it in the broadest context possible, moving a step away from its purely intrapsychic meaning: regardless of what it signifies for each individual, it's also one of the various contemporary ways through which an experience can be expressed through the body and within social groups.

I've mentioned earlier that before today's psychiatric view of self-harm, cutting had different meanings. For example, it was part of religious rituals that included scarification, bloodletting, or self-flagellation (Favazza, 2011). Favazza explains that self-mutilation, including cutting, has cultural roots and tends to aim towards 'the correction or prevention of destabilizing conditions that threaten people and communities' (p. 281). Cutting rituals thus generally occurred to 'promote healing, spirituality, and social order' (p. 281). Scarification was also done for medical or aesthetic purposes (p. 191) or during coming-of-age ceremonies (p. 283). For example, Tiv females of Nigeria used to be inscribed as they entered puberty, 'to ensure the continuity of life' (p. 192), while the Kagoro boys of Papua New Guinea underwent skin cutting (and other forms of wounding) in rituals where they were 'reborn as men' (p. 193).

Sarah Chaney (2017) also references bloodletting, an important historical medical procedure that resembles today's self-harm but served a completely different purpose. It's worth noting that this practice is not totally in the past: Favazza (2011) describes recent instances of bloodletting (by venipuncture) as an unusual type of NSSI (p. 78), specifically in women with a history of eating disorders. He offers an account of one of these women who

> began bloodletting in her senior year of medical school and claimed that it reduced tension and gave her a sense of control and satisfaction. She also believed that it helped her to lose weight (she removed a liter of blood each time).
>
> (p. 78, citing Parkin & Eagles, 1993)

Sarah Chaney (2017, p. 42) discusses historical practices of bloodletting, which were believed to alleviate pain, headaches, and other physical issues (p. 48). Patients would, at that time, often report 'supernatural voices' instructing them to 'go and be cupped' (thus blood-let through cutting). Hearing this historical description, any clinician working today with self-harming adolescents will be reminded of their patients' descriptions of 'voices' urging them to cut themselves, which we now interpret within a completely different contextual framework.

Blood has always been imbued with powerful meanings, associated with life, death, and purification. For young women, blood marks also the onset of their adult sexual and reproductive life, with the arrival of their periods. Until the 19th century, bloodletting was a mainstream, widely accepted practice (Chaney, p. 42), considered for years a beneficial and 'natural process' (p. 44), believed to balance body and soul. In contemporary contexts, we can see parallels with adolescents' fascination with body-horror films and their blood and gore. We might also think of cutting – and the blood that comes out – as representing an opening toward the internal world, making what's inside visible externally, with the blood metaphorically signifying the inner experience and creating a concrete relationship to it.

Religious self-flagellation, historically practiced in groups, is also worth mentioning here. Sarah Chaney (2017, p. 40) describes various activities which we would now view as forms of self-harm, involving public self-flagellation as a form of celebration, contrasting with the individual nature of modern self-harm (2017, p. 50). Favazza (2011) also gives examples of religious self-flagellating within cults, for instance, through the use of leather whips, often with an epidemic character (2011, p. 58–59). This practice occurred, for example, amongst followers of Saint Francis, starting in 1260, spreading to Germany and then increasing during the 14th century, sometimes framed as a 'voluntary act of penance' within a Christian context (2011, p. 58). Over time, Church and state authorities restricted flagellant activities, though Favazza points out that instances of self-flagellation still occur today (2011, p. 60).

Following the historical trajectory of cutting even briefly makes it clear that, contrary to the modern perception of self-harm as a private and isolated act, it has, in fact, always carried a notable collective or group-based aspect, both historically and in the current context. I will now turn to how this collective aspect of cutting manifests among today's adolescents.

A looping effect in adolescent self-harm

Self-harm in its contemporary form is cyclical. It happens like this:

Young people's cutting generates discussions (both online and offline) about self-harm. These discussions, in turn, contribute to changes in teenage behaviour through heightened cultural conversations and preoccupation with risk and crisis. The associated social concern – and, occasionally, excitement and fascination – among adolescents and those around them results in a 'looping effect', to take philosopher Ian Hacking's term (2006). Hacking described how all mental health conditions are shaped in this way: the classification of a phenomenon frames it in a specific way (e.g. cutting seen as self-harm and then classified as a psychiatric illness). The cycle continues with individuals engaging in the behaviour, relevant institutions like CAMHS teams, schools, and media outlets recognising and treating it, and thus inadvertently reinforcing the looping effect by referring to self-harm in a particular way. Through this process, cultural, lay, and professional attitudes, and ultimately, knowledge itself, are constructed, encompassing both 'expert knowledge and popular knowledge, shared by a significant part of the interested population' (Hacking, 2006).

For psychoanalytic therapists, what's of particular interest is how individual suffering, always messy and unique to each of us, is 'tidied up' and categorised into specific syndromes. Aligning ourselves with the adolescents we see and understanding the often traumatic and complex realities they externalise in this way need patience, curiosity, and availability. Tidying what's happening within a set of assumptions – 'This is self-harm', 'This is what it means (risk, aggression, pathology . . .)', and 'Here's how we will handle it' – can feel easier.

Social media and the looping effect

The proliferation of social media has amplified this looping effect, leading to a heightened awareness of self-harm narratives among today's adolescents. This also impacts Child and Adolescent Mental Health Services (CAMHS), social services, and schools, shaping both the stories adolescents share in clinical settings and the perspectives of clinicians. Adam Phillips once mentioned an anorexic patient who, on entering his office, already seemed to know 'everything about anorexia' there was to know, seeming to surpass his own knowledge (2000, p. 291). With self-harm it can be similar.

Self-harm memoirs, fictional accounts, representations on social media and traditional media, along with everyday discussions in both online and offline groups, collectively create an environment where adolescents become well-versed in self-harm narratives, despite its ostensibly private nature. As a result, adolescents who self-harm often approach treatment with a preconceived understanding of the implications of their cutting: they perceive it as serious, risky, linked to suicide, and demanding an urgent response – and they also assume that others share these perceptions. They expect (as they have heard repeatedly) that cutting can relieve pain, numb feelings, and create visible scars, identifying them as a 'self-harmer'. The list of what is perceived and accepted as a given when it comes to cutting evolves over time, but my main point here is that it's recognisable by all involved within the cultural contexts where it occurs.

Self-harm: a physical urge or a psychic activity?

Amongst the shifting sociocultural perspectives on cutting as they have evolved over the years, two main themes have persisted in different forms. They still exist today in psychiatric/psychological conceptualisations of the phenomenon.

One model views self-harm as an uncontrollable impulse – a primitive, instinctual, bodily urge – rather than a psychological process. This perspective focuses on mastering the impulse and resulting behaviour rather than understanding it.

By contrast, the second model interprets self-harm as motivated by psychic (both conscious and unconscious) intentions, suggesting a degree of agency and control. Most psychoanalytic models of self-harm fall within this framework; however, the attribution of motivation can be (and has at times been) misused and taken completely concretely to dismiss people who self-harm as 'seeking attention', 'faking it', etc., as if any degree of agency equates 'doing it on purpose'. As a pushback response, both clinicians and patients tend to prefer framing self-harm as an uncontrollable urge, to avoid blaming the self-harmer, equating any indication of internal motivation to blame.

The distinction between self-harm and suicidality

The knowledge of (and discourses around) self-harm that has built over time has long distinguished it from suicide, something that's been recognised since the Victorian era (Chaney, 2017, p. 52). However, modern public discourse often, perhaps surprisingly, conflates these concepts (Favazza, 2011, p. 13; Chaney, 2017, pp. 56–57), including in crisis intervention services, where self-harm and suicide are frequently considered closely related categories. This perception is likely reinforced by the fact that the same clinical teams usually handle both suicidality and self-harm.

This conflation can't help but affect how adolescents themselves perceive self-harm today. For example, younger adolescents who engage in superficial cutting might claim they are *cutting in order to kill themselves*. They may then feel intensely dissatisfied if they sense that a clinician is implying that their self-harm doesn't indicate suicidality, reading this as not taken seriously. Though they understand on some level that their cutting isn't fatal, teenagers, I've noticed, often implicitly use it as a way to signal their deep distress, drawing on (through the existing looping effect of conflating self-harm with suicide) the *perceived seriousness of their situation*. This makes sense, as sometimes it can feel like the only way they can be heard. Their wish to show us how serious things are should be carefully considered clinically. It is highly risky if we don't.

In practice, though, high demands on services and sometimes lack of experience among clinicians can result in adolescents' gestures, intended 'to mobilize or cause changes in other people's behavior' (Miller, 2021, p. 6) being overlooked rather than properly attended to. This oversight can lead to the escalation of the behaviour or, conversely, to an unnecessary overreaction when a more measured response could have been more helpful. These distinctions are not always easy, the stakes are high, and the process requires time, therapeutic experience, and thinking space. All this is hard to come by in resource-starved institutions, with the push towards 'managing/holding risk' (i.e. eliminating it quickly), coupled with a tendency to deny the complexity of the behaviour.

To summarise the key points so far: first, self-harm can more usefully be viewed as a symptom rather than a disorder; second, it's best understood within an interpersonal and sociocultural context rather than as a private activity; third, attention must be given to the individual's psychological experience that leads to the manifesting symptom; fourth, self-harm is distinct from suicidality; and finally, it's important to acknowledge and respect the adolescent's interpretation of their behaviour, particularly if they want to equate it to a wish to die: this needs to be heard very carefully.

A psychoanalytic and sociocultural formulation on self-harm

Self-harm through cutting, whether indicative of longstanding pathology or something that happens temporarily, is seen psychoanalytically as an attempt to communicate through the body rather than through words (Horne, 2018). Although some argue that bodily communication is more pathological than verbal communication, it is still much better than not communicating at all and withdrawing. After all, communicating distress through the body happens to all of us as our earliest experiences in infancy. It's not by chance that Freud (1923) described the ego as fundamentally a 'body ego'.

In adolescence, this turn to the body is even more central. Ladame (1995) suggested that enactments during adolescence mirror the internal process of dreaming in adults (see also Tzikas's chapter in this book, which explores this further). Self-harm, as an enacted expression of something internal, can be understood developmentally as something more likely to occur in adolescence than in adulthood.

The hope within self-harm

In certain instances, particularly during adolescence, self-harm may paradoxically hold a hopeful message, representing an insistent demand for something to be *heard and addressed*, as Anna Motz has argued (2010). This idea reminds us of Winnicott's thoughts on delinquency and the antisocial act, which underline the implicit *request for a response* that we can read between the lines of these acts:

> In the hopeful moment . . . the environment must be tested and re-tested in its capacity to stand the aggression, to prevent or repair the destruction, to tolerate the nuisance, to recognize the positive element in the antisocial tendency.
>
> (Winnicott, 1956/1992, p. 314)

This wish for 'hearing' what the self-harm is saying is something the therapist can really focus on, regardless of whether they work briefly or longer-term, rather than centring the work on risk management.

A psychoanalytic, developmental, psychosocial framework

When evaluating self-harm, beyond our psychoanalytic theories, it's useful to take into account three other distinct dimensions during the assessment and treatment process (see Figure 6.1). For each of these three axes, I'll offer a clinical vignette or imaginary scenario to show what I mean.

First and most importantly, the *developmental context of self-harm* is crucial. Self-harm in adolescence is completely different from that in early childhood or adulthood. Even within adolescence, there are differences; self-harm at 13 is different from self-harm at 18. Although no clear, absolute lines divide developmental stages, treating, say, a 40-year-old who self-harms regularly as similar to a 14-year-old who self-harms is completely misguided: a self-harming 40-year-old is a much rarer and usually more serious situation. Similarly, a toddler's outburst would be seen completely differently than an outburst in a 45-year-old. All this may appear obvious, yet in my experience the developmental perspective can easily be overlooked in modern CAMHS teams that are increasingly diagnostic and

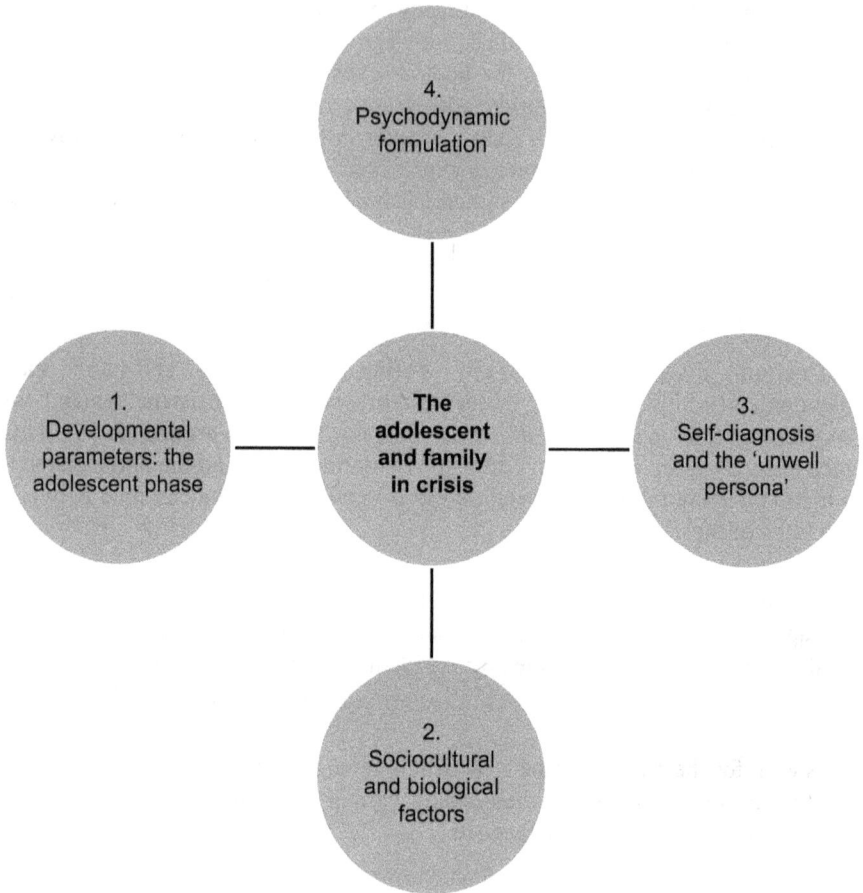

Figure 6.1 Dimensions to consider during the assessment and treatment of self harm

symptom-focused, leading to references, for example, to self-harming 13-year-olds as 'emerging personality disorders'.

A 13-year-old year girl spends time on Snapchat with her group of friends. A few in the group self-harm and belong to a 'self-harm-Tok' collective that they all follow. They post and share pictures of their cuts and discuss their understanding of various mental health issues – for example, what sleep positions indicate ADHD. They use the phrase 'I want to kill myself' openly, and often, and explain when asked that it's okay to use this expression as their friends then 'really get' how bad it's been for them. They support each other fiercely and loyally through continuous texts and calls, asking each other if 'they're safe' and often staying on the phone with each other with an open line all night.

And now imagine this same scenario with a group of 50-year-old women engaging in the same behaviours. A developmentally based formulation, which may include diagnostic elements, is essentially a working hypothesis to be considered as part of a thorough history. A diagnosis, on the other hand, often limits the professional's options, leaving little room to manoeuvre as the picture changes. The Independent psychoanalytic perspective, based on Anna Freud's and Winnicott's ideas on maturation (Freud, 1958; Winnicott, 1968/1971), holds this developmental perspective as central. Next, we must consider *the sociocultural and biological factors* that may be shaping the observed behaviour, such as cultural views on self-harm within the adolescent's community and friends, their online experiences, family dynamics, and any neurodevelopmental traits that may play a role. For example, young people with rigid temperaments, including those who today would be seen as having autistic traits, may be prone under certain conditions to engage in riskier or more persistent self-harm than their so-called 'neurotypical' counterparts. Sometimes this is because they have a more concrete understanding of self-harm and how others will 'read it'. The impact of widespread social media misinformation on self-harm and mental health diagnoses should be taken into account here, particularly for this vulnerable group, as it can lead to self-harm through a different route. The following clinical vignette shows how this can happen:

A 16-year-old male adolescent with significant autistic features asks me if I think it would be morally wrong for him to use a razor belonging to his dad to cut himself. I ask him to explain what this means to him. He pauses and, before answering, says that he continues to self-harm now even though he no longer really feels the urge to do it. I am surprised and ask him to explain.

With the honesty that characterises him, he says, 'If I stop now, people would think I don't have a difficulty anymore, and then I can't come to CAMHS anymore'. He adds, 'Self-harm, you know, means someone has a mental health problem'. He then returns to his original question: his father hasn't agreed to him using the razor for self-harm, and the razor doesn't belong to him.

We discuss this further. I explain to him that self-harming isn't needed for my continued support at CAMHS. I consider his depression serious and requiring ongoing care, and this isn't linked to the self-harm. I add that self-harm is only one way he can express his distress: there are others. I suggest that, as he's not feeling the urge to self-harm now, maybe he could consider stopping, with a clear agreement on my part that this won't signify a lessening of his problems.

He accepts this with relief; this settles the question, he tells me, of using his father's razor in an immoral way. And it settles the question of the self-harm altogether.

For our psychoanalytic formulation, we also need a third element: the recognition that young people today often arrive to us *with a self-diagnosis already in mind* and specific ideas about its implications (Acheson & Papadima, 2023). The self-diagnosis needs to be explored, not just out of respect for the adolescent's perspective – showing an interest in what interests him – but also because sometimes their self-diagnosis might be correct! Having said that, a self-diagnosis shouldn't stop us from developing our own formulation, which might, in some cases, differ significantly from the views of the teenager or their parents.

This possibility of a difference in opinion that can be voiced and explored can easily be overlooked in the current NHS focus on co-production of assessment and treatment, which can sometimes be taken concretely, with the clinician feeling pressured to validate a formulation (a self-formulation) they may not agree with. The following example shows the kind of negotiation that can happen in these situations:

Case Example

I meet a 14-year-old girl together with her parents for their first appointment at CAMHS. The girl introduces herself and quickly tells me she's certain she has bipolar disorder. She has extensively researched this online and found it extremely helpful relating to others with similar symptoms.

I'm interested in this and ask her what she's noticed. She describes feeling intense mood swings, 'out of nowhere'. She wants to consider medication and a formal diagnosis. I notice that while this discussion is going on, her mother grimaces and scoffs. Her father is silent and withdrawn, with a stony expression.

I underline the word 'intense moods' and ask her detailed questions – when they occur, what changes them, what the moods are specifically. I avoid, though don't dismiss, the word 'bipolar'.

We talk about the girl's wider life: she tells me she used to self-harm occasionally. She returns to the 'bipolar' symptoms and says she doesn't think there are triggers. She emphasises this: 'There's no reason for them to happen, that's why I'm convinced it's bipolar rather than trauma'. I emphasise the unpredictability of the mood swings. I say they sound a bit like the weather in the UK: you always need to carry a raincoat to be prepared, as they come out of nowhere. What's her equivalent of a raincoat? She laughs.

Out of the corner of my eye, I continue to observe the parents, who seem increasingly irritated with their daughter's descriptions. I thus turn the discussion directly to the mental illness terminology used and ask the girl to explain what she means by 'bipolar' and 'trauma', as I may have my own definitions and we might not mean the same thing. I notice the parents now are more willing to enter the discussion.

Her mother jumps in and says she completely disagrees with the idea of bipolar disorder: her daughter doesn't have a mental illness! She would know if she did. The girl raises her voice, 'It's how my brain works, and Mum just doesn't get it – she has no idea about mental health!' The mother looks at me seeming helpless. Before this escalates any further, the father chips in and says he's noticed the moods tend to occur on Sundays. We all puzzle over this for a bit, wondering why Sundays, and the mood in the room shifts.

After the Sunday discussion, the girl softens and turns to me: 'If this isn't bipolar', she says, 'maybe ADHD or ASD? My physics teacher once mentioned ADHD as my schoolwork is never consistent, and I struggle to focus'.

The discussion continues, in this and the following sessions. Over time, as my work with this family develops, I help the parents find a way to communicate with their daughter without dismissing her self-assessments, but also without concretely validating the labels either. We discuss that the language their daughter uses is important to her – it shows her interest and passion in the world she lives in – and doesn't mean what the parents attribute to it: it's not attention-seeking, it's an interest in finding her identity, and it's the language this generation uses.

Over time, as we explore the specific experiences their daughter has and as they connect better, the labels fade away.

Levels of severity

A final aspect to consider in our formulation of self-harm is its *level of severity*, and this has been briefly mentioned in an earlier chapter of this book (chapter 2), but it's worth mentioning here too. A psychiatric study by Uh et al. (2021) outlines the diverse manifestations of self-harming severity. The authors identify two distinct pathways of self-harm at age 14.

The first group is described as the 'psychopathology' pathway, associated with early and persistent emotional difficulties. This category includes major self-injury, which may be sometimes caused by psychosis, involving experiences such as identification with religious figures, purification, punishment for sins, or psychotic commands (Favazza, 2011, p. 292–293; citing Large et al., 2009). Serious stereotypic self-injury also occurs among institutionalised people, including some with learning difficulties or autism (p. 294). It's important to remember that even within CAMHS or private settings – not exclusively in institutions – certain instances of self-harm in young people with autism, though not applicable to all neurodiverse young people, can be highly risky.

The second type of self-harm described by Uh et al. (2021) is referred to as the 'adolescent risky behaviour' pathway. Adolescents in this category may self-harm temporarily, without it necessarily signifying deeper, entrenched pathology. According to the authors, this is a significant subgroup of self-harming adolescents and much larger than those with longstanding difficulties. Working well with these adolescents requires a developmental rather than diagnostic treatment approach. This is an area where shorter-term interventions focusing on adolescent processes, peer relations, and family dynamics can be most effective (chapter 13 in this book) – at the stage when the self-harm 'has not yet reached a static, entrenched state and retains more of a potential hope for communication' (Brady, 2014).

If the network around an adolescent perceives transient self-harm as more serious than it is, this may inadvertently strengthen a self-harming identity, raising questions about iatrogenic harm that can occur when there is excessive emphasis on mental illness (Foulkes & Stringaris, 2023). Many times, I've met young people who experimented with self-harm in early adolescence but continued on this path for years, due partly to the looping effect of the intense reactions in their environment to the cutting. Self-harm can sometimes, despite all good intentions, become a recognised shorthand within a friendship circle, school, CAMHS team, or family to indicate 'I'm not doing well'. So leaving it behind ends up having a cost too.

Different types of self-harm

As part of our assessment, we need to consider the various clinical presentations of self-harm, each requiring a different clinical approach. I've grouped them here into six types, though these are by no means cut-and-dried categories but, rather, groupings I've noticed over time. I'm sure there are additional types of self-harm beyond those I describe here.

Self-harm as a coping mechanism providing temporary relief

Armando Favazza (2011) has extensively discussed the skin's role as a meeting point between outer and inner, 'a message center or billboard' (p. 186) – where emotional states can be expressed (p. 186). He suggests that through cutting the skin, there can be a 'brief relief from anxiety' (p. 295). This type of cutting is described as a method to manage overwhelming emotions and is believed to bring immediate, albeit temporary, relief from distress as well as offering a level of control and a valve to release built-up tension. Favazza (2011) says:

> Deliberate self-injury of the skin, a morbid self-help behavior, indicates that a person is attempting to cope with some form of emotional distress such as intense anxiety, depersonalization, suppressed rage, or fear of abandonment.
>
> (p. 186)

From a psychoanalytic perspective, multiple factors may lead to the use of the body (and skin) to express feelings in this way. Fonagy and Target propose that

> the absence or distortion of this mirroring function may generate a psychological world in which inner experiences are poorly represented, creating a desperate need for alternative ways of containing psychological experience.

This would include self-harming as a coping mechanism through action (Fonagy & Target, 2000).

Jeanne Magagna (2008, pp. 120–121) discusses numb and depersonalised psychic states leading sometimes to a 'wish to obtain relief . . . through cutting the self or injuring the self in some other way'. This occurs in many cases of self-harm, in an effort to 'feel real', as we are often told by adolescents.

Considering, though, Hacking's idea of the looping effect, we need to keep in mind that self-harm as a method to express or manage emotions is well known among adolescents, some of them explicitly believing it can be a helpful 'coping mechanism'. This form of self-harm can be continuously reinforced by online descriptions of the 'coping mechanism' idea, posing questions as to whether its ability to help teenagers cope with their emotions comes from the act itself or the ideas about it (Mokrini et al., 2012; Tracy, 2016). Adolescents have, in fact, often told me, when we discuss their self-harm, that they've read that it can help them cope, either through social media or from friends who told them it can 'be a release for their feelings'.

A 'both/and' approach is helpful here: young people *can and do* use cutting to numb their feelings and manage overwhelming thoughts, *and at the same time*, they may fall into this particular way of 'coping' because they've heard many others do so before them – and may then continue to 'cope' in this way partly because of the responses this behaviour evokes in others, with an excessive focus on coping mechanism discussions, that despite the intentions, continues to place the self-harm at the centre of attention.

As therapists, we can approach this form of self-harm without adopting the position of an authoritative expert who instantly recognises what's going on, recommends alternative coping strategies (cold water, rubber bands, etc.), and closely monitors the scars and occasions of self-harm, labelling them 'unhealthy' coping mechanisms. We also can't presume that the young person we are seeing *wants* 'healthier coping mechanisms' or, for that matter, wants to stop cutting. Often they want to continue. We can meet them where they are, becoming curious about the function of the self-harm for them and not taking on the full responsibility ourselves for whether they stop or not.

I've noticed that, once we truly accept that preventing an adolescent from cutting isn't possible (in an absolute sense), and once efforts to make it stop lose their urgency, the adolescent often gradually stops mentioning their self-harm. They then begin to understand, step by step, that self-harm doesn't provide the answers they expected it would and, in fact, causes numerous problems with parents and teachers. These adults, the adolescent now notices, usually respond with increased restrictions and monitoring, which affects their independence.

This phase of realisation often starts, I've noticed, when the adolescent observes that the adults around them 'hate their self-harm'. The work of change often starts with a shared curiosity as to why they think this disapproval exists. A neutral stance from us is important here. I've been surprised by how often adolescents who self-harm haven't considered that their parents don't share their view of self-harm as an effective coping mechanism for dealing with difficult emotions – such can be the strength of adolescents' belief sometimes in the efficacy of cutting 'to manage emotions'.

This curiosity can lead to an increase in the adolescent's wish for more independence and for being treated like an adult. In turn, this can lead them sometimes, step by step, to a pragmatic decision to stop cutting to avoid further monitoring and babying. In my experience, this is usually one of the most straightforward, surprising, but in fact developmentally positive ways the adolescent can stop self-harming – with a gradual move towards the reality principle and the realisation that the self-harm doesn't achieve the magical solution that was promised.

This can be a deeply satisfying process to observe: I often feel in such situations that the work is done by the adolescent, with me alongside them observing and supporting their movement forward towards these realisations. But once again, I need to stress that this depends on us as therapists not 'buying into' the idea that self-harm is any kind of coping mechanism or agonising over listing alternatives. Instead, we need to let the adolescent figure what solutions will help them, trusting that they'll realise eventually that cutting – like any 'magic solution' – is largely smoke and mirrors. Real solutions lie elsewhere.

Of course, sometimes the adolescent unconsciously doesn't want independence: they may wish to be treated like a younger child, and thus may regress through the cutting. Sometimes, that is, adolescents may unconsciously seek exactly this excessive monitoring and looking after.

This leads me to the second grouping of self-harm via cutting, closely linked to relationships, the expression of frustration, and anger.

Self-harm as an expression of anger, in the context of arguments

A very different form of self-harm occurs often during arguments between parents and adolescents. This immediately conveys that there is still work to be done in that relationship, indicating that something earlier – being replicated in the present moment – is not quite resolved.

It happens like this: in the heat of a shouting match, the teenager retreats to the bathroom and cuts themselves or threatens to do so. Anna Motz highlights the paradoxical nature of self-harm in these cases, as a means of 'using injury to create healing and withdrawal into the self as an attempt to make contact with others' (Motz, 2010). The wished-for 'contact' attempted through the self-harm comes dressed up as anger and attack against the self but implicitly is calling to the parents.

The parental response tends to be equally intense. The teenager may be accused of 'attention seeking', 'being influenced by friends', 'going through a phase', 'being hormonal', 'blackmailing them', or 'acting crazy'. Parents may tell us they want to give up and can't parent their adolescent as they are 'holding them hostage' through the cutting and threats (sometimes through overdosing too). Beneath the fury and frustration lie helplessness and guilt, which may be projected onto the teenager, who is then seen as retaliating against them.

Within arguments, this type of self-harm becomes a powerful signal: 'Don't push too hard or things will get worse!', or in a gentler version: 'This is what I need to do for you to see how much pain I'm in'. The scene of the argument, the cutting, and the parents' reactions – sometimes ending in an A&E visit – encapsulate all the pent-up emotions that neither adolescent nor parent can express in words.

Similar scenes occur in schools. The figure of the out-of-control, threatening, unruly, self-harming adolescent can lead to impasses during the school day, creating urgency for staff to either overreact (sending them to A&E) or underreact (ignoring the teenager's behaviour altogether). Both responses reflect a difficulty thinking and reacting in a measured way. The urgent goal becomes keeping the adolescent *safe*, which equates to stopping their self-harm, but this can paradoxically escalate it, sometimes leading to the adolescent avoiding school altogether.

This is difficult terrain. The therapist must navigate the urgency and intensity of the situation, help contain it, while at the same time creating a space where underlying issues can be heard and explored, avoiding a focus solely on whether the self-harm stops. The first step is to secure 'buy-in' from parents and/or school – agreement that stepping back and thinking together, rather than only reacting, can be useful. Once the whole network (and, eventually, the adolescent too) shares this goal, the work can begin.

Self-harm as indicating an enjoyment of blood: A link to the prehistory of bloodletting as healing

Blood holds a significant, symbolic place in self-harm. The wish to see, smell, and touch blood can be linked to past practices of bloodletting, which were once seen as healing, as I've discussed previously.

In self-harming adolescents, the sight and smell of blood can sometimes bring an imagined sense of *cleansing* or externalisation of feelings, making them visible and undeniable, leading to a feeling of excitement and fascination with the blood. The sensory reality of blood can intensify the psychological experience of self-harm, and some young people are drawn to this experience.

Body modification, in some cases, might belong within this wider category of self-harm. There are distinctions here to take into account. Alessandra Lemma (2010) notes that modification of the body can at times be a source of learning, or as form of acting out, distinguishing between actions that feel authentic and compulsive actions that don't allow thought or feeling. She reminds us that 'cutting tells a tale, as do tattooing and piercing' (Lemma, 2010). There have been many adolescents I've known through the years who are drawn to both body modification and the sight and smell of blood, while others engage in the same behaviours in a far more unthinking, numbing, compulsive way.

This category of cutting can be thought of as an abject experience, as Julia Kristeva describes (1980/2024), involving both fascination and horror when faced with the body's raw physicality, its reality. This theory has been used to explain the fascination with horror movies (which adolescents are often drawn to). Developmentally, this fascination with the body's physicality can be appropriate to some degree, given all the bodily changes, making this form of cutting (however distressing it may be to those who observe it) more transient and less pathological than other forms.

Self-harm as group bonding: delineating the 'in-group' from the 'out-group'

It's well documented, particularly within mental health institutions and educational settings, that self-harm can become the basis for an identity that offers recognition and a sense of belonging within groups. This phenomenon can evoke intense reactions from those on the 'outside' of these groups, especially in inpatient settings. Favazza (2011, p. 213), citing Podvoll (1969), says:

> [S]elf-injurers in a hospital quickly assume an identity equated with their acts. The label cutter or slasher confirms a distinctive, functional role. Although self-cutting may lead to a personal sense of calmness, it evokes 'feelings of unbearable intensity' in caretakers and challenges staff roles and hospital structure.
>
> (p. 213)

There is a difference between the severity of problems and the seriousness of harm in different settings. A hospital setting can differ vastly from a school setting, though the group-based dynamics may be similar. Uh et al.'s findings (2021), discussed earlier, reflect previous research by Favazza (2011, p. 219), showing that

> the current generation of young student self-injurers . . . have lower rates of childhood sexual or physical abuse; show strengths in the areas of family, peers,

and school; are psychologically healthier; and stop their NSSI more rapidly (6 months to 2 years).

(pp. 219-220)

This, with social contagion being a factor in how they begin, hopefully makes the exit route clearer than for those in inpatient facilities.

It can be an enormous challenge to help teenagers in such groups find new ways of bonding and pledging 'allegiance' to the group without relying on conversations around mental health and self-harm. These forms of belonging are now amplified through the expansion of online life. As discussed earlier, socially transmitted clusters of mental health problems or behaviours are abundant – the most serious being the spread of suicidality, as seen classically in the wave of suicides inspired by Goethe's *The Sorrows of Young Werther*, where the hero kills himself: 'In an attempt to stem what was seen as a rising tide of imitative suicides, anxious authorities banned the book in several regions in Europe.

(Phillips, 1974; cited in Marsden, 1998)

At the extreme edges of this phenomenon, there have been tragic examples of mass suicides, such as those that happened within the Jonestown cult (Chidester, 2003). Sociogenic epidemics involve the way 'thoughts, actions, and feelings spread in epidemic-like-patterns' (Kirsch, 2012). The work of Christakis and Fowler (2009) on social networks offers further explanation for how these processes work. Socially spread self-harm among adolescents has been well-documented in the literature (e.g. Jarvi et al., 2013; Kirsch, 2012; Rosen & Walsh, 1989). Whitlock et al. (2006, p. 3) compare this to the spread of anorexia in the 1980s, when 'heightened cultural visibility through the mass media rendered [it] an available emotional outlet for individuals with receptive predispositions'.

Self-harm as a self-punishing act indicating depression

This is a more serious form of self-harm. Cutting that happens within the context of a significant depressive episode can, however, be misunderstood, seen as minor delinquency or attention seeking, dangerously underestimating the strength of the depression driving it. This is often because the self-harm in these cases lacks the group-based or 'loud' character of the types described earlier and thus may be overlooked.

Sometimes, this type of self-harm can be one of the few external symptoms indicating an underlying deep depression that may not be obvious otherwise to spot. This form of self-harm has a closer link to suicidality, aligning with Karl Menninger's classic ideas from his 1938 book 'Man against himself' (Menninger, 1938), where he argued that self-harm sometimes can be an unconscious mechanism for avoiding suicide by directing the suicidal impulse onto a part of the body as a substitute for the whole. He named this 'focal suicide', underlining the negativism and death drive within the act of cutting.

We can see how different this is than the earlier forms of self-harm I described, which are more connected to the life force, communication, connection, and even hope. This final type of self-harm tends to occur more often in isolation, compared to the previous forms, and is often found in adolescents with a harsh superego and unachievable ego ideal, who experience thoughts of worthlessness (often described as 'voices') and a wish to die. Sometimes this form of self-harm can indicate practice for suicide.

An example of this type of self-harm was noted in the final days of the American poet Sylvia Plath, who, before her death from suicide, practiced and prepared for her final act both with self-harm and extensive self-neglect (Chaney, 2017, p. 177).

Conclusion: self-harm as a communication

Understanding self-harm through all these different lenses allows us to reconceptualise this behaviour, examining it case by case, person by person. In its current 'epidemic' form, where self-harm is often – tragically – the quickest means of engaging the attention of therapists and mental health services, it becomes all the more crucial to listen carefully to the story the person behind the cutting tells us, stepping away from both overreaction and the even more dangerous underreaction.

Self-harming adolescents have complex stories to tell, yet their narratives are often confined within the socially recognised, over-familiar story self-harm holds in the cultural imagination. What remains unsaid is the deeper, unique story of each young person we might be lucky enough, one day, to hear.

Note

1 Alessandra Lemma (2017) as well as Lemma and Caparrotta (2014) have covered in their work the role of the body in contemporary psychoanalytic thought as well as working within a digital environment, as psychotherapists, and what factors we need to consider.

References

Acheson, R., & Papadima, M. (2023). The search for identity: Working therapeutically with adolescents in crisis. *Journal of Child Psychotherapy*, 49(1), 95–119.

American Psychiatric Association. (2013). *Diagnostic and statistical manual of mental disorders* (5th edition). Arlington, VA: American Psychiatric Publishing.

Andover, M. S., Primack, J. M., Gibb, B. E., & Pepper, C. M. (2010). An examination of non-suicidal self-injury in men: Do men differ from women in basic NSSI characteristics?. *Archives of Suicide Research*, 14(1), 79–88.

Angelotta, C. (2015). Defining and refining self-harm: A historical perspective on nonsuicidal self-injury. *The Journal of Nervous and Mental Disease*, 203(2), 75–80.

Arendt, F., Scherr, S., & Romer, D. (2019). Effects of exposure to self-harm on social media: Evidence from a two-wave panel study among young adults. *New Media & Society*, 21(11–12), 2422–2442.

Berk, M. S., & Clarke, S. (2019). Safety planning and risk management. In: *Evidence-based treatment approaches for suicidal adolescents: Translating science into practice* (pp. 63–84). American Psychiatric Pub.

Biernesser, C., Sewall, C. J., Brent, D., Bear, T., Mair, C., & Trauth, J. (2020). Social media use and deliberate self-harm among youth: A systematized narrative review. *Children and Youth Services Review*, 116, 105054.

Bogousslavsky, J. (2020). The mysteries of hysteria: A historical perspective. *International Review of Psychiatry*, 32(5–6), 437–450.

Bollas, C. (2000). *Hysteria*. Routledge.

Borsch-Jacobsen, M., & Brick, D. (1996). Neurotica: Freud and the seduction theory. *October*, 76, 15–43.

Brady, M. T. (2014). Cutting the silence: Initial, impulsive self-cutting in adolescence. *Journal of Child Psychotherapy*, 40(3), 287–301.

Brausch, A. M., Williams, A. G., & Cox, E. M. (2016). Examining intent to die and methods for nonsuicidal self-injury and suicide attempts. *Suicide and Life-Threatening Behavior*, 46(6), 737–744.

Bresin, K., & Schoenleber, M. (2015). Gender differences in the prevalence of nonsuicidal self-injury: A meta-analysis. *Clinical Psychology Review*, 38, 55–64.

Chaney, S. (2017). *Psyche on the skin: A history of self-harm*. London: Reaktion Books.

Chapman, A. L., & Rosenthal, M. Z. (2016). *Managing therapy-interfering behavior: Strategies from dialectical behavior therapy*. American Psychological Association.

Chesler, P. (2018). *Women and madness*. Chicago Review Press.

Chidester, D. (2003). *Salvation and suicide: An interpretation of Jim Jones, the Peoples Temple, and Jonestown*. Indiana University Press.

Christakis, N. A., & Fowler, J. H. (2009). *Connected: The surprising power of our social networks and how they shape our lives*. New York: Little, Brown and Company.

Chung, E. (2009). The neurobiology of self-harm. In: *Self-harm in young people: A therapeutic assessment manual* (p. 49).

Cummins, T. M., English, O., Minnis, H., Stahl, D., O'Connor, R. C., Bannister, K., McMahon, S. B., & Ougrin, D. (2021). Assessment of somatosensory function and self-harm in adolescents. *JAMA Network Open*, 4(7), e2116853–e2116853.

Cybulski, L., Ashcroft, D. M., Carr, M. J., Garg, S., Chew-Graham, C. A., Kapur, N., & Webb, R. T. (2021). Temporal trends in annual incidence rates for psychiatric disorders and self-harm among children and adolescents in the UK, 2003–2018. *BMC Psychiatry*, 21, 1–12.

Demazeux, S., & Singy, P. (2015). *The DSM-5 in perspective*. New York: Springer.

Dutta, C. (2015, January 7). Teaching unions warn of self-harm epidemic among students. *The Independent*. http://www.independent.co.uk/life-style/health-and-families/health-news/teaching-unions-warn-of-self-harm-epidemic-among-students-9961669.html

Farkas, B. F., Takacs, Z. K., Kollárovics, N., & Balazs, J. (2024). The prevalence of self-injury in adolescence: A systematic review and meta-analysis. *European Child & Adolescent Psychiatry*, 33(10), 3439–3458.

Favazza, A. (2011). *Bodies under siege: Self-mutilation, nonsuicidal self-injury, and body modification in psychiatry and culture* (3rd edition). Baltimore: Johns Hopkins University Press.

Fonagy, P., & Target, M. (2000). Playing with reality: III. The persistence of dual psychic reality in borderline patients. *The International Journal of Psycho-Analysis*, 81(5), 853.

Foulkes, L. (2024). *Coming of Age: How adolescence shapes us*. Random House.

Foulkes, L, & Stringaris, A. (2023). Do no harm: Can school mental health interventions cause iatrogenic harm? *BJPsych Bulletin*, 47(5), 267–269. https://doi.org/10.1192/bjb.2023.9

Freud, A. (1958). Adolescence. *The Psychoanalytic Study of the Child*, 255–278.

Freud, S. (1896). Aetiology of hysteria. *The Standard Edition of the Complete Psychological Works of Sigmund Freud*, 24, 1953–1974.

Freud, S. (1923). The ego and the id. In: *The standard edition of the complete psychological works of Sigmund Freud* (Vol. 19, pp. 1–66). London: Hogarth Press.

Freud, S., & Breuer, J. (1895). *The standard edition of the complete psychological works of Sigmund Freud, Volume II (1893–1895): Studies on hysteria*. Hogarth and the Institute of Psycho-Analysis.

Gillies, D., Christou, M. A., Dixon, A. C., Featherston, O. J., Rapti, I., Garcia-Anguita, A., Villasis-Keever, M., & Christou, P. A. (2018). Prevalence and characteristics of self-harm in adolescents: Meta-analyses of community-based studies 1990–2015. *Journal of the American Academy of Child & Adolescent Psychiatry*, 57(10), 733–741.

Gilman, S. (2013). From psychiatric symptom to diagnostic category: Self-harm from the Victorians to DSM-5. *History of Psychiatry*, 24(2), 148–165.

Gould, M., Jamieson, P., & Romer, D. (2003, May). Media contagion and suicide among the young. *American Behavioral Scientist*, 46(9), 1269–1284.

Hacking, I. (2006, August 17). Making up people. *London Review of Books*, 28(16).

Hartas, D. (2024). Wellbeing, psychological distress and self-harm in late adolescence in the UK: The role of gender and personality traits. *European Journal of Special Needs Education*, 39(2), 201–218.

Hawton, K., Knipe, D., & Pirkis, J. (2024). Restriction of access to means used for suicide. *The Lancet Public Health*, 9(10), e796–e801.

Hodge, L., & Baker, A. (2021). Purification, punishment, and control: Eating disorders, self-harm, and child sexual abuse. *Qualitative Health Research*, 31(11), 1963–1975.

Horne, A. (2018). *On children who privilege the body: Reflections of an Independent psychotherapist*. Routledge.

Horne, O., & Csipke, E. (2009). From feeling too little and too much, to feeling more and less? A nonparadoxical theory of the functions of self-harm. *Qualitative Health Research*, 19(5), 655–667.

Jarvi, S., Jackson, B., Swenson, L., & Crawford, H. (2013). The impact of social contagion on non-suicidal self-injury: A review of the literature. *Archives of Suicide Research*, 17(1), 1–19.

Kernberg, O. F. (2012). Overview and critique of the classification of personality disorders proposed for DSM-V. *Swiss Archives of Neurology and Psychiatry*, 163(7), 234–238.

Keyes, K. M., & Platt, J. M. (2024). Annual research review: Sex, gender, and internalizing conditions among adolescents in the 21st century-trends, causes, consequences. *Journal of Child Psychology and Psychiatry*, 65(4), 384–407.

Kirsch, P. M. (2012). *The influence of social contagion and technology on epidemic non-suicidal self-injury*. http://digitalscholarship.unlv.edu/award/8

Kristeva, J. (1980/2024). *Powers of horror: An essay on abjection*. Columbia University Press.

Krohn, A. (1978). *Hysteria: The elusive neurosis*. New York: International Universities Press.

Ladame, F. (1995). The importance of dreams and action in the adolescent process. *International Journal of Psychoanalysis*, 76, 1143–1153.

Large, M., Babidge, N., Andrews, D., Storey, P., & Nielssen, O. (2009). Major self-mutilation in the first episode of psychosis. *Schizophrenia Bulletin*, 35(5), 1012–1021.

Laye-Gindhu, A., & Schonert-Reichl, K. A. (2005). Nonsuicidal self-harm among community adolescents: Understanding the "whats" and "whys" of self-harm. *Journal of youth and Adolescence*, 34, 447–457.

Lemma, A. (2010). *Under the skin: A psychoanalytic study of body modification*. Routledge.

Lemma, A. (2017). *The digital age on the couch: Psychoanalytic practice and new media*. Routledge.

Lemma, A., & Caparrotta, L. (eds.). (2014). *Psychoanalysis in the technoculture era* (p. 134). London: Routledge.

Lilley, R., Owens, D., Horrocks, J., House, A., Noble, R., Bergen, H., Hawton, K., & Kapur, N. (2008). Hospital care and repetition following self-harm: Multicentre comparison of self-poisoning and self-injury. *The British Journal of Psychiatry*, 192(6), 440–445.

Liu, B. P., Lunde, K. B., Jia, C. X., & Qin, P. (2020). The short-term rate of non-fatal and fatal repetition of deliberate self-harm: A systematic review and meta-analysis of longitudinal studies. *Journal of Affective Disorders*, 273, 597–603.

Lloyd-Richardson, E. E., Perrine, N., Dierker, L., & Kelley, M. L. (2007). Characteristics and functions of non-suicidal self-injury in a community sample of adolescents. *Psychological Medicine*, 37(8), 1183–1192.

Lothane, Z. (2001). Freud's alleged repudiation of the seduction theory revisited: Facts and fallacies. *The Psychoanalytic Review*, 88(5), 673–723.

Magagna, J. (2008). Attacks on life: Suicidality in self-harm in young people. In: S. Briggs, A. Lemma, & W. Crouch (eds.), *Relating to self-harm and suicide: Psychoanalytic perspectives on practice, theory and prevention*. London & NY: Routledge.

Marsden, P. (1998). Memetics and social contagion: Two sides of the same coin? *The Journal of Memetics: Evolutionary Models of Information Transmission*, 2. https://web.stanford.edu/~kcarmel/CC_BehavChange_Course/readings/Additional%20Resources/social%20contagion/Social%20Contagion.htm

McKenzie, K. C., & Gross, J. J. (2014). Nonsuicidal self-injury: An emotion regulation perspective. *Psychopathology*, 47(4), 207–219.

Menninger, K. A. (1938). *Man against himself*. Harcourt, Brace.

Miguel, E. M., Chou, T., Golik, A., Cornacchio, D., Sanchez, A. L., DeSerisy, M., & Comer, J. S. (2017). Examining the scope and patterns of deliberate self-injurious cutting content in popular social media. *Depression and Anxiety*, 34(9), 786–793.

Miller, D. N. (2021). *Child and adolescent suicidal behavior: School-based prevention, assessment, and intervention*. Guilford Publications.

Mokrini, F., Waeyenberge, L., Viaene, N., & Moens, M. (2012, March 5). Promises behavioral health. *Suffering Silently: Using Self-Injury as a Coping Mechanism*. https://www.promisesbehavioralhealth.com/mental-health/self-injury-as-a-coping-mechanism/

Moran, P., Chandler, A., Dudgeon, P., Kirtley, O. J., Knipe, D., Pirkis, J., Sinyor, M., & Christensen, H. (2024). The Lancet Commission on self-harm. *The Lancet*, 404(10461), 1445–1492.

Motz, A. (2010). Self-harm as a sign of hope. *Psychoanalytic Psychotherapy*, 24(2), 81–92. https://doi.org/10.1080/02668731003707527

Motz, A., & Jones, H. (2009). The paradox of self-harm. In: *Managing self-harm: Psychological perspectives* (pp. 42–52).

Nock, M. K. (2010). Self-injury. *Annual Review of Clinical Psychology*, 6(1), 339–363.

Norris, J. (2025 in press). *(Overcoming) attacks on thinking: The importance of psychoanalytic thinking in surviving systemic fragmentation of the public mental health sector*. JCP.

O'Sullivan, S. (2016). *It's all in your head: Stories from the frontline of psychosomatic illness*. Random House.

Osuch, E. A., & Payne, G. W. (2008). Neurobiological perspectives on self-injury. In: *Self-injury in youth* (pp. 79–110). Routledge.

Ougrin, D., Wong, B. H. C., Vaezinejad, M., Plener, P. L., Mehdi, T., Romaniuk, L., Barrett, E., & Landau, S. (2021). Pandemic-related emergency psychiatric presentations for self-harm of children and adolescents in 10 countries (PREP-kids): A retrospective international cohort study. *European Child & Adolescent Psychiatry*, 1–13.

Papadima, M. (2019). Rethinking self-harm: A psychoanalytic consideration of hysteria and social contagion. *Journal of Child Psychotherapy*, 45(3), 291–307.

Parkin, J. R., & Eagles, J. M. (1993). Blood-letting in bulimia nervosa. *The British Journal of Psychiatry*, 162(2), 246–248.

Patalay, P., & Gage, S. H. (2019). Changes in millennial adolescent mental health and health-related behaviours over 10 years: A population cohort comparison study. *International Journal of Epidemiology*, 48(5), 1650–1664.

Phillips, A. (2000). On eating, and preferring not to. In: A. Phillips (ed.), *Promises, promises* (pp. 282–295). London: Faber & Faber.

Phillips, D. P. (1974, June). The influence of suggestion on suicide: Substantive and theoretical implications of the Werther effect. *American Sociological Review*, 39, 340–354.

Podvoll, E. M. (1969). Self-mutilation within a hospital setting: A study of identity and social compliance. *British Journal of Medical Psychology*.

Richardson, B., Surmitis, K., & Hyldahl, R. (2012). Minimizing social contagion in adolescents who self-injure: Considerations for group work, residential treatment, and the internet. *Journal of Mental Health Counseling*, 34(2), 121–132.

Rosen, P. M., & Walsh, B. W. (1989). Patterns of contagion in self mutilation epidemics. *American Journal of Psychiatry*, 146, 656–658.

Sarchiapone, M., Mandelli, L., Iosue, M., Andrisano, C., & Roy, A. (2011). Controlling access to suicide means. *International Journal of Environmental Research and Public Health*, 8(12), 4550–4562.

Showalter, E. (1985). *The female malady: Women, madness and English culture, 1830–1980.* New York: Pantheon Books.

Showalter, E. (1997). *Hystories: Hysterical epidemics and modern media* (Vol. 2). Columbia University Press.

Stotland, N. L. (2004). Women's bodies, doctors' dynamics. *Journal of the American Academy of Psychoanalysis and Dynamic Psychiatry*, 32(1: Special Issue), 181–191.

Stupples, B. (2015, February 28). Self-harm is not just attention-seeking: It's time to talk openly about the issue. *The Guardian*. https://www.theguardian.com/lifeandstyle/2015/feb/28/self-harm-is-not-just-attention-seeking-self-harm-awareness-day

Therrien, A. (2018). Fifth of 14-year-old girls in UK "have self-harmed". *BBC News Website*. https://www.bbc.co.uk/news/health-45329030

Tracy, N. (2016, August 26). Self-injury cutting: Cutting yourself to relieve emotional pain. *Healthy Place Website*. https://www.healthyplace.com/abuse/self-injury/selfinjury-cutting-cutting-yourself-to-relieve-emotional-pain

Uh, S., Dalmaijer, E. S., Siugzdaite, R., Ford, T. J., & Astle, D. E. (2021). Two pathways to self-harm in adolescence. *Journal of the American Academy of Child and Adolescent Psychiatry*, 2021(12), 1491–1500. https://doi.org/10.1016/j.jaac.2021.03.010

Veith, I. (1965). *Hysteria: The history of a disease*. Chicago: University of Chicago Press.

Whitlock, J. L., Powers, J. L., & Eckenrode, J. (2006). The virtual cutting edge: The internet and adolescent self-injury. *Developmental Psychology*, 42, 3.

Winnicott, D. W. (1956/1992). Delinquency as a sign of hope. In: *Collected papers: Paediatrics through psychoanalysis*. London: Karnac/The Institute of Psychoanalysis.

Winnicott, D. W. (1968/1971). Contemporary concepts of adolescent development and their implications for higher education. *Playing and Reality*, 139.

Zetterqvist, M. (2015). The DSM-5 diagnosis of nonsuicidal self-injury disorder: A review of the empirical literature. *Child and Adolescent Psychiatry and Mental Health*, 9, 1–13.

Chapter 7

Moving towards a psychoanalytic formulation when assessing the risk of suicide in adolescents in crisis

Nikolaos Tzikas

In Greek, the word 'crisis' (κρί[cri]-ση[sis]) carries a dual significance. It can refer to a state of turmoil, but also to the exercise of judgement in evaluating a situation. As psychoanalytic practitioners encountering an adolescent in crisis, we must grasp the nature of the crisis while simultaneously assessing potential risks. This dual approach is essential for building a psychoanalytic formulation that allows us to understand and create meaning regarding the adolescent crisis and its associated risks.

In this chapter, I introduce a way of formulating risk that I've called the 'Threefold Insight for Evaluation Risk' (TIER) model. I have developed this as a way of guiding myself when assessing adolescents at risk of suicide. This model provides a structured framework for evaluating risk in a clinical setting, comprising three distinct layers.

The first layer follows Peta Mees's (2016) approach to generic assessments, exploring external factors and their impact on the adolescent's life. The second layer considers specific risk factors relevant to adolescent crises and history, and finally, the third layer turns to the adolescent's internal world and functioning, in relation to their risk presentation.

To demonstrate the potential wider clinical application of the TIER model, I will present three composite case examples. These examples will highlight the model's application and underscore the critical role of dynamic psychoanalytic formulation in risk assessment.

My argument here is that the TIER framework offers a simple yet comprehensive approach to psychoanalytically informed frontline risk assessment and formulation. In doing so, it attempts to bridge generic assessment techniques with psychoanalytic understanding, combining elements from Mees's (2016) work on generic assessments with an exploration of both external factors and internal dynamics. This integrated approach can enhance our ability to manage risk and develop meaningful formulations for adolescents in crisis, moving away from the current standard practice in risk assessment of tick-boxing exercises and safety planning, and moving towards an understanding of the meaning of the risk.

DOI: 10.4324/9781003592778-10

Therapeutic work within risk evaluations

Engaging in exploratory work with adolescents in crisis offers valuable insight into their initial expressions and communication. This way of working moves away from certain standard crisis team practices, such as focusing only on the crisis rather than the whole personality of the young person, assigning a diagnosis, or providing generic skills and strategies that may not be suitable for every adolescent in crisis. In this exploratory way of thinking, the emphasis instead is on building a connection with the young person and establishing the initial therapeutic alliance, which will make a big difference to what comes next. In this way, the assessment process can serve as both a critical and a creative experience, offering an opportunity to co-construct meaning with the adolescent and to gradually, jointly reach a formulation.

When assessing a young person in crisis, we have to navigate a complex interplay between their immediate crisis, their past and current challenges, their external environment and influences, and their internal experiences. Given their developmental stage, adolescents experience, even in the best of circumstances, significant fluctuations in emotional and physical development, which constantly shape their evolving psychic experience, and that, too, needs to be taken into account. Therefore, a 'psychoanalytic formulation' (McWilliams, 1999, 2012) aims to understand the core problems, behavioural tendencies, defence mechanisms, and recurring patterns an adolescent presents with at a specific time, giving us an overall idea of the adolescent's emotional world and motives. Perry et al. (1987) suggest that dynamic formulation, alongside clinical diagnosis, share a key purpose: 'to provide a succinct conceptualisation of the case and thereby guide a treatment plan' (p. 543). Through the ongoing, evolving relationship between therapist and patient that happens during the stage of formulation, we can gain deeper insights into why specific modes of functioning have emerged and what the current risk may relate to.

Expression through the body

As noted by several authors in this volume, adolescents are often action-oriented rather than reflective, navigating in many occasions their inner conflicts through physical expressions. Winnicott's (1949/1975) concept of 'personalisation', which examines adolescents' return to a *bodily sense of self*, highlights this tendency to process and express emotions through the body. Campbell and Hale (2017) refer to this as a 'withdrawal from others into the body', which is seen as a necessary developmental phase for adolescents, despite the difficulty it can cause for a time. During periods of crisis, this withdrawal into the body can manifest as a fluctuating state between integration and disintegration as the adolescent works toward a more stable and cohesive identity, a process that may include myriad emotions and bodily acting-outs while it's unfolding.

Therefore, when we are in the consulting room with an adolescent who presents in a crisis, our main task as psychoanalytic psychotherapists when trying to understand what's going on is, firstly, to observe their emotional experience in as much detail as we can. Later in this chapter, I will discuss what this involves further. The next step is to determine and make meaning of these experiences (Bion, 1963). As we know, close and careful observation is essential in making a psychoanalytic formulation about our patients, rather than quickly acting, offering solutions, and reaching an understanding of the adolescent's actions prematurely. What I'm arguing here is that an exploratory stance that also acknowledges the seriousness of the young person's risky act is important, even in those states of urgency that adolescents in crisis present us with.

Crafting a psychoanalytic case formulation aims, more widely, to deepen our understanding of the adolescent before us, guiding the direction and tone of the treatment, regardless of whether it ends up being long- or shorter-term. McWilliams (1999) emphasises that this process is more artistic and inferential than strictly diagnostic, encouraging us to conceptualise key aspects of the young person's process of growth within the formulation. These aspects include their development of insight, agency, identity, self-esteem, emotional regulation, ego strength, self-cohesion, as well as their capacity for love, work, play, and finally, their overall sense of emotional wellbeing.

A setting ready to receive: preparing the therapeutic space for adolescents in crisis

Before discussing the parameters for creating a formulation, as we're assessing our adolescent patients in crisis, we first need to make sure we've created a space that offers them the opportunity to *escape and find respite*, away from their crisis and problems in the outside world.

Practically, this can involve offering access to drawing materials, fidget toys, Lego, or card games. All these items can serve as a form of emotional refuge for adolescents, particularly when they're experiencing significant distress. Such materials can also serve as a helpful manoeuvre, offering a buffer from emotional pain and enabling adolescents to create a necessary mental space, away from the intensity of the therapeutic interaction. Otherwise, we might fall into the trap of too much emotional intensity developing during the period of assessment, potentially leading to the physical discharge of this intensity, or acting out through the body, or even leading to the young person disengaging altogether. The use of such materials can often encourage a shift from physical action to a more playful, constructive engagement in the presence of an attentive therapist, who is then felt to be *not too close and yet not too far*.

Developing the TIER framework

When assessing a young person, it is crucial to consider several parameters. In doing so, the most important thing to keep in mind is that assessing risk is always *dynamic*, due to adolescents' volatile and dynamic emotional experiences (Cantrell et al.,

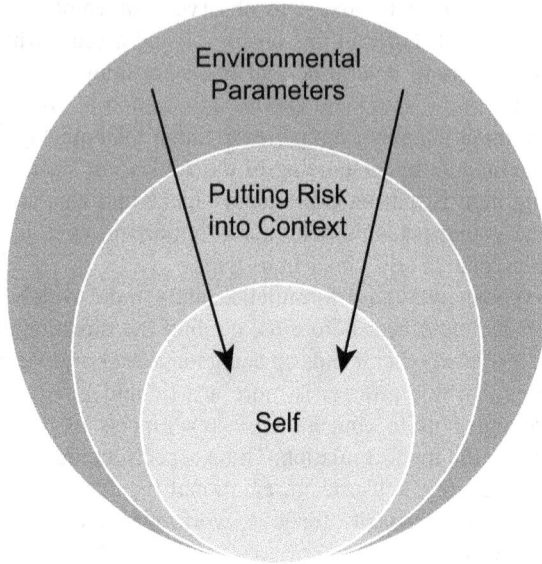

Figure 7.1 Threefold Insight for Evaluating Risk (TIER).

2024). Adolescents' experiences are always in flux, so it is necessary to always hold in mind a developmental perspective that considers both environmental factors and the adolescent's internal world.

As I mentioned earlier, I envisage this as a framework, which I've named the 'Threefold Insight for Evaluating Risk' (TIER) model, which can be used to guide adolescent risk assessment, starting from external considerations and leading on to more internal ones. The TIER framework, outlined in Figure 7.1, I think can help structure the complex interplay of external and internal factors in a way that supports a nuanced understanding of the adolescent in crisis. This framework can serve as a mental guide for clinicians, allowing them to consider most of its key parameters within the first, or at most the first two, clinical sessions.

Environmental parameters – understanding the context

To effectively assess risk in adolescents, it's essential to consider the broader environmental factors that shape their lives, as these can significantly impact mental health and can contribute to crises. For instance, some adolescents may experience temporary states of despair around periods of intense academic pressure, such as exams. During these times, the stress they feel can become overwhelming, heightening their feelings of anxiety and even despair.

Another key factor here is family dynamics. Adolescents often feel a growing distance from their parents, partly as they seek independence and new relationships outside the family, but at other times because family relationships may already be strained. This growing sense of distance from parents can deepen during adolescence, intensifying any pre-existing tensions (Schnettler & Steinbach, 2022). Winnicott (1968, 1971) highlights that adolescence is a period marked by emotional immaturity and a struggle for self-discovery.

Peer relationships also play a critical role during this developmental stage. For many adolescents, the quest for social belonging can bring additional stress, leading to feelings of loneliness or even social exclusion when they struggle to find a supportive peer group. Peer groups can also play a significant role in risk-taking behaviour during adolescence (Knoll et al., 2015). As discussed in Papadima's chapter (chapter 4 of this volume), the social dimensions of understanding risk and self-harm are important to keep in mind. Occasionally, we see adolescents in our work who belong to groups that engage in self-harm together, or participate in online suicide groups.

In recent years, there have been intense debates around whether social media impacts adolescent mental health and, if so, why and to what degree. Some studies indicate that excessive use of social media may have adverse effects on adolescents' mental health (Purba, 2023; Haidt, 2024). Other research highlights both the potential risks, but also the benefits, such as enhancing adolescents' sense of belonging and developing social connections (West et al., 2023). What is clear is that increased online engagement connects adolescents in a continuous way with peers and exposes them to a vast amount of information and input. This can arguably feel overwhelming, not only to adolescents, but also to adults too. At times, we also know that social media presents unrealistic standards for appearance, success, and popularity, while also exposing young people to cyberbullying and harmful comparisons. For adolescents, who are in a critical phase of identity formation, one wonders if digital interactions in particular can heavily influence their self-perception, which could pose risks by heightening their vulnerability to mental health crises.

The following figure (Figure 7.2) presents in summary the factors that need to be taken into account in the risk assessment process of the adolescent.

Overall, combined with other stressors – academic pressures, family dynamics, peer relationships – social media and other digital influences can add to a cumulative burden for the adolescent, especially during a time of identity formation and the struggle to find oneself.

Protective factors

In assessing external elements when it comes to adolescent mental health, it's crucial to also recognise protective factors alongside these risk elements (Dickens & O'Shea, 2018). Protective factors encompass any positive aspects of the environment that can buffer against stress and foster resilience. Supportive family bonds, trusted friendships, positive school experiences, and involvement in activities that promote belonging all play essential roles in reinforcing an adolescent's mental wellbeing. Encouraging connections with mentors, engagement

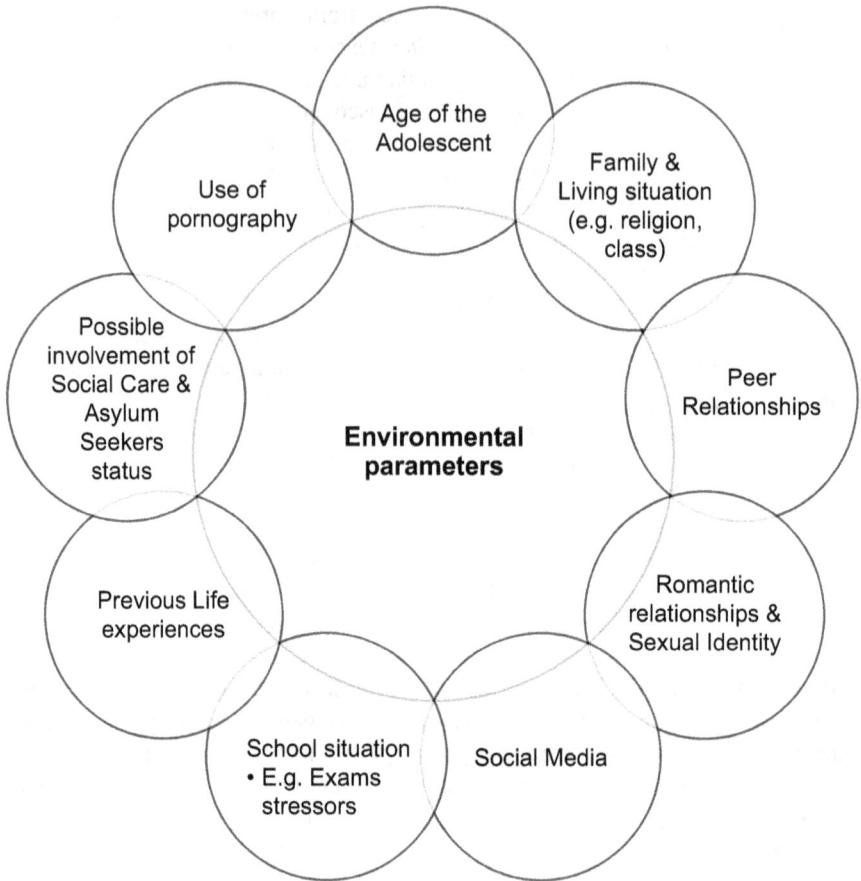

Figure 7.2 Environmental parameters.

in hobbies, community involvement, or finding positive social groups – offline or through healthy online interactions – can further bolster resilience. By identifying these protective factors alongside risk factors, clinicians can develop a more holistic understanding of the adolescent's environment, building on their formulation of the environmental parameters on the self.

By creating a map of the adolescent's environment and engaging them in an open exploration of this landscape, the therapeutic relationship offers a valuable opportunity to revisit both external challenges and protective factors. This process allows therapists and adolescents to deepen their understanding of the present crisis by connecting past experiences with the current situation. Through this integrative approach, the therapist can more effectively address the immediate crisis and thoughtfully assess all the factors that may contribute to risk or mitigate it.

Parameters around risk

When working with adolescents in crisis, we need to understand risk in its context and consider all the following, as shown in Figure 7.3.

Other chapters in the book have delved into the nuanced distinctions and different meanings of overdose and self-harm (via cutting). However, as part of our assessment, it is also crucial, as a first step, to consider and rule out whether the adolescent is experiencing psychosis, or whether they have a formal diagnosis that might exacerbate their suicidal state of mind, or whether they may be using alcohol or drugs. Campbell and Hale (2017) highlight that individuals with a history of suicide attempts are at greater risk of reattempting, so we need to have this information. Additionally, the loss of a family member or a close relative may act as a trigger, plunging the adolescent into despair and identifying with the lost object, which risks making them move towards suicidal ideation.

A primary goal of risk assessment is for the clinician to understand the adolescent's current situation clearly. This involves exploring how long the young person has felt in crisis and whether they have formed a suicide plan. Questions about the presence of a plan and its specifics provide insights into the extent of their suicidal ideation.

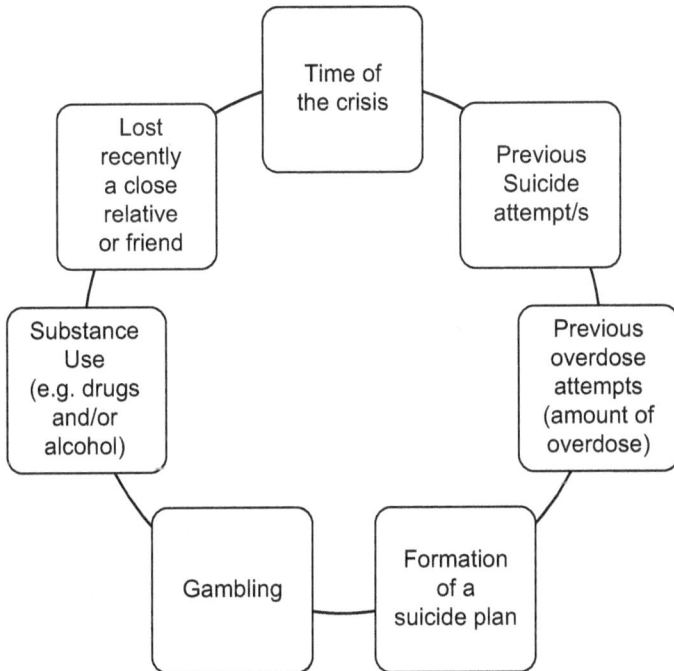

Figure 7.3 Parameters around risk.

For instance, if the adolescent mentions a vague thought of dying without a specific plan, it often indicates that suicidal ideation remains a conceptual notion rather than a fully developed intent, at least up to this point. Conversely, a well-defined plan reveals a deeper level of engagement with the idea of suicide, necessitating a more urgent and tailored response.

Understanding environmental parameters and contextualising young people's risk help us identify external pressures and protective factors that may influence their mental health. This knowledge is essential as a baseline in determining whether suicidal ideation or plans exist. But in addition, it is crucial to understand each patient's unique characteristics to develop personalised plans and risk assessments. This can only be achieved by deeply understanding their individual ways of being. Therefore, it's crucial to try to understand each young person's sense of self.

The self

In times of crisis, it's equally crucial to understand both the external factors influencing an adolescent's life and those affecting their internal world. This comprehensive approach is pivotal to our formulation process, providing us with vital information about the adolescent's urgent need for help, their strengths, and their challenges. By integrating these external and internal perspectives, we can develop over time a more nuanced formulation, addressing both the immediate concerns and the underlying issues that may be contributing to the crisis.

Adolescents experience emotional turmoil due to physical, hormonal, and emotional changes, as well as, in some cases, underlying primitive anxieties, resulting in emotional disarray. As the overwhelmed psyche seeks release, the body can serve as an outlet, reflecting both internal organisation and/or disorganisation (Rosenberg, 1991), and a crisis could present an opportunity for psychological reorganisation. Some crises may lead adolescents toward disintegration, while others may end up restoring the psyche's equilibrium. Assessing all these different outcomes and acknowledging that life is dynamic and constantly evolving is crucial during the process of formulation. The complicated relationship between psyche and soma always influences the psychosomatic aspect of crisis, offering insights into the adolescent's self-organisation (Marty, 1968). Adolescents may respond to their traumatic experiences by seeking escape or, alternatively, by developing new coping strategies, ultimately choosing life over death. The emergence of internal conflicts related to sexuality also plays a crucial role during this process, as adolescents grapple with their sexualised bodies and their relationships with others (McDougall, 1986). A key focus during assessment is to identify any underlying developmental and growth arrests that may be affecting the process of identity formation. In doing so, we also need to assess their duration, keeping in mind that the process of maturation can be remarkably uneven. For example, a young person can have well-developed capabilities in some areas yet suffer from a crippling deficit in the area of sexuality or the capacity to mourn or to be alone. Fixation is not a simple, unidimensional thing.

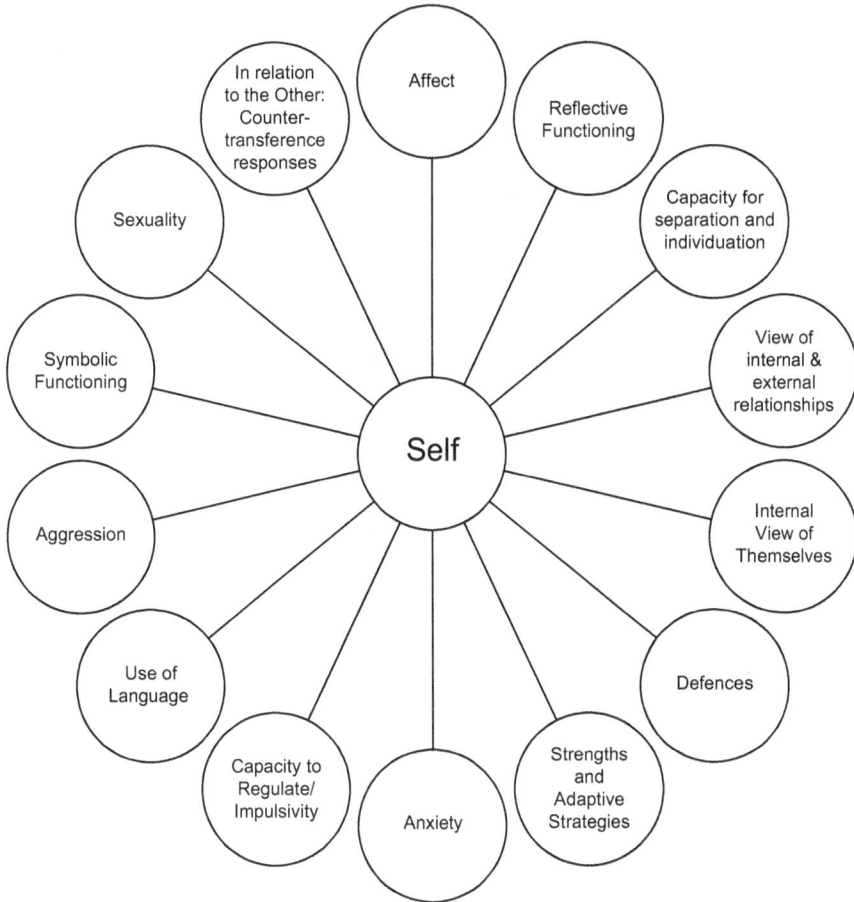

Figure 7.4 The self.

Therefore, assessing young people in crisis involves determining, over time, their ability to cope with tasks at their current developmental stage. Understanding the adolescent's resources and whether they can effectively utilise the therapeutic relationship is also crucial. The following characteristics and information, shown in Figure 7.4, can be considered during the assessment period.

Of course, utilising all this in practice is easier said than done! Therefore, to illustrate this process further, I will now describe three composite examples of young people and will try to formulate a psychoanalytic approach to demonstrate how I think about risk. I hope these examples, together with the preceding framework, can prove helpful in clinical practice with adolescents.

Firstly, I will describe each case separately, thinking of the parameters shown in the preceding table. Then, I will continue with the different risk levels each case presented, according to the aforementioned parameters and in relation to the experience of their internal objects. Finally, I will try to show the way this process works, as a whole, in assessing risk.

Suzanna

The first case I'll present is of a 16-year-old girl whom I will call Suzanna.

Suzanna comes in after her first significant overdose of 25 tablets of ibuprofen and five tablets of codeine. She comes into the room for the first time. She initially appears very calm and content and tells me that she feels carefree, not caring about anyone or anything, and at peace: nothing is currently weighing on her.

I ask her whether there was a time she remembers caring about something or someone.

She tells me that she used to care about people, but she kept feeling 'shit'. That's when she used to turn to alcohol and drugs to numb the pain. But since then, she doesn't care and feels that everything is great. She doesn't understand why she should come here, since she has been making sensible choices since last week.

I wonder out loud if there is a fear that, by coming here, she will feel rejected again.

She responds in a humorous way, telling me, 'We need to wait and see, I guess, about that'. She seems more connected now.

Her tone then changes. She tells me that she feels lonely most of the time, distant from her parents and emotionally detached from her boyfriend and friends, although she is 'addicted to online chatting with people who share similar interests with her'. She repeatedly tells me that she doesn't expect much of people in real life, as they are never committed to the friendship/relationship as much as she. But she never tells them and always waits for them to move away, without her actively taking the role of disappointing someone.

We transition from discussing friends to talking about school, where she consistently achieves good grades – in fact, she excels.

Towards the end of the session, we touch upon the issue of her recent overdose. She tells me that she also self-harms – this is because she doesn't deserve anything good. She doesn't deserve to be happy. As she shows me the self-harming marks, she tells me she feels worthless and feels there's 'a void' in herself.

We are approaching the end of the session. I notice I've been feeling protective and 'motherly' towards her, assuming she is vulnerable and fragile, not allowing anyone to approach her emotionally.

In the last couple of minutes, she tells me that she is a big 'fuck-up' – but it's not her fault. I ask what she feels she has 'fucked up', and she says, 'Pretty much everything and everyone around me'. She gives me this metaphor of reading a book that was named 'the best book of the year': you are excited to read it, but actually the book is 'shit'.

I mention that her metaphor implies other people informed her about reading the book and that it is not her fault if it is 'shit'. Consequently, she feels let down by them. She responds that she might recognise a difference between people actually letting her down and her perception that people might have let her down. She jokes, 'Do I sound mad? That's why people probably people leave me'. In the last minute, she tells me about a dream she recently had.

In considering a psychoanalytical formulation for Suzanna, I will use the following parameters from Figure 7.4: underlying anxiety, defences, sense of self, use of aggression, and level of symbolic functioning.

Suzanna's experiences reveal profound anxiety rooted in themes of rejection, isolation, and emotional closeness. Her self-perception – marked by feelings of emptiness and a belief that she does not deserve anything good – reflects an internal conviction of unworthiness when it comes to connection or happiness. This anxiety may stem from relational failures, where her attempts at closeness were, in the past, met with disappointment. Her statements 'I'm a big fuck-up' and 'It's not my fault' encapsulate the ambivalence fuelling her anxiety: she feels profoundly responsible for her perceived failures, while also recognising the role of external relational dynamics in shaping her sense of inadequacy. This internal conflict amplifies her anxiety, creating cycles of self-blame and relational withdrawal.

To manage her overwhelming feelings, Suzanna seems to be employing a number of defences. She reverses affect, masking her pain with a facade of being 'carefree'. Projection also plays a role, as she externalises her disappointment and attributes her negative self-perception to others, expecting abandonment rather than risking rejection by leaving first. Additionally, substance and alcohol use serves as a way to numb these emotions.

Suzanna's internal sense of self seems to be dominated by worthlessness and hopelessness, with a pervasive belief that she can't help but 'fuck-up' everything. This self-perception is deeply influenced by environmental failures, which she internalises and channels into self-directed aggression. Her self-harm and overdosing behaviours highlight the influence of a harsh, punitive superego that drives her self-destructive tendencies.

In my countertransference, Suzanna has evoked feelings of parental care and a desire to nurture her. These responses may reflect her relational style, characterised by a longing for nurturing connections, tempered by a deep fear of rejection and abandonment. Within the therapeutic relationship, Suzanna has demonstrated ambivalence, testing my availability through both humour and guardedness. This dynamic underscores her struggle to navigate emotional closeness while managing the fear of being let down.

In the 'here and now' of therapy, Suzanna has exhibited a capacity for symbolic thinking, using metaphors to articulate unmet expectations and relational disappointments. My interpretation – distinguishing between actual let-downs and her perception of being let down – resonated with her. This prompted reflection on her fears and anxieties, including the possibility that her actions might push people away. By the session's end, Suzanna mentioned a dream, a significant moment that suggested a growing openness to emotional exploration and connection. Perhaps the timing of this disclosure also reflected her ambivalence toward deeper emotional work, while signalling a desire to maintain a connection between sessions.

In applying the TIER framework, several key environmental factors emerge as significant. Suzanna has maintained connections with her friends, boyfriend, and family, despite experiencing feelings of distance; importantly, these relationships at this point remain intact. Her engagement with social media provides her with a vital sense of belonging, and she performs well academically. All these elements serve as protective factors, indicating that Suzanna is functioning effectively in a number of areas of her life.

Regarding risk, this incident marks her first overdose, and her instances of mild self-harming suggest a controlled method of coping. She has previously used alcohol and drugs to numb emotional pain, reflecting an awareness of her defensive mechanisms aimed at mitigating distress. Furthermore, Suzanna demonstrates emotional insight, symbolic capacity, and the ability to elicit care from others, as well as a wish for emotionally connecting with others – attributes that are promising for establishing a therapeutic relationship. These qualities can facilitate a balanced approach to managing her psychological wellbeing and promote personal growth.

Rudy

In contrast, cases such as Rudy's, which I'll describe now, highlight different personality dynamics that are more prone to acting on suicidal thoughts.

Rudy, a 17-year-old, arrived at our clinic following his second suicide attempt, in which he had consumed a mixture of alcohol, drugs, and medication. Before the attempt, he had sent goodbye messages to both his cousin and a friend. Alarmed by these messages, these young people informed his mother, who promptly took him to the emergency department.

When Rudy arrives for his first session two days after the incident, he barely makes eye contact with me. His gaze is fixed somewhere distant, as though speaking requires immense effort. His body language indicates someone who is exhausted: his slouched posture and slow movements convey a profound emptiness, as if life itself has been drained from him.

As he shuffles into the room, it feels like I'm reaching out across an unbridgeable chasm. As time passes, each attempt to connect seems to vanish into a void.

Initially, Rudy says very little, offering only brief, hesitant responses. Gradually, he begins to open up about his life, revealing the extent of his struggles. He describes a strained relationship with his family, with whom he lives, but from whom he feels profoundly disconnected. Though employed, he hasn't been to work in days, further isolating himself. A recent breakup has intensified Rudy's loneliness, leaving him feeling abandoned and convinced that everyone had turned against him. Every answer he gives to my questions underscores his lack of emotional or physical support.

When we discuss his suicide attempt, I feel an overwhelming worry about his safety. Rudy expresses no remorse for the act and admits he had hoped it would succeed. When I gently explore his thoughts and fantasies surrounding the attempt, his responses are unsettling. While some young people might describe feelings of wanting to 'escape' or express curiosity about death, Rudy's perspective is starkly devoid of such nuance. He states, 'Well, I just wish I'd be dead by now – just gone – and that I'd never have woken up. Death or life, it's all the same. I don't mind being dead. I haven't felt alive for a long time, anyway. If it happens, no one will be sad about me. I won't be sad about me'.

His words are steeped in hopelessness, leaving me experiencing, in the countertransference, a deep sense of despair. Rudy is not merely afraid of emotional and psychological breakdown; he is already living it. He explains that he didn't feel a specific urge to die but, rather, an acceptance of death as inevitable – a state he has already come to embrace.

Rudy's affect was notably flat throughout the session, with no emotional vitality. He didn't express remorse or sadness for his previous suicide attempt, with a lack of emotional processing in discussing it. His emotions seemed to be numbed and were so confusing that life and death appeared to feel the same to him, reflecting a sense of a deadened internal world.

At first, in our meeting, even an underlying anxiety was not possible to sense or think about, Rudy's anxiety indicating an experience of insignificance. Though his strained family relationships and recent breakup brought some upset that was evident in the way he talked, these relationships and his feelings about them seemed cut off, with a quality of emotional disconnection encompassing all aspects of his communication. This reflected a withdrawal from anxiety about relationships, rejecting their significance, and the significance of life in a wider way.

There was a strong sense of defensiveness in Rudy, including withdrawal, complete denial of affect, and depersonalisation. He had a perception of himself as fundamentally undeserving of care or attention from others, believing that his existence or disappearance wouldn't matter to them. This utter lack of life implied that feelings of hope or connection were non-existent, with a resignation towards death. His self-directed aggression didn't seem to be fuelled by active hatred, but rather indicated a surrender to his perceived insignificance and devalued sense of self, with his aggression manifesting in the absence of a will to survive or to live.

Unfortunately, the lack of symbolic functioning I could sense in Rudy was also profound, with life literally feeling drained and devoid of meaning, and with his statement of 'death or life, it's all the same' signifying a collapse of symbolic functioning, where the capacity to invest in meaning or purpose had disintegrated.

Though Rudy's lack of a premeditated plan might at first glance have seemed positive, his previous suicide attempt and what he had talked about in the session showed that he was at risk of acting on his suicidal thoughts when they came up, contributing to a sense of urgency and inevitability in his actions, away from any processing of or regulating emotions. My countertransference of deep worry and fear for Rudy's safety also underlined his inner conviction of helplessness that trapped him in isolation, away from anything meaningful.

Overall, Rudy's presentation describes the fragmented and depleted world of a young person who has already faced a breakdown, and his sense of death's inevitability reflects a collapsed self. His belief that no one cared, his cut-off ties from his parents, his second suicide attempt within a very short period of time, as well as his strong belief that he or anyone else wouldn't care if he existed, together illustrate a dangerous, complex reality with no protective factors. His symbolic functioning and emotional regulation were also profoundly impaired, making him unable to process any emotions or to invest in life. All those characteristics showed a young person at a point of breakdown, with another suicide attempt highly possible.

In contrast, the next case highlights a very different emotional landscape, one marked by heightened emotional intensity and volatility. While Rudy's struggles were rooted in withdrawal and detachment, Marianna's difficulties, which I'll discuss now, stemmed from her tumultuous relational patterns and intense fears of abandonment.

Marianna

Marianna, a 16-year-old girl with a long history of suicide attempts and self-harm, was referred to our service two years ago. It was decided then to consider psychotherapy, and she came in for her first session.

At first, she appears confident and well put together. However, within a few minutes, she begins fidgeting with her fingers and repeatedly fixes her hair, as if something is bothering her that she can't quite express.

Keeping in mind her recent suicide attempts, I ask how things are going for her. She responds enthusiastically, saying everything is 'great': her parents are 'amazing', she 'loves them so much', and things are going well with school and friends. She speaks with apparent self-awareness, emphasising how well she understands herself and how emotionally insightful she is.

In my countertransference, I find myself drawn in, carried along by her narrative and almost believing it. For a moment, I feel convinced that everything, indeed, is fine. But almost immediately, I have a visceral reaction, a mental jolt that reminds me to wait and look deeper. I gently ask her, 'It sounds like everything is really good right now. Is there anything you feel you need from therapy?'

She responds that she feels it would be good to have someone 'capable' to talk to and appreciates having someone who will listen. But almost immediately, the perfect image she's presented so far begins to crumble. She suddenly shifts her tone, saying, 'But why should I waste my time talking to someone who probably doesn't understand anything I've gone through?' She calls me 'useless' and claims she already knows everything there is to know about herself.

Then she suddenly spirals, venting about her deep resentment toward her parents, whom she now describes as 'awful'. She blames them entirely for everything, saying her friends are 'terrible' too; they 'never text', they're 'always caught up in their problems', and they 'never really listen'.

Marianna's initial confidence at the beginning revealed a façade of experience and a defence against deeper underlying anxiety, which seemed tied to relational conflict. This was apparent as her tone shifted and her self-assurance was quickly shattered, revealing her resentment towards her parents and friends. Her pervasive sense of dissatisfaction and emotional neglect from others seemed to be fuelling her anxiety, further making her feel ambivalent towards anything and everyone.

Primitive defences seemed to be at play, such as idealisation and devaluation, with abrupt shifts between the two, which seemed to be protecting her psyche from feelings of disappointment and hurt. This kind of disappointment instead was projected outwards and onto others. Her way of claiming she knew everything about herself could be understood as a defence of intellectualisation, protecting against feeling vulnerable and avoiding a deeper exploration of her difficulties with another mind. Those defences appeared to be used because of Marianna's fragmented sense of self. Her attempt to convince herself and others that she 'knew everything', coupled with her apparent disillusionment about her relationships, suggested a deep conflict and a dichotomy pointing to a fragile sense of self. This led her to feelings of isolation, resentment towards others, and frustration.

Her dramatic fluctuations of intense emotions, love and confidence followed by anger and frustration, indicated difficulties in emotional regulation, reflecting a lack of a stable emotional world. This inability to regulate signalled a difficulty in integrating complex feelings, leaving her trapped in cycles of wanting to be emotionally close to others and immediately moving further and further away. Although not overtly demonstrated, her rapid shifts in emotional tone and behaviour suggested a young person who was highly impulsive and who could react disproportionately to perceived slights or emotional neglect. This might lead her to direct her aggression outwards towards others, turning the emotional intensity of her experience into resentment and blame. In order to punish her objects, she self-harmed, overdosed, and attempted suicide. I think that my countertransference experience of a push–pull dynamic reflected Marianna's capacity to draw me into her narrative, creating a false sense of connection that was then shattered when feelings of resentment and abandonment emerged.

Marianna's unstable and fragmented sense of self resulted in a cyclical pattern of emotional pain, leading her to challenges with emotional regulation, impulsive reactions, and dramatic fluctuations between feelings of love and hate. Her shifting emotional states towards external and internal objects significantly impacted her risk level, as these shifts were a key factor in her suicide attempts and self-harm, which were strongly influenced by relational connections.

TIERing it all together: mapping the adolescent alchemy in crises

While all three clinical cases involve young people who are experiencing profound emotional distress, their presentations of risk, self-harm, and suicidal ideation are very different in terms of their psychological dynamics, emotional regulation, impulsivity, and relational patterns. We can observe a key difference between the three cases in each adolescent's experience of their internal objects.

Suzanna's psychological state can be described as an arrested state of melancholia, centred on the loss of her internal objects. She mourns these objects deeply yet retains a capacity for attachment, rooted in her relational patterns and her need to feel meaningfully connected.

In contrast, Marianna oscillates between love and hate towards her internal and external objects. This constant vacillation creates emotional volatility and impulsivity, with severe consequences for her relationships and mental state. While Suzanna demonstrates the ability to attach herself to others and process loss to some degree, Marianna's oscillation gives rise to a sadomasochistic relationship with her objects. Her suicidal acts embody this duality: an expression of both love and hate.

On the one hand, suicide represents 'altruistic love', an attempt to free her objects from the burden of her presence. On the other hand, this is an act of profound aggression, inflicting significant pain on her objects by ending her life. This confusion and ambivalence fuel the extreme volatility in her mental state, increasing the risk of repeated self-harm or violence toward herself and her objects. Marianna struggles to differentiate herself from others, remaining enmeshed with her objects. Suzanna, by contrast, experiences the loss of her internal objects, which signals some degree of separation and an emerging capacity to form new, meaningful connections. However, Marianna's intense projections engulf the therapeutic relationship, creating a threatening and non-separate state for both her and the therapist, making the idea of developing a therapeutic relationship highly difficult and complex.

Rudy's case presents a stark contrast to both Suzanna and Marianna. For him, both the internal and external worlds feel depleted, leaving him with an empty, lifeless affect that mirrors the experience of a person already dead. Unlike Marianna, who exhibits emotional intensity, or Suzanna, who shows a capacity for connection, Rudy demonstrates no attachment to his objects, no sense of self, and no vitality. He lacks aggression – an energy that might signal life – and shows no evidence of sexuality or defensive structure. Rudy's presentation is profoundly concerning, aligning with Bion's (1962) concept of *nameless dread* – a state beyond repair. His contemplation of suicide is not framed as an act of aggression or an attempt to resolve emotional conflict but as a pull toward Freud's (1920) idea of the death instinct: a longing to return to an inorganic state. In Rudy's case, the act of self-destruction is not about inflicting pain on others or himself but about seeking an end to existence altogether.

Building towards a psychoanalytic formulation can be instrumental in guiding us toward appropriate and effective care planning. For instance, Suzanna appears capable of engaging in therapy; she can tolerate the emotional difficulties that may arise and use the therapeutic space constructively. In contrast, for Marianna and Rudy, the situation is more complex.

For Marianna, a different approach may be more suitable – one that combines individual therapy with parallel parent work, with regular review meetings where intense feelings such as love and hate can be acknowledged and contained. This could also involve collaboration with the school, advocating for the appointment of a mentor for Marianna and fostering a more holistic support system around her.

In Rudy's case, the priority is managing the acute risk of suicide and keeping him alive. He would likely benefit from regular psychiatric as well as psychotherapeutic reviews, potentially involving a combination of consultations and medication to stabilise his mood. Engaging both parents and the school is essential, aiming to establish a consistent, small core group around him. This group would meet regularly and, where possible, coordinate across services, even involving the local crisis team for periodic phone check-ins. While this may seem intensive, Rudy's presentation highlights the necessity of such a comprehensive approach, one that addresses the gravity of a situation where the stakes are quite literally life and death.

The TIER model offers a structured yet flexible framework for assessing suicide risk in adolescents through a psychoanalytic lens, integrating external influences, underlying risk factors, and the adolescent's internal world. By adopting an exploratory rather than reactive stance when faced with adolescents at risk, we can move beyond surface-level assessments and standard safety checklists, enabling a deeper understanding of the adolescent's crisis and its underlying meaning. Psychoanalytic formulation thus becomes not only a tool for risk assessment but also a crucial framework for conceptualising and designing an appropriate care plan tailored to the young person's needs. Furthermore, it serves as a vital means of therapeutic engagement, facilitating the co-construction of meaning with the adolescent and supporting their journey toward psychological integration and development.

References

Bion, W. R. (1962). The psycho-analytic study of thinking. *International Journal of Psychoanalysis*, 43, 306–310.

Bion, W. R. (1963). Chapter Five. *Elements of Psycho-Analysis*, 4, 17–21. Basic Books.

Campbell, D., & Hale, R. (2017). *Working in the dark: Understanding the pre-suicide state of mind*. Routledge.

Cantrell, A., Sworn, K., Chambers, D., Booth, A., Buck, E. T., & Weich, S. (2024). Factors within the clinical encounter that impact upon risk assessment within child and adolescent mental health services: A rapid realist synthesis. *Health and Social Care Delivery Research*, 12(1), 1–107.

Dickens, G. L., & O'Shea, L. E. (2018). Protective factors in risk assessment schemes for adolescents in mental health and criminal justice populations: A systematic review and meta-analysis of their predictive efficacy. *Adolescent Research Review*, 3(2), 95–112. https://doi.org/10.1007/s40894-017-0062-3

Freud, S. (1920). Beyond the pleasure principle. *The Standard Edition of the Complete Psychological Works of Sigmund Freud*, 18, 1–64. Hogarth Press and the Institute of Psycho-Analysis.

Haidt, J. (2024). *The Anxious Generation: How the Great Rewiring of Childhood is Causing an Epidemic of Mental Illness*. Penguin.

Knoll, L. J., Magis-Weinberg, L., Speekenbrink, M., & Blakemore, S. J. (2015). Social influence on risk perception during adolescence. *Psychological Science*, 26(5), 583–592.

Marty, P. (1968). A major process of somatization: The progressive disorganization. *International Journal of Psychoanalysis*, 49, 246–249.

McDougall, J. (1986). Identifications, neoneeds and neosexualities. *International Journal of Psychoanalysis*, 67, 19–30.

McWilliams, N. (1999). *Psychoanalytic case formulation*. Guilford Press.

McWilliams, N. (2012). Beyond traits: Personality as intersubjective themes. *Journal of Personality Assessment*, 94(6), 563–570.

Mees, P. (2016). A psychoanalytic child psychotherapy contribution to generic assessments. *Clinical Child Psychology and Psychiatry*, 21(1), 133–144.

Perry, S., Cooper, A. M., & Michels, R. (1987). The psychodynamic formulation: Its purpose, structure and clinical application. *American Journal of Psychiatry*, 144(5), 543–550. https://doi.org/10.1176/ajp.144.5.543

Purba, A. K. (2023). The relationship between social media use and adolescent health-risk behaviours (Doctoral dissertation, University of Glasgow).

Rosenberg, B. (1991). Les relations du narcissisme avec la deuxième théorie des pulsions. *Revue française de psychanalyse*, 55, 103–109.

Schnettler, S., & Steinbach, A. (2022). Is adolescent risk behavior associated with cross-household family complexity? An analysis of post-separation families in 42 countries. *Frontiers in Sociology*, 7, 802590.

West, M., Rice, S., & Vella-Brodrick, D. (2023). Adolescent social media use: Cultivating and constraining competence. *International Journal of Qualitative Studies on Health and Well-Being*, 18(1), 2277623.

Winnicott, D. W. (1949/1975). Chapter XIX. Mind and its relation to the psyche-soma. *Through Paediatrics to Psycho-Analysis*, 100, 243–254. Routledge.

Winnicott, D. W. (1968). Adolescent immaturity. *Home Is Where We Start From: Essays by a Psychoanalyst*, 150–166. W.W. Norton & Company.

Winnicott, D. W. (1971). Chapter 11: Contemporary concepts of adolescent development and their implications for higher education. *Playing and Reality*, 17, 138–150. Tavistock Publications.

Part 3

Chapter 8

Reconfiguring adolescent–parent psychotherapy

Empowering relational dynamics to promote adolescent health and growth

Ruth Schmidt Neven

Introduction

This chapter presents a recalibration of our understanding of work with parents of adolescents, reconfiguring the essential interactive nature of this relationship. It identifies the parent–adolescent relationship as one that is, by its nature, deeply intertwined with respect to unconscious processes. These processes become powerfully enacted both in the service of health and growth and in the service of negative experiences and identifications. The task of the therapist is therefore to identify and unravel the complexity of the parent–adolescent relationship.

This approach is in contrast to the generally accepted – and still, I think, limited – approach to what is commonly described as 'parent work' or 'work with parents' within the field of psychoanalytic child psychotherapy. Work with parents has traditionally been perceived as an adjunct to the main focus of child psychotherapy, in which the child or adolescent and their problems take centre stage. In clinical experience, however, we observe that the most enduring therapeutic outcomes for the adolescent or young person rely not only on their changing perceptions of themselves, but also on a significant shift in the way their parents come to view themselves in relation to the adolescent. While structural factors – such as the loss in the UK of the psychiatric social worker profession and the increasing fragmentation of NHS multidisciplinary teams – have made sustained parent work harder to embed in some services, this has at times been compounded by a wider professional culture, both within child psychotherapy and across MDTs, that has been slow to fully recognise the therapeutic centrality of parent work.

I describe five essential components that give rise to the necessity for the reconfiguration of adolescent–parent psychotherapy. The first is attention to the *developmental task* and those elements which are inherent to the task of adolescence (Schmidt Neven, 1996, 2016); the second is attention to reframing the adolescent's problem as an *opportunity* that has a dynamic meaning in parental relationship terms, rather than one that is perceived purely in individual pathology-based linear terms. The conceptual framework of presenting the problem as an opportunity creates a more dynamic framework for therapeutic exploration, rather than one that is solely focused on risk. The latter inevitably leads into medicalised symptomatic

DOI: 10.4324/9781003592778-12

descriptions, as well as, of course, medicalised diagnoses of the young person (Schmidt Neven et al., 2002).

The perception of the problem as the opportunity leads to the third element in this reconfiguration, which is the *widening of the therapeutic frame*. This not only reinstates the role of parents but also pays attention to the everyday experience of the young person within their school, community, and wider cultural context, dimensions that were recognised notably by Winnicott in 'The child, the family and the outside world' (1964/2021). In describing the fourth element in the reconfiguration of adolescent–parent therapy, I suggest that while long-term therapy may be appropriate in some situations for troubled adolescents, time-limited psychotherapy can often resonate more appropriately with the adolescent developmental task, as well as with viewing this period through the lens of developmental transition, which necessarily implies the active participation of parents.

Finally, the fifth essential element takes a values-based stance with respect to the need for parents to assert good authority in relation to their adolescent child, as well as to provide a proper duty of care towards them at a time of major social and technological change.

The marginalisation of parents in the therapeutic process

Attention to the dynamic interaction between children and their parents – including adolescents – has at times been somewhat marginalised in the field of child and adolescent psychotherapy and in some of the accompanying literature and research. Earlier models of training for child psychoanalytic psychotherapists could resemble a kind of therapeutic boarding school for the patients, in which parents were often kept at a distance and received formal feedback only occasionally, perhaps once a term, on their child or adolescent's progress. Sometimes, parents were seen separately by another therapist, but the information passed between the respective therapists tended to remain factual and carefully circumscribed, prioritising the perceived need to, above all else, protect the child's individual therapy. Historically, terms such as 'parent guidance' or 'mother guidance' reflected a discourse confirming this orientation – the primacy of the individual therapy project – leaving little doubt about who possessed the 'right knowledge' about the child or adolescent and who needed to be guided towards this 'knowledge'.

I have addressed this problem (Schmidt Neven, 2017) in the context of challenging articles of faith concerning the practice of individual child psychotherapy laid down by the innovative founders of the profession more than a century ago. How we conduct therapeutic assessments today, in the 21st century, of adolescents with complex mental health needs, requires a different line of approach. If we are to focus on the adolescent – either to the exclusion of parents or with their minimal involvement – then we must provide robust justification for this position that is in line with all current treatment modes.

It is interesting to note in this respect how little impact the clinical experience of a practitioner as significant and prolific as Donald Winnicott has had on child psychotherapeutic training in this regard. As Reeves (2003) points out, Winnicott recognised over his long career that many of the presenting problems in the child (and adolescent) represent 'a latent displaced expression of parental states'. Indeed, Winnicott became increasingly convinced by the young person's natural capacity for growth and healing, given the right environmental provision, and less convinced of the indispensability of full-scale child analysis. In several of his writings (1958, 1964, 1965), he articulated this in terms of an 'economics of therapy', not in the sense of limiting the therapy, but at the deepest level, of promoting what fits the child and young person within the family.

Edwards and Maltby (1998), in a seminal paper, concur with this view and comment on how an interactive, parent-inclusive approach removes the burden from the child or young person of being the nominated patient. They point out how much can be achieved in short-term focused therapy with children and their families, where the unconscious itself can be "surprised" without lengthy interventions.

Deborah Marks (2020) also argues for greater recognition of the importance of work with parents in child psychotherapy and its positive impact on prevention through time-limited intervention. She describes a refreshed perspective of perceiving parenthood itself as 'the patient' in the therapeutic encounter. In this context, she states that distinctions between conscious and unconscious levels of therapeutic engagement become 'artificial and restrictive' (p. 23).

The arrival of family therapy and our growing understanding of the family as a system is different from the type of adolescent–parent therapeutic interaction I describe here. However, it is salutary to note again how this systemic understanding has not always been fully filtered down into child and adolescent therapeutic training, which, in many settings, remains primarily focused on the individual child and adolescent. Family therapist David Campbell (2013), referring to the complexity of family interrelationships, put it succinctly: 'We used to think that the family had a problem, and now we think that the problem has a family. Or the problem has a system around it' (Campbell, 2013, pp. 47–49).

It is therefore difficult to avoid the conclusion that the persistence of an individually focused therapeutic model, often with limited parental involvement, continues to reflect aspects of a more traditional medical model of treatment and cure.

Keeping parents at the margins of therapeutic work comes fully to the fore when working with adolescents and young people, where their exclusion is often perceived as therapeutically justified. In such cases, parental exclusion takes on a position aligned with a sense of virtue, framed as preserving the rights of the adolescent, and supporting their need to move into a state of independence. However, this can risk becoming a default position. A significant number of psychotherapists have displayed an eagerness to uncouple the adolescent and young person from their parents that is often premature and may deny them the opportunity to work through the challenges of transition that inevitably involve their parents. Negotiating transition represents a cornerstone of the adolescent developmental task (as I describe in more detail in what follows), the absence of which leads to a stalemate for the adolescent and often to poorer outcomes.

At times, the involvement of parents in this context is even perceived as a potential contaminant of the 'purity' of the individually focused therapeutic experience. Following on from the IMPACT study by Goodyer et al. (2011) which evaluated the treatment of adolescent depression, Whitefield and Midgley (2015) described a subsidiary study that included interviews with five CAMHS clinicians reflecting on their experiences of working with the parents of these adolescents as part of the research protocol. In their paper, they question as 'a matter of debate' whether parent work should include a focus on their own childhood experiences.

Their findings highlight the anxieties of some of the therapists who struggled with stepping out of the confines of what they perceived to be their essential therapeutic task of 'protecting' the adolescent's treatment. Whitefield and Midgley (2015) describe the expressed concern of child psychotherapists about intruding on revelations about parents' own histories, and their uncertainty about having permission to do so, while simultaneously feeling confronted by the parents' vulnerability and neediness. These reflections point to the ongoing complexity of integrating parent work into settings shaped by an individual treatment frame.

The comments of the child psychotherapists in this study indicate a degree, perhaps, of resistance around fully taking into account the powerful impact of the essential interactive process between the adolescent and their parents, and the possible relational meanings of the adolescent's symptoms in these dynamic terms. In their commentary, Whitefield and Midgley touch on how the potential for what they describe as 'intertwining' – the mutual influence between parent and adolescent – was at times negatively interpreted by the psychotherapists as a possible competition between the parents' needs and those of their adolescent child.

Whitefield and Midgley (2015) differentiate parent work and psychotherapy as though this is a meaningful distinction, with the latter considered to be primarily applicable to the child or adolescent. Most significantly, the authors acknowledge how parent work in general has a peripheral status in our profession, with a lack of guidelines, training, and supervision. The rather worrying phrase 'Learn as you go' mentioned by the child psychotherapists in this study is accompanied by the authors' suggesting that parent work may require what they refer to as 'different parameters' (p. 276), in which the transference relationship specifically is not encouraged. I have previously commented (Schmidt Neven, 2018) on the methodological problems I see associated with the IMPACT study on adolescent depression (Goodyer et al., 2011) and the possible reasons for the less-than-hoped-for outcomes of this study. I made the point then that keeping parents at the margins, which took place in this research, represented an apparently neat construct for research purposes, namely, that of an exclusive focus on psychopathology in the individual adolescent. However, the limited engagement with the parents appeared to contribute not only to a high adolescent dropout rate but also to a denial about the essential interactive process at hand between the adolescents and their parents. I commented further at that time that the exclusive focus on the problematic symptoms in the adolescent generated a reductionist, instrumental approach that is at odds with a meaning-making psychoanalytic or psychodynamic framework.

The marginalising of parents becomes even more pertinent when the adolescent or young adult presents as being at high risk with respect to their mental health. It is not uncommon for professionals in this context to assert that they have 'no time' to involve parents, given what they perceive to be the urgent need of the young person for their attention. This in itself conveys enormous confusion about the presenting problem, as well as confusion about the nature of the primary therapeutic task when it comes to risk management. It avoids the important question of who is, in fact, in charge of the adolescent, namely, the parents or the professionals, and who has a duty of care for the young person?

The last 20 years have disappointingly reflected, more widely, a revisionist conservative approach to understanding mental health and emotional problems. There has been a move away from prevention towards supporting individual medicalised conceptualisations, often under the guise of 'evidence-based practice'. This is the avowed intention, for example, of Ian Goodyer (2014), the principal researcher of the IMPACT study, who has advocated both for drug treatment and for what he described as individual 'behavioural phenotyping' for the treatment of adolescent depression.

This revisionist medicalised approach has contributed to the delegitimising of the role of prevention, which traditionally has always involved parents in a central role (Schmidt Neven, 2008). It has limited learning from earlier preventative projects and programmes, such as the UK national organisation 'exploring parenthood' (Schmidt Neven, 1990/1994). Exploring parenthood, through its group work and partnership between parents and professionals, utilised a psychodynamic approach whereby specialised knowledge could become common knowledge. Most importantly, its emphasis was on empowering parents to build on their own experiences and to own what they know. These are essential elements that form part of the primary therapeutic task, which is that the best outcome is not solely for the psychotherapist to understand the problems of the adolescent but to work empathically alongside their parents to enable them to do so themselves (Schmidt Neven, 1995).

The developmental task: adolescents and parents in transition

The concept of *the developmental task* is central to a consideration of our understanding of the ages and stages of human development from birth to early adulthood, focusing as it does on the essential interrelationship between child and parent for the successful achievement of these tasks: from the managing of bodily functions, through to sleeping, separation, learning, and the capacity for empathy. During adolescence, we recognise the importance of two further developmental tasks in the making, namely, the extension of the capacity for self-regulation and identity formation (Schmidt Neven, 2005a).

Arising in part from Donald Meltzer's (1967) ideas of 'developmental and task confusions', I have elaborated on the use of this framework of developmental tasks in under-fives counselling, in assessment and therapy, and in time-limited psychodynamic therapy with children and adolescents (Schmidt Neven, 2005a, 2005b, 2017). Meltzer acknowledges that the original term 'confusions of zones and modes' is borrowed from the work of Erik Erikson and his lifespan model of human development (1968). Meltzer has used the term 'geographical and zonal confusions' primarily in reference to analytic work in the transference. I have found these terms to also be highly applicable to the ways in which we can both understand and interpret the essential nature of human development, in terms of the tasks that must be achieved at the various ages and stages, from birth through to young adulthood.

Adolescence and early childhood have much in common, both in developmental terms with respect to significant bodily changes and the achievement of mastery and in evoking at times intense, turbulent emotion. Zonal, geographic, and task confusions that remain unresolved from earlier times manifest in adolescence in the form of body preoccupations. These may include eating disorders, high levels of anxiety about separation, and confusion about roles – concerning who is the parent and who is the child.

It is also salutary to note in this respect Meltzer's comments (1989) about how the past focus of psychoanalysis on understanding psychotic processes in adult patients drew us into a cul-de-sac. As he explained, this is because psychoanalytic thinking contributed to our understanding of how the mind can go utterly wrong in its functioning but contributed little to how it can go right. Instead, Meltzer asserts the centrality of growth and development as the drivers of therapeutic inquiry. There is a parallel here with medical training, in which trainees do not commence with the diagnosis of pathology but with an understanding of how the body normally functions.

This conceptual framework overlaps, of course, with Anna Freud's 'developmental lines' (1982) with respect to recognising behaviour that is relevant and appropriate for each age and stage. The fundamental premise of the developmental task in my own formulation is that all developmental transitions are perceived as dynamic and interactive. They rely for their success on evoking the need for transition simultaneously in parents, in order for the child to achieve a successful outcome. In other words, the capacity for change in the adolescent is intrinsically connected with the capacity for change in their parents and caregivers (Schmidt Neven, 2002).

We recognise that the adolescent or young person and their parents have been, since birth, engaged in a deeply interactive and enactive relationship – one that carries complexity, ambivalence, including both positive and negative attributes, and profound mutual influence. In this respect, the position sometimes taken in psychotherapy settings – that adolescent and parent therapy must be carried out entirely separately – can risk being out of touch with the reality of families' experience and the interdependence that shapes adolescent development. The trepidation expressed by child psychotherapists in Whitefield and Midgley's study (2015) – concerning the potential for intertwining between the needs of the adolescent and those of their parents – far from undermining the therapeutic project, is precisely what requires therapeutic attention.

Some simple examples may throw light on this essentially interactive process. We may find parents who ascribe all their child's problems to the stage of adolescence itself, when they have been in denial about the child's problems from the very early years. For example, they may have found it difficult to set boundaries or to have reasonable expectations of their child. They may have dismissed their child's annoying behaviour in the earlier years as 'that's just Billy'. However, they become pained when Billy, now grown in size in adolescence, makes his behaviour impossible to ignore. I have likened this to parents who go into their garden and discover a strange large plant that has taken root which they don't recall having planted.

Billy, in developmental terms, is of course neither mentally nor emotionally in a state of adolescence but remains fixed at a much earlier stage of development. In other words, he has not begun the process of working towards the adolescent developmental task. There are other examples of how children who have lived in their families in a state of benign parental indifference, or what is sometimes described as 'flying below the radar', discover their developmental shortcomings painfully exposed once they move into secondary education. Their hopes of starting out anew in secondary school become dashed when they find themselves completely at a loss in the new school environment and end up refusing to attend. This may lead to their problem becoming formulated as (for example) school refusal, when it more likely represents symptoms of the underlying feelings of helplessness of the young person who has been so ill-prepared for this new phase of their development that requires attention.

In line with Winnicott's dictum about the presenting problem in the child or young person as representing 'a latent displaced expression of parental states' (cited in Reeves, 2003, p. 6), we enter here into the realm of powerful emotional enactments with which psychotherapists will be familiar. We may find an adolescent boy who becomes the 'golden penis' for his mother in the absence of a mature parental sexual relationship; the father who insists on 'reincarnating' his son in his own image, away from the influence of the mother; or the mother who pulls her daughter into a convoluted identification with her, in which neither can achieve any degree of separation. This may lead to a high degree of acting out on the part of the young person in order to free themselves, which can present us with concerns about levels of risk. In turn, the concern about risk becomes the primary focus and diverts our attention from the complex antecedents of the behaviour.

Donald Campbell (2020) refers to the contribution of Mervin Glasser in helping us understand the dilemma in which the adolescent or young person finds themselves. Glasser (e.g. 1992) formulated this dilemma in relation to the 'core complex', a universal life cycle process involving the child's capacity to manage independence primarily from the mother. In situations in which this process of developing independence and individuation becomes compromised through anxiety about separation from, and loss of, the mother, various intrapsychic processes come into play. These involve both a longing to merge with the mother and a simultaneous fear of engulfment by her, with a resultant loss of identity.

Glasser points to how the entrapment for the young person in this continuing destructive cycle can lead to the acting out of aggression as well as suicidal behaviour.

In these predicaments, it may be tempting to help the young person uncouple themselves entirely from their parents and treat them separately, but we need to recognise the omnipotence inherent in this position. As psychotherapists, it is not our task to supersede the role of parents. By doing so, we run the risk of uncoupling the young person from their moorings. Instead, our therapeutic task lies in understanding the meaning of the adolescent's presentation in the context of an important communication to their parents and helping parents understand and respond adequately to this communication.

In a new century, it is also important to consider the role of the mother traditionally writ large in the psychoanalytic literature, as though operating outside of any essential connection with a partner, namely, the father of the child. The language we need to use in involving parents therefore needs to change. It must include *fathering* and *partnering* routinely and at the centre, and the concept of the parenting team as a core principle for the promotion of child and adolescent mental health.

The presenting problem as the opportunity

It is important to note in the course of assessment of adolescents who present with emotional and psychological difficulties that certain fault lines in the personality that become marked and persistent may indicate the presence of prodromal elements, or early signs and symptoms of a more severe and specific mental disorder (Kelleher et al., 2012).

However, the behaviour of the vast majority of young people referred for assessment and psychotherapy, including those who are deemed to be at suicidal risk, may be construed despite their disturbing presentations to represent enactments of unresolved and problematic relationship issues with parents and caregivers. As numerous psychoanalytic and other clinicians have explained (Blos, 1968; Coleman, 2011; Laufer & Laufer, 2019; Winnicott, 1965), adolescence is typically understood as a time of turbulence and emotional intensity, where we may find ourselves as clinicians concerned about the state of mind of the young person one moment while recognising at the next moment that the storm has passed.

Reframing the presenting problem of the adolescent as *the opportunity* opens up an entirely new and dynamic level of interaction. This is one in which we perceive the problem through an interactive lens that gives rise to a conversation that is at once synonymous with the developmental task. These conversations move us from a linear individual pathology focus to one that avoids blame and acknowledges both the centrality of past history, and that of the unconscious in the search for meaning. Ideally, it can lead to actual structural alterations in the way in which parents reconstruct the family.

For example, a previously well-functioning adolescent, in their last years of schooling, becomes apathetic, consistently refuses to hand in work, and eventually fails exams. The school is at a loss to know what to do and calls in the parents. The parents call in the psychotherapist to help the adolescent with instructions, to set them on the correct path towards academic achievement. The psychotherapist discovers in the course of their exchange with the adolescent and their parents that the father had mapped out a blueprint for the future life of the adolescent and has very definite ideas about how this will be achieved. It becomes clear that the adolescent does not want to fulfil the blueprint but feels trapped, not wishing to disappoint their father. They have used their dropping out of school studies as a kind of compromise solution. The mother, who presented herself initially as entirely dominated by her husband, has an extraordinary moment of insight in one of the joint meetings with the adolescent. She stands up for the first time to her husband, disagrees with the blueprint plan, and says she recognises that she must use her authority as the mother to free her child from the predicament in which they find themselves.

This example demonstrates how, in a sense, 'the child is in the parent and the parent is in the child'. Here the father had hoped to create a pathway for their child's development that contains within it elements of his own unfulfilled childhood hopes and aspirations. The mother, by contrast, moves from a position of acquiescence and dependence on her husband to use her authority as an adult and parent. This example illustrates how the negotiating of transition becomes a double task for both the adolescent and their parents.

The presenting problem, however challenging, both for children and adolescents, creates a unique opportunity to gain insight into parental history and what I call the 'working scenario' of everyday family life. One such challenging presentation is that of obsessive-compulsive disorder, which may present in an acute form in adolescence. From a psychodynamic perspective, we may hypothesise that the intensity with which obsessive belief is pursued provides important information about a possible diversion from deeper concerns that cannot be expressed. The obsessive behaviour may be considered a kind of temporary staging post in adolescence for the thoughts, wishes, and fears that are too dangerous to be articulated through normal channels.

A young person may find themselves at odds, for example, with the stated identification of the family culture, with respect to particular religious adherence. Secretly, they may refer to the religious adherence as a 'fairy tale' but dare not openly challenge their parents. Their obsessive and often ritualistic behaviour may be perceived as a compromise solution.

When we view what I describe as 'embedded problems' of this type – that have their antecedents, at least in part, in family relationships – we move from a problem-centred focus to a *person-in-relationship-centred* focus. This is particularly helpful in contrast to a solely biomedical construction of the problem that sets the young person on the trajectory of mental health patient.

Central to the presentation of all obsessive-compulsive behaviours is the recognition that the young person and their parents – and other family members – are trapped together in the problem. For example, the adolescent may insist their parents support the rituals that form part of their obsession and may become furious and threatening if the parents refuse. Since the young person feels controlled by their anxiety, they put their energies into trying to control the people around them. By taking a meaning-making stance, we recognise that the rigidity and insistence of the young person about their self-perception have already pervaded the parents' thinking, who end up walking on eggshells around their child. If we are to help the adolescent, we must help their parents to cease being the servants of the obsession and work towards containing their anxiety.

The particular strength of the adolescent–parent approach that I identify in all therapeutic work is that it provides the necessary scaffold and safety net to contain the anxiety both of the young person and their parents. The scaffold, as a holding and containing framework, is also essentially concerned with providing the facilitating environment for the developmental priorities of the young person. This necessitates attention to a detailed assessment process, one that must involve parents. By taking a parental history, we may discover how the particular vulnerability of the young person, for example, may be connected with severe illness in parents, a stillborn child, or longstanding parental communication difficulties.

In taking a psychodynamic, meaning-making perspective of the adolescent's obsessive behaviour and rituals, we may discover how these reflect aspects both of parental history and concerns, and come to embody the ways in which the young person is trying to explore and make sense of these concerns. For this reason, we would explain to them that we understand how much they need this behaviour, and we would not force them to give it up. The adolescent may be relieved to hear this, which, in turn, may lead them to begin to acknowledge the defensive function of the behaviour. In one such example, an adolescent with body-based obsessive behaviours, on being informed that the therapist would not wrest these obsessive behaviours from them, responded by creating an extraordinarily detailed drawing of their various tics and obsessions. This detailed drawing became the first step in their capacity to take distance from the obsessive tics.

In addition, by responding to the problem as the opportunity and recognising the adolescent experience as one of transition towards health and growth, we have a greater chance to disentangle these conflicts both for the young person and their parents before they become solidified in adult life.

Finally, a word about confidentiality. While we need to take a protective and confidential approach where required, this cannot always be guaranteed in situations of high risk. We also need to be vigilant about what may be a slavish adherence to confidentiality that becomes used as a way of justifying the lack of communication with parents. Clinical experience indicates that young people have a great longing to be understood by their parents; they also want the psychotherapist to be able to hold the complexity of the whole picture.

Widening the therapeutic frame

Working with adolescents, particularly those at high risk, requires that we widen what I call the field of inquiry, which leads, in turn, to *widening the therapeutic frame*. The frame encompasses not only parents but also communicating with the people in the world that the young person inhabits, particularly the school. This, of course, is carried out with the informed consent of both the adolescent and their parents. We recognise that adolescents may present very differently in the school setting than in the home setting, which assists us to avoid jumping to premature conclusions about the presenting problem.

Widening the field and the therapeutic frame enables us to gather an accumulation of findings that allow for greater depth of understanding as well as for the better management of crises. Teachers in the educational environment are under huge pressure, and by offering containment to teaching staff, we provide a collaborative experience that extends the containing, holding function and contributes to better outcomes for young people. The psychotherapist in this process has the function of case manager as well as that of therapist, both of which are ascribed equal value.

There are times when, due to the resistance of the young person, the possibility of therapeutic engagement may be limited. In these situations, we may find ourselves instead having to create *a therapeutic scaffold* around them. For example, an adolescent with longstanding chronic pain for which no organic cause can be found has been out of school for some time. They present to the therapist as fearful of giving up this problem that has a secondary protective function for them, with respect to managing family difficulties. Their parents enrol them in a new school in another town, hoping that this will make for 'a fresh start'. The therapist fears that without support, the young person will relapse and return to their position of incapacity. With the parents' consent, the therapist involves key staff members at the school who are immensely relieved to be part of a treatment plan in which they can help manage the transition of the young person into the school community.

Time-limited psychotherapy and its benefits

We can see how reframing the problem of the adolescent and young person as the opportunity rather than as psychopathology, making parents central to the therapeutic task, understanding the context and developmental meaning of the presentation, and widening the frame to include the school and other relevant services, provide the adolescent and young person with the resources that contribute to a therapeutic scaffold.

Essential to this position is recognising that we are working with a young person in developmental transition, and as such, we are on the side of their inherent capacity for growth and change, rather than solely on the pathological construct of their behaviour. A time-limited approach is particularly apposite in this context, relying as it does on our conviction that, as psychotherapists, we can facilitate radical change, even in a short space of time, by working collaboratively with the key people involved, rather than placing all the burden for change on the adolescent or young person.

Additionally, the psychotherapist is relieved of having to shoulder the burden of creating effective change for the adolescent alone. Their task instead is one of trusting the process and of eliciting and promoting the inherent capacity for development and change in both the adolescent and their parents. It has its parallel in infant–parent relationships, in which, when parents' anxiety is contained, they are able to elicit from the infant what already exists in potential and what Daniel Stern refers to as 'the infant's formidable capacity' (Stern, 1977, p. 33).

When we take a different perspective of time, we also discover that the adolescent and their parents can work productively together in the time between sessions and can helpfully 'fill in the gaps'.

Acknowledging the centrality of the core developmental task and the dynamic nature of change and growth for young people means that we utilise a different framework with respect to time and to what constitutes 'cure'. As Shedler (2006) reminds us, successful psychotherapy is not confined to frequency of sessions or lying on a couch. It 'is an interpersonal process, not an anatomical position' (p. 7).

Time-limited psychotherapy, in this context, makes a demand on the therapist to be active and communicative at all times, in which communication, reflection, and observation are all of a piece and are shared with the adolescent and their parents. This leads, ultimately, to the making of connections, which is the cornerstone of the therapeutic process and sets in train an often entirely new perspective about how behaviour can be understood.

In addition to this, engaging in a more dynamic manner with time (which never stands still) has the potential to engage positively with the idea of a time limit to the therapy as opposed to maintaining an open-ended experience in the unrealistic hope of finding a permanent 'cure' or total personality change. It also instils trust in the therapeutic process that has taken place and affirms and empowers the adolescent and their parents to believe in their own capacity to bring about positive change. This has significant implications as well for acknowledging the duty and responsibility of parents, which I discuss in more detail in what follows.

The flattening of hierarchy between adolescents and their parents

We live in changing times, and these changes contribute to the way in which parents and adolescents commence their formal engagement with the more adult aspects of life. In Western societies, families face myriad problems associated with loss of community and social cohesion, something which was particularly exposed in the worldwide Covid-19 pandemic. The isolation of many parents, poverty, inequality, and economic instability are further stressful factors. However, the most radical change to the parenting task has come from the explosion of information technology (IT). This not only has affected the speed and level of our communication but also has contributed to how we think, feel, and experience our relationships.

One of the most significant implications of the ubiquity of information technology is that, for the first time in our cultural history, it serves to flatten the traditional hierarchy between children, adolescents, and their parents, since all have equal access to what IT has to offer. This leads to the blurring of boundaries between childhood and adulthood that tends to muddle roles. The area of play so specific to the childhood experience becomes both oddly contracted and, at the same time, expanded to include the adult world. For example, this is the case in online gaming, in which both children and parents often participate simultaneously.

The issue of maintaining appropriate parental authority is also challenged through the proliferation of social media. Adolescents can turn to myriad alternative authority figures outside of their parents' control, or even awareness. The impact of the availability of these alternative locations of authority often leads to a sense of urgency to hurry through childhood to assume more adult and, in many cases, prematurely defined identities, particularly with respect to sexuality.

Foundational assumptions regarding how childhood and adolescence are construed may no longer be as enshrined as we would like to believe. The period of childhood and adolescence itself has become contracted, in a move towards premature independence that belies the need for nurturance and containment. The safeguarding of the crucial 20th-century paradigm of distinct developmental time periods that allow children to be children and adolescents to be adolescents, so hard-fought for by educationalists and theorists of child development, is in danger of becoming traduced by a seductive marketing and advertising culture embedded as it is in the technology industry.

The search for identity in a world in which appearance and reality become increasingly blurred creates a particular burden for adolescents and young people. Acheson and Papadima (2023) refer to adolescents' search for identity in current times in the context of an increasing tendency for them to try to frame and understand their distress through mental health diagnoses and the use of psychiatric diagnostic-type explanations. This extraordinary turn of events constitutes a complete about-turn with respect to earlier community concerns regarding the negative implications of labelling. It deserves our careful attention.

The pressing need for adolescents to define themselves in psychiatric terms may arise from their immersion in the cyberuniverse. However, when we consider the implications of the flattening of hierarchy, we may question whether the need on the part of the adolescent for rigidly formulated explanations of ordinary emotions reflects, at least in part, an opting out on the part of parents from providing the kinds of explanations and understanding they require.

It is not unusual for parents to feel themselves at a loss to know how to help their preoccupied, depressed, even suicidal adolescent children. This is not a criticism of parents but points to the need to recognise that the adolescent's capacity to successfully explore their maturational process is intrinsically connected with their parents' own capacity to do so.

The flattening of hierarchy between parents and, in particular, their adolescent children contributes, at least in part, to parents' potential neglect of the need to attend to their own continuing development as mature adults.

Frank Field (2010), the longstanding anti-poverty campaigner, more recently shifted his attention to the problem of the poverty of child–parent relationships, particularly to the under-nurturing of children. Field emphasised the need for attention to the early years of development and how this informs later development, through establishing parenting courses and placing 'parenting and life skills' into the school curriculum.

In the therapeutic encounter we find many parents who have failed to comprehend the absolute position of their duty of care and how this is expressed through the exercising of good parental authority. In many cases, they confuse having authority which is vested in them by virtue of their parenting role with being authoritarian. When parents are confused about the authority vested in them by virtue of their parenting role, they become confused about how to exercise good facilitating authority with respect to their adolescent children.

Psychologist Haim Omer (1999) describes the need for what he calls 'the parental presence' and the need for parents to reclaim their leadership role. He refers to the importance of the 'parental anchoring function' in early childhood, based on presence, self-control, support, and structure, which is of equal importance in parenting adolescents.

It is in this context that psychotherapists need to recalibrate the meaning of the presenting problem and sidestep taking over the parenting role for the adolescent, however tempting at times that may be. Additionally, an over-readiness to rely on uncovering psychopathology rather than on the meaning of the symptom may find parents spending their time in the therapist's waiting room, which is not the correct space for active parenting.

Empowering parents

Empowering parents raises the question of how we can help them to opt in and to take ownership of the authority vested in them to support the developmental transition of their adolescent. This requires both a clinical and a values-based stance on the part of the psychotherapist. Taking a values-based stance implies that parents must be assisted to use and develop their sense of judgement about what is appropriate for their adolescent as a matter of course, and to take responsibility where needed to establish boundaries. This is of particular importance with respect to helping parents assert boundaries between real and 'virtual' life within the family.

Overall, the task of all psychotherapy is to help people find their own voice. This holds particularly true in adolescent psychotherapy, but it is also true for parents. Helping parents to find their own voice and own what they know generates a level of containment for their adolescent children and sets the scene for reflective communication that has the potential to promote resilience for the future.

The clinical stance for the psychotherapist in working with parents to achieve this outcome requires that they be clear about the need to work with both parents wherever possible and to avoid a position that colludes with existing splits between the parents, or with a traditional view that reinforces the mother's sole responsibility for parenting. By excluding or avoiding the involvement of the father, we work with one hand tied behind our backs, since the adolescent may have very different relationships with each parent. Bringing about therapeutic change involves a three-dimensional perspective.

Ultimately, taking an active and interactive approach with parents to address adolescent difficulties generates a greater sense of mastery over relationship problems and enables knowledge and understanding to flourish in the service of development and growth.

References

Acheson, R., & Papadima, M. (2023). The search for identity: Working therapeutically with adolescents in crisis. *Journal of Child Psychotherapy*, 49(1), 95–119.

Blos, P. (1968). Character formation in adolescence. *The Psychoanalytic Study of the Child*, 23(1). Taylor & Francis.

Campbell, D. (2013). Reflections to questions over time: David Campbell in interview with Charlotte Burck. In: C. Burck, S. Barratt, & E. Kavner (eds.), *Positions and polarities in contemporary systemic practice: The legacy of David Campbell* (pp. 47–49). Systemic Thinking and Practice Series. London: Karnac Books.

Campbell, D. (2020). *The core complex, violence and perverse solutions: Mervin Glasser's contribution to psychoanalysis*. London: Routledge.

Coleman, J. (2011). *The nature of adolescence* (4th edition). Hove: Routledge.

Edwards, J., & Maltby, J. (1998). Holding the child in mind: Work with parents and families in a consultation service. *Journal of Child Psychotherapy*, 24(1), 109–133.

Erikson, E. H. (1968). *Identity, youth and crisis*. New York: Norton.

Field, F. (2010). *The foundation years: Preventing poor children from becoming poor adults*. London: HM Government.

Freud, A. (1982). *Psychoanalytic psychology of normal development: The international psycho-analytical library* (C. Yorke, ed.). The Hogarth Press and the Institute of Psychoanalysis.

Glasser, M. (1992). Problems in the psychoanalysis of certain narcissistic disorders. *The International Journal of Psycho-Analysis*, 73(3), 493.

Goodyer, I. (2014, August 11–15). *From phenotypes to therapeutics: Sub-typing depressed youth to aid treatment success and be ready for treatment failure*. Address given to the 21st World Congress of IACAPAP, Durban, South Africa.

Goodyer, I., et al. (2011). Improving Mood with Psychoanalytic and Cognitive Therapies (IMPACT): A pragmatic effectiveness superiority trial to investigate whether specialized psychological treatment reduces the risk for relapse in adolescents with moderate to severe unipolar depression: Study protocol for a randomized controlled trial. *Trials*, (12), 175.

Kelleher, L., Murtagh, A., Molloy, C., Roddy, S., Clarke, M. C., Harley, M., & Cannon, M. (2012). Characterisation of prodromal risk syndromes in young adolescents in the community. A population-based clinical interview study. *Schizophrenia Bulletin*, 38(2), 239–246. https://doi.org/10.1093/schbul/sbr164

Laufer, E., & Laufer, M. (2019). *Adolescence and developmental breakdown: A psychoanalytic view*. Maresfield Library: Routledge.

Marks, D. (2020). Fostering parental growth and enhancing the therapeutic alliance: Key tasks for the child psychotherapist. *Journal of Child Psychotherapy*, 46(1), 20–34.

Meltzer, D., in Astor, J. (1989). A conversation with Donald Meltzer. *Journal of Child Psychotherapy*, 15(1).

Meltzer, D. (1967). *The psychoanalytical process*. Perthshire: Clunie.

Omer, H. (1999). *Parental presence: Reclaiming a leadership role in bringing up our children*. Zeig Tucker and Thelsen, Publishers.

Reeves, C. (2003). *Creative space: A Winnicottian perspective on child psychotherapy in Britain*. Paper presented at a workshop of the European Psychoanalytic Psychotherapy in the Public Sector Conference: Stockholm; published in *Insikten*, No. 4, September 2003.

Schmidt Neven, R. (1990/1994). *Exploring parenthood: A psychodynamic approach for a changing society*. Melbourne, Australia: Australian Council for Educational Research Ltd.

Schmidt Neven, R. (1995). Developing a psychotherapy clinic for children, parents, and young people at a large paediatric hospital in Australia. *Journal of Child Psychotherapy*, 21(1), 91–120.

Schmidt Neven, R. (1996). *Emotional milestones: From birth to adulthood. A psychodynamic approach*. UK: First published by Australian Council for Educational Research and Jessica Kingsley.

Schmidt Neven, R. (2002). Integrative therapy: The dialogue with the unheard child. *Psychotherapy in Australia*, 8(4), 54–62.

Schmidt Neven, R. (2005a). *Core principles of assessment and therapeutic communication with children, parents and families: Towards the promotion of child and family wellbeing*. London and New York: Routledge, Taylor &Francis.

Schmidt Neven, R. (2005b). Under fives counselling: Opportunities for growth, change and development for children and parents. *Journal of Child Psychotherapy*, 31(2), 189–208.

Schmidt Neven, R. (2008). The promotion of emotional well-being for children, parents, and families; What gets in the way? *Educational and Child Psychology*, 25(2), 9–18. British Psychological Society.

Schmidt Neven, R. (2016). Recalibrating our models: Time-limited psychodynamic psychotherapy with children and adolescents: Towards a paradigm shift. *New Associations*, (20).

Schmidt Neven, R. (2017). *Time-limited psychodynamic psychotherapy with children and adolescents: An interactive approach*. London and New York: Routledge, Taylor & Francis.

Schmidt Neven, R. (2018, Summer). IMPACT study response. *Association of Child Psychotherapists Bulletin*, (269).

Schmidt Neven, R., Anderson, V., & Godber, T. (2002). *Rethinking ADHD – an illness for our time: Integrated approaches to helping children at home and at school*. First published: Crows Nest, NSW: Allen & Unwin.

Shedler, J. K. (2006). *That was then, this is now: An introduction to contemporary psychodynamic therapy* (pp. 1–47). www.psychsystems.net/Publications/Shedler

Stern, D. (1977). *The first relationship: Infant and mother*. The Developing Child Series. Cambridge, MA: Harvard University Press.

Whitefield, C., & Midgley, N. (2015). "And when you were a child?": How therapists working with parents alongside individual child psychotherapy bring the past into their work. *Journal of Child Psychotherapy*, 41(3), 272–292.

Winnicott, D. W. (1958). *Collected papers: Through paediatrics to psychoanalysis*. London: Tavistock.

Winnicott, D. W. (1964/2021). *The child, the family, and the outside world*. Penguin UK.

Winnicott, D. W. (1965). *The maturational processes and the facilitating environment*. London: Hogarth.

Chapter 9

Reaching for the unreachable

Working with parents of adolescents who struggle to engage

Victoria Hayward and Paul Bell

As child and adolescent psychotherapists, we spend many years training in how to work with young people who are struggling with their mental health, reflecting on how to support them with their relational difficulties and how to create a therapeutic space that can foster change and growth. But what do we do when young people don't want to see us, when they are unwilling or unable to engage in psychotherapy or, for that matter, therapy of any kind? What can we do that can impact their worsening state of mind, their increased risk-taking, or their deteriorating relationships? How can we reach the unreachable?

By their very nature, adolescents often don't take up the offer from adults of the things they most need. Whilst this is part of the task of separation and individuation so crucial in this developmental phase (Blos, 1960), this resistance can also result in intense conflict, both internal and external; rejection; and ultimately, the loss of the possibility of shift and change. It can be all too easy for clinicians and overstretched mental health services to play into these projections from the adolescent and stop offering interventions or close cases, labelling them as 'difficult to engage' and arguing that they 'can't help them if they won't help themselves'. However, just as Winnicott highlights in reference to the mother–infant dyadic relationship, so too adolescents do not 'exist in isolation separate and independent. . . . [T[hey come with parents, carers, significant adult figures' (Bailey, 2006).

The concept of parent work is very much embedded in child and adolescent psychotherapy, with an extensive body of writing and clinical material demonstrating the value of parents having their own space to reflect on their child, the challenges they face, and the dynamics within the family structure (Jarvis, 2005; Tsiantis, 2000). However, as Bailey (2006) emphasises, the parent work typically is offered alongside a young person's individual psychotherapy, enabling a separate parallel place for the parent who is excluded from the therapy. It is far less common – at least in the UK – for parent work to be offered by child and adolescent psychotherapists when the adolescent in question is not having therapy themselves. But there is a steadily growing body of evidence supporting the efficacy of this kind of parent work (Slade, 2005; Shuttleworth et al., 2017). In fact, when an adolescent is in real crisis, this may be the only intervention possible.

DOI: 10.4324/9781003592778-13

Falling off the developmental track – what do we mean by 'crisis' in adolescence?

There are various ways of using the word 'crisis' in the context of adolescent presentations. Most commonly in mental health services and among clinicians, this term typically refers to a young person reaching a breaking point, alongside an escalation in risk to self, often in the realm of self-harm or suicidality (Fonagy & Target, 1996). There are, of course, breakdowns of other sorts in adolescence that require urgent assistance, and where the risk does not pertain to physical self-harm or suicide but rather to a risk of significant deterioration or complete collapse of the adolescent's relationships. Such situations often manifest as increased volatility in the home environment and high stress levels for those caring for the young person.

Furthermore, we would argue that depending on context and timing, the notion of developmental arrest can be understood as representing a crisis just as much as more overt indications of adolescent breakdown, like deliberate self-harm. Indeed, many of the parents we meet in our clinical work report that whilst their adolescent may not be seen as at imminent risk to themselves (and thus does 'not meet criteria for referral' or is 'not hitting the threshold' in the terminology of under-resourced health services), the impact of not fully engaging with the external world and continuing along the rapid developmental pathway of adolescence toward adulthood can be just as critical. Both adolescents and their parents can be acutely attuned to the speed and flexibility of their adolescent peers in adapting to new environments, reacting to social dynamics of increasing complexity, and managing the complex psychosocial intricacies inherent in romantic and sexual relationships, which are typical of the adolescent period. When, due to either environmental or internal psychological reasons (or often both), an adolescent perceives themselves as failing to meet the standards set by their peers, developmental arrest becomes more likely. Without appropriate intervention, this issue can become entrenched and concerning.

This brings to mind the phrase 'failure to thrive', used by medical professionals to describe infants whose growth has faltered and who are at the lower ends of normative developmental metrics. The shame, worry, and guilt that can be felt by parents hearing this phrase seem also pertinent when considering parents' responses to faltering progress in their adolescent's development. The rapid pace of growth and the importance of developmental windows of opportunity in both infancy and adolescence have long been recognised and understood in psychoanalytic theory and clinical work and are gaining increasing levels of empirical support from the neurosciences too (Sharp et al., 2011). Both infancy and adolescence can, in our view, be critical periods of potentially high risk in the minds of parents supporting their children. As such, we would argue that an adolescent who has fallen off the developmental track – unable to fully engage in education, peer relationships, or family interactions – is equally in crisis. So we will be using the term 'crisis' in this chapter to encompass all of the aforementioned situations where the adolescent is in intense difficulty, whether physically or emotionally.

Lastly, following on from Winnicott's point outlined earlier, we suggest that when an adolescent can be described as being in crisis, then it is likely that the parent presenting to our service is in crisis too. When parents bring their child to us for treatment in child psychotherapy (or, as is the case in this chapter, bring to us the absence of their child and seek the treatment themselves), they have reached an understanding, often after much consideration, that external help is required to solve the problem before them. We are well acquainted with the guilt and worry that arise as a consequence, and of how these are understood and managed clinically in the context of parallel parent work alongside a child engaged in therapy. However, if the young person is not engaged in treatment themselves, the anxiety experienced by parents is likely to be of a somewhat different character.

Firstly, the absence of a trained, observing clinician in regular weekly contact with an at-risk adolescent can heighten the anxiety experienced by the parents, leading to a feeling that they are managing entirely on their own. Secondly, the blurring of generational boundaries inherent in adolescence characterised by the push and pull between infantile and adult states of mind, early attachment concerns, and more adult defensive manoeuvres can altogether create a unique struggle in grasping one's role as a parent in ways that are unique to this developmental stage and entirely unfamiliar to the style of parenting required for babies and younger children. Thirdly, for many parents, the negotiation of their own adolescence and the resolution of typically adolescent internal conflicts can be an ongoing task. Being thus presented with a teenager engaging in high-risk behaviours or who is disengaging from the social world altogether can prove provocative for parents whose own unresolved adolescent difficulties remain influential at both a conscious and an unconscious level.

It is also important to remember that parental identity is established over the course of many years; an adolescent crisis can be experienced as a challenge to parental identity itself. Many parents accessing support report that they 'no longer know their child' or that their relationship with them used to make sense but is now unrecognisable. The unease and shame associated with a suddenly ineffective parental identity and competency can not only be destabilising but also, in some cases, contribute to the difficulties of the adolescent in crisis. As such, thinking about issues with identification, sameness, and difference must be grasped quickly and practically if one is to be of help.

Given all this, it's reasonable to surmise that the crisis observed extends beyond the internal world of the adolescent and is likely to be present and influential in the mind of the parent also. Therefore, in such cases, a clear and structured understanding of parental experience is required.

The central tasks of parent work

Adolescence is a loose, unstructured, hazy time developmentally; there is thus a good argument for the value of offering a structured and clear framework for working with parents. In this chapter, we think about and describe clinical work using a time-limited model first developed by Open Door – a voluntary sector counselling and psychotherapy service for adolescents and young adults – and written about fully elsewhere (Jarvis, 2005; Jarvis et al., 2004; Desatnik et al., 2021). A brief account of the model follows for clarity.

Open Door's Approach to Parenting Teenagers (referred to as APT hereafter) is a brief (6–8 sessions) manualised model of therapeutic intervention for parents of adolescents. It was developed at Open Door Young People's Consultation Service in Haringey, London, and was initially offered as an intervention to parents who were worried about their adolescent but where the adolescent themselves was not accessing therapy (though it has since been broadened for application to a wider range of contexts, including use as a model of parallel parent work where clinically indicated). The aim of APT is to assist parents in thinking about how they are parenting their teenager, and to help them parent more effectively and establish a more balanced relationship with their child (Jarvis et al., 2011).

The theoretical basis for APT is broad, incorporating multiple perspectives, including psychoanalytic developmental theory on the tasks of adolescence, attachment theory, mentalization, and behavioural modelling. Central to the model, from both a technical and theoretical perspective, is the use of a standardised psychometric instrument that measures parental stress – the Stress Index for Parents of Adolescents (SIPA) (Moreira & Canavarro, 2014). This is a 111-point questionnaire designed to elucidate and enumerate the specific stresses inherent in parenting teenagers. Whilst other measures are available for assessing broad parental stress at the time of writing, the SIPA is the only validated measure that assesses the parental stresses that are specifically tied to the adolescent developmental stage, making this instrument extremely useful to the clinician offering APT to parents of adolescents in crisis.

The SIPA measures parental functioning and stress across a range of subdomains, yielding clinically relevant information on parental understanding of adolescent mental health, normative development, and parenting roles (amongst other things). The SIPA is used at the beginning and end of the intervention, and the scores are then discussed and compared. Importantly, when beginning APT work, the clinician will outline that the target of the intervention is neither the parent and their mental health nor the adolescent and their mental health but, rather, the adolescent–parent relationship. A broad measure of the quality of this relationship is provided by the SIPA, and the APT clinician draws attention to this figure in early sessions. The APT therapist will outline that the most effective way for a parent to support their adolescent child in crisis is to develop and promote their relationship with them. Over the course of the work, this involves encouraging the parent to imagine the perspective of the young person, reflect on their own experience as an adolescent, and consider the powerful conscious and unconscious forces influencing their child's behaviour, as well as beginning to understand and tolerate the mental states that underpin this.

The model also incorporates techniques more usual in cognitive behavioural therapy, including psychoeducation and modelling, whereby the therapist provides information on typical adolescent development and psychology and offers help and advice in structuring behavioural or relational experiments designed to facilitate changes in the dynamics of the adolescent–parent relationship. Such experiments might range from making a cup of tea and asking for a chat, to helping complete a UCAS form, or to encouraging an adolescent to access therapy themselves. The adolescent in question is also invited to join in the work and may attend one or two sessions (after the initial sessions with the parent(s) have occurred and a working relationship has been established). The way in which the adolescent is invited by the parent – and this invitation re-attempted if needed – serves to further develop communication between parent and adolescent.

At all times, the manner of communication is more important than the content or result. It is this focus on the communication and the relationship that typifies the APT modality. We would also argue that while this way of working may be described as 'psychoeducation' from a more cognitive-behavioural stance, it can also be considered 'interpretation in the displacement' from a psychoanalytic perspective, whereby instead of making a direct interpretation pertaining to the parent and our understanding of their unconscious processes, we utilise a gentle and less potentially persecutory way of putting our understanding to them.

There can often be an impediment to even beginning the work, for, as Trevatt emphasises, 'parents can feel that to come to a service for parents is an admission of failure and are embarrassed to admit it' (Trevatt, 2009, p. 313). In order to counter this reaction and to be able to create a working therapeutic alliance, he describes how the therapist must reframe this notion, highlighting the bravery it has taken to ask for help, underlining that accessing parent work is actually a positive indication of a capacity to responsibly parent. In doing so, the therapist begins the central task of helping the 'parent to "parent" more effectively by offering containment to them and to their own sometimes overwhelming feelings of loss of control, authority, and a sense of structure' (Trevatt, 2009, p. 313) while simultaneously attempting to hold both the needs of the parents and the needs of the adolescent in mind. Of course, as Trevatt highlights, this can be a 'precarious balance to achieve' (p. 223).

Case study – Mr A

Mr A was concerned about his son Nico, aged 18, who he felt was disintegrating mentally. He described him during the referral phone call as 'falling apart on every level'. Nico had been getting worse for the past year. He had stopped attending college for some months now, had poor self-care and personal hygiene, refused to leave his room for meals, but would binge-eat junk food in the middle of the night, experienced disordered sleep, and had become extremely isolated. He was non-communicative with Mr A, to the point that he had to talk to him through his closed bedroom door – unable to get him to leave his room – and he would only grunt or ignore him in response when he spoke.

Nico was refusing all offers of support, both from Mr A and from college, and his father felt he was heading towards shutting him out completely. He was thus asking for support from us, to know how to help Nico, given this rapid deterioration. Nico had been open to mental health services previously but had not attended the sessions he was offered. Although Nico was struggling immensely and increasingly was not able to engage in life, Mr A was told by the crisis team that he did not meet the threshold for intervention.

When we met, Mr A described a complex and distressing early history for Nico, whom he and his ex-partner, Mr Z, had adopted when he was six years old. He described him as having experienced extreme poverty and deprivation, as well as neglect and abuse in his early life. Although he had initially adjusted well to the adoption and bonded with Mr A, he had struggled increasingly over the years, acting out with aggression at home and at school, engaging in risky behaviours, and then almost fully withdrawing from education, family, and peers as he progressed through adolescence. To add to the already-painful situation, Mr A's relationship had broken down last year, and Mr Z now had almost no contact with Nico.

In our early sessions, Mr A spoke to me about desperately wanting to be able to communicate with Nico, to feel more capable and confident in his ability to support him, and – holding back some tears – to get some kind of pleasure out of parenting again. It seemed important for Mr A to have a space in which to think about his ambivalence towards Nico, and I wondered with him about the ordinary mourning of the loss of the 'younger Nico', with whom he had felt such a connection but who now rejected him so vehemently. I reflected on a central conflict of adolescent development with Mr A, namely, the need to develop autonomy and independence and to reject the authority of adult figures in order to achieve separation, but also the simultaneous pull back to infancy and a wish to regress and be looked after, in fear of the unknown and uncertainty of growing up (Blos, 1960). We thought about how easy it might be, in turn, for him then to respond to these sorts of projections by rejecting Nico further, thus confirming his fears that he might be unwanted and unlovable.

In addition to thinking about the internal and unconscious processes at play, it seemed important to offer Mr A ways of reconnecting with

Nico in the dire external reality they were both experiencing. We spoke at length about the value of trying initially to begin by rebuilding everyday neutral communication, rather than tackling the enormity of the very real and serious issues that were clearly on both of their minds and that were impeding Nico's functioning. Mr A went away from this session with a plan to try to offer to make Nico a hot chocolate as a way of initiating some kind of non-confrontational communication, a seemingly simple gesture, but one which had the potential to be the first step on a significant journey towards repairing their strained relationship. We thought in detail about the ways in which he might do this and how we might understand things from Nico's perspective if he still refused to speak with Mr A.

Mr A returned for our third session and spoke of how he had tried the experiment we had set, giving a coherent narrative of how he had approached things and, ultimately, of a positive outcome. While Nico had initially ignored the offer of a hot drink, as we had discussed in preparation for this, Mr A had subsequently gone back to let him know he had made some biscuits if he wanted to come down for one. To his surprise, Nico had joined him in the kitchen, and they had even made 'chit-chat' while having a biscuit and a drink. He went on to speak about how Nico had also subsequently joined him for dinner on one occasion that week. He felt they had been able to make light conversation on that occasion too.

Although Mr A was able to reflect with me on how different things were beginning to feel with Nico compared to how they had been just a few weeks ago, he subsequently became emotional as he spoke about his ongoing concerns for Nico. He also spoke about how his own experiences growing up had been tough but that he had dealt with it, whereas he felt his own child was not able to manage life in the way other people's children were. It felt important again to acknowledge and think together about his highly ambivalent feelings towards Nico and the context in which his son might be struggling to manage life, feelings that were perhaps exacerbated for Mr A by having adopted a boy who did not grow up to fulfil the fantasy of who he might become. While this is a topic also regularly encountered in parent work with birth parents, it felt important to acknowledge the additional complexity here given the context of adoption. This was followed by a discussion about the ordinary developmental challenges adolescents are likely to face in how they manage things, but also the importance of remembering that, for

Nico, some of these areas of difficulty were likely to be intensified, given his early history.

When Mr A returned the following week, he spoke of noticing that Nico had appeared a little more animated this week, even leaving their home on one occasion to meet up with a friend, whom he subsequently invited back to their flat but checked with his father if this was okay first. As Mr A described this, it was clear he was rather proud of this small gesture. I commented on this, particularly given that it seemed hard for him at times to notice and acknowledge the positive in Nico when so much felt negative. He agreed that was true and felt it was because every time something was going well and he began to be hopeful, things would then take a turn for the worse again. We thought together about the protective aspect of how he was approaching things in his mind, but also how unfortunate it was, too, as it precluded him from being able to enjoy the times that were pleasurable. It also seemed helpful to Mr A to consider together the non-linear developmental trajectory of adolescence and to normalise the likelihood that there would be many ups and downs on Nico's path to adulthood.

In the remaining sessions, Mr A continued to report gradual but significant improvements in his communication and relationship with Nico. He had joined Mr A for dinner again, and on another occasion, they had jointly played a computer game. We spent time thinking about why Nico might struggle with failure and a worry about doing things wrong, hence his difficulty with engaging in education. It seemed helpful to Mr A when I spoke of a protective way in which teenagers might not even attempt something for fear of not succeeding. This also linked in Mr A's mind to a sense for Nico that he might be the cause of his parents' separation, having not been special enough in his own mind to keep Mr Z's interest. Interestingly, Mr A also reported that there had been an incident earlier in the week where he had got cross at Nico and had shouted at him but had then walked away to calm down before returning to apologise and resolve things, which he had managed successfully. Thinking with him about this in the context of the value of rupture and repair (Tronick & Gianino, 1986) seemed helpful and something that he had not really considered in that way before. This also allowed us to think about the paralysing effects of guilt and incompetence, particularly at junctures where an external source of perceived criticism might meet with an internal critical voice, and how, although to an extent these feelings go hand in hand with being a parent, allowing the volume to get too loud risks drowning out the capacity a parent does actually possess (Fonagy et al., 1991).

The ending was complicated and somewhat painful, as endings so often are. While Mr A was able to recognise a marked improvement in certain areas with Nico, he was also overwhelmed by financial worries and his own mental health. He was, however, able to think about how, even though things were far from perfect, he could already see some significant shifts that had begun to occur:

> 'Coming here has been incredibly helpful. I've felt genuinely supported and understood. The blend of practical suggestions – like exploring how to handle certain conversations with him – and your knowledge of adolescence has really helped. When you're parenting a struggling teenager, it can feel very lonely. These sessions reminded me that I'm doing my best.'

In many ways, Nico and Mr A are a perfect example of the families we see and support with this kind of non-parallel parent work. Nico is, as a young man, very much in the throes of the slow crisis of developmental arrest, as described previously. Mr A's worries about his efficacy as a parent, coupled with ambivalent feelings around the unrecognisable adolescent in front of him, are typical examples of the static, sometimes hopeless dynamics facing clinicians. Finding a way to bring some flexibility to entrenched relational dynamics hampered by miscommunication is the first task of APT work.

Fonagy and colleagues' work (Fonagy & Allison, 2014) outlining the development of – and obstructions to – mentalization provides key theoretical understanding for what makes APT such a valuable parent work intervention. Mentalization is described as the imaginative process by which we make sense of the behaviour of others and ourselves as being underpinned by mental states (Sharp et al., 2011). Mentalization in adolescence has been written about extensively elsewhere (Rossouw & Fonagy, 2012), but for the purposes of this chapter, it is important to keep in mind the ways in which this capacity to imagine and represent other people's mental activity can be bolstered and undermined in both adolescents and their parents, with particular reference to attachment stress.

In the work with Mr A, we consistently see the therapist offering Mr A potential ideas about the psychological dynamics underlying Nico's withdrawal and perceived rejection. Importantly, the therapist balances academic understanding of typical adolescent concerns (psychoeducation) with a curious and contingent perspective on the individual family, acknowledging uncertainty as a consequence of respecting the specificity of the dynamics between Mr A and his son and both of their respective histories. This curious and imaginative perspective is typical of the empathetic and thoughtful stance that the therapist both explicitly and implicitly encourages Mr A to take with his son.

This account also highlights many of the key differences between APT work and the kind of parallel parent work more typically offered by child and adolescent psychotherapists. It is notable that while Nico's early history is acknowledged by the therapist as being an important factor in understanding his current mental health and is brought into the sessions when appropriate, extensive detailed examination of this does not form the main focus of the work. In a brief treatment such as APT, time restraints are such that the focus of the work must necessarily be towards what is likely to have the most immediate and sustainable impact on parent–child dynamics, namely, re-establishing communication and strengthening the parent–adolescent relationship. It is also important to note the specificity of goal-setting with Mr A and the way in which the therapist works to bolster Mr A's confidence to try something new with his son. The seemingly small act of offering a hot chocolate to Nico leads to a sequence of events opening the gates to authentic communication between father and son. Mr A perseveres following the initial rejection of the offer (modelling resilience and persistence), which in turn leads to the wished-for non-confrontational communication.

The therapist's attention to Mr A's state of mind – the ambivalence toward, love for, dedication to, and anxiety around his son – seems to be key to the positive outcome reported by Mr A. Fonagy and Allison (2012) suggest that we are only able to effectively mentalize the other if we ourselves feel held in mind and understood to be unique points of subjectivity. This is true of parents managing adolescents in crisis, as well as the adolescents themselves. By offering and modelling a mentalizing stance, the APT therapist is able to explicitly and implicitly offer new ways of thinking about a young person in crisis, which might shift communication into more helpful domains.

Case study – Miss B

Miss B referred herself to the parent service due to struggling in her relationship with her 15-year-old daughter, Maryam. She described a complete breakdown in communication with Maryam, where they now would barely speak. She described the two of them 'like strangers co-existing under one roof'. Miss B felt that Maryam was extremely unmotivated, would sleep all day and then play computer games all night. There had been an acrimonious separation with Maryam's father when she was young, following domestic violence, and she was aware that Maryam still had a difficult relationship with her father, who continued to struggle with his mental health and alcohol addiction. Miss B, however, felt that she simply couldn't relate to the way in which this was affecting Maryam. She spoke of not letting her own difficult past and childhood trauma define her and that she did not want it to be that way for Maryam, who she felt saw herself as a victim and couldn't move on from the difficult relationship with her father and what had happened in the past at all.

Miss B let me know that Maryam had historically self-harmed and had experienced suicidal ideation. She was not sure whether she was still hurting herself or experiencing these thoughts, as Maryam would barely speak to her. Although Maryam had at one point been open to mental health services, she had found it hard to build a relationship with professionals and had been discharged after one or two appointments. Miss B described that Maryam had become extremely withdrawn socially and had not met up with friends in a long time. She also described how Maryam could become extremely confrontational and aggressive at home, especially with her younger siblings, and that Miss B felt she was walking on eggshells at all times.

In our first session, we discussed whether Miss B might feel able to invite Maryam to join one of our sessions in the coming weeks, which she was reluctant to do for fear of being met with rejection or denigration. However, having thought together about the way in which she might proffer such an invitation, the following week, Miss B spoke of her surprise that Maryam had indeed agreed to join us in a fortnight. We used the intervening sessions to try to understand what might be happening for Maryam, both in terms of the challenges of ordinary adolescent development and also regarding her experiences with her father and why it might be difficult for Miss B to empathise with this given her own history. Miss B was also feeling very unsupported as a working single mother at this time, and we soon noticed certain patterns that repeatedly led to conflict between her and Maryam.

Maryam joined us for our fourth session together. She sat in the room slumped in a chair with her hood up. While it took some time and effort to help her feel able to talk, she did contribute to our discussion and was able to tell me about the ways in which she felt judged and berated by her mother. What was apparent to me was that both Miss B and Maryam harboured a wish for things to be different between them and to be able to communicate better. I highlighted this observation to them both. In particular, Maryam wanted to be able to speak to Miss B about things that were important to her but not be treated like a child.

In the subsequent sessions, Miss B described a gradual and ongoing improvement in her relationship with Maryam. There were fewer moments of conflict or full-blown arguments, and while Maryam still did not always do as Miss B asked, we were able to think about why this was hard for Miss B to accept and how she might understand it. Miss B let me know she was finding the sessions helpful, as our discussions enabled her to feel she was not 'shouldering the parenting burden' by herself. She had successfully initiated a conversation with Maryam for them to start thinking about her education. She felt especially proud that, when Maryam had said she wanted to apply for an apprenticeship rather than go to college to study A-levels, Miss B had only responded positively and encouragingly rather than highlighting the challenges of this, which was something she would have done in the past and that she felt would have led to a row between them.

In our final session together, Miss B spoke of how Maryam had asked for her advice on a project she was doing. Miss B felt thrilled to be asked and to have her opinion valued. She spoke of how much less tense things were at home, but how she still constantly doubted herself and found it hard as a single parent. The work we had done around ordinary feelings of guilt and incompetence in parents and our discussions about adolescent development had been helpful. She said, 'Speaking with you made me see that she's her own person – she doesn't have to follow my path'.

There was a significant improvement, according to Miss B, in her communication with Maryam and a reduction in every category of the SIPA she had completed and that we had co-interpreted at the start and end of the intervention. She and Maryam had even planned to have a day out together the following month. Miss B was grateful for the sessions, speaking of the work together being informative in bite-sized, manageable amounts, not overwhelming, and allowing her to have a better understanding of her daughter.

The description of Miss B and Maryam as 'strangers co-existing' typifies the pain of a parent and child isolated from one another but living under the same roof. The account of Maryam as a young person in need of support but unable to meet statutory service requirements for 'engagement' will likely be familiar to anyone working clinically with adolescents in crisis. Miss B's decision to seek help in improving communication between her and her daughter speaks to the hope that someone might be able to see things differently, to offer a way of relating and engaging that might mould to their family rather than the other way around. Maryam's attendance at session four is interesting, particularly given the descriptions of her as someone who tends to disengage from services. Perhaps Maryam was curious about the professional that her mother had been meeting with and about what may have been discussed at these meetings.

Britton (2004) provides a contemporary account of the Oedipal situation that is highly relevant for work with parents of adolescents. He outlines the developmental achievement involved in allowing oneself to tolerate observing a (parental) relationship from which one is excluded, whilst also acknowledging participation in a dyadic relationship that is itself observed by a third party. The hostile, static atmosphere initially described by Miss B in relation to Maryam is suggestive of a dyadic relationship that had not been able so far to accommodate a third thinking position from which the relationship and its complex dynamics could be observed. The APT therapist, by providing this triangulating space, could enable and encourage new perspectives to be taken. Maryam can observe her mother and the APT therapist considering the difficulties at home, and the therapist can observe both sides of a conflict that had previously only been represented by Miss B's perspective.

We might postulate that the provision of a third triangulating perspective enabled Miss B and Maryam to more effectively observe each other's position within a hitherto conflicted and static dyadic relationship. The APT therapist was able to observe this, but also reflect and connote what was shared by both Miss B and Maryam, namely, the wish to communicate with each other more effectively. The positive changes reported by Miss B at the conclusion of the work can be seen as stemming from the external third directing attention toward what is shared rather than what is different. Miss B's statement that '[Maryam's] her own person – she doesn't have to follow [Miss B's] path' further highlights the way in which fixed, non-mentalizing accounts of Maryam's behaviour and identity can be loosened in the context of direct work with a parent.

Case study – Mr and Mrs C

When Mr and Mrs C first came to the service, they presented in such opposing ways that it was hard momentarily to reconcile in my mind that they were dealing with the same situation. While Mr C appeared utterly deflated, distressed, and worn down with concern and frustration about their 16-year-old daughter, Shanice, Mrs C presented as calm, upbeat, and confused as to why Shanice could not simply be happy.

Mrs C had grown up abroad and described how, in her own cultural background, mental health was 'not a thing'. They both spoke of Shanice's volatility and extreme mood swings, her withdrawal from them (and rejection of her father in particular), her perception that they constantly criticised or shouted at her, and her increasing reluctance to attend school. They had observed indications that she was self-harming, but struggled to engage her in talking about this. Although they had organised private therapy for her, she had stopped attending after only a short time.

Her early developmental history gave some indication of the longstanding nature of the difficulties. She was described by her parents as a baby and child who had often presented as fractious and prickly, difficult to soothe, and prone to emotional dysregulation, though she had always succeeded in building relationships with her peers. However, once she had hit adolescence, things had deteriorated further, and now Mr and Mrs C felt they needed some help. While it was clear that in their own couple relationship things were strained, the one thing they could agree on was what they wanted from the parent work: to feel more united as parents and more confident in de-escalating situations with Shanice before they reached a peak.

It felt especially important to create a space in which the splitting of Mr and Mrs C's ambivalence towards Shanice could be named and thought about, in the hope of something more integrated being built (both internally and as a couple) (Klein, 1946).

While Mrs C worked so hard at remaining 'positive' about Shanice and the situation they found themselves in, Mr C said he could barely remain in a room with his daughter; the anger and hatred she left him feeling seemed almost visceral. We thought together about a more ordinary parental experience of being able to hold both positive and negative emotions towards the adolescent simultaneously (Klein, 1935). What gradually became clear in these discussions was that Mr C felt overly identified with the parts of Shanice that, in turn, caused him distress. In perceiving the unpalatable parts of himself in her, he tried to manage this unwanted experience by rejecting Shanice altogether and distancing himself. Mrs C conversely struggled to identify at all with Shanice: 'We're complete opposites in every way', she would say with a broad smile. She needed help to recognise that which she could feel more connected to and identified with, in order to be in touch with the more painful parts of Shanice's own experience.

Shortly after we began meeting, the crisis escalated. Shanice's school contacted her parents to say that a friend had reported finding a note she had written that made reference to wanting to end her life. As advised by the school, her parents took her to A&E; once there, she confirmed that she had been harming herself severely and secretly for many months and had frequent suicidal thoughts. After an assessment, she was deemed safe to go home, though she was to be monitored and reviewed over the coming weeks by the crisis team.

What was interesting to think about with Mr and Mrs C when they attended their next session and described all this, was that, during the protracted hospital visit, Shanice had allowed her father to sit with her. She had even, at one point, reached for his hand to hold. Mr C had been moved by this seemingly small act of connection, and for the first time since we had begun meeting, he spoke with tenderness about his daughter. He talked with sincerity about the confusion he felt when faced with a child who, in some ways, appeared so independent, defiant, and grown up, and yet there were moments now where he could glimpse the little girl he had once felt connected to.

I made a link with his observations and what I perceived as a central conflict of adolescent development – the wish to be big and, at the same time, the wish to remain small, pushing and pulling against each other through this non-linear developmental journey. Mr and Mrs C could really identify with and reflect on this description of what might be going on for Shanice, and we spent the remaining time discussing the importance of them being able to create some scaffolding for her during this turbulent stage, respecting and supporting her need for psychological autonomy and independence while also holding firm but benign boundaries and showing her warmth, in order to attend to the more vulnerable younger part of herself.

In the subsequent sessions, Shanice's parents seemed to be more unified in their appraisal of, and feelings about, the situation with Shanice. Though she continued to display some volatile outbursts, these were handled with greater sensitivity and balance by her parents. On one such occasion, not only did they succeed in de-escalating the circumstances in a way they had never managed previously, but it also resulted in Shanice sitting down with them and articulating further details of the ways in which she had been struggling. While painful to hear, it felt like a reparative moment

> where communication had been re-established, and in which both Shanice
> and her parents were able to recognise that pain and miscommunication
> could ultimately lead to something other than rupture.

The account of work with Mr and Mrs C highlights the importance of theoretical breadth within the APT model and the need for responsiveness on the part of the therapist in utilising the theoretical framework that most appropriately fits the clinical situation. The therapist quickly identifies the highly split positions occupied by Mr and Mrs C, with the father holding all the rage and hostility and the mother experiencing an aloof calm, devoid of the emotional intensity felt by her partner. We might understand this as a reflection of Shanice's internal experience – oscillating between a cut-off calm version of herself that might be able to manage day-to-day life (to a point) on the one hand and a furious, aggressive part of herself that erupts in private moments of punitive self-harm on the other.

It appears that the therapist, through developing their relationship with the couple, was able to help Mr C identify that what he found most provocative in Shanice's behaviour were the actions that reminded him of disavowed intolerable parts of his own identity. A process of projective identification resulted in Mr C identifying with the projected hostile parts of Shanice and then responding aggressively from a position of anger, thus reinforcing to Shanice that there were aspects of her personality which were beyond the pale (Klein, 1946). The link here to secretive private self-harm seems clear.

There is also something typical here of normative adolescent development, namely, the use of projection to defend against unwanted parts of the self and also to split parents so that a combined, integrated thinking position had become impossible. However, the extent to which this would escalate, with the ultimate involvement of a crisis team, demonstrates how rapidly these adolescent internal crises can evolve from a point of concern to a matter of life and death. The developments that both Shanice and her parents made subsequently in being able to communicate with each other more effectively seem to be substantial improvements, offering a more hopeful route out of crisis. It may be that the APT therapist enabled Shanice's parents to see each other's perspective more clearly, thereby reducing the split-off and polarised positions in reality and, through more integrated and collaborative parenting, facilitating better integration in Shanice's mind. This led to her becoming more able to articulate her needs using words rather than action.

Final reflections

In all three of the case studies presented, the APT therapist strives to help parents find new ways of thinking about their adolescent child's motivations, struggles, and behaviours, and to unstick the rigid and unhelpful patterns of interaction that have brought families to seek help in the first place. Often, parents will approach therapeutic work expecting to be given knowledge or skills to deploy at home. This often masks a fantasy that the professional has privileged information that will readily solve problems. While in some minor ways this may be true – and the psychoeducation component of APT speaks to this – the real work lies in helping parents shift from positions of rigidity (whether hostile, ashamed, guilty, or confused) to more thoughtful positions in which they are open to new ways of understanding things. Of course, many factors will influence the viability of this, not least parental attachment styles, early experience, and parents' own experience of adolescence, as well as cultural and familial styles. However, shifting the focus away from behaviour and onto mental states and relationships enables parents to see both their child's perspective and, more importantly, their role in the formation of that perspective – a crucial step towards working towards the possibility of movement and change.

The concept of epistemic trust (Fonagy & Allison, 2014) is particularly helpful for understanding the processes of change within successful APT work. Epistemic trust describes the particular kind of trust that we might develop and employ when assessing whether or not to take in new information from any given person, whether they are a parent, a friend, or a therapist. The social aspect of epistemic trust is key to understanding who it is we can learn from and what they might teach us. In a therapeutic context for parents of adolescents, the therapist's goal is to establish themselves in the mind of the parent as someone who might have helpful knowledge to offer them that may initially contradict their originally held beliefs about the nature of their adolescent child's difficulties but may actually serve to develop the adolescent/parent relationship in ways which ultimately help them both.

Throughout APT, the relationship between parent and adolescent is central and often referenced explicitly as the vehicle of change for the young person. This is made explicit through the assessment of the aforementioned SIPA scores. Indeed, we might understand positive changes in these scores to represent mutual improvements in epistemic trust between parent and child – parents feel less rigid in their understanding of their children and more curious about new explanations while developing confidence that their child might teach them something real about themselves. For their part, adolescents under optimal circumstances come to feel that a parental perspective can be flexible and attuned enough to provide information or ways of being which might help alleviate their distress. Mr C's experience of Shanice reaching to hold his hand poignantly suggests that something in the way they understand and experience each other has changed for the better.

The scenarios and cases presented in this chapter illustrate the complexities and varied challenges of working with parents of adolescents who are in crisis or disengaged from therapeutic support themselves. The APT model offers a structured yet flexible clinical framework that incorporates multiple theoretical perspectives to address the unique needs of each family. By keeping the focus on the parent–adolescent relationship and utilising psychoanalytic theory and understanding, while also incorporating some mentalization-based therapy techniques and cognitive-behavioural approaches, the therapist can facilitate significant improvements in communication and relational dynamics. This, in turn, supports the adolescent's developmental trajectory and overall mental health, demonstrating the value and efficacy of such an approach to parent work in child and adolescent psychotherapy and, most importantly, the possibility of effecting significant change for adolescents in crisis, even if they are not in therapy themselves.

References

Bailey, T. (2006). There's no such thing as an adolescent. In: M. Lanyado, & A. Horne (Eds.), *A Question of Technique* (pp. 123–137). Routledge.

Blos, P. (1960). Separation and individuation in adolescent psychological development. *The Psychoanalytic Study of the Child*, 15, 163–188.

Britton, R. (2004). The Oedipus Complex Today: Clinical Implications. In: J. Steiner (ed.), *The Oedipus Complex: Solutions or Resolutions?* (pp. 17–32). Karnac Books.

Desatnik, A., Jarvis, C., Hickin, N., Taylor, L., Trevatt, D., Tohme, P., & Lorenzini, N. (2021). Preliminary real-world evaluation of an intervention for parents of adolescents: The Open Door Approach to Parenting Teenagers (APT). *Journal of Child and Family Studies*, 30(1), 38–50.

Fonagy, P., & Allison, E. (2012). What is mentalisation? The concept and its foundations in developmental research and social-cognitive neuroscience. In: N. Midgley, & I. Vrouva (Eds.), *Minding the child* (pp. 11–34). Routledge.

Fonagy, P., & Allison, E. (2014). The role of epistemic trust in the development of self. In: P. Rochat (Ed.), *The self in infancy: Theory and research* (pp. 124–141). Elsevier.

Fonagy, P., Steele, M., Steele, H., Moran, G. S., & Higgitt, A. C. (1991). The capacity for understanding mental states: The reflective self in parent and child and its significance for security of attachment. *Infant Mental Health Journal*, 12(3), 201–218.

Fonagy, P., & Target, M. (1996). Predictors of outcome in child psychoanalysis: A retrospective study of former patients. *Journal of the American Psychoanalytic Association*, 44(1), 27–77.

Jarvis, C. (2005). Parenting problems: Research and clinical perspectives on parenting adolescents. *Journal of Child Psychotherapy*, 31(2), 181–197.

Jarvis, C., Trevatt, D., & Desatnik, A. (2011). *Open Door Approach to Parenting Teenagers: APT*. Unpublished training manual, Open Door. London.

Jarvis, C., Trevatt, D., & Drinkwater, D. (2004). Setting up and evaluating a therapeutic parent consultation service: Work in progress. *Journal of Clinical Child Psychology and Psychiatry*, 9(2), 221–235.

Klein, M. (1935). A contribution to the psychogenesis of manic-depressive states. *International Journal of Psycho-Analysis*, 16, 145–174.

Klein, M. (1946). Notes on some schizoid mechanisms. *International Journal of Psycho-Analysis*, 27, 99–110.

Moreira, H., & Canavarro, M. C. (2014). Stress Index of Parenting Adolescents (SIPA): Psychometric properties of a brief multidimensional measure. *Journal of Child and Family Studies*, 23(8), 1314–1325.

Rossouw, T. I., & Fonagy, P. (2012). Mentalization-based treatment for self-harm in adolescents: A randomised controlled trial. *Journal of the American Academy of Child and Adolescent Psychiatry*, 51(12), 1304–1313. https://doi.org/10.1016/j.jaac.2012.09.018

Sharp, C., Pane, H., Ha, C., Venta, A., Patel, A. B., Sturek, J., & Fonagy, P. (2011). Theory of mind and emotion regulation difficulties in adolescents with borderline traits. *Journal of the American Academy of Child & Adolescent Psychiatry*, 50(6), 563–573.

Shuttleworth, J., Britton, J., Keenan, A., & Thomaidis-Zades, K. (2017). Thinking psychoanalytically about mental health services for children, adolescents, and their parents. In: A. Vaspe (Ed.), *Psychoanalysis, the NHS and mental health work today* (pp. 45–62). Routledge.

Slade, A. (2005). Parental reflective functioning: An introduction. *Attachment & Human Development*, 7(3), 269–281.

Trevatt, D. (2009). Adolescents in mind. *Journal of Child Psychotherapy*, 35, 311–314.

Tronick, E. Z., & Gianino, A. (1986). Interactive mismatch and repair: Challenges to the coping infant. *Zero to Three*, 6(3), 1–6.

Tsiantis, J. (Ed.). (2000). *Work with Parents: Psychoanalytic Psychotherapy with Children and Adolescents*. Karnac Books.

Chapter 10

Working with schools to support adolescents in crisis

Rachel Acheson and Catherine Campbell

As has been reflected elsewhere in this book, in recent years, adolescent mental health has been widely perceived to be in crisis. Rates of self-harm (Cybulski et al., 2021), suicidality, and suicide attempts (Royal College of Paediatrics and Child Health, 2020) are on the rise, with a 65% increase in hospital admissions for children and young people due to mental health concerns between 2012 and 2022 (Ward et al., 2025). In parallel, there have been cultural shifts in how mental health difficulties are perceived. There are now more open conversations about mental health in the media, in schools, and amongst young people themselves, resulting in reduced stigma. While these changes may have many positive aspects – such as more young people feeling able to ask for mental health support – they may also have led to an increase in the perception of negative emotions, which may then be understood through the lens of a mental health disorder (Acheson & Papadima, 2023).

The focus of this chapter is on how child and adolescent psychotherapists, and indeed, other mental health professionals, can work with school staff to support adolescents in crisis. We believe it is important for those working therapeutically with adolescents to be concerned with what happens in schools, and with their patients' experience of the educational environment. While most of us will have had experience of school environments personally (through our own or our children's attendance), and some will have worked in schools prior to training, it is important to recognise that much has changed in the education system in relation to mental health over recent years. Cultural and political shifts have increased both the perceived and actual responsibility of schools to be concerned with this aspect of their pupils' lives, and while some in the teaching profession may welcome this change, others may feel ill-equipped and under-resourced to take on this challenge.

While in the UK there is no legal requirement for schools to have mental health services, many schools are now offering some type of mental health support, in the form of counselling, therapy groups, and psychoeducation (Argent, 2021; Barwick, 2002). The 2017 Green Paper 'Transforming children and young people's mental health provision' (Department for health and department for education, 2017) recognised the key role of schools and colleges in early intervention when it comes to students' mental health and proposed the introduction of designated leads of

DOI: 10.4324/9781003592778-14

mental health within these settings. Funding has subsequently been made available for Mental health support teams (MHSTs) within schools, which are usually run by local Clinical commissioning groups (CCGs) and staffed by education mental health practitioners (EMHP). This new initiative has employed and trained Band 4 NHS staff with undergraduate degrees to postgraduate diploma (PGDip) level, aiming to offer low-intensity interventions such as cognitive-behavioural therapy and guided self-help in groups or one-to-one meetings.[1]

The idea behind locating MHSTs in schools was that they would provide ready access to mental health support for young people with mild to moderate mental health difficulties, thereby alleviating pressure on CAMHS, which would then only see cases that were more severe and/or complex. It was also hoped that schools would use this resource to help prevent escalation of mental health difficulties. Subsequent reviews of the project (Ellins et al., 2023) have identified both strengths and weaknesses in its design, acknowledging that staff were sometimes not equipped to manage the complexity of the work they were faced with, and that some schools have not been adequately resourced to engage with the MHSTs.

Another guiding force in how mental health is thought about within schools is the statutory guidance from the Department for education (DfE), 'Keeping children safe in education' (KCSIE, Department for education, 2024b). It sets out the legal responsibilities that govern all schools and colleges in England when carrying out their duties to safeguard and promote the welfare of children under the 18, as well as outlining best practice when it comes to managing safeguarding issues and limiting risk. This document is updated on an annual basis to keep pace with new safeguarding challenges (e.g. online abuse, radicalisation, and peer-on-peer violence) and has developed significantly in recent years, tripling in length between 2015 and 2022.

Despite – and in some ways, because of – its comprehensiveness, KCSIE has faced criticisms, particularly with regard to the increased workload it can place on staff who may not feel resourced to implement its recommendations effectively (King, 2022). In addition, this document may represent an unintentional shift in focus, with the stated purpose of schools – to provide education – being usurped by a different purpose: to promote young people's wellbeing and development.

In this chapter, we address the challenges faced by school staff who interact with adolescents in distress and reflect on how child and adolescent psychotherapists can support schools in understanding and responding to these difficulties. Due to the consistent and close contact school staff have with their students, they are in a unique position to offer insight into young people's state of mind and behaviour and play a key role in supporting their recovery. However, this position can become overwhelming when a young person is in crisis, and school staff need to be recognised and embraced as vital parts of the network in order for this to be sustainable. We will thus consider here the ways in which child psychotherapists and schools can work together to understand and support young people struggling with their mental health, particularly when they are in crisis.

By using case vignettes, we hope to shed light on the kinds of dynamics that can occur when a student is in crisis, whether due to self-harm, suicidality, or school attendance difficulties. Before delving into these, we would like to first consider the importance of understanding adolescents' inner worlds, by looking at ordinary adolescent development, particularly as it pertains to school life.

Adolescent development

The understanding of adolescent development contributes to our understanding of *how* adolescent risk behaviours can present within schools. Adolescence is a period of profound growth and transformation – a bridge between the psychic worlds of childhood and adulthood. This can be experienced as exciting, but it can also be fraught with anxiety and disappointments. Freud (1905) positions adolescence as both a renewal and a reorganisation of the psychic structures formed during earlier developmental phases. Margot Waddell (2002) encapsulates the complexity of the adolescent transition, observing:

> For adolescents the psychic agenda is a demanding one: the negotiation of the relationship between adult and infantile structures; the transition from life in the family to life in the world; the finding and establishing of an identity, especially in sexual terms; in short, the capacity to manage separation, loss, choice, independence, and perhaps disillusionment with life on the outside.
>
> (p. 140)

In ordinary development, the adolescent psyche grapples with the resurgence of earlier conflicts and impulses, juxtaposed with the demands of forging a new identity, propelled by biological changes and sexual development. Freud's conception of adolescence highlights the reawakening of infantile desires and the profound reworking of Oedipal dynamics, which had been temporarily subdued during the latency period. These re-emerging conflicts are not simply a return to earlier stages but a recontextualisation within a developing framework of adult sexuality and autonomy.

This back-and-forth movement can be observed in the adolescent's emotional and relational world, which inevitably informs their experience of school life. At times, an adolescent may quite normally exhibit regressive behaviours, seeking the comfort and safety of parental care. At other times, they may completely reject such comforts, seeking instead to assert their burgeoning sense of self in relationships outside the family. This struggle mirrors the broader psychoanalytic understanding of development as non-linear, characterised by advances and retreats that ultimately – and hopefully – foster integration.

To facilitate the move towards greater independence, risk-taking plays an important role. It enables the adolescent to develop a more robust sense of self, where experimentation with one's limits can be experienced. In her book 'Coming of age: how adolescence shapes us' (2024), Lucy Foulkes argues that adolescents don't partake in risky behaviour mainly because of their sense of invincibility (as is often assumed); rather, they may proceed to take risks regardless of the potential dangers – which they're mostly aware of – in order to fit in and maintain social standing. Thus, risk-taking can play an important role in adolescents' social development and identity formation, as part of the process of belonging and fitting in during this period. Foulkes also highlights that overprotecting adolescents can hinder their ability to manage anxiety and develop resilience, as well as undermine their sense of belonging in their peer group.

The task of establishing an identity, especially in sexual terms, is central to adolescent development. Freud emphasised that the integration of sexual drives within a cohesive sense of self is not a straightforward process driven solely by biology and hormones, but one fraught with ambivalence and anxiety, as well as the pleasures that sexuality brings. Adolescents during these years must navigate the gradual weakening of childhood identifications while forming new attachments and ideals. This process is deeply tied to the adolescent's capacity to tolerate separation and loss. Separation from parental figures, both literal and symbolic, is essential for growth but can often be experienced as destabilising.

Waddell's (2002) observation that adolescence entails grappling with 'disillusionment with life on the outside' speaks to the inevitable confrontation with reality that can't be avoided during this stage. Fantasies of omnipotence or perfect fulfilment, carried over from childhood, will most likely be challenged by the demands of external relationships and societal expectations. While this normal disillusionment can often provoke anxiety or defensive retreat, it also eventually offers the possibility of greater realism and emotional growth.

From our position as child and adolescent psychotherapists who have worked in various settings with adolescents, we know that they come to the attention of school staff or CAMHS when something has disrupted the ordinary adolescent trajectory we have described. In many cases, instead of healthy risk-taking, something more concerning may be starting to develop. Although the behaviours that bring adolescents to the attention of therapists or school counsellors are not necessarily indicators of serious mental illness, they do need to be addressed and understood. To think about this in more depth, we will now move to an exploration of how adolescent crisis and risk can present and how we, as child psychotherapists, think about working with these difficulties within a school setting or within CAMHS teams alongside school staff.

Adolescent crisis

In this chapter, we define crisis and risk as they pertain to the phenomena of self-harm and suicidality, which encompass both thoughts and attempts in adolescence. While often conflated in conversations about adolescent crisis, self-harm and suicidality are two distinct phenomena. Psychoanalytic theory emphasises the unconscious communication with the object inherent in both, defining self-harm as 'damaging and torturing the self's body to torture the mind of the other. By contrast, suicide aims to kill the self's body to create a permanent epitaph in the mind of the other' (Campbell & Hale, 2017, p. 97). But we believe that during adolescence there are also many forms of self-harm and suicidality that can be strongly influenced by culture (Le Breton, 2017). With both self-harm and suicidality, it is therefore critically important to understand the context in which these occur.

Crises during adolescence sometimes emerge as expressions of profound internal conflict, signalling a breakdown in the adolescent's ability to manage overwhelming emotions, unmet developmental needs, or unresolved relational traumas. Drawing on psychoanalytic theory, such crises can be understood as manifestations of a disrupted self-structure, where the adolescent's ego may struggle to mediate between internal drives and external realities. However, the self-harming act may, in some cases, be misunderstood as purely destructive, when in fact it can paradoxically serve as a means of psychic survival – an attempt to exert control, to articulate unspoken pain, and even to reconnect with a sense of aliveness in the face of psychic deadness. For some, it can also be a means of experimentation. Risk-taking, in this context, can reflect the adolescent's ambivalent negotiation of life and death, driven by the interplay of Thanatos (the death drive) and Eros (the life drive), as conceptualised by Freud (1920). In addition, aggression against one's body may also serve as an unconscious attempt by the adolescent to achieve other important aims, such as prompting others to notice, listen to, or worry about them.

While self-harm symptoms may seem similar on the surface, we must always be curious about their meaning, and we emphasise the importance of understanding this meaning for each individual and family, and avoiding assumptions about what it signifies. By situating self-harm and suicidality within this framework, we aim to view an emerging crisis as a communication that needs to be understood. Although for some adolescents self-harm and suicidality can be signs of longer-term psychiatric illness, for many, the self-harm and suicidal thoughts subside relatively quickly, once they get a sense that their communication has been understood.

Thus, a psychotherapeutic approach that seeks to address both internal conflicts and explore the broader social factors in the young person's life – including family, friends, and school – can be a particularly effective way of containing risk and preventing further escalation.

However, for teachers supporting students in crisis, the experience can understandably be fraught with anxiety. We would now like to take a closer look at the kinds of challenges that can arise in such situations and think about how we might understand them from a psychoanalytic perspective.

Challenges faced by school staff working with adolescents in crisis

In 2023, we had the opportunity to present a version of this chapter at a conference titled 'Therapeutic work in schools'. Hearing directly from school leaders and safeguarding officers about the challenges they face in their work was illuminating, with many expressing concerns about the growing pressure within schools to fill the gaps left by cuts to social care and NHS mental health services.

What also emerged was a perception that the social contract between schools and families has broken down post-pandemic – an observation that was also recently voiced by former Chief Ofsted inspector Amanda Spielman. She defined this social contract as an 'unwritten agreement (that) sees parents get their children to school every day and respect the school's policies and approach' (Ofsted, 2023). Government data shows that many pupils have struggled to return to the classroom full time following prolonged periods at home during the pandemic, with a 150% rise in the number of pupils classed as 'severely absent' during the 2023/24 academic year, compared to pre-pandemic levels (Office for National Statistics, 2024). *The Guardian* has reported that this trend can be strongly attributed to a rise in mental health issues and that parents are 'unduly cautious' when keeping their children off school (Adams, 2024). While many schools have introduced group mental health interventions, recent research suggests these may be harmful to those who are already at risk (Guzman-Holst et al., 2025).

School staff may feel more attuned than mental health professionals to the day-to-day realities of increasing rates of child poverty in the UK, which currently stands at 30% (Department for Work and Pensions, 2024). As a result, many teachers have found themselves regularly stepping beyond their role in education, feeling at times as though they must also function as therapists, social workers, and even surrogate parents – often without adequate time or training to perform these functions. Unsurprisingly, this (along with poor pay and increased bureaucracy) has contributed to record numbers of teachers leaving the profession, with many teaching posts currently vacant (Department for Education, 2023).

At times, teaching staff may also find themselves pulled out of their usual teaching role when dealing with a student who may, for example, have disclosed self-harm or suicidal thoughts. In our experience as child and adolescent psychotherapists, the effect that adolescents have on the teaching staff can be profound. While many who are drawn to teaching or working in schools may consciously feel they want to support young people, we have observed over the years how staff can often be drawn to act beyond their roles and responsibilities when it comes to their care of these young people. There are many obvious reasons for this, including increased incidence of emotional difficulties in young people, inadequate resources within schools, and long CAMHS waiting lists.

However, these realities aside, as psychoanalytic practitioners we recognise that school staff will be affected by the pupils they work with on an unconscious level, too, and when these pupils are in a mental health crisis, this effect may be acute. Legislation, such as KCSIE, seeks to outline a school's role and responsibility in relation to pupil welfare, but what is less clear is how school staff can navigate the human interactions that constitute supporting pupils emotionally, and how this differs from what other settings (family, social services, CAMHS, etc.) might offer.

In a therapy setting, we can take time to observe unfolding dynamics between ourselves and the adolescents we work with, alongside benefitting from training and ongoing clinical supervision that equip us to make use of our observations. Even with these structures in place, highly skilled psychotherapists can, at times, find themselves acting out. Within schools, time for exploration can be limited, as school staff are balancing multiple responsibilities while at the same time having to think about all the students, not just one. This means there is often little space for reflection when a crisis emerges for one student, making it considerably more likely that school staff are left alone to manage the anxiety that such a crisis can evoke.

As we know, anxiety that cannot be made sense of and contained is likely to be defended against in various ways. It is not surprising that school staff may need to defend against anxiety in order to continue operating in other parts of their jobs. The characteristic ways we have observed school staff manage these anxieties include over-identifying with their students, splitting within and between teams, and at the extreme end, denial, repression, and grandiosity. These tendencies can sometimes result in undermining parental authority or in neglecting the necessary involvement of parents.

Over-identification with young people in crisis

Over-identification with a young person who is struggling can happen both in a therapy setting and in a school setting. In a school setting, it can lead staff to unconsciously protect themselves against the anxiety arising from crisis situations by, in some cases, over-offering support to the student, as we explore later. The over-identification reflects the understandable wish to help and sometimes even to rescue the young person.

As psychoanalytically trained professionals, we are taught to observe and take note of the times we are moved to act outside the boundaries of the therapy. It's true that sometimes, when working with adolescents in an acute crisis, stepping outside the therapy framework may be temporarily necessary. For example, we may sometimes ask a young person to remain in the clinic and be collected by a parent following a difficult session. Such a decision could have many possible meanings, which need to be thought about, with consideration given to the change in the therapeutic frame this entails.

By comparison, the school day and all the contacts with teachers and school staff through which aspects of a young person's emotional life are unveiled are considerably more complex and less structured. Students and teachers will often share spaces such as dining halls and spend time together in semi-formal settings, such as school trips and extracurricular activities, all of which allow important relationships to develop but, at the same time, create complexities in terms of how risk is handled.

In all settings, including schools, being confronted with an adolescent in distress can lead to a strong wish to do what one can to support them. This is what can lead to over-identification with the adolescent. As the following example shows, in school settings this dynamic can become particularly complicated:

Mrs Lyons is a full-time English teacher in a secondary school, with her own young family at home. She recently joined the school and is enjoying getting to know the school culture, other staff, and pupils. She has a form class of Year 8 pupils, one of whom, Zara, has been referred to CAMHS due to self-harm by cutting and suicidal thoughts.

Zara frequently becomes emotional during the school day and often needs to leave class. The school policy is that Zara should attend the medical room when in distress, but Zara then becomes frustrated with the nursing staff, who often encourage her to return to class.

Mrs Lyons is called in to support Zara. Unsure of how to proceed, she suggests that Zara spend time in her department office while she calms down. This soon becomes a pattern, and while, according to school policy, Zara should not be allowed in this part of the school, she is soon spending large parts of the day there. Other staff members are understandably unhappy about this situation, as they feel they have lost a valuable area to work in and have private conversations. Meanwhile, Mrs Lyons feels increasingly stuck and frustrated by the situation. She wants to help Zara but also feels imposed upon and under pressure to 'resolve' the situation. As Mrs Lyons is unable to support Zara in returning to the normal support structures on subsequent days, Zara's behaviour soon leads to her regularly intruding on her time and staff-only spaces.

As all this unfolds, and despite Mrs Lyons's efforts, Zara doesn't seem to be improving.

While Mrs Lyons is, of course, attempting to support Zara in this scenario, she is also allowing boundary-breaking to become habitual in a way that ultimately is not supportive. Rather, what is happening ends up reinforcing the idea that the normal environmental provision of a classroom, teacher, and if need be, medical room is *not sufficient* to contain this young person.

One can imagine that Mrs Lyons may have initially been responding to a need in Zara for 'something more' (Stern et al., 1998). The initial offer may have represented a moment of meeting between her and the student, similar to what can occur in therapy, as described by Lanyado (2017). The normal relationships within a school environment, such as the one a form teacher may have with a pupil, are incredibly important for pupil welfare, as they allow pupils to be known and understood as individuals within an institution and mean that individualised responses, such as the one described earlier, can sometimes occur and be useful.

We can wonder why the setting of certain boundaries felt difficult for Mrs Lyons. Was it her own position as a mother of young children that meant she was more readily in touch with Zara's needs and therefore less able to entrust her to the care of others? Or was it her lack of familiarity with the school and her sense of overwhelm that meant she may have identified with Zara's wish for her own quiet space?

On a simple level, we can surmise that Mrs Lyons may not have had the time and support she needed to think in detail about how best to support her pupil. When questioned, she would express a fear that the supportive relationship she had with Zara would break down if she tried to set limits to her behaviour, and that this constituted a risk.

However, by weakening her relationship with the other support structures in school that were already readily available to her, Mrs Lyons ended up contributing to a situation where Zara's wellbeing became dependent on her presence. This also created a split in the team, where Mrs Lyons became over-identified with Zara's needs, meaning that other staff members disconnected from this student and thus underestimated the risk she posed to herself.

At times like these, when a situation becomes out of hand, staff members or school policies around managing adolescents' mental health difficulties can often swing too far the other way. For example, we have been involved in cases where, after a situation such as the one described previously, a teacher may then end up completely withdrawing the offer of support to a young person, rather than remaining involved, albeit with boundaries in place. This swing from overidentification with the pupil to withdrawal of involvement is likely to leave the young person feeling confused or abandoned.

Setting limits and offering support

We have also encountered schools that, in an effort to provide appropriate support to their pupils, develop policies that put troubled young people either on a 'behavioural' pathway, or a 'mental health' pathway, where the first involves clear behaviourally based rewards and punishments, while the latter involves empathic understanding and a considerably looser interpretation of school rules. The reality, though, is that each pupil presents their own complex picture of strengths and difficulties, of 'behaviour' and 'mental health', with various variations and fluctuations within one and the same person. And while it is important for pupils to have an understanding of what reactions their behaviour will elicit within the school environment, it is also important that these responses are overseen by an individual or team, with the capacity to think and feel what is being communicated. The following example shows how a school can be supportive of a pupil in crisis while also setting limits to their behaviour:

Carris is in Year 9 and is a looked-after child in a long-term foster placement. Her birth mother re-initiated contact in the last year, after four years of them not having seen each other. It becomes clear that Carris is sensitive, emotional, and quick to anger after these contact meetings and has been struggling with her friendships as a result.

It has recently come to light that Carris has been self-harming by burning her fingertips and cutting the base of her feet. Following a visit with her mother over the weekend, Carris storms out of a science class after swearing at the teacher, who has asked her to stop chatting. She goes to the medical room and becomes very emotional there but is able to accept comfort from the nursing staff.

Carris spends the rest of the morning there, and after a conversation with her form tutor at lunch, they agree that she will return to class that afternoon. They meet together with her science teacher the following day so that Carris can have the opportunity to apologise, and they agree to a lunchtime detention that she sits the following week.

Although it is not the responsibility of schools to treat the emotional difficulties of students, they play a vital role in providing support through their day-to-day containment, fostering through these ordinary interactions emotional regulation and helping students develop self-awareness. In the earlier example, we note that Carris has had several opportunities to reflect on her behaviour with trusted adults, as well as to reflect on the impact she has on those around her. The school's willingness to connect with Carris in her moment of distress, as well as to foster opportunities for growth while doing so, have meant that they are supporting her in staying safe, without compromising her overall emotional development.

However, the defences that can occur against the anxiety evoked by such situations, as described earlier, may, in some cases, mean that schools feel fearful when confronting adolescents in crisis. When that occurs, this can deprive students of the valuable benefits that a supportive and containing school environment can offer.

To address the kind of complex dynamics described, we propose that schools operate on a strong assumption of joint work with families and external agencies from the outset. When NHS services are overstretched, with long waiting lists, and schools are also dealing with their own additional pressures, time for these networks to think together can be limited. But these contacts – even through a brief email or quick telephone call – ultimately go a long way toward allowing the development of joint formulation and avoiding splitting, where one group or one person feels they are carrying all the burden of concern. This brings us to a closer exploration of the way CAMHS and schools can work together.

Joint work

When schools are feeling overstretched, it is easy to overlook or underestimate some fundamental ideas that most school staff, given the right support, time, and space, can use to contain an adolescent in crisis. Some of these ideas may sound basic: they include the importance of listening to students and validating their concerns while also respecting their need for privacy; they also involve encouraging the young person to get back to class within a reasonable time frame (as much as possible). When these simple steps are followed consistently, they can provide a containing function within the school. The symbolic message of these interventions is, of course, that *it is possible to work through difficult feelings.* However, 'to offer containment requires the adults, whatever their role, to be open to the feeling states of the children and young people without being overwhelmed by them' (Youell, 2006, p. 60).

All this can sound easier said than done, but it is not always clear to the adults (including therapists and parents) how at risk a young person is. For schools to think together with CAMHS about this can be helpful and possibly 'offer a degree of containment to the container' (Youell, 2006, p. 61).

Traditionally, psychotherapy with adolescents has placed emphasis on the task of separation/individuation of the young person and has prioritised the individual space for the adolescent. Often, parent work and close liaison with school were only offered at a later stage of treatment, when and if it was deemed necessary. While individual work is undoubtedly important, when working with adolescents in crisis, strengthening the circles of support around the young person from the outset is also a crucial aspect in understanding and addressing the crisis, thus reducing risk (see chapter 13 of this book).

Ruth Schmidt Neven makes the argument for greater parent involvement during the secondary school years:

> Often parental involvement is encouraged in primary school, but actively discouraged in secondary schools as it is seen as preventing the young person from becoming independent. This signifies confusion about the nature of independence and about the joint learning tasks for adolescents in secondary school . . . [Y]oung people cannot move into independence until they have been appropriately dependent.
>
> (Schmidt Neven, Podcast: The new ecology: A whole classroom, whole school, whole community approach, 2003)

Structures that already exist, such as Team around the family (TAF) meetings – where school staff, parents, and other agencies such as CAMHS and social services meet – are crucial. In these meetings, the network around the young person comes together to collectively think about the adolescent in crisis; these meetings play an important role in enabling a joint formulation to be worked on and can enhance clarity about the difficulties and ways to support the young person. When a jointly constructed formulation is held in mind by the network, it reduces the risk of splitting and enables a more containing response to concerning behaviour and situations.

As psychotherapists, we draw heavily on our countertransference feelings in the therapy room to help us understand the feelings we experience 'as a result of the patient's influence on [our] unconscious' (Freud, 1910, p. 144), which can include an 'empathic resonance with the patient's felt conflicts' (p. 61). We use our countertransference to gain a deeper understanding of ourselves as therapists, of our patients, and of the relationship between us.

Work discussion groups

Taking this a step further, professionals can benefit from noticing and being curious about the feelings evoked in them by the other – including, in this case, the student in crisis. Many schools have seen the benefits of work discussion groups for their staff members, particularly when dealing with situations involving adolescents at risk that evoke strong feelings (Jackson, 2002, 2008).

These discussion groups allow a safe space for staff to reflect on their concerns about what's occurring with their students. They can also allow them to voice the feelings a particular young person may stir up in them, including sympathy, guilt, panic, incompetence, frustration, anger, or denial – all of them useful feelings to be aware of. When such feelings are brought to light and can be thought about, they are less likely to be acted upon in an unthinking way.

A therapist who runs such a group can work together with the school staff to make sense of these feelings and understand what they might mean in relation to a particular young person. Jackson and Berkley (2020) write powerfully about the value of psychoanalytically informed thinking spaces for school leaders (through the medium of executive coaching), in helping them be aware of the unconscious dynamics at play within their school and to develop their self-awareness. Interventions like these by psychoanalytically trained clinicians can also help bring into consciousness the powerful dynamics of transference and countertransference that often arise between students and staff during a crisis.

Campbell and Hale (2007) have written about the impact that an individual's self-harm can have on institutions, which is particularly apt when thinking about schools:

> In the act of self-mutilation, the object (now the therapist or institution) is both sought and clung to in desperate need, and at the same time attacked in violent reprisal and to escape intrusive control. . . . [This] stimulates in us as professional staff simultaneous and dramatically opposed emotions – protective concern versus dismissive anger, cynicism and reprisal, affection versus revulsion. Our minds struggle and frequently fail to make sense of these contradictory experiences reflecting as they do the experiences of the patient. The professional's burnt out state of mind may function to remove them from situations that are felt to be traumatic.
>
> (Campbell & Hale, 2007)

When school staff are supported in noticing their reactions and feelings – which include their countertransference in relation to the students – it contributes to being able to provide a containing function both for the young person and for the member of staff. We have found Bion's concept of container–contained (1959, 1962) a useful way to think about what we can offer. Through being available to school staff (on the end of the phone, in meetings, etc.), building a relationship, and being receptive and interested in their perspective (including countertransference material), we have been able to offer true containment through alpha function. This allows unconscious communications (beta elements) to gradually become thoughts, which can then become part of a shared formulation that can inform next steps.

School staff who feel they have been understood and contained then often feel they have greater capacity to understand and contain the adolescent. Difficult feelings are then less likely to be acted upon or to get projected back into the young person, or into other parts of the network around the child.

Safety planning

The care and concern for students, coupled with the understandable anxiety in the professional network when it comes to risk, can sometimes lead to complicated and highly restrictive safety plans. We would argue that at times these plans offer a *false* sense of safety, as they may lull staff into thinking they can *do* something to stop the young person from hurting themselves. This can, in some cases, reinforce further regression in the adolescent, leaving them feeling controlled, rather than understood. In turn, feeling controlled can prompt further self-harming action in a student.

There is also the risk that the safety measures (such as frequently checking bags for implements that could be used for self-harm) may either provoke excitement in the young person, increase their anxiety, or lead them to feel that the only way to get the support they need is by acting out through self-harm. There have been students over the years who have explicitly explained all these possibilities to us in therapy sessions.

Instead, we feel that the emphasis should ideally be on a less rigid, more relational approach to monitoring risk. This is not to suggest that safety plans are unnecessary. In fact, there are many things that can be helpful to include in them. For instance, it can be helpful to construct a safety plan that might involve parents collecting or dropping off the teenager at school for a period of time or making sure the young person knows who within the school they can contact in a crisis. In more severe cases of self-harm, or in the case of a suicide attempt, it would be important for the young person to be taken to the Accident and emergency department (A&E). However, other measures, such as the daily bag checks mentioned earlier, or regular checks for self-harm scars on arms, might be less helpful to include, as they focus more specifically on the symptom.

Safety planning must take account of a young person's need to have their anxiety recognised, while balancing this against the need for development and independence. We would encourage any plan to be actively reviewed, with the way the child responds to the plan being a central consideration, alongside incorporation of ordinary risk-taking.

It is also important to notice when a young person might seem withdrawn but does not create strong feelings in the adults around them. This may indicate that projective processes are not operating, meaning that the difficult feelings the young person may be experiencing are not being unconsciously communicated, received, and absorbed by the adults around them. The risk here is that the young person may slip under the radar, which can lead to their needs being missed or overlooked.

When a young person does not make enough of an impact on the adults around them, sometimes the first indicator of a crisis can tragically be a suicide attempt. Many psychotherapists have worked with young people who may be overlooked, particularly in a busy school setting. For all these reasons, the countertransference feelings a young person evokes in their therapist can offer helpful information for them to share with the school, as it can encourage school staff to pay closer attention to this young person. It may also encourage staff to notice and reflect on their own feelings that might be evoked by the young person.

What young people in crisis need from schools

Freud (1930) famously wrote that for a person to be happy, they need to be able to love and work. Winnicott (1971) later added being able to play to this list. For adolescents, *school is their work* and one of the central features of their lives. As for play, in adolescence this might involve social interaction, experimentation with one's identity, and ordinary risk-taking behaviour. School plays an important role in providing an environment where adolescence can 'play', and a breakdown in the adolescent's capacity to play can be a sign of developmental difficulty. Therefore, we feel it is important to maintain the perception of education and the school environment as essential and positive parts of a young person's life.

Often, when adolescents are in crisis, they can struggle with different aspects of the school environment – its rigidity, demands, and expectations; the need for conformity; the exams and tests; as well as the social dynamics these all represent. There are situations where there is a poor fit between specific pupils and schools, which can be hard to resolve, as the young person's struggles with school are intertwined with their broader difficulties. However, it is important for schools and teachers to keep firmly in mind that in the vast majority of cases, the school environment is not the cause of the distress or crisis but may be the setting within which the distress manifests.

We feel that, in most cases, there should be a strong expectation that young people continue to attend school during periods of mental instability and, when possible, that the school try to make necessary adjustments to support this. Ultimately, though, this is often dependent upon the resources available to the school to manage pupils having these difficulties. Such resources can be physical – such as being able to offer separate quiet spaces for a pupil to spend part of their day – but more often they are staffing-related, such as having enough staff within the school who are available to offer thoughtful support in a timely manner, to liaise with family and other professionals, and when needed, to enforce benign boundaries.

The important question in most cases is: what adjustments would allow a student to continue attending school, and for the school to continue to function for that young person in a meaningful way? School is a place where cognitive, social, and emotional development happens and can hopefully continue. It also needs to be an environment that doesn't place intolerable demands on a student or provoke acting-out behaviours. What this means in practice will be specific for each young person. The key thing to keep in mind is the danger that steps taken to contain risk may also stifle development and encourage unhelpful regression. School staff, educators, and mental health professionals all need to acknowledge that their good intentions (such as overly restrictive safety planning, or time off school) could, in some cases, be misdirected and, though providing some short-term relief, may not represent the best interests of the student in the longer term.

School staff who become involved with these young people are likely, as we've discussed, to experience strong emotional responses to their distress. This can lead to even the most psychologically minded adults temporarily feeling restricted in their capacity to think. Adolescents in crisis want to be understood, but this is different from those around them taking what they say at face value. It is therefore vital that, in such situations, the adults involved can keep a separate space in their mind to digest and understand what is being said. We would encourage school staff to turn a well-known phrase on its head: *'Don't just do something, stand there'*. This 'standing there' allows time for thinking to take place.

School avoidance

The rise in the number of children absent from school seems to reflect the wider rise in mental health problems among young people in recent years. There has been a steep rise in the number of young people classed as severely absent from education following the Covid-19 pandemic. A large portion of these absences are thought to be anxiety-related, with children eligible for free school meals or on educational healthcare plan showing up as disproportionately absent from school (Centre for Young Lives, 2024). The number of children being home-schooled has also risen by over 10,000 between 2023 and 2024, with mental health difficulties increasingly being cited as a reason for this (Department for Education, 2024a).

Since the Covid-19 pandemic, there has been a particularly high rate of absences on Fridays (Weale, 2023), which seems to correlate with more parents working from home at the end of the week. Perhaps this is an indicator of underlying difficulties around separation from parents and home, which one might speculate have been exacerbated by the pandemic.

There can, of course, be other reasons for school attendance problems, such as social difficulties and bullying. In the digital age, young people can find themselves humiliated, exposed, and shamed on a wide scale. For instance, physical fights in the past may have been witnessed by a handful of adolescents in the playground, but in today's society, fights are often filmed and rapidly circulated throughout the school and beyond on various social media platforms. In our experience, schools work hard to help students when cases of bullying occur. Yet understandably, situations like this can make young people feel isolated and afraid of returning to school. In extreme cases, it might be necessary for a young person to transfer to another school, although the online world can also make it increasingly hard for young people to make a fresh start in a new environment.

At present, in the UK, parents can face fines if their child is persistently absent from school. Yet the current figures on absences indicate that these sanctions may not be helping. The sanctions certainly do not address the underlying difficulties that lead children and adolescents to miss school. So how can child psychotherapists work together with schools to support young people, particularly when they are in crisis and not attending school?

When a young person engages in self-harm, parents often feel trapped in a delicate balancing act, unsure of how to set boundaries without worsening the situation. The fear that imposing limits might escalate the self-harm can leave parents feeling powerless, leading them to avoid necessary interventions – such as restricting phone use at night. Over time, this hesitancy to enforce boundaries can inadvertently reinforce a pattern of regression, where the adolescent retreats further into isolation. The bedroom becomes both a refuge and a prison, making the eventual transition back to school and broader social engagement increasingly difficult.

For an adolescent who is struggling to move from the inside world of their bedroom to the outside world of school, a certain degree of healthy splitting needs to take place. This helps them tolerate emotions that threaten to overwhelm them by idealising certain people or things and denigrating others, allowing the adolescent to manage emotions that may, on the surface, seem contradictory (for example, anxiety about one's rapidly changing body), while also maintaining a healthy narcissism. In his paper 'Fetishism' (1928), and later in 'Splitting of the ego in the process of defence' (1940/1964; Freud, 1938), Freud discusses the ways in which two opposing thoughts can co-exist through the process of disavowal and repression. Here, 'the attitude which fitted in with the wish and the attitude which fitted in with the reality [exist] side by side' (pp. 155–156).

Adolescence is widely thought of as a time when greater separation from one's family needs to occur to allow for the adolescent's formation of identity through their mental and physical development. The school setting and what it can offer in terms of peer groups can greatly aid the adolescent's development. However, the pandemic caused many adolescents to spend prolonged periods of time at home (with their families) and out of school – potentially reinforcing a greater regression than would ordinarily occur.

For young people who struggled with school before the pandemic, the extended periods at home may have felt like a relief, but anxiety was likely to be heightened when asked to return, as is demonstrated in the following vignette:

Lucy, a 15-year-old, was referred due to suicidal thoughts and school-related anxiety. She was raised by her loving and supportive mother but had little contact with her father. It seemed that Lucy and her mother had always struggled to separate. At nursery, she would cling to her mother in floods of tears. Despite her mother's attempts to reassure her, nothing seemed to help, and in desperation to leave in time for work, her mother recalls eventually prying Lucy off her legs and pushing her through the nursery doors. She could hear Lucy wailing as she walked off to work in tears.

Things improved slightly in primary school, but the difficulties resurfaced when Lucy started secondary school.

Lucy described the way she'd be crying at the school gates, not wanting to go in. Initially, school was understanding and would allow her mother to come in with her and stay for a while. However, when the crying and reluctance to attend school persisted, Lucy felt they were losing patience with her. Her mother was stressed by the situation, and Lucy remembers a member of staff saying, 'Look how upset you're making your mother'. Lucy tells me, 'This only made me feel worse'.

This response from the member of staff, which was most likely said out of desperation, reinforced Lucy's worst fears, namely, the damage she was doing to her mother, and worries about what would happen to her mother when she was not with her. The frustration felt by this member of staff (who had, up to a point, been supportive) got pushed back into Lucy, who was left feeling that the difficulty was all on her. Psychotherapy was needed to help Lucy and her mother understand and work through these difficulties, and liaising with school was also an important aspect of the work.

Not having to go to school during the pandemic was a relief to Lucy. Her mother described how Lucy emerged from lockdown like a butterfly, going from an overweight young teen in braces and glasses to a beautiful young woman. Returning to school was not easy but was initially helped by Lucy finding a peer group. For the most part, she enjoyed learning and did not have any academic difficulties. However, the difficulties with school attendance reignited when Lucy and her best friend were ousted from their friendship group.

Lucy struggled to get to school in the mornings and was often leaving school early as she suffered frequent panic attacks whilst there. To her, it felt like these came out of the blue. However, exploring these panic attacks in more detail revealed a pattern – often they were triggered when Lucy would unexpectedly find herself alone at school. On one occasion, her best friend had to leave school early; on another occasion, it was the subtle shifting of her friend's attention away from her: *'I was talking to my best friend, then she turned her head away as if she were distracted. Suddenly, I felt like I couldn't breathe'*. This was the same friend with whom she often felt a sense of claustrophobia.

For Lucy, relationships were often experienced in an adhesive way, and separation was experienced as a type of tearing apart (Bick, 1968). It became clear that, for the most part, school was not the problem; it was simply the setting where Lucy's early infantile anxieties about separation surfaced.

Aggression is necessary for separation to occur; however, in the case of Lucy, school became the repository for the projected feelings of anger and aggression, which could not be acknowledged in her idealised relationship to her mother.

Concluding thoughts

In India, students as young as thirteen often travel far from home to attend coaching centres that prepare them, amongst thousands of other young people, for the notoriously difficult exams that determine whether they will be able to study for a prestigious, well-earning career in medicine or engineering. Poorer families will use their life savings to send their children to these centres, in the hope that this experience will secure a better future for them. Sadly, but perhaps not surprisingly, suicide rates are disproportionately high in India (at one coaching centre, more than 100 students have taken their lives in the past ten years, while 2023 saw the highest yearly rate, with at least 25 suicides).

There are likely to be many reasons for this: the pressure to succeed, the intense study schedules, separation from family and friends, as well as the social contagion element of suicide amongst this population. But another factor that has been identified is the risk around not being *seen* or known as an individual. Classes comprise of hundreds of students and teachers who do not know their names (Khare, 2023).

As newly qualified psychotherapists starting our work in an adolescent crisis team, we remember the fear we felt at the time about working with adolescents who were at risk of suicide. It was hard to escape the thought of how devastating it would feel to work with a young person who does eventually kill themselves. We were curious to know how more senior members of the team – who had been working with self-harming and/or suicidal young people over decades – assessed and addressed these risks. The advice given to us by one of the consultant psychiatrists in our team was seemingly simple and perhaps even obvious, but it was incredibly helpful to keep in mind when thinking about protective factors. He asked:

Can the young person connect with you and you with them? Does he or she have other people in their life whom they feel connected to?

It is perhaps not surprising that, in the UK, over a third of adolescents who have taken their own life were not known to mental health services (National Childhood Mortality Database, 2021).

Although the coaching centre example is extreme for the UK context, it highlights the value of connection, belonging, and community. We believe that many schools can and do offer this sense of belonging and connection to their students while, at the same time, encouraging them to step out of their comfort zones and manage the ordinary anxieties of life. However, at a time when the aspirational language of both education and children's mental health is growing ever more sophisticated, it is easy for these simple things to sometimes be overlooked.

Schools have much to offer pupils, beyond standard educational provision, and this is especially true for adolescents in crisis. However, for this to be effective, staff need to have the necessary time and support to connect with pupils, work collaboratively with external agencies, and maintain appropriate professional boundaries. Our experience of working with school staff is that through offering them containment in the Bionian sense (1959, 1962), they are then better able to understand and contain the acting-out behaviours. This, in turn, provides positive developmental opportunities for the young person while also increasing the likelihood that they will continue attending school. Strengthening the link with school staff can also, in turn, contain the therapist's anxieties as a more accurate picture of the young person's strengths, difficulties, and sources of support emerges. This can provide a helpful basis for individual psychotherapy or strengthen ongoing therapeutic work.

Note

1 For more information on this programme, please visit the NHS website https://www. england.nhs.uk/mental-health/cyp/trailblazers/#_Mental_Health_Support.

References

Acheson, R., & Papadima, M. (2023). The search for identity: Working therapeutically with adolescents in crisis. *Journal of Child Psychotherapy*, 49(1), 95–119. https://doi.org/10.1 080/0075417X.2022.2160478

Adams, R. (2024, June 4). Mental health is main cause of rising absences in England, say headteachers. *The Guardian*. https://www.theguardian.com/education/article/2024/ jun/14/mental-health-anxiety-absences-pupils-schools-covid-pandemic-headteachers

Argent, K. (Ed.). (2021). *Child psychoanalytic psychotherapy in primary schools: Tavistock approaches*. Routledge.

Barwick, N. (Ed.). (2002). *Clinical counselling in schools*. Routledge.

Bick, E. (1968). The experience of the skin in early object relations. In: M. Harris Williams (ed.), *Collected papers of Martha Harris and Esther Bick*. The Roland Harris Trust.

Bion, W. R. (1959). Attacks on linking. *International Journal of Psychoanalysis*, 40, 308–315.

Bion, W. R. (1962). The psycho-analytic study of thinking. *International Journal of Psychoanalysis*, 43, 306–310.

Campbell, D., & Hale, R. (2017). *Working in the dark: Understanding the pre-suicide state of mind*. Routledge.

Centre for Young Lives. (2024, December 12). *Centre for Young Lives report warns poverty and hardship are preventing some children from attending school amid big*

increases in persistent and severe absence among children receiving Free School Meals
[Press release]. https://www.centreforyounglives.org.uk/news-centre/centre-for-young-
lives-report-warns-poverty-and-hardship-are-preventing-some-children-from-attending-
school-amid-big-increases-in-persistent-and-severe-absence-among-children-receiving-
free-school-meals

Cybulski, L., Ashcroft, D. M., Carr, M. J., Garg, S., Wilton, L., & Kontopantelis, E. (2021).
Temporal trends in annual incidence rates for psychiatric disorders and self-harm among
children and adolescents in the UK, 2003–2018. *BMC Psychiatry*, 21, 229. https://doi.
org/10.1186/s12888-021-03235-w

Department for Education. (2023). *School workforce in England*. https://explore-education-
statistics.service.gov.uk/find-statistics/school-workforce-in-england/2023

Department for Education. (2024a, February 19). *Elective home education*. https://explore-
education-statistics.service.gov.uk/find-statistics/elective-home-education/2023-24

Department for Education. (2024b). *Keeping children safe in education*. https://www.gov.
uk/government/publications/keeping-children-safe-in-education-2

Department for Work and Pensions. (2024). *Households below average income: An analysis
of the UK income distribution – FYE 1995 to FYE 2023*. https://www.gov.uk/government/
statistics/households-below-average-income-for-financial-years-ending-1995-to-2023/
households-below-average-income-an-analysis-of-the-uk-income-distribution-fye-1995-
to-fye-2023#children-in-low-income-households

Department of Health and Department for Education. (2017). *Transforming children and
young people's mental health provision: A green paper*. https://assets.publishing.service.
gov.uk/media/5a823518e5274a2e87dc1b56/Transforming_children_and_young_
people_s_mental_health_provision.pdf

Ellins, J., Hocking, L., Al-Haboubi, M., Newbould, J., Fenton, S. J., Daniel, K., Stockwell,
S., Leach, B., Sidhu, M., Bousfield, J., McKenna, G., Saunders, K., O'Neill, S., & Mays,
N. (2023). Early evaluation of the children and young people's mental health trailblazer
programme: A rapid mixed-methods study. *Health and Social Care Delivery Research*,
11(8), 1–137. https://doi.org/10.3310/XQWU4117

Foulkes, L. (2024). *Coming of age: How adolescence shapes us*. Doubleday.

Freud, S. (1905). Three essays on the theory of sexuality. In: *The standard edition of the
complete psychological works of Sigmund Freud Volume VII (1901–1905): A case of
hysteria, three essays on sexuality and other works* (pp. 123–246). Hogarth Press and the
Institute of Psycho-Analysis.

Freud, S. (1910). The future prospects of psycho-analytic therapy. In: *The standard edition
of the complete psychological works of Sigmund Freud* (Vol. 11, pp. 139–151). London:
Hogarth Press.

Freud, S. (1920). *Beyond the pleasure principle* (Standard edition, Vol. 18, pp. 7–64). Hogarth
Press and the Institute of Psycho-Analysis.

Freud, S. (1928). Fetishism. *The International Journal of Psycho-Analysis*, 9, 161.

Freud, S. (1930). *Civilization and its discontents*. Hogarth.

Freud, S. (1938). Splitting of the ego in the process of defence. *The Standard Edition of the
Complete Psychological Works of Sigmund Freud*, 23, 271–278.

Freud, S. (1940/1964). *Splitting of the ego in the process of defence*. The Standard Edition of
the Complete psychological Works of Sigmund Freud, 23, 275–278. Hogarth Press and the
Institute of Psychoanalysis.

Guzman-Holst, C., Davis, R. S., Andrews, J. L., & Foulkes, L. (2025). Scoping review:
Potential harm from school-based group mental health interventions. *Child and Adolescent
Mental Health*. https://doi.org/10.1111/camh.12760

Henry, G. (1974). Doubly deprived. *Journal of Child Psychotherapy*, 3(4), 15–28. Hogarth
Press and the Institute of Psycho-Analysis. https://doi.org/10.1080/00754179708257300

Jackson, E. (2002). Mental health in schools: What about the staff? *Journal of Child
Psychotherapy*, 28(2), 129–146. https://doi.org/10.1080/00754170210143762

Jackson, E. (2008). The development of work discussion groups in educational settings. *Journal of Child Psychotherapy*, 34(1), 62–82. https://doi.org/10.1080/00754170801900191

Jackson, E., & Berkeley, A. (eds.). (2020). *Sustaining depth and meaning in school leadership: Keeping your head*. Routledge.

Khare, V. (2023, October 23). Kota: Stricter rules for India student hub after suicides. *BBC News*. https://www.bbc.co.uk/news/world-asia-india-67167036

King, H. (2022, November 19). Safeguarding: Pressure on designated leads is alarming. *Schools Week*. https://schoolsweek.co.uk/safeguarding-pressures-on-designated-leads-is-alarming/

Lanyado, M. (2017). Putting down roots: The significance of technical adaptations in the therapeutic process with fostered and adopted children‡. *Journal of Child Psychotherapy*, 43(2), 208–222. https://doi.org/10.1080/0075417X.2017.1323947

Le Breton, D. (2017). Understanding skin-cutting in adolescence: Sacrificing a part to save the whole. *Body & Society*, 24(1–2), 33–54. https://doi.org/10.1177/1357034X18760175

National Childhood Mortality Database. (2021, October). *Suicide in children and young people*. https://www.ncmd.info/wp-content/uploads/2021/11/NCMD-Suicide-in-Children-and-Young-People-Report.pdf

Office of National Statistics. (2024). *Pupil absence in schools in England*. https://explore-education-statistics.service.gov.uk/find-statistics/pupil-absence-in-schools-in-england/2023-24-autumn-and-spring-term

Ofsted. (2023). *The annual report of his Majesty's Chief Inspector of Education, Children's Services and Skills 2022/23*. https://www.gov.uk/government/publications/ofsted-annual-report-202223-education-childrens-services-and-skills/the-annual-report-of-his-majestys-chief-inspector-of-education-childrens-services-and-skills-202223

Royal College of Paediatrics and Child Health. (2020). *State of child health*. London: RCPCH.

Schmidt Neven, R. (Host). (2003). The new ecology: A whole classroom, whole school, whole community approach [audio podcast episode]. In: *Centre for child and family development*. https://mysoundwise.com/soundcasts/1598761684402s

Stern, D., Sander, L., Nahum, J., Harrison, A., Lyons-Ruth, K., Morgan, A., Bruschweiler-Stern, N., & Tronick, E. (1998). Non-interpretive mechanisms in psychoanalytic therapy: The "something more" than interpretation. *International Journal of Psycho-Analysis*, 79, 903–921.

Waddell, M. (2002). *Inside lives: Psychoanalysis and the growth of the personality* (Rev. edition). Karnac.

Ward, J. L., Vazquez-Vazquez, A., Philips, K., Settle, K., Pilvar, H., & Cornaglia, F. (2025). Admissions to acute medical wards for mental health concerns among children and young people in England from 2012 to 2022: A cohort study. *The Lancet Child and Adolescent Health*, 9(2), 112–120.

Weale, S. (2023, March 8). Schools in England seeing more pupil absences on Fridays. *The Guardian*. https://www.theguardian.com/world/2023/mar/07/schools-in-england-seeing-more-pupil-absences-on-fridays

Winnicott, D. W. (1971). *Playing and reality*. London and New York: Routledge.

Youell, B. (2006). *The learning relationship: Psychoanalytic thinking in education*. Routledge.

Chapter 11

Ripples of containment

How CAMHS teams manage anxiety in the midst of adolescent crisis

Rebecca Bolam

In this chapter, I explore an organisational structure I have observed in generic Child and Adolescent Mental Health Services (CAMHS) that I believe develops in response to overdetermined pressures on services, exacerbated by alarming and risky adolescent presentations. I specifically describe the dynamics in a team where one member becomes an *un-appointed container*, serving as the predominant source of unconscious containment for the team. As a result of the reverie that occurs between colleagues, I consider how Canham's (2002) concept of a 'group state of mind' can develop and proliferate. I go on to consider the requirement for a *like-minded colleague* to whom the un-appointed container can turn for support, thereby enabling the group state of mind to be sustained.

I begin by exploring the root and nature of unconscious pressures brought into a service by adolescents who pose a risk to themselves, and the way that a service can become structured around these anxieties. This chapter is developed from my professional doctorate in child psychotherapy (Bolam, 2023) and from my observations of team dynamics.

The time of adolescence

Adolescence is a time of internal and external turmoil, a time when the push and pull of contradictory desires for autonomy and dependence emerge (Midgley et al., 2015). Infantile dilemmas resurface alongside the emergence of the biological and emotional need for independence and separation from parents or carers (Tonnesman, 1980). The journey of adolescence is one of uncertainty and upheaval, until an ill-defined endpoint is reached, marking the move into adulthood (Stambler, 2017).

The need for separation from parents, from whom genes are inherited, is a process at the core of the success of life on earth; it ensures that procreation takes place between those who do not share genes, and in this way, a species' health and success is promoted (Dawkins, 1976). In humans, the biologically unusual delay in this process – that which we name latency – has given the human race an opportunity to grow, learn, and develop so that the separating individual is more mature compared to other species. This has contributed to humans becoming sophisticated and highly successful. Nonetheless, separation remains emotionally

DOI: 10.4324/9781003592778-15

linked to infancy, and an adolescent reaching sexual maturity not only has to contend with questions about their own readiness for adulthood and a painful separation from caregivers, but also must manage resurfacing infantile dilemmas that remain to be processed.

Catty (2021) describes adolescence as a time of crisis during which young people are caught between past experiences and an unknown and unknowable future. Catty argues that for the adolescents of today, the challenge is great, as it is set against a 'maelstrom of a culture' (p. 3) in which the previously predictable milestones for young people, such as 'to find work, buy a home, or even, perhaps, retire' (p. 189), are no longer certain and are often portrayed in a catastrophising way in the press.

The explosion of largely unregulated social media has further intensified these challenges for adolescents. The risks of this technology are wide-reaching and include manipulation by criminals, exposure to distressing content, and adverse impacts on brain development linked to the overuse of screens and reduced socialisation (Acheson, 2022).

But perhaps just as concerning is the constant recording through videos and photographs of the normal trials and errors of adolescence. Mistakes do not fade in people's memories but instead hold the double threat of being widely shared instantaneously and stored online in perpetuity. In short, the challenges of adolescence are numerous and complex, as internal tasks intersect with a changing and demanding landscape of external pressures. For those who have experienced deficits in early care, this experience can be particularly difficult.

Deficits in early care and development of communication

Communication in early infancy is essential for survival. The helpless infant is primed to relate from birth and learns to adapt to the specific environment of their caregiver in ways that promote proximity and elicit care (Music, 2016, p. 23). This successful strategy requires adaptation to the mother's mental state, her specific capacity to provide care, and her own distress tolerance (Campbell, 2005). Constitutional variations in the 'capacity of the ego to tolerate anxiety' exist in both the mother and the infant, but experience and adaptation are paramount (Klein, 1946). As such, the infant may soon learn to weigh lightly on their caregiver, as urgent projections may evoke fear and result in reduced proximity, and so less care. Other infants may need to adopt powerful communication strategies in order to have an impact upon their caregivers and elicit an ordinary level of care.

Strategies developed in infancy are repeated and honed over time, and in this way, the personality of the child, adolescent, and then adult is formed, shaped by the particular nature of the environment. However, within the context of environmental change linked to age and development, not least increased physical freedom and agency, strategies that were essential for survival in infancy may prove to be maladaptive later on. As such, they could be both dangerous to the individual and disruptive to relationships.

Bion's (1962a) concept of reverie defines a central aspect of this process. Infants respond to unpalatable and uncomfortable sensations, which Bion named beta elements, that are perceived as threats to the developing early ego. In order to promote survival, these must be expelled. The expelled elements are then met by a recipient, often a parent, into whom they are projected. The recipient draws upon their alpha function to make sense of the beta elements and convert them into knowable alpha elements. These are then returned to the infant, who no longer perceives them as a threat to their ego due to their now digested and understood form.

In good enough development, cues from the baby's movements, vocalisations, and identification with projections help a parent to comprehend, or identify, an approximation of the baby's experience, and therefore their needs (Bion, 1962a). Physical and psychological aspects are intertwined, as sensations may relate to physical needs, such as hunger, and the understood psychic sensation is returned to the infant alongside food. Through this process, the infant has the opportunity to introject the parent's capacity to understand, which promotes the development of their own capacity to understand, namely, alpha function (Bion, 1962a).

For some parents, the experience of being on the receiving end of an infant's projections can be difficult, and consequently, sufficient experiences of attuned reverie do not occur. These infants are left with urgent and unknown stimuli and are not afforded the opportunity to develop a capacity for alpha function themselves, depriving them of the opportunity to develop this as an internal source of support to be drawn upon in later life. In the extreme, Bion (1962b) describes *nameless dread*, which develops as a result of a repeated lack of maternal reverie, leaving an infant with meaningless, frightening sensations that pose a threat to the ego and so, in phantasy, to life itself. In reality, an infant who is not responded to appropriately *is* at risk of death, so the desire to avoid this psychic situation is also to avoid the reality of death.

As adolescence marches on and psychic dilemmas of the past re-emerge, the links to a feeling of true helplessness are clear. In combination with the desire for freedom and the complexities of navigating newfound sexual urges and physical freedom from the parents, this dual task can easily become overwhelming and dangerous. The tools at the disposal of young people are those learned in infancy and, as such, can include powerful and urgent communication techniques. In other circumstances, they may include more closed-off responses characterised by directing the urgency and aggression towards the self or the body. It is common for adolescents to split the body from the mind and to use it as a holding place for projections arising from these complicated internal experiences (Bell, 2001).

New tools or capacities enabled by the agency and freedom of an adult-sized body can result in alarming and dangerous acts against the body, including harming and killing it. Motz (2010), however, highlights the hope in self-harm as expressing an object-seeking activity and a desire to communicate, holding in some cases a desire for belated mastery of the difficulties of infancy (Tonnesman, 1980). However, strategies essential for survival in infancy may now hinder the task of adolescence. Alarm-evoking behaviours and an inability to be in contact with or process one's own feelings using alpha function can leave an adolescent in distress.

Structures around risk

Those accessing mental health services relay their experiences through conscious and unconscious communication, bringing anxieties into the midst of the CAMHS team. The task of receiving communications from adolescents in distress is difficult. In fact, when researching how child psychotherapists respond to risky adolescents, I found that, despite not being explicitly asked, the difficulties and personal impact of working with this patient group in a CAMHS service overshadowed all interviews (Bolam, 2023).

Partly as a consequence of this, the response of CAMHS clinicians to patient communications is orientated around overt risks, such as suicidal intent, and involves *doing* something to curtail the dangers and specifics of the risks. In reality, though, unconscious communications also affect how clinicians respond. These responses may be less familiar to clinicians but have an equal (or potentially more powerful) bearing on how a patient is responded to, particularly when they are unprocessed and uncomfortable. Managing external predicaments such as safety planning can alleviate the clinician's, and perhaps the patient's, anxiety in the short term as, understandably, there is an unconscious desire to turn away from raw, hopeless and painful anxieties evoked by the unconscious forces at play (Waddell, 1989). Yet a focus on *doing* something, with the overt aim of minimising risky behaviours, can lead to services becoming structured around risk management, leaving little time or emphasis on understanding the true nature of the difficulties faced by the adolescent. Where this becomes the norm, uncomfortable unconscious communications can remain unknown and can unwittingly amass a burdensome psychic load on clinicians, with no obvious channel for their processing and alleviation.

Pressures on NHS services

The chronic underfunding of the NHS has placed CAMHS services under unprecedented pressure, as the demand for services outstrips supply. Inquests have revealed that these pressures contribute to 'serious and systemic CAMHS failures', leading to patient deaths (Doughty Street Chambers, 2024). Baraitser and Brook (2021) highlight the impact of changing societal pressures including increasing inequality, which deepen the difficulties faced by the NHS and lead to unhelpful outcomes when these issues are politicised. These authors explore the relationship between the temporalities of care and the concept of care within a crisis-stricken system, where there is a pull against a 'waiting-with' mentality. This is offered as an alternative to taking action, such as implementing 'transformations' that don't appear to add up, given the context of a funding crisis (p. 3).

Reflecting this, Osserman and Lê (2020) describe how a move towards 'efficiency' tends to be prioritised above the needs of patients, and the time required to care for them is less available. Wright (2022) describes the shift of services towards crisis management, leading to a more focused and often less nuanced patient care. This shift holds the possibility of change as normal operating systems are paused. Overt justifications linked to insufficient funding or a change in demand (such as during the coronavirus pandemic) may mask a deeper desire to avoid the pain and discomfort of patients' experiences. In their wake, a situation ensues, creating a 'temporality upon which one can act, and in which critique and thus change are possible' (p. 316).

However, Wright (2022) argues that in a 'crisis-stricken care system', in which the crisis has become 'chronic and enduring', the outcome often differs from this. The advantages of a temporally linked deficit being efficiently managed are replaced by a stripped-down offer of care that de-prioritises time for thought and reflection and holds no hope of change. Space and nuance that allow for thought and consideration of each situation are lost, and not only does patient care diminish, but individual clinicians can feel alone and isolated from one another. Projective defences against anxieties build, and the impact on individuals can negatively affect organisational dynamics.

This is a ripe environment for Canham's (2002) 'gang state of mind' to develop. Here, differing views can become defended and entrenched, as blame and responsibility for obvious dysfunctions in the team are apportioned to others. It is difficult in such a context for members of a team to examine their own deficits, leading to a greater need to disavow anxieties (Canham, 2002). Those who raise them can become 'a lightning rod' for blame (Bolam, 2023, p. 85). A gang state of mind can then cause further focus on crisis management, perpetuating the problem.

As Waddell (1989) describes, so fittingly for current CAMHS services, 'doing' avoids the pain of contact with feelings that can be so hard to manage, while 'thinking' can be anxiety-provoking. However, she argues that thinking about anxieties must take place for things to feel better: 'Pain can be more easily borne, ultimately, if it can be thought about' (p. 2). This is particularly difficult to do when there are limited support structures in place, and Kraemer (2015, p. 146) warns that reflective groups and other spaces made available for thinking about patients are routinely resisted, as 'there seems to be an inherent fragility about meetings whose purpose is to reflect rather than to produce'. Roberts (2019) explains that 'our neurological response to new information can be experienced as unpleasant, leading to repressing what disrupts the stories we have been using to make sense of our lives and our organizations'. This amounts to the development of strong defences against change, and a shift away from a gang state of mind is resisted, owing to the rigidity around the function of keeping anxieties at bay.

This unhappy situation isn't necessarily inevitable. Here, I want to describe a particular dynamic that can develop in response to overdetermined organisational pressures that is more optimistic, akin to Canham's group state of mind (Canham, 2002, p. 113). This state is linked to Klein's depressive position (1940/1998, 1946) and describes a group dynamic in which different points of view can be tolerated along with associated tensions and ambivalent feelings. It can enable a team to function and, under certain circumstances, allow this mode of functioning to proliferate.

The un-appointed container

Despite considerable pressures, certain individuals within CAMHS teams *are* able to maintain their capacity to think. Following is a composite vignette about a psychotherapist I've named Clara, an experienced clinician who retains her ability to think. It draws together clinical observations with findings from my doctorate.

Clara

Clara is the lead psychotherapist in a generic CAMHS team. She is one of the longest-standing members of the team and has been working in the NHS for nearly 25 years. In addition to the delivery of psychotherapy, Clara offers support to the wider team by holding regular supervision groups for colleagues and leading team-wide discussions about difficult cases. Alongside one of the psychiatrists, Clara offers individual consultation slots to colleagues about specific patients. The team manager asked that these be limited to four per month, but the demand is much higher, and Clara has recorded offering ten consultation sessions in a single month. In addition, team members often seek Clara out for informal support, and there is a joke that she is the team's mother.

Clara recognises that her warmth and aptitude to support colleagues lend her to this role. She also recognises that her way of doing things means that she has an influence on how team members relate to one another. Team members convey and report a sense of ease in their views on patient decisions when they have been shared and validated by her, meaning that their capacity to offer their minds to patients increases and they are less burdened by their own anxieties about the cases. As well as this, Clara is aware that her psychological training has led her to understand aspects of team functioning in ways that are not always obvious to the senior managers. Consequently, she is often sought out to support thinking about aspects of the team dynamics.

This position is not always easy for Clara; there used to be an experienced family therapist in the team with whom Clara could share thoughts and offer mutual support. Together they used to be able to influence aspects of how the team functioned, and during that time, useful systems had been put in place, such as reflective group meetings.

All this has been much more difficult since the family therapist left. Clara feels depleted and has noted that she herself is rarely offered informal support by colleagues. She is now considering leaving the team, despite her deep love for the work and for the NHS.

Clara is an example of someone I describe as an *un-appointed container*. By virtue of their training, experience, personal qualities, or a combination of all these factors, individuals like Clara not only appear to have the capacity to contain their own anxieties in relation to the work but also can offer this to fellow team members. This reflects Bion's (1961) assertion that 'sophisticated skill' is required by those participating in a productive group (a work group), which 'is possible only to individuals with years of training and a capacity for experience that has permitted them to develop mentally' (p. 143). It appears that this isn't consciously decided upon but relates to a propensity for a particular role, or a *valency*, as described by Bion (1961).

The un-appointed container offers support in both formal settings, such as case management, reflective discussion meetings, and supervision, as well as informal settings, like chats in the corridor where aspects of a case might be raised or reflections on team dynamics commented on. While advice and thoughts can be shared during these interactions, I am not referring here to this conscious and practical process. Instead, I focus on the capacity of these individuals to contain unconscious anxieties through non-verbal aspects of their interactions with colleagues. They are sought out by various members of the team, including those more senior to them, and can hear and understand anxieties ostensibly related to patients, as well as personal issues. The recipients may find themselves relieved of an unconscious burden and so may return to this individual even if they don't fully understand why.

Through this process, the receiving clinicians have an experience of their anxieties and uncomfortable projections from patients being understood, processed, and returned to them in a digested form. Now less burdened by anxieties, they are able to contend with their own deficits and vulnerabilities and can acknowledge and accept the vulnerabilities of colleagues. Mirroring the development of alpha function in infants, this reverie conveys the capacity for alpha function. The receiving clinicians are, in turn, able to offer containment to other colleagues. This process can alter the dynamics of a team as a proliferation of the capacity to contain anxieties ripples out from the un-appointed container into the entire team. Facilitating the capacity to remain in the depressive position engenders a culture that allows for thinking, valuing differing views and depressive concern, which are at the heart of Canham's group state of mind (Canham, 2002, p. 113).

Reverie between colleagues such as this may become necessary, owing to the overwhelming volume of urgent and unbearable projections that CAMHS teams are in receipt of from patients. As discussed earlier, these communications can amass amongst clinicians and may arise from patients' necessary capacity to evoke alarm. They may hold within them such things as the terror of a defenceless infant's nameless dread.

When combined with anxieties and organisational pressures linked to long waiting times, unprecedented underfunding, and the 'crisis of time' in the current adolescent population (Catty, 2021), this load can become almost unbearable. The nature of adolescents' unmet needs can lead to the organisation being required to function in a parental role, offering a vessel into which projections can be deposited. These projections are then met by clinicians whose own infantile needs and deficits may be stirred by the experience. In turn, as Clara was referred to as the 'mum of the team', individuals seek a mother-like container where infantile dilemmas and discomfort can be held.

It follows that the availability of a colleague who can provide this support is essential. Importantly, if these processes are not understood or acknowledged, these necessary aspects of a team may not be established or valued and maintained within the structure. Where this role remains unacknowledged, there is a mirroring of adolescent functioning, where the need for a parental container is disavowed and the 'parent' is left holding the uncomfortable projections, just as the un-appointed container is left with them.

Anxieties in the organisation

Generally, containment of anxieties in organisations would be expected to exist within a vertical structure, rather than through the peer-to-peer route described here. Psychoanalytic understanding of organisational dynamics, or the processes that develop in response to anxieties affecting an organisation, have built upon Isabel Menzies-Lyth's consultation to a failing hospital ward in 1988 (Menzies-Lyth, 1988). Through observation of interactions within staff groups and between staff and patients, she observed insufficient acknowledgement of the impact on nurses as recipients of unsettling projections from patients. Opportunities for supervision and discussion about these were not provided. Instead, anxieties remained with the nurses, and blame for the team's failures was located with them. Recommendations were offered based around increased understanding of the unconscious processes alongside mechanisms to manage these but were not taken up (Halton, 2015).

Later, Halton (2015, p. 36) describes the positive impact of vertical movement of anxieties through an organisation via supervision, offering containment of anxieties at the National Orthopaedic Hospital. Here, change became possible as recommendations were taken up. This was attributed to the senior ward sisters' capacity to reflect upon and understand the experiences of junior staff members. Anxieties were able to flow up the organisation and be contained by more experienced colleagues, and an improvement in organisational function and patient care was seen.

A vital component of this system is the capacity of senior members of staff to make practical changes to the organisation. Mosse (2019, p. 1) explains that the organisation functions as a social system with concurrent unconscious dynamics at play. Therefore, the psychoanalytic view of organisational functioning must be considered alongside the social view, and as Mosse states, the 'social and the psychoanalytic perspectives must be deployed together if real change is to be effected' (p. 1).

The social aspects of management and operational decisions provide a structure for organisational tasks, which, if deployed without knowledge of the involved unconscious processes, can be two-dimensional (Mosse, 2019). Mosse warns that if looked at alone, the psychoanalytic understanding of an organisation can 'heighten people's awareness of and sensitivity to unconscious processes, but it will not create the conditions in which such awareness can be used, and staff will therefore become ever more depressed and frustrated' (p. 1). The capacity to alter organisational processes mirrors physical responses to an infant's distress, such as the offer of milk. This offer both alleviates the discomfort and aids the infant in the process of sense-making and in alpha function development. Without the actual milk, the infant neither develops nor grows.

Those in managerial positions in CAMHS, who hold the responsibility for implementing social change, may not recognise the presence of unconscious dynamics within the team. This may relate to the particular training of an individual that does not focus on unconscious processes and the consequent limited knowledge, experience, or skills required to recognise and manage unconscious processes, or to disseminate this capacity. However, given the structure of CAMHS teams, those in management are often particularly exposed to the huge pressures of upward justification of the value and productivity of their service, despite insufficient funding. Self-preservation in the face of this pressure may thus manifest as a denial of the true nature of anxieties, in order to prevent overload. This inadvertently leaves a gap in team functioning that, I am arguing, can sometimes be filled by the un-appointed container.

As I have argued elsewhere (Bolam, 2023), the response to this is largely dependent upon the specific climate of each organisation. In particular, where an organisation is not able to recognise the need for anxieties to be addressed, a destructive gang state of mind can develop. For instance, those who raise the presence of anxieties can be felt to be 'upsetting the apple cart' (Bolam, 2023, p. 84) and can evoke a further denial of the presence of anxieties, described in stark terms by a study participant as 'akin to adolescents to split off, project and deny their anxieties when they themselves are unable to hold them' (p. 85).

Similarly, it may be in certain cases that there is some recognition of the requirement for this function by those in management positions. As one psychotherapist explained, 'as part of the role, beyond the spoken part, was that you would help contain institutional anxiety and the anxiety for other clinicians' (Bolam, 2023, p. 84). More optimistically, it may be, as it is for Clara, that the need for and capacity to manage unconscious aspects of the work *is* acknowledged, and the un-appointed container can function to a greater extent, with managers seeking advice and support from this person.

I argue that where the structure and atmosphere of a team enable clinicians to address unconscious processes, this state of mind can ripple out into the wider team, and clinicians appear less burdened by the workload and can be freer to think about their patients, leading, as reported in my research, to an improvement in the quality of care. Where no value is placed on addressing unconscious aspects of the work by managerial structures, the opposite has been found to be true (Bolam, 2023). Nonetheless, as described earlier, an understanding of unconscious processes without the capacity to alter the social structures of the team can lead to dissatisfaction and be unhelpful.

In order for this system to be sustainable, it is key that the un-appointed container has status within the team, which allows for their recommendations to be followed, that is, for managers to incorporate their thinking into structural systems and changes. As seen in the vignette, this setup can be changeable, dependent upon relationships amongst particular individuals within the team and their specific perspective and experience.

It is more likely for this working relationship to become established between those who have been in a team longer and have had the opportunity to build mutual trust and understanding. A stable team in which there is low staff turnover has the benefit of staff members who have come to know each other well, with trusting relationships building over time. Through repeated experiences with one another, both professionally and through informal interactions (like a shared tea break), mutual understanding and knowledge can develop, and strong bonds can be formed amongst staff.

This is a self-preserving situation. Mathisen et al. (2021) found in their research that psychosocial aspects of the work environment had a significant impact on staff turnover across more than 2,500 hospital staff. In particular, job satisfaction was identified as a principal aspect of this, and it was suggested that where this is prioritised, the turnover is lower. It doesn't come as a surprise that relationships between colleagues are important in workplaces in general, but perhaps particularly so when working with patients, and all the more so with the disturbed states of mind encountered in CAMHS services. The move towards working from home, expedited by the coronavirus lockdowns, can ease the working week, but can also threaten the ability to build meaningful relationships with colleagues. With less contact, there was, during that time, an impact on building mutual trust, on learning from one another, and ultimately, on patient care.

Sustained with a like-minded colleague

When examining the impact of risky adolescents on child psychotherapists in CAMHS services, I have observed the value clinicians place on the presence of at least one person within their team who holds a similar psychological perspective with them, including an understanding of unconscious processes (Bolam, 2023). The phrase *like-minded colleague* was used to describe a colleague with 'a capacity to hold and think about aspects of the work, particularly risk, rather than to be quick to take action, even when the pain and anxiety of not acting was difficult to bear' (p. 86). The value of this kind of colleague was far-reaching and included 'greater confidence in decision-making, particularly around risky patients, leading to a reduction in anxiety; improved understanding of patients as they could be thought about in greater depth; greater capacity to understand and process unconscious material' (p. 88).

This set-up was rarely formal but involved someone with whom they had developed a relationship and whom they could trust and turn to for support. The presence of this individual enabled the clinician to think about and hold the anxieties and projections of risky adolescents, without the need to move to action too quickly. Interviews in which clinicians reported a strong alliance with at least one like-minded colleague involved fewer thoughts about the organisational denial of anxieties. My research did not attempt to determine causation, and a broader study would be required to fully understand the factors at play (p. 87). Nonetheless, whether it was a cause or a consequence, it appeared that those who reported having a like-minded colleague were less affected by difficult organisational dynamics. This gives an indication that the un-appointed container is less burdened when they have a like-minded colleague; consequently, their offer to the team is more sustainable.

Expanding on this concept, I would like to draw together my findings to suggest that what was described as a like-minded colleague can be a fellow un-appointed container holding the same or similar functions. To ensure the sustainability of the position of the un-appointed container, I suggest that it's essential to have a minimum of one like-minded colleague. Within this set-up, there will naturally be variations in the extent to which each individual can offer support to one another, as well as to team members unfamiliar with unconscious dynamics, and to sustain this function within the team. It may be that one of the two individuals has a greater capacity for this role, by virtue of their inherent qualities or accumulated experience, thus becoming the un-appointed container while turning to their colleague for support themselves, without the latter acting as co-container for the team. In certain situations, it may be that a figure in the management team can offer the support of a like-minded colleague and, as such, may have the capacity to influence social aspects of the team functioning.

The flow of patients, and with them the flow of anxieties arriving in the organisation, is at the very centre of the service's purpose. Therefore, the need to sustain a group state of mind is a perpetual task in a dynamic system. The provision of a container to process and manage these anxieties is not static but must be continually offered. So my suggestion, as I have shown, is that the un-appointed container be then continually drawn upon. In order to do this, an un-appointed container requires support themselves. Where a like-minded colleague is present, the un-appointed container is less burdened, and so their offer is more sustainable. Where this is absent, the personal impact on the un-appointed container is significant and negative and may lead to burnout and to them leaving the team. Bolam (2023) describes how a clinician's post with a CAMHS team became untenable after their like-minded colleague left, eventually leading to their own departure from the team.

Collapse of containment

The set of circumstances described here, when working well, can allow an organisation to function and to achieve its tasks. However, this is precarious and reliant upon certain dynamic attributes which, by nature, are liable to change. As such, the system can tip over and collapse, which would be particularly likely in an organisation where a gang state of mind begins to establish.

Such a collapse can begin in one part of the system and cascade across the team. For example, if the un-appointed container no longer has supportive and productive links with management and so has no influence on social structures, or in the absence of a supportive like-minded colleague, it is likely that the un-appointed container is unable to fulfil the function of the role without undue personal detriment. These changes may take place as a consequence of staff changes, or changes in organisational structure that are more likely in a less stable team, with high staff turnover. The delicate balance that has enabled the team to be self-containing can thus dissolve; a perpetuation of the gang state of mind can then develop, and an unravelling of effective support structures can happen, as individuals become defensive and less trusting of each other.

Instead of the un-appointed container being a source of support, on the contrary, and as described by Mosse (2019), in such situations they can come to be seen as the source of disturbance. I have argued that in these circumstances, a negative spiral can ensue, whereby those who were able to notice and report upon unconscious dynamics in the team were perceived as the problem: 'it's a lightning rod for, you know, it angers people when you're felt to be destructive to the unconscious functions of the system' (p. 85). In these situations, supervision groups are not taken up or can be hijacked by other matters, and it is felt that the organisation is in a defensive state, in which denial of the difficulties becomes necessary. This leads to the role becoming untenable, and they end up having to leave the team. The team thus loses those who have the capacity to acknowledge anxieties, and denial of their presence becomes the safest way to operate, leading to a gang state of mind, an increasing unconscious burden for clinicians, and a reduced quality of care for families.

This situation is difficult for a team to recover from. An understanding of the processes at play and the power of unconscious communications that are being brought into the organisation is a helpful way to reduce pressures on individuals and to value and promote this service within an organisation. This requires that all levels of the organisation prioritise space and time for thought and reflection, alongside social and structural change.

Summary

The particular pressures that the NHS is under and the pressures on adolescents combine and blast through the CAMHS clinic doors. Clinicians and management structures are inclined towards operational approaches that deny the presence of unconscious anxieties. Nonetheless, the projections that amass from these patients remain within clinicians who, where possible, seek out and unofficially appoint a team member to provide containment. Where a sufficiently skilled and experienced clinician exists in a team, they have the capacity to contain these anxieties. Not only do they offer this to colleagues, but un-appointed containers also pass on the capacity to contain, and through this a group state of mind can develop, in which a team can function productively, and patient care is high quality. However, the un-appointed container cannot offer this in perpetuity, and the presence of a like-minded colleague is essential for their health and wellbeing. Further, a productive team dynamic relies upon a responsive social structure that acknowledges and adapts to unconscious psychological processes. In times of crisis, it can be very difficult to justify time for thought, but this is essential to enable the team to function.

References

Acheson, R. (2022). Research digest: Digital technology and its impact on child mental health. *Journal of Child Psychotherapy*, 48(3), 422–435.

Baraitser, L., & Brook, W. (2021). Watchful waiting: Temporalities of crisis and are in the UK National Health Service. In: V. Browne, J. Danely, & D. Rosenow (eds.), *Vulnerability and the politics of care: Transdisciplinary dialogues.* Oxford University Press.

Bell, D. (2001). Who is killing what or whom? Some notes on the internal phenomenology of suicide. *Psychoanalytic Psychotherapy*, 15(1), 21–37.

Bion, W. R. (1961). *Experiences in groups.* London: Tavistock Publications.

Bion, W. R. (1962a). *Learning from experience.* London: Heinemann.

Bion, W. R. (1962b). A theory of thinking. *International Journal of Psychoanalysis*, 43, 306–310.

Bolam, R. (2023). When to wait and when to act? An exploration of child psychotherapists' work with risky adolescents (Professional Doctorate Thesis, Tavistock and Portman NHS Foundation Trust and University of Essex).

Campbell, D. (2005). Perversion-sadism and survival. In: S. Budd, & R. Rusbridger (eds.), *Introducing psychoanalysis: Essential themes and topics* (pp. 231–245). London and New York: Routledge.

Canham, H. (2002). Group and gang states of mind. *Journal of Child Psychotherapy*, 28(2), 113–127.

Catty, J. (2021). Out of time: Adolescents and those who wait for them. *Journal of Child Psychotherapy*, 47(2), 188–204.

Dawkins, R. (1976). *The selfish gene.* Oxford University Press.

Doughty Street Chambers. (2024). *Serious and systemic CAMHS failures contribute to death of 17-year-old with autism and ADHD.* Retrieved May 5, 2024 https://www.doughtystreet.co.uk/news/serious-and-systemic-camhs-failures-contribute-death-17-year-old-autism-and-adhd-maya-sikand

Halton, W. (2015). Obsessional-punitive defences in care systems: Menzies Lyth revisited. In: D. Armstrong, & M. Rustin (eds.), *Social defences against anxiety: Explorations in a paradigm* (pp. 27–38). The Tavistock Clinic Series. London: Karnac Books.

Klein, M. (1940/1998). Mourning and its relation to manic-depressive states. In: *Love, guilt and reparation and other works 1921–1945* (pp. 344–369). Vintage Press.

Klein, M. (1946). Notes on some schizoid mechanisms. In: *Envy and gratitude and other works 1946–1963* (pp. 1–24). Vintage Press.

Kraemer, S. (2015). Anxiety at the front line. In: D. Armstrong, & M. Rustin (eds.), *Social defences against anxiety: Explorations in a paradigm* (pp. 144–160). The Tavistock Clinic Series. London: Karnac Books.

Mathisen, J., Nguyen, T., Jensen, J. H., Rugulies, R., & Rod, N. H. (2021). Reducing employee turnover in hospitals: Estimating the effects of hypothetical improvements in the psychosocial work environment. *Scandinavian Journal of Work Environment and Health*, 47(6), 456–465.

Menzies-Lyth, I. (1988). *Containing anxiety in institutions: Selected essays* (Vol. 1). London: Free Association Books.

Midgley, N., Parkinson, S., Holmes, J., Stapley, E., Eatough, V., & Target, M. (2015). Beyond a diagnosis: The experience of depression among clinically-referred adolescents. *Journal of Adolescence*, 44, 269–279.

Mosse, J. (2019). Making sense of organizations – the institutional roots of the Tavistock approach. In: A. Obholster, & V. Z. Roberts (eds.), *The unconscious at work: A Tavistock approach to making sense of organisational life* (2nd edition, pp. 1–8.). Routledge.

Motz, A. (2010). Self-harm as a sign of hope. *Psychoanalytic Psychotherapy*, 24(2), 81–92.

Music, G. (2016). *Nurturing Natures: Attachment and children's emotional, sociocultural and brain development* (2nd edition). Routledge.

Osserman, J., & Lê, A. (2020). Waiting for other people: A psychoanalytic interpretation of the time for action. *Wellcome Open Research*, 5, 133.

Roberts, V. Z. (2019). Afterword. Consulting to oneself. In: A. Obholzer, & V. Z. Roberts (eds.), *The unconscious at work: A Tavistock approach to making sense of organizational life* (2nd edition, pp. 251–254). London: Routledge.

Stambler, M. (2017). 100 years of adolescence and its prehistory from cave to computer. *Psychoanalytic Study of the Child*, 70(1), 22–39.

Tonnesman, M. (1980). Adolescent re-enactment, trauma and reconstruction. *Journal of Child Psychotherapy*, 6(1), 23–44.

Waddell, M. (1989). Living in two worlds: Psychodynamic theory and social work practice. *Free Associations*, 1(15), 11–35.

Wright, F. (2022). Making good of crisis: Temporalities of care in UK mental health services. *Medical Anthropology*, 41(3), 315–328.

Chapter 12

Cries in crisis

Holding looked-after adolescents and their networks in mind

Eftychia Apostolidou, Victoria Nicolodi, and Nikolaos Tzikas

Introduction

All three authors have worked as child and adolescent psychotherapists in looked-after children teams within Child and Adolescent Mental Health Services (CAMHS) and/or adolescent crisis teams. In doing this work, we have continually faced the challenge of supporting young people in care, whilst also navigating the responses of the systems surrounding them. By exploring the adolescent's perspective, we aim to 'be light upon the shadow', to use Lemn Sissay's beautiful words (2023), and to illuminate the interplay between their development, their past traumas, and the external pressures they encounter while trying to foster a therapeutic experience.

This chapter delves into the experiences and developmental challenges faced by young people in care, aiming to understand how systems interpret and respond to them. Drawing on a Winnicottian framework, particularly his famous assertion that '[t]here is no such thing as an infant' (Winnicott, 1960/1984, p. 39), and incorporating Bailey's (2006) extension of this statement to her work with parents of troubled adolescents, we recognise that the risk that adolescents in care present with serves as a form of communication that doesn't exist in isolation. This communication manifests through risk, reverberating throughout the fabric of the experiences of adolescents in care and the professional network surrounding them.

By building on the foundational concept that a baby does not exist in isolation, we propose that looked-after adolescents should be thought about and understood in relation to their environment. This involves mutually influencing communication with the professional network and the systems around them.

Language matters: context for looked-after children and adolescents in the UK

The term 'looked-after children' refers to those under local authority care due to significant environmental challenges, such as abuse or neglect (NSPCC, 2023a). These circumstances can lead to a range of mental health issues that can persist into adulthood (York & Jones, 2017).

DOI: 10.4324/9781003592778-16

In the UK, the acronym LAC brings up associations with the word 'lack'. The linguistic resemblance of the two words, *LAC and lack*, feels like a Freudian slip (Freud, 1901) – a societal unconscious response reflecting a (misguided) perception of children who are missing something fundamental: structure, a safe environment, and stable external support and internal objects. The euphemistic nature of this term is ironic, as it theoretically indicates the care these children receive from local authorities but, in fact, refers to children whose very predicament stems from a profound lack of adequate care.

Literature grounded in the experiences of children who have been in care highlights the profound impact of *language* throughout their lives. Various reports have identified the risks of using the acronym LAC, suggesting it can exacerbate feelings of low self-esteem, increase stigmatisation and 'othering', foster a sense of professional depersonalisation, and create barriers to meaningful engagement (TACT, 2019; NSPCC, 2023b).

Language, when used thoughtfully, can accurately reflect the complexity of children's experiences with compassion and respect. Conversely, it can also perpetuate harmful narratives, portraying children in care as a *problem* or as inherently lacking something fundamental, instead of recognising the role of their environments and systems in failing to provide adequate support (Capes, 2024). Addressing these challenges requires a commitment to ongoing reflection, an effort towards semantic reframing, and changing the way we discuss and support children and young people in care (Janzen, 2023; Pierre, 2024).

Inspired by a report drafted by Surrey youth voice (TACT, 2019) which describes the preferred terminology for care-experienced children and young people, we have opted in this chapter to use the terms 'adolescents in care' and/ or 'looked-after adolescents'. This choice was made based on our reflections on the relevant literature about the brave young people we have met on our journeys as child and adolescent psychotherapists in NHS CAMHS teams. We hope that this terminology recognises the individuality and potential of these young people, while also acknowledging the complex systemic and relational factors that shape their experiences.

'There is no such thing as an adolescent in care': reframing crises as cries

Adolescents in care are at a notably higher risk for suicidal thoughts and actions, given the profound emotional, relational, and developmental disruptions many of them have experienced. It's unsurprising that they engage in self-harm and suicidal behaviours at higher rates than their non-looked-after peers (Hamilton et al., 2015; Evans et al., 2017; Jewett et al., 2025). In our work, we frequently hear from foster carers, social workers, specialist and mainstream schools, and mental health professionals, who report that these adolescents often experience crises, bringing with them risk, distress, and feelings of confusion, fear, and lack of safety, shaping their relationships with those around them.

How can we understand *risk* in this context? We go back to Winnicott's influential statement 'There is no such thing as a baby . . . only a baby with its mother', which emphasises that an infant exists within a relationship with a primary caregiver rather than in isolation. Extending this foundational idea, we propose the parallel concept that there is 'no such thing as an adolescent in care' who can be understood independently of their surrounding network. This aligns with Bailey's (2006) perspective on adolescents not existing outside their family context. Adolescents in care and their support systems are deeply intertwined in a dynamic, mutually influential relationship, making it impossible to understand them separately. Risky behaviours in adolescents in care, often expressed in 'a crisis', are also not isolated, reverberating through their environment, shaping and being shaped by the professional network meant to support them.

Understanding these behaviours within the context of the adolescent–network interaction is crucial. Taking Winnicott's concept of the facilitating environment (1965), the network should 'hold' and 'handle' adolescents while providing a 'good enough' transition to adulthood that fosters development and connectedness. By attending to both physical and emotional needs, adolescents can develop security and resilience. This experience mirrors early infancy.

We know that babies communicate distress through crying – a fundamental tool for eliciting care, attention, and connection (Bowlby, 1969). The baby's cries act as a 'melody of connectedness', prompting a response from the caregiver. Emotional needs in infancy can be received and met within a nurturing relationship and environment. Over time, through experiences of gradual frustration, babies develop emotional regulation and a tolerance for reality (Stern, 1985). However, when a baby's cries are met with neglect or persistent inconsistency, they may shut down, seek comfort through physical means, or escalate to inconsolable crying, reflecting unmet and uncontained needs (Wright, 2009). This early relational pattern can set the stage for how distress is experienced and expressed later in life.

Adolescents in care have had a variety of early experiences as infants, which inevitably shape how they signal their need for care. Some adolescents may communicate by crying, while others might resort to inconsolable crying in the form of a crisis, seek comfort through their behaviour, or move straight to shutting down. The manner in which these signals are met by the professional network is crucial to the adolescent's experience. Just as an infant's cries serve as a fundamental form of communication requiring a particular caregiver response, such expressions from adolescents in care also call for a change in the professional network's response.

Instead of seeing crises in adolescents as behavioural disruptions or enactments, they need to be recognised as powerful expressions of need, communications of their internal world, emotional pain, or unresolved trauma. Although these crises can be seen as signals requiring an attuned, network-wide intervention, they often appear in ways that can be confusing to caregivers and professionals, possibly eliciting frustration, distress, or denial, and making all involved want to turn away or misconstrue them. It's essential to recognise these crises as forms of 'cry communication', rather than mere behavioural disturbances, in order to understand and respond to them in a meaningful way.

Addressing these crises effectively requires a shift in perspective – moving from surface-level, punitive, or reactive responses to examining the underlying distress and needs expressed by these crisis behaviours with curiosity.

The adolescent's emotions and experiences, shaped by early attachment ruptures and traumatic relationships, profoundly influence the system's response to them. In turn, the system's reactions further shape the adolescent's emotional world. This reciprocal dynamic extends beyond immediate professional networks and is embedded within broader factors, such as societal attitudes, historical trauma, poverty, cultural narratives, and systemic inequalities (Treisman, 2024). These wider influences shape both the adolescent's experiences and the system's capacity to respond effectively.

Therefore, crises should be seen as signals of distress resulting from a complex interplay between the young person and their professional network within a specific socio-political environment. Understanding these behaviours as indicators of underlying issues, rather than meaningless acting out, requires professionals – including social workers, mental health specialists, and caregivers – to look beyond the immediate crisis and consider its meaning in a broader context.

Navigating looked-after networks: holding or hindering in crisis

Beginning to work in specialist teams for looked-after children and adolescents within NHS Children and Adolescent Mental Health Services (CAMHS) can be overwhelming. Engaging with professional networks is often marked by confusion and disorganisation, being confronted by a whirlwind of names, systems, and unfamiliar structures – a chaotic world that demands swift navigation. This experience may mirror that of young people entering care, as they encounter a world filled with new people, different professionals, unclear expectations, and uncertain plans. Similarly, professionals entering this field must quickly adapt to a multifaceted network of individuals, teams, and organisations tasked with supporting adolescents and children in care (Gibbs, 2006).

The professional network surrounding young people in care in the UK is extensive and multifaceted, incorporating various professionals and organisations responsible for the welfare, development, and wellbeing of these children (Department for Education and Skills, 2006). These networks may include:

Social services. Integral to the network, with professionals such as social workers, team managers, service managers, and placement officers. These roles focus on coordinating care, assessing needs, and overseeing the child's placement and welfare.

Caregivers. Individuals responsible for the day-to-day care and stability of the child, which may include foster or residential carers. Family members, such as parents or relatives, may also be involved, particularly in situations involving kinship care arrangements.

Education professionals. Key figures include class teachers, school heads, and the special educational needs coordinator (SENCO), each of whom plays a crucial role in supporting the young person's educational progress, managing learning or behavioural needs, and collaborating with other professionals to ensure appropriate support for the child.

Health and mental health services. This encompasses GPs, local authority or independent paediatricians, child psychologists, mentors, youth support workers, LAC nurses, local or specialist NHS CAMHS (Child and Adolescent Mental Health Services) staff, as well as other specialist workers, like occupational or speech and language therapists (SLTs). These professionals address the physical and mental health needs of young people and work closely with other professionals to provide integrated care.

Legal representatives. Lawyers, judges, and guardians ad litem protect the rights of children and young people in legal matters, ensuring their best interests are maintained.

Additional support services. These can include independent or local authority fostering agencies, social work agencies, local authority virtual school staff who support educational outcomes for looked-after children, advocacy services, and various charities and non-profit organisations specialising in child welfare.

This complex network doesn't exist in a void; it is deeply influenced and constrained by societal and systemic factors, including the UK's chronic underfunding of services, workforce shortages, and the instability caused by policy changes. These constraints trickle down to young people in care, affecting their day-to-day experiences and the responses from those tasked to support them. The professional group surrounding looked-after children and adolescents is often too large to enable effective communication, and there are differing views within it.

Besides its size, the network's often unstable nature presents huge challenges. Adolescents often experience changes in professionals – such as social workers and foster carers – due to factors like staff turnover, team re-organisations, professionals' long-term sick leave due to stress, or other reasons (Shulman, 2008). The rapidly changing structure of these networks makes them vulnerable to unconscious re-enactments of trauma within professional interactions, echoing the dynamics of the young person's past experiences (Emanuel, 2002; Lanyado, 2017; Solomon, 2020; Sprince, 2000). Combined with the inherent complexities of these networks, these disruptions can lead to breakdowns in communication. Such breakdowns inevitably affect everyone involved and impair the network's ability to provide consistent, solid support (Conway, 2009). Understanding how relationships within these networks often break down requires examining the psychodynamics of group functioning.

Psychoanalytic thinking offers a framework to better understand the dynamics within professional networks surrounding children in child protection, foster care, and adoption, as well as the powerful impact of children's past traumatic experiences on multi-agency communication in the care system. Bion (1952) and Menzies (1960) have studied group functioning, particularly how groups receive, experience, and respond to unconscious communications through projections. It has been suggested that primitive defence mechanisms, such as splitting, projection, and denial, are unconsciously used by children and adolescents in care to cope with their experiences; these same defences can be activated in the professionals and networks around them (Witkon, 2012).

Britton (1981) applied these ideas to professional networks in child and family services, showing how professionals might unconsciously replicate the primitive defence mechanisms used by children and families to manage anxiety. He also noted that professionals within the network may unconsciously identify with different family members at various times, influencing their actions and interactions. Professionals and carers may thus be drawn into the projections of looked-after young people, entangled in the child's unconscious efforts to externalise their distress. This can lead to cycles of conflict and misunderstanding, damaging the very relationships meant to provide stability and healing. This instability can exacerbate existing challenges during critical periods and, of course, can lead to crises.

In response to these crises, professionals might identify with the adolescent's vulnerability and adopt protective or even rescuing behaviours, while others may focus on the adolescent's defiance or aggression, triggering punitive reactions.

We have discussed how making the transition (or being pushed) into adulthood is a critical experience for adolescents in care. Anecdotal experience and research (Blackmore et al., 2020) indicate that crises often escalate for these adolescents as they approach significant transitions, such as moving between placements, moving to independent living at 16, or turning 18. At those times, crises can intensify. The natural anxieties around these transitional periods are projected onto the professionals, who themselves may be under stress and carrying their own attachment histories and experiences. This can lead to the activation of primitive defence mechanisms to avoid the pain of loss, like splitting, projection, and denial within the professional group (Blackmore et al., 2020; Boswell & Cudmore, 2014).

Consequently, professionals in these situations may notice they're acting in uncharacteristic ways, behaving unprofessionally or outside their role (Sims, 2018). Misunderstandings, emotional exhaustion, and tensions among caregivers can echo the dysfunction experienced by the adolescent in their original family context, perpetuating instability. The pressure on professional networks is further amplified when they must respond to these dynamics amidst heavy workloads and time pressures. These experiences can have a powerful impact on the transitions that are happening and, at times, on the adolescent's placement itself (Harkin & Houston, 2016).

Through these dynamics, the professional network can end up contributing to the neglect and deprivation already experienced by children in care. Emanuel's (2002) concept of 'triple deprivation' provides a comprehensive framework for understanding the compounded layers of deprivation that children in care face. This builds upon the earlier concept of 'double deprivation' introduced by Henry (1974), which describes two primary sources of deprivation: the first stemming from external, uncontrollable factors, such as familial and systemic failures, and the second arising from the child's development of psychological defences that inhibit them from effectively seeking or accepting external support.

Emanuel's addition of a third layer highlights how professional networks can inadvertently contribute to a child's neglect. This involves the professionals' responses and projected anxieties that we've already discussed. This dynamic reflects how even well-meaning support systems can struggle with the psychological demands placed on them, potentially reinforcing the child's existing feelings of deprivation and isolation. The challenge for the professional network lies in withstanding and metabolising these dynamics without succumbing to the pull of the projections.

During periods of crisis, adolescents might be especially prone to projecting and splitting their intense and often overwhelming anxieties onto professionals and other adults around them, thereby placing significant strain on the relationships within the caregiving network. This relational instability within the professional network has the potential to compound the neglect and deprivation the adolescent has already experienced. Adolescents in care may then be particularly vulnerable to any perceived tension among the adults surrounding them; even minor relational discord can at times further destabilise these young people, intensifying their sense of imbalance and loss of control (Vilegen et al., 2023).

We will illustrate these ideas with three case examples: George, Maya, and Kayla. These cases are not exhaustive or representative of best practice, but they offer a snapshot of experiences from working with adolescents in care and their professional networks.

Escalating cries: how professional networks can become swept up by projections

George is a composite case example illustrating the aftermath of a placement breakdown – an experience of environmental failure – and its profound impact on the young person. This case outlines how the system reacts to such crises, revealing the interplay between individual experiences and systemic responses.

George, a 14-year-old in long-term foster care following multiple placement breakdowns, initially presented to the clinic with self-harming behaviours and suicidal ideation. Over time, his risk behaviours escalated. He had struggled with failed attempts to reconnect with his biological parents and had then moved to a new foster care placement after a previous one broke down, given that George's risk had become unmanageable; because of all this, he became increasingly dysregulated. He began engaging in highly risky activities, such as walking onto train tracks, attacking a person in public with a knife, and seeking out older people online, later disclosing experiences of sexual assault. Following a week of such behaviours, the social worker invited me to a network meeting to discuss his case.

Upon joining the meeting, I was confronted by a large group of professionals – about 20 people from 20 different organisations. The meeting was initially chaotic, as half the time was spent introducing the professionals and clarifying the roles of each.

It quickly became evident that referrals had been made to various services at the same time, each focusing on a specific aspect of George's presentation, with no effort until this point to link them all up. Each professional framed their contribution according to their area of expertise. These contributions often reflected an 'imaginative identification', with professionals speculating on how their specific approach could address George's behaviour.

George had recently been diagnosed with both ADHD and ASD, and throughout the meeting, these labels were repeatedly cited as shorthand explanations for his behaviour: 'George's behaviour is a consequence of his ADHD brain' or 'This behaviour is typical of someone with ASD, so we must adapt our approach accordingly'. As the discussion unfolded, I felt increasingly disoriented and frustrated. The George I had been working with in therapy seemed lost amidst these labels and fragmented perspectives, and I struggled to think of his individual experience.

We can now speculate on what might have triggered George's escalated risk. George's loss of yet another placement may have brought him in contact with his constant experience of being removed, from his birth family to multiple foster placements, an experience that positions him in a cycle of re-experiencing loss and rejection. Each placement breakdown can amplify George's sense of abandonment and reinforce a core belief that he is difficult to manage. With every rupture, another layer of environmental failure deepens George's psychological breakdown, heightening his emotional dysregulation and risky behaviours.

George's escalation in risk could also be viewed as an expression of unprocessed anger toward the failing systems around him. Simultaneously, it may signal an unconscious longing for a stable environment that can contain his risk. Another dimension of George's risk lies in his interpersonal boundaries, which may signify his difficulty in knowing what safety truly means. This could stem from the ruptured early attachments and the repeated changes in caregivers throughout his life, leaving him without an internalised sense of security.

The meeting of professionals in response to George's crisis seemed chaotic and incoherent, reflecting the system's struggle to contain his deep, unprocessed anxieties, fears, and pain linked to his losses. Splitting acts as a significant defence mechanism in this context: by unthinkingly adding more and more professionals to George's care network, the difficult experience of his escalation becomes, in a sense, diluted. When overwhelmed, the network's holding function splits off different parts of George's experience and projects them onto various professionals, each tasked with a specific aspect of his care in a mechanistic way, with elements of magical thinking. However, this process of splitting depletes the network's holding function, losing sight of the emotional complexity George presents as one whole person and reducing him instead to a fragmented collection of bits.

The reliance on ADHD and ASD diagnoses as shorthand explanations for George's risky behaviour, while to some degree helpful in understanding certain aspects of his experience, becomes reductive in fully capturing his challenges. This approach reflects a defensive, rigid stance that prevents deeper engagement with the overwhelming, traumatic past that George carries. Focusing on labels can obscure the system's ability to address the deeper roots of George's difficulties and acts as a defence mechanism for the professionals, simplifying George's complex emotional state and managing the anxiety surrounding his care.

George's increasing risk and the system's fragmented response illustrate a mix of projection, splitting, and environmental failure when faced with his emotional complexity, rooted in unprocessed trauma and loss. Reframing George's escalating 'crises' as a form of communication is crucial for understanding his behaviour and providing the needed containment.

George's growing distress and loud cries for help starkly contrast with Maya's withdrawal and emotional shutdown, a description of which follows. While George struggles to process the instability of his life, his response to yet another placement breakdown is an outward expression of his pain, amplifying his emotional crisis.

Muted cries: re-sparking the professional network

Yet distress does not always take a loud or explosive form. For Maya, reactions to trauma were present in a different way, through retreating inward and becoming emotionally numb. As Alvarez (2010) notes, severely traumatised young people may adopt a 'deadening' defence to shield themselves from the unbearable pain of repeated disappointments:

Maya had moved through multiple placements across different boroughs, with her journey marked by instability and neglect. Her upbringing had been challenging, shaped by moments of love and companionship within her family, alongside incidents of abuse and neglect; her disclosure of sexual abuse by an extended family member had come through a drawing in her art class. However, her family had denied the allegations and had framed Maya as 'the problem', accusing her of 'making up stories'. In response, she had run away from home several times.

Maya then moved out of borough, living with multiple family members until coming into care at 17, at which point she was also referred to CAMHS. The timing of the referral, on the cusp of Maya leaving care, carried an air of procedural haste, emphasising the need to 'offer her something' before she turned 18. She was referred at this point due to depression, low mood, panic attacks, and intense suicidal ideation.

Maya missed her first appointment and didn't let the receptionist know. I phoned her and acknowledged that it was the first time we were speaking. She said she was unwell and had forgotten about the appointment. Her tone of voice sounded flat and low. I suggested that she might be sceptical about help – or that anybody could help – as she had been so let down in the past . . . Why would this be any different? Maya responded, 'Yeah, what is the point of me seeing you? We won't have enough time anyway'.

This moment underscores the critical importance of recognition and social witnessing in addressing Maya's experiences. Her hesitation reflects personal defences, but also an understandable mistrust of systems that have consistently failed her. As Music (2009) notes, neglected children often appear disengaged, with their flat and lifeless demeanour masking profound emotional pain. Without recognising these underlying dynamics, their silent struggles can be overlooked, perpetuating cycles of institutional failure.

When she began attending care coordination sessions, Maya's guarded demeanour and lack of energy were palpable. Her suicidal thoughts and feelings of worthlessness seemed tied to a deep-seated belief that she was a burden. She spoke sparingly about her struggles and conveyed a sense that 'no one can really help'. Her mistrust of the world seemed justified: she had been repeatedly failed by adults and the systems that were meant to protect her. As her 18th birthday approached, her engagement became tenuous, and eventually, she stopped attending sessions altogether.

The network's response was swift: her absence was interpreted as an indication of her readiness to move on, a sign that she no longer needed support. I felt bewildered and shocked, as if I were mad for believing Maya needed more support. It seemed to me that her withdrawal might be a defence against the vulnerability of seeking help that she feared might not come or would not prove reliable. Maya's retreat perhaps echoed both the dynamics of neglect and adolescent conflict: how can a young person risk showing they need help when experience has taught them that help may vanish just when it's most needed? In Maya's case, her efforts seemed consumed by managing the void left by a lifetime of unmet needs and unresolved trauma:

I presented my concerns at a network meeting, emphasising that Maya's withdrawal was likely an expression of fear and unresolved trauma rather than an indication of independence, especially within a system that encourages quick moves and adaptation. I highlighted the similarity between Maya's earlier experiences – her family's denial of her abuse and dismissal of her disclosures – and the system's current approach. Both seemed to push her away during moments of vulnerability, reinforcing her belief that she was unworthy of care, love, and time. The network's response shifted after the meeting, as we were able to reflect together on how Maya's seemingly stable behaviour – being thrust into independence without adequate preparation – created immense pressure on her.

Music (2022) describes how neglected children fall into 'desparked states', where their capacity to seek help becomes compromised by layers of mistrust and self-protection. In the meeting about Maya, we had reflected on her previous comments about feeling 'thrown into an abyss', capturing the mismatch between her developmental stage, her emotional experience, and the expectations placed on her. Slowing things down seemed essential. I reached out to her social worker, who admitted to feeling rejected by Maya's disengagement. Together, we explored the ambivalence on both sides – Maya's fear of connection and the social worker's frustration at her withdrawal. The social worker agreed to write Maya a card, acknowledging their relationship and offering a chance for closure. Similarly, Maya's foster carer reflected on her own feelings of rejection and arranged a goodbye meeting.

These dialogues of recognition and reconnection, though small, began to address Maya's feelings of being discarded. This process also involved recognising and addressing the systemic barriers that had led to her disengagement. The neglect Maya had experienced was not only internal but also institutional, reflecting the broader social disparities that had limited her access to consistent care and support. Music (2022) discusses the necessity of initial 'safening' within the therapeutic relationship, as well as re-sparking connections, but this concept also extends to the professional network. To help with this, I spoke to different parts of the network but also acknowledged the systemic barriers that had shaped Maya's mistrust and disengagement. Without this acknowledgement and re-sparking, Maya's needs would have remained unmet, reinforcing her belief that she was undeserving of care.

Supervision was essential in exploring my acute reaction when the network initially decided to step down, helping me differentiate between my countertransference and Maya's experience of abandonment. Reflecting on how the network's defences mirrored her family's denial enabled me to advocate for a buffer period, facilitating a smoother transition. We created a plan that included

254 Psychoanalytic Crisis Work with Adolescents

ongoing involvement from her professional advisor, social worker, foster carer, and birth mother. This process required an intentional effort to witness and challenge systemic disparities, while fostering collaboration within the network. The dual recognition of intersubjective and structural neglect was vital to keeping Maya in mind and creating continuity and vitalisation (Alvarez, 2012) within the network. Neglect is not merely a relational issue; it is intertwined with societal and institutional systems. Addressing both dimensions allowed us to begin re-sparking hope and connection for Maya.

Cries of trauma

Kayla, aged 14, entered care a year ago following a disclosure at school of the severe emotional and physical abuse she had endured at home. She reported that her mother struggled with alcohol abuse, while her father was controlling, resulting in a volatile and unsafe household environment. Kayla felt neglected and unloved, believing her parents favoured her younger sister and directed their disdain and aggression toward her. Being removed from her family initially brought a sense of relief for Kayla, as her first foster placement provided a nurturing environment where she felt safe and heard. While still on an interim care order, she was moved to a longer-term placement with a foster carer who was already caring for another foster child. Kayla did not feel that the new foster care could understand her in the same way.

In parallel, Kayla was referred to CAMHS for an ADHD assessment. During the urgent initial assessment due to her high risk, Kayla reported feeling unsafe and very anxious about going outside and attending school. She was worried she might bump into unsafe people on the street and reported hearing voices and having intrusive thoughts that 'told' her at times to jump out of the window in her room or off a bridge, or at other times to hurt others. Our MDT determined that addressing ADHD was not the priority, as Kayla needed to feel safe in the placement and at school.

To support the placement, weekly review meetings were held with Kayla's social worker, the foster carer, and their supervising social worker. With support, Kayla also attended her care coordination sessions, where she began reflecting on the neglect she experienced. She described dangerous, unsafe incidents at home and stories of being left alone for long periods with access to her mother's alcohol and cannabis, getting out of the window at home and falling off the roof, or leaving home and wandering the streets late at night.

These disclosures were a key part of her early CAMHS sessions, where she shared vivid memories of her home life, expressing a mix of anger, sadness, and confusion. Similar to the case of George, despite these disclosures, the network was predominantly focused on CAMHS assessing for an ADHD diagnosis.

This focus may reflect an unconscious attempt to use the diagnosis as a vessel for the projections and disturbance, allowing professionals to distance themselves from thinking about the terrors and neglect Kayla was communicating. Though Kayla did not share these experiences with her social worker, she knew about the professional meetings and that information was being communicated, which she found reassuring. For Kayla, this might have been the first time for her to feel thought about by adult minds; the network's attempts at thinking about her experience and communications offered a sense of being 'held' by a parental couple.

Meanwhile, the ongoing court proceedings for a full care order seemed to create ambivalent feelings for Kayla – on the one hand, she didn't want to return home, yet on the other hand, she was terribly worried about what this would mean for her future and identity. On the day the care order was finalised, feeling increasingly anxious, Kayla left the placement for an entire day without any communication and returned the next day. She later shared that she had wandered around the city on buses and had slept rough in the park while feeling confused and suicidal. The finalisation of the full care order marked a tipping point for her, leading to a day of crisis expressing her cry over her experience of being at a loss and wandering alone, not belonging, unclaimed, and unanchored.

Shortly after the care order was granted, Kayla's social worker, whom she had grown to trust, was replaced. This also marked a turning point in the placement. Kayla's sense of connection to the carer began to erode. Her behaviour became unpredictable, characterised by anger, mistrust, and withdrawal. The foster carer, though compassionate, struggled to manage the escalating tension and started getting drawn into re-enacting past dynamics. She eventually gave notice, citing concerns for the other foster child's safety. While social care was unable to find a new placement, Kayla's state of mind shifted; she was afraid and felt unsafe and constantly persecuted, not wanting to live in that placement anymore, as if she did not need anyone.

The social worker's change had deeply unsettled Kayla, reigniting feelings of loss, neglect, abandonment, and uncertainty. This brought Kayla back into the dynamics of her birth family; she started to perceive her foster home as mirroring her previous experiences, believing that her foster carer favoured the other child in the home and interpreting certain interactions as dismissive or rejecting. The professional network around Kayla unfortunately collapsed under the pressures and also became 'actors' in the re-enactment of Kayla's trauma. Her experience of feeling rejected, unwanted, and abandoned, given the unclear local authority plan, was terrifying for Kayla, who, to preserve her psychic integrity, communicated that she did not want to be dependent on anyone, as it is very risky.

During this time, Kayla's psychic solution was to spend nights in local parks. She found these spaces peaceful, a stark contrast to the turmoil she felt in the foster home. For Kayla, the parks symbolised a paradoxical sense of safety: by choosing the risks, she felt she could reclaim control over her life. This echoed her early experiences of danger at home, reframed as something she could manage on her terms.

> Kayla was able to reflect on this in sessions, although she continued going out to the parks. She communicated to me some suicidal thoughts and plans, as well as mentioning new acquaintances that raised my alarm in terms of potential exploitation, as Kayla had been receiving expensive gifts. In the network meetings, we thought about what Kayla might be expressing through her risky behaviours while also supporting the carer in holding Kayla's need for feeling wanted and cared for. Although Kayla didn't seem concerned about herself, the network around her was holding the anxiety about her risk and safety. Kayla communicated that she found this reassuring: it made her feel that people cared.
>
> In one CAMHS session, Kayla arrived stoned and drunk, admitting she had turned to substances that morning to cope with her overwhelming emotions. I shared these concerns with her social worker, who, in a rushed way, took immediate action and reprimanded her. Kayla interpreted this response as judgemental and dismissive, leading her to stop attending CAMHS sessions. She expressed her anger, betrayal, and disappointment towards me; she hated me 'for everything' I had done. Shortly after, unexpectedly, social care arranged a new out-of-borough placement: the transition happened hastily, within a few days, with no goodbyes.

Kayla experienced me as the source of all that had gone wrong, projecting onto me all the badness. I became another uncaring, harmful object, like those from her past, reinforcing her belief that no one can be trusted or truly understand and care for her. There was a level of confusion between her and me: 'Who did what?' The loss of our relationship and the continued instability in her living situation left her increasingly isolated. Despite voicing a desperate need to be claimed by someone – to feel truly seen, valued, and wanted – she became further removed from supportive relationships. Her feelings of intense anger and confusion, communicated to me, made me feel I had done something terrible and was left with feelings of shame and injustice. These feelings were hard to shake off as the case then moved on, with social care not responding to offers for any closing meetings.

Both Kayla and George showed strong loyalty to their biological families, helping them to avoid feeling like an 'unwanted child' (Hodges, 1990). However, this loyalty made forming new relationships challenging, leaving them in emotional limbo and suspicious of new relationships. According to Youell (2012), identifications with birth parents and family may weaken during the latency years but can then resurface in adolescence as part of identity formation and rebellion, complicating their relationship to foster parents as they navigate their loyalties and attachments. This was especially evident for Kayla, who was placed in foster care during her adolescence, intensifying both her feelings of suspicion and loyalty towards her parents.

The meaning of cries: psychic wounds, breakdown, and moving on

Adolescence, as explored in previous chapters, is a period of significant emotional and physical transformation. It is marked by the search for identity and independence, often leading to a distancing from familial structures and processes of differentiation and individuation. Successfully navigating these developmental tasks requires a stable and secure environment where young people can regress when needed and can rely on trusted adults for support (Blos, 1967). They must also rehearse the vital process of rupture and repair within consistent and containing relationships in their systems (Stern, 1985). Without safety and environmental continuity, 'the natural healing that comes with time and gradual maturation' (Winnicott, 1963) is significantly hindered or even absent.

The cases of George, Maya, and Kayla demonstrate how the breakdown of family life and multiple placements can lead to profound relational, historical, and developmental trauma, disrupting the fundamental experiences of adolescence (Conway, 2009). For George and Maya, there were multiple instances of placement and relationship changes. They endured both the disintegration of their families, but also frequent failures within the very system meant to support them, with moves from one placement to another whenever challenges arose. These changes exacerbated their ongoing sense of instability and abandonment. Similarly, while Kayla faced adversity within her family for years, a crucial breakdown at a pivotal stage in her development further deepened her sense of unsafety and insecurity.

In all three cases, there had been a striking pattern of profound discontinuity over the years, both in the young people's internal worlds and their external realities. Their unresolved past traumas continuously resurfaced, influencing their interactions with professionals within their support networks. Simultaneously, the systems and professionals meant to support them inadvertently re-enacted these traumas, perpetuating instability through repeated relationship and placement breakdowns. As a result, new sequences of trauma were experienced and internalised by these young people, leaving their inner worlds in a state of flux, characterised by fractured and sporadic connections that felt neglectful and uncaring.

George, Maya, and Kayla had faced deep-seated feelings of loss and rejection from professionals, making it challenging to establish a stable foundation for growth. Their relationships had been disrupted, reinforcing cycles of insecurity and impermanence due to past and present attachment failures that continued to surface. This pattern was particularly evident in the cases of Maya and Kayla, where systemic failures were re-enacted, leading them to abruptly leave relationships that they had just started to develop, often without closure. Consequently, despite their best intentions, they each time internalised yet another 'failing object', reinforcing their sense of powerlessness and adopting defensive behaviours during adolescence.

As a result, adolescents in care such as these may come to believe, in the end, that they are 'too difficult to manage', intensifying their existing feelings of being unloved and neglected. The cumulative weight of all these experiences profoundly complicates the process of mourning (Bartram, 2003). For Maya and Kayla in particular, saying goodbye in any context had become a fraught task, as mourning for them was intertwined with guilt, anger, and confusion. They might have felt responsible for their circumstances while simultaneously resenting the caregivers and systems that had failed them. This unresolved grief had left their internal worlds fragmented and chaotic, while professionals working with them found themselves experiencing similar emotional turmoil, as poignantly illustrated in Kayla's case.

We see a complex interplay of both external and internal difficulties unfolding in the cases of George, Maya, and Kayla, with significant implications for their psychological development and risk presentation. For many looked-after adolescents, experiences of disconnection and instability create a fertile ground for crises that may appear contradictory or confusing to carers and professionals. These crises are often rooted in emotional distress, with behaviours such as self-harm, violence, or risky activities emerging – sometimes after years of internal struggle – as coping mechanisms to manage feelings of worthlessness, rejection, or trauma.

As seen in the example of all these three cases, the risks faced by adolescents in care can extend beyond self-harm and suicidal behaviours. They may also include violence expressed through high-risk and impulsive activities, involvement in gangs, increased vulnerability to child exploitation, sexual abuse, grooming, or risky online behaviours. The high-risk activities that George, Kayla, and Maya had engaged in were not only driven by external pressures and exploitation but also served as coping mechanisms to manage their internal distress. For some adolescents, such behaviours can provide a sense of belonging, an escape from emotional pain – as Kayla described – or a way to mask feelings of worthlessness. In this way, engaging in risk-taking can offer a temporary sense of control or validation in an environment where they otherwise feel powerless and insignificant.

The contradictory nature of these adolescents' behaviours – at times aggressive or self-harming, at other times engaging in risky behaviours or defying authority – reflected their turbulent struggle for identity and development, as well as a re-enactment of their past traumatic experiences (Canham, 2004). By placing themselves in dangerous situations, they externalised their internalised neglect and abusive attachment constellations, sometimes even becoming the recipients of further abuse. George and Kayla, in particular, exhibited intense shifts between acting out and withdrawing, caught in a cycle of seeking control, testing boundaries, and reacting to feelings of abandonment, rejection, and fear. This pattern reflected a dual drive: the thrill and excitement of danger, paired with the compulsion to repeat the familiar trauma, reliving feelings of fear and risk. Ultimately, these adolescents were attempting to assert some sense of control over chaotic and overwhelming emotions.

The vulnerability of adolescents in care is exacerbated by the lack of targeted mental health and suicide prevention interventions, as mental health crisis services often fail to address their specific and nuanced needs (Ball et al., 2024). Instead, rather than addressing their complex emotional needs and states with depth and understanding, systemic responses frequently reinforce defensive mechanisms that hinder meaningful support. In moments of crisis and heightened risk, professional networks surrounding adolescents in care often respond reactively to their unprocessed and intense emotional turmoil.

In George's case, a significant issue was the compartmentalisation that had emerged within the professional network. The constant influx of new professionals and the overreliance on diagnostic labels diminished the emotional significance of his experiences. This fragmentation not only disrupted continuity of care but also mirrored George's own internal fragmentation, amplifying his distress. Rather than engaging with the depth of his emotional struggles, professionals had compartmentalised his difficulties, treating isolated symptoms instead of addressing their root causes. This 'divide and conquer' approach prevented a holistic understanding of his needs and distanced him from meaningful, sustained support.

A similarly damaging form of systemic fragmentation is the frequent turnover of professionals, often dismissed as inevitable or inconsequential. However, as Kayla's vignette illustrates, these changes force young people to try to form new attachments when they are already emotionally depleted. This disruption not only affects the young person but also weakens the professional network itself. When professionals fail to build strong working relationships with each other, enactments and misunderstandings can emerge, further complicating the support process. Effective care requires professionals to form stable, collaborative relationships – spaces where mutual understanding, coordination, and even disagreement can be processed constructively. Without these foundational relationships, the system can become increasingly fragmented, leaving young people to navigate an unstable and disjointed support network on their own.

In Maya's case, we saw a reversal of affect and a disavowal – defence mechanisms used by the system to justify disengagement, both changing the meaning of Maya's actions to its opposite and denying the meaning behind it. Rather than recognising her withdrawal as an expression of fear and vulnerability, professionals misinterpreted it as a sign that she no longer required support, ultimately leading to case closure. This reflected a broader societal tendency to push such adolescents toward independence prematurely, disregarding their emotional realities and developmental needs.

The expectation that young people in care should rapidly transition into independence is so ingrained that it often goes unquestioned. However, Maya's experience, along with that of many other adolescents in care, highlights a fundamental systemic flaw: the abrupt transition to independence at age 18. Despite research demonstrating that brain development continues well into the mid-20s (Blum et al., 2012), the current system expects young people to become fully self-sufficient the moment they reach legal adulthood (Häggman-Laitila et al., 2018; Rogers, 2011). This pressure creates an inherent dilemma – why should a young person emotionally invest in a foster carer or professional when they know that the relationship has an expiration date? The inevitability of severed attachments reinforces their sense of instability and disconnection, making it even more difficult to trust and engage with support systems.

Ultimately, these systemic defences – whether through forced independence, professional fragmentation, or disavowal of emotional needs – severely limit our ability to engage with the deeper psychological needs and experiences of young people like George, Maya, and Kayla. By failing to acknowledge and work through these complexities, the system perpetuates instability rather than providing the consistent, attuned support these adolescents need – pushing them further into crisis rather than helping them find stability and healing.

Hearing, translating, and metabolising the cries

At the heart of meaningful work with adolescents in care is recognising their crisis as an unheard 'cry', whether distressed, loud, or muted. These cries often manifest through challenging behaviours, withdrawal, or disengagement, which can be easily misinterpreted. Reframing crises as communication enables professionals to move beyond surface-level behaviours and better understand the adolescent's internal world and unmet needs.

Slowing down the network responses to create thinking spaces allows professionals to pause, be curious, and reflect on what these crises and cries mean. Curiosity can facilitate thinking from the young person's perspective (Robinson et al., 2020) and mentalizing (Vliegen et al., 2023) – interpreting behaviours as expressions of the adolescent's emotional state. This can help professionals engage with the adolescent's unconscious communications in a deeper way.

For example, in Maya's and Kayla's cases, the carer and social worker had spaces to reflect and process Kayla's actions; similarly, in Maya's situation, a smaller professional network served as the core group, effectively guiding the broader network. This facilitating environment, where the adolescent's unconscious communications could be reflected on, helped establish spaces where these young people could feel thought about and understood.

Therefore, professionals can create a 'holding environment/network' that provides consistent, attuned, and responsive care to mitigate the destabilising effects of trauma, transitions, and anxieties about loss (Winnicott, 1965). For instance, disruptive behaviours might be reframed not as 'misbehaviour' but as expressions of anxiety, fear, or vulnerability. Aggression may reflect inner turmoil, and self-harm might be a defensive response to uncontained anxiety. This allows a team to understand the unconscious relational dynamics at play, deepening the understanding of the adolescent's emotional experiences and needs.

Understanding network dynamics is also crucial for improving support for looked-after adolescents more widely. Reflective consultations, such as those facilitated by child and adolescent psychotherapists working in LAC teams in CAMHS, enable exploration of the professional network's dynamics around the case at hand (Robinson et al., 2020). Thinking with the network gives time for processing complex emotions and understanding the pressures that hinder effective professional communication (Emanuel, 2002; Lanyado, 2003; Solomon, 2020), which can reduce the risk of destructive re-enactments in the network (Cregeen, 2008; Rocco-Briggs, 2008).

Reflecting on this kind of consultation, Sprince (2000) describes gaining insight into how powerfully clients project into social workers, causing fieldworkers to identify so strongly with families that they can't think clearly. This shows the pressures professionals face and highlights the importance of greater awareness of unconscious identifications (Britton, 1981). A shift in perspective allows professionals to reflect on their own experiences, feelings, and roles within the network and their responses to the adolescent's communication and how they may contribute, unknowingly, to the adolescent's distress. Synthesising insights from all professionals helps the network develop a holistic view that can better contain the looked-after adolescent in crisis.

Alongside mentalization, advocacy ensures the adolescent's voice is heard within the complex web of professional systems. Looked-after adolescents are often silenced by systemic neglect or overwhelmed by bureaucratic processes. Advocacy amplifies the adolescent's voice, translating their cries into meaningful action within the network. It challenges narratives that pathologise the adolescent, reframing behaviours in the context of trauma considering historical injustice as well as broader systemic inequalities.

Think of the example of Maya, where a wider narrative about the imperative move of the looked-after adolescence into adulthood coloured how professionals viewed and responded to her. Advocacy within the network, as in her case described, shifted the focus from blaming the adolescent to understanding their broader struggles.

Adolescents in care often embody systemic injustice, with their pain misunderstood or dismissed. Professionals can address this by bearing witness to the layers of historical, cultural, and systemic trauma underlying their experiences. Shifting from asking 'What is wrong with you?' to 'What has happened to you – and to your people?' (Ghosh Ippen, 2019) situates the adolescent's cries within a broader societal, historical, and intergenerational context, fostering a more compassionate response.

Ultimately, maintaining a curious, mentalizing, and advocating approach cultivates a 'consistent, positive, thinking and caregiving network' around the young person (Boston & Szur, 1983, p. 5). This allows professionals to stay connected to the painful issues they work with daily (Sprince, 2000), safeguarding the adolescent against further breakdowns. Such an approach requires consistent reflective practice to thoughtfully recognise and respond to complex emotional experiences, ensuring the integrity of the caregiving network to offer a holding environment for adolescents in care.

References

Alvarez, A. (2010). Levels of analytic work and levels of pathology: The work of calibration. *The International Journal of Psychoanalysis*, 91(4), 859–878.

Alvarez, A. (2012). *The thinking heart: Three levels of psychoanalytic therapy with disturbed children*. Routledge.

Bailey, T. (2006). There's no such thing as an adolescent. In: M. Lanyado, & A. Horne (eds.), *A question of technique: Independent psychoanalytic approaches with children and adolescents* (pp. 181–199). Routledge.

Ball, W. P., Anderson, C., Black, C., Gordon, S., Lackenby, M., Murchie, M., Ostrovska, B., & Butler, J. E. (2024). Mental health service use in children at risk of significant harm: A record linkage study of a child protection register. *Social Science & Medicine*, 353, 117057.

Bartram, P. (2003). Some Oedipal problems in work with adopted children and their parents. *Journal of Child Psychotherapy*, 29(1), 21–36.

Bion, W. R. (1952). Group dynamics: A re-view. *The International Journal of Psychoanalysis*, 33, 235–247.

Blackmore, J., Burns, G., Waters, C. S., & Shelton, K. H. (2020). "The very first thing that connected us to him": Adopters' experiences of sharing photographs, "talking" albums and other materials with their children prior to meeting. *Adoption & Fostering*, 44(3), 225–241.

Blos, P. (1967). *The adolescent passage: Developmental issues*. New York: International Universities Press.

Blum, R. W., Bastos, F. I., Kabiru, C. W., & Le, L. C. (2012). Adolescent health in the 21st century. *The Lancet*, 379(9826), 1567–1568.

Boston, M., & Szur, R. (1983). *Psychotherapy with severly deprived children*. London: Routledge.

Boswell, S., & Cudmore, L. (2014). "The children were fine": Acknowledging complex feelings in the move from foster care into adoption. *Adoption & Fostering*, 38(1), 5–21.

Bowlby, J. (1969). *Attachment and loss: Volume I. Attachment*. London: Hogarth Press.

Britton, R. (1981). Re-enactment as an unwitting professional response to family dynamics. *Psychotherapy with Families: An Analytic Approach*, 48–58.

Canham, H. (2004). Spitting, kicking and stripping: Technical difficulties encountered in the treatment of deprived children. *Journal of Child Psychotherapy*, 30(2), 143–154.

Capes, K. (2024). Don't call me a case: Love languages and the care experience. In: R. Pierre (ed.), *Free loaves on Fridays: The care system as told by people who actually get it* (pp. 29–40). Unbound.

Conway, P. (2009). Falling between minds: The effects of unbearable experiences on multi-agency communication in the care system. *Adoption & Fostering*, 33(1), 18–29.

Cousins, W., Taggart, L., & Milner, S. (2010). Looked after or overlooked? An exploratory investigation of the mental health issues of adolescents living in state care in Northern Ireland. *Psychology, Health & Medicine*, 15(5), 497–506.

Cregeen, S. (2008). Workers, groups and gangs: Consultation to residential adolescent teams. *Journal of Child Psychotherapy*, 34(2), 172–189.

Department for Education and Skills. (2006). *Working together to safeguard children: A guide to inter-agency working to safeguard and promote the welfare of children*. The Stationery Office.

Emanuel, L. (2002). Deprivation 2 3. *Journal of Child Psychotherapy*, 28(2), 163–179.

Evans, R., White, J., Turley, R., Slater, T., Morgan, H., Strange, H., & Scourfield, J. (2017). Comparison of suicidal ideation, suicide attempt and suicide in children and young people in care and non-care populations: Systematic review and meta-analysis of prevalence. *Children and Youth Services Review*, 82, 122–129.

Freud, S. (1901). The psychopathology of everyday life: Forgetting, slips of the tongue, bungled actions, superstitions and errors. In: *The standard edition of the complete psychological works of Sigmund Freud* (Vol. 6, pp. vii–296). Hogarth and the Institute of Psycho-Analysis

Ghosh Ippen, C. (2019). Wounds from the past: Integrating historical trauma into a multicultural infant mental health framework. In: C. H. Zeanah (ed.), *Handbook of infant mental health* (4th edition, pp. 134–153). Guilford Press.

Gibbs, I. (2006). Working with the looked-after child and his network. In: M. Lanyado, & A. Horne (eds.), *A question of technique: Independent psychoanalytic approaches with children and adolescents* (pp. 99–111). Routledge.

Häggman-Laitila, A., Salokekkilä, P., & Karki, S. (2018). Transition to adult life of young people leaving foster care: A qualitative systematic review. *Children and Youth Services Review*, 95, 134–143.

Hamilton, D. J., Taylor, B. J., Killick, C., & Bickerstaff, D. (2015). Suicidal ideation and behaviour among young people leaving care: Case-file survey. *Child Care in Practice*, 21(2), 160–176.

Harkin, C., & Houston, S. (2016). Reviewing the literature on the breakdown of foster care placements for young people: Complexity and the social work task. *Child Care in Practice*, 22(2), 98–112.

Henry, G. (1974). Doubly deprived. *Journal of Child Psychotherapy*, 3(4), 15–28.

Hodges, J. (1990). The relationship to self and objects in early maternal deprivation and adoption. *Journal of Child Psychotherapy*, 16, 53–73.

Janzen, M. D. (2023). Stigmatized: In/Forming identities of children in Care. *Power and Education*, 15(3), 274–290.

Jewett, P. I., Taliaferro, L. A., Borowsky, I. W., Mathiason, M. A., & Areba, E. M. (2025). Structural adverse childhood experiences associated with suicidal ideation, suicide attempts, and repetitive nonsuicidal self-injury among racially and ethnically minoritized youth. *Suicide and Life-Threatening Behavior*, 55(1), e13084.

Lanyado, M. (2003). The emotional tasks of moving from fostering to adoption: Transitions, attachment, separation and loss. *Clinical Child Psychology and Psychiatry*, 8(3), 337–349.

Lanyado, M. (2017). Putting down roots: The significance of technical adaptations in the therapeutic process with fostered and adopted children. *Journal of Child Psychotherapy*, 43(2), 208–222.

Menzies, I. E. (1960). A case-study in the functioning of social systems as a defence against anxiety: A report on a study of the nursing service of a general hospital. *Human Relations*, 13(2), 95–121.

Music, G. (2009). Neglecting neglect: Some thoughts about children who have lacked good input, and are "undrawn" and "unenjoyed". *Journal of Child Psychotherapy*, 35(2), 142–156.

Music, G. (2022). *Respark: Igniting hope and joy after trauma and depression*. Mind-Nurturing Books.

NSPCC. (2023a). *Annual report and accounts 2022/23*. https://www.nspcc.org.uk/globalassets/documents/annual-reports/NSPCC-Annual-Report-2022-2023.pdf

NSPCC. (2023b, October 27). *Why language matters: Why you should avoid the acronym "LAC" when talking about children in care*. NSPCC Learning. https://learning.nspcc.org.uk/news/why-language-matters/looked-after-children

Pierre, R. (ed.). (2024). *Free loaves on Fridays: The care system as told by people who actually get it*. Unbound.

Robinson, F., Luyten, P., & Midgley, N. (2020). The child psychotherapists' role in consultation work with the professional network around looked after children. *Journal of Social Work Practice*, 34(3), 309–324.

Rocco-Briggs, M. (2008). "Who owns my pain?" An aspect of the complexity of working with looked after children. *Journal of Child Psychotherapy*, 34(2), 190–206.

Rogers, R. (2011). I remember thinking, why isn't there someone to help me? Why isn't there someone who can help me make sense of what I'm going through? "Instant adulthood" and the transition of young people out of state care. *Journal of Sociology*, 47(4), 411–426.

Shulman, G. (2008). Unconscious dynamics in systems and networks: Introduction. In: D. Hindle, & G. Shulman (eds.), *The emotional experience of adoption: A psychoanalytic perspective* (pp. 71–77). Routledge.

Sims, L. (2018). What happens in the making of an adoptive family? Rethinking matching in adoptions from care. Doctoral Dissertation in Collaboration with CORAM BAAF. University of Sussex.

Sissay, L. (2023). *Let the light pour in: Morning poems*. Canongate Books.

Solomon, R. (2020). The professional couple, the consultant, and the outside world. In: A. Roy (ed.), *A for adoption: An exploration of the adoption experience for families and professionals* (pp. 83–100). Routledge.

Sprince, J. (2000). Towards an integrated network. *Journal of Child Psychotherapy*, 26(3), 413–431.

Stern, D. N. (1985). *The interpersonal world of the infant: A view from psychoanalysis and developmental psychology*. Routledge.

TACT. (2019). *Language that cares: Changing the way professionals talk about children in care*. https://tactfostering.org.uk/content/uploads/2019/03/TACT-Language-that-cares-2019_online.pdf

Treisman, K. (2024). *Trauma-informed health care: A reflective guide for improving care and services*. Jessica Kingsley Publishers.

Vliegen, N., Tang, E., Midgley, N., Luyten, P., & Fonagy, P. (2023). *Therapeutic work for children with complex trauma: A three-track psychodynamic approach*. Routledge.

Winnicott, D. W. (1960/1984). The theory of the parent-infant relationship. In: *The maturational processes and the facilitating environment* (pp. 37–55). Routledge. (Original work published 1960).

Winnicott, D. W. (1963). Struggling through the doldrums. In: D. W. Winnicott (ed.), *The child, the family and the outside world* (pp. 201–208). Penguin Books.

Winnicott, D. W. (1965). *The maturational processes and the facilitating environment*. Hogarth Press.

Witkon, Y. (2012). A crisis mental health intervention service: An innovative model for working intensively with young people on the edge of care. *Journal of Child Psychotherapy*, 38(2), 154–169.

Wright, J. L. (2009). The princess has to die: Representing rupture and grief in the narrative of adoption. *Psychoanalytic Study of the Child*, 64, 75–91.

York, W., & Jones, J. (2017). Addressing the mental health needs of looked after children in foster care: The experiences of foster carers. *Journal of Psychiatric and Mental Health Nursing*, 24(2–3), 143–153. https://doi.org/10.1111/j

Youell, B. (2012). The expressed wishes and feelings of children. In: A. Briggs (ed.), *Waiting to be found: Papers on children in care* (pp. 135–151). London: Routledge.

Part 4

Chapter 13

Brief psychodynamic psychotherapy for adolescents and their families in crisis

A pilot study[1]

Maria Papadima, Catherine Campbell, Nikolaos Tzikas, and Fembe Nanji-Rowe

Introduction: presenting the pilot project

This chapter describes our experience of a two-and-a-half-year pilot project, which we conducted as part of our work in the adolescent team at Enfield CAMHS (Service for Adolescents and Families in Enfield, SAFE), in London, UK.[2] The project introduced a brief psychodynamic intervention for young people and their parents experiencing a crisis, consisting of up to 12 sessions. For the purposes of this chapter, we refer to *crises* as those involving suicidality or moderate to severe self-harm. Often, such crises lead teenagers to visit the emergency department (Bommersbach et al., 2024; Poyraz Fındık et al., 2022). There are many other forms of crises, of course; but here we specifically focus on crises related to suicidality and self-harm, to give a taste of our day-to-day work in our clinic.

An applied psychoanalytic approach

Our intervention is grounded in psychoanalytic concepts, with observation, transference, and countertransference as central pillars (Lia, 2017; Luborsky & Barrett, 2006; Sandler et al., 1970). We have also been influenced by systemic ideas, which highlight the interactive and interdependent nature of family dynamics (Hanna, 2018; Massey, 1986; Selvini et al., 1980; Sexton & Stanton, 2016).

We have opted for using the term 'psychodynamic' when referring to our therapeutic work with adolescents and their families in our clinic. While our work draws on psychoanalytic principles, it adopts an applied way of working that fits a CAMHS[3] context, joining others before us who have adapted psychoanalytic ideas across varied settings (Axelrod et al., 2018; Esman, 1998; Lemma & Patrick, 2010; Rowan, 2003; Schmidt Neven, 2017).

This pilot project emerged from our effort to continue offering psychodynamic treatment to adolescents (aged 13–18) and their parents who attend in crises. We believe in the value of this approach as part of the adolescent crisis service offer, as we hope to show in this chapter.

DOI: 10.4324/9781003592778-18

Background

This time-limited model for crisis was borne out of our experiences as ACP[4]-trained psychoanalytic child psychotherapists within an adolescent team. The therapeutic approach we developed over time reflects adjustments we made to our previous practice. In this section, we explain these adaptations, the rationale behind them, how they were implemented in our clinic, and offer ideas about contexts where we believe this therapeutic approach might be suitable for young people and families.

This way of working did not stem from theoretical or clinical ideas alone; instead, it was a direct response to the practical challenges we faced in recent years within our NHS adolescent crisis team, made worse by the destabilising effects of the Covid-19 pandemic (Bouter et al., 2023; Panchal et al., 2023; Wolf & Schmitz, 2024) and years of economic austerity measures in the UK (Cummins, 2018; Hunter, 2018). These issues, combined, deeply affected adolescents, their families, and the NHS as a whole; so it became clear to us that we needed to think 'outside the box' and try new approaches in our work.

As psychoanalytic child and adolescent psychotherapists working in a crisis team, we were already grappling with some key questions: could we balance our heavy caseloads with the wish to contribute meaningfully in the midst of the broader NHS staffing and funding crisis? Could we provide something valuable to our service while staying true to our psychoanalytic background?

A crisis as an opportunity

Through this pilot project, which started at the tail end of the pandemic, we answered these questions in the affirmative. Despite the pain and turmoil involved, we came to see that a family crisis, especially in high-risk situations involving self-harm or suicidal ideation, represents a unique opportunity to uncover meaning for both the young person and their parents, by allowing critical themes to be articulated in the moment when defences against psychic pain are lowered and thus awareness is temporarily more open about what is going on under the surface. This offers space to potentially reduce risk relatively quickly (Campbell & Hale, 2017; Schmidt Neven, 2017; Yakeley, 2018).

Throughout the project, we gained a deeper appreciation of the role that child and adolescent psychoanalytic psychotherapists can play in crisis teams. Rather than viewing a crisis in the adolescent and their family as a negative event or a set of symptoms to be managed, we could seek practical ways to integrate our therapeutic approach into crisis work. This identified the point of crisis as an opportunity to elicit a developmental shift in the family, with parents actively participating in the changes – one of the major findings we adopted from Schmidt Neven's work (2010, 2017). As such, our goal became to rethink the 'crisis work' we were already doing, moving towards an in-depth psychodynamic approach grounded in observation, use of transference and countertransference phenomena, and the collaboration of two psychotherapists on each case.

Positioning this intervention

The work that we describe here is best initiated early in the journey of a crisis, regardless of how big or small the manifestations of the crisis appear. As such, it aligns with the typical NHS adolescent crisis pathway, aiming for a first appointment within two weeks of referral, and could be considered as one of the frontline options for families in crisis. The intervention, we believe, offers a viable alternative going beyond the prevailing risk management strategies, which often rely on rigid safety planning, detached from therapeutic understanding. This brief psychodynamic intervention aligns with the NICE guidelines on self-harm (2022), which emphasise the value of a holistic psychosocial assessment.

Before a detailed discussion of our pilot project, including its context, structure, and initial findings, we want to start with some thoughts about the wider societal crisis within which these current problems in adolescence are occurring, and how we think we can work with them psychoanalytically in the NHS. From there, we will discuss some recent literature on brief psychotherapy work, followed by a detailed examination of three main pillars central to the brief psychodynamic psychotherapy intervention, which we summarise as:

1. The general usefulness of time-limited psychodynamic work in crisis
2. The active involvement of parents in adolescent crisis work
3. The close collaboration of two therapists in crisis work

The wider context

In this section we refer to the existing gap in knowledge around psychotherapeutic crisis work as a frontline option in NHS CAMHS crisis services, in the context of the increasing rates of psychological difficulties in adolescence.

The adolescent mental health crisis

Reflecting the broader vulnerability of adolescents to mental health challenges, the World Health Organization (WHO, 2021) estimates that approximately 14% of teenagers worldwide suffer from emotional disorders, with depression, anxiety, and behavioural issues being the most prevalent. The number of young people needing emergency care has surged, with a 29% increase in contacts with mental health services in England between December 2019 and April 2021 (Edwards et al., 2024). These developments underline the pressing need for expanded crisis interventions to address these difficulties proactively before they escalate further. However, there's an ongoing debate on the best ways to 'spot' and prevent the progression of suicidality (Garland & Zigler, 1993; Gibbons, 2023, 2024).

Data from NHS Digital (2020) also show a steady growth in these problems among children aged 5–19, with one in six impacted in some way, up from one in nine in 2017. Suicide tragically ranks as the fourth leading cause of death among

15- to 19-year-olds worldwide (WHO, 2021), making its prevention an international imperative (WHO, 2014).

In previous decades, teenagers' crises more often centred on externalising behaviours, such as drunk driving, drug use, or other forms of risk-taking – along the lines of Holden Caulfield in 'The Catcher in the rye' by Salinger (1951), or Bruce Springsteen's 1975 anthem 'Born to run'. But things have changed. Since around 2010, there has been a striking expansion in internalising difficulties, such as anxiety and depression (Haidt, 2024). Today's struggling teenagers, when presenting to crisis teams, typically may be self-harming or considering suicide.

As this growing crisis progresses, stretched services and high demand have led to lengthy waiting times for children and young people needing help, compounded by ongoing issues in social care and education (Salisbury et al., 2023). The House of Commons Health and Social Care Committee (2021) has warned that the delays in support may be causing manageable problems to escalate into crises due to waiting lists and high thresholds for accessing care in the NHS.

When considering how to respond to this, we need to keep in mind that adolescence is often the time that mental illness emerges (Jones, 2013; Ormel et al., 2015), making it crucial to distinguish between prodromal signs of severe, long-term mental illness and transient difficulties (Kelleher et al., 2012; Lång et al., 2022). In the case of self-harm in adolescents, Uh et al. (2021) have shown that most young people presenting in crisis do not develop entrenched mental health problems, a hopeful idea to keep in mind.

It is particularly within this field – crisis presentations that most likely will not lead to longstanding issues – that our psychodynamic psychotherapy intervention for adolescents and their families finds its place.

The need for urgent mental health support for adolescents

Despite the stated need for urgent interventions, we don't know enough about what works and what does not in the context of today's mental health crisis when it comes to therapeutic crisis interventions (Washburn et al., 2012). The formalised risk reduction approach is what is mainly explored in the literature (Edwards et al., 2024; Glenn et al., 2015), but we need more contextualised, in-depth, clinically informed ideas, given that adolescent mental health has become a top policy priority in the UK and internationally (The NHS Long Term Plan, 2019; WHO, 2021).

Within the limited existing literature on time-limited adolescent–parent therapy for risk, we note: a family-based crisis intervention in the emergency department (Ginnis et al., 2015; Wharff et al., 2012, 2019); an ultra-brief acute crisis model based on Interpersonal Psychotherapy (IPT) (Adini-Spigelman et al., 2024; Haruvi Catalan et al., 2020); and an integrated model combining individual and family therapy, working on emotional regulation, school attendance problems, and relapse prevention (Wijana et al., 2021). Another relevant intervention combines parent training with cognitive-behavioural therapy for teenagers over 8–10 sessions

(Dekel et al., 2021). Time-limited psychodynamic models do exist, such as those based on mentalization ideas (Rossouw, 2013; Rossouw & Fonagy, 2012), Stephen Briggs's short-term therapy for adolescents (Briggs et al., 2019), and Short-term psychoanalytic psychotherapy (STPP) for young people with depression (Goodyer et al., 2011), offering helpful insights that we've drawn on.

Despite the evidence on how useful psychodynamic psychotherapy can be for understanding and addressing self-harm and suicidal ideation (Briggs et al., 2019; De Maat et al., 2013; Fonagy et al., 2015), specific ideas in this field remain limited, with a paucity of evidence, both in the form of case studies and in the empirical field. A gap thus exists in specific psychodynamic crisis interventions that consider both the centrality of parents' support in understanding and addressing the adolescent's problems, but also the wider sociocultural environment in which adolescents grow up and the ways it shapes their subjectivity and family experiences, as well as their friendship and wider cultural interactions. All this comes into the material the therapist listens out for in the room.

Addressing this gap is critical since child and adolescent psychotherapy is a core profession within multidisciplinary NHS CAMHS; a solid evidence base is essential for continuing our work in crisis contexts, which forms a substantial portion of CAMHS daily responsibilities. Psychoanalysis has continuously evolved (Shedler, 2023), and it's within this framework of change and growth that we built this therapeutic intervention for adolescents and families in crisis.

We now turn to the foundational assumptions of our project.

The foundational principles of the pilot project

In this section, we outline the key values and principles (see Figure 13.1) underpinning our pilot project, highlighting its distinctive elements compared to other models and its areas of alignment. By keeping these principles in mind and adopting some or all of them in their practice, we believe clinicians can offer better quality care to families in crisis. This is why we start with these principles before outlining the sequence of appointments and detailing the 'logistics' of this way of working. These values and principles are at the heart of our psychotherapy intervention, shaping its overall structure and approach.

Time-limited psychodynamic psychotherapy for adolescents and parents in crisis

While certain adolescents need long-term psychotherapy, not all require such extensive treatment, nor do they always *want it or expect it* when coming to clinics like ours. As Peta Mees (2015) points out, a detailed assessment or a few short encounters is often all that proves possible when a family comes to CAMHS. This can be for several reasons, some related to the family and others related to service limitations, including limitations in education, social services, and NHS provision.

Beyond issues of capacity and engagement, it's also the case that brief psychotherapy can be a developmentally suitable option for young people (Edlund &

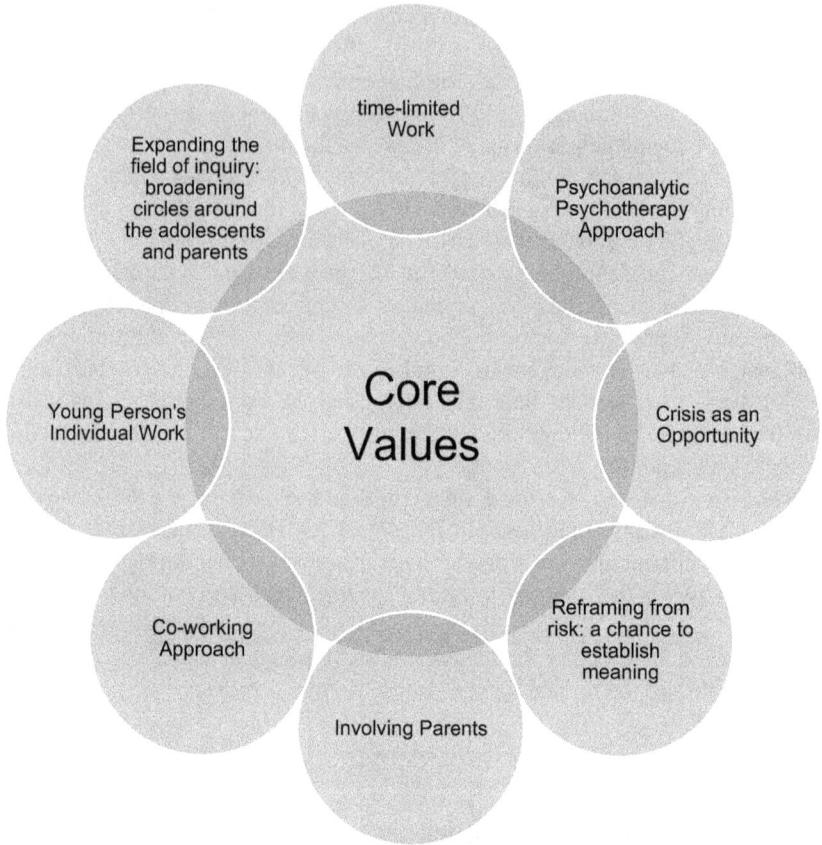

Core Values

- time-limited Work
- Expanding the field of inquiry: broadening circles around the adolescents and parents
- Psychoanalytic Psychotherapy Approach
- Young Person's Individual Work
- Crisis as an Opportunity
- Co-working Approach
- Reframing from risk: a chance to establish meaning
- Involving Parents

Figure 13.1 Core values of our model.

Carlberg, 2016; Gatta et al., 2019), and it has been shown to be helpful for those self-harming or experiencing suicidal thoughts (Briggs et al., 2019; Catty, 2021).

The main theoretical framework we have adopted – viewing *adolescent crises as opportunities for therapeutic engagement* (Schmidt Neven, 2017) – represents a significant shift from the conventional NHS divide, where crisis work and psychotherapy often operate in silos. This is particularly the case with psychoanalytic psychotherapy approaches, which tend to be excluded from preventative and frontline services and are regarded as follow-on options when other interventions (presumed to be better-suited) have been exhausted.

However, psychoanalytic training equips clinicians to create and maintain a reflective space and sustain critical thinking even in the face of emotional turmoil – qualities that are essential in crisis work; this is a resource, we believe, that is under-utilised in the NHS context, and we hope that the work we present in this chapter can contribute towards a different way of thinking about this.

By intentionally merging these two fields, risk support and therapy, we not only promote the integration of therapy into crisis work but also argue for a redefinition of the role of *adolescent crisis intervention* itself. Instead of viewing crises as moments to be quickly stabilised and left behind, we see them as critical junctures in a developmental journey. They allow us a rare opportunity to gain access to underlying issues in real time. This can potentially have a powerful impact on the family and adolescent's developmental trajectory, going beyond symptom management.

Crisis as an opportunity

The term *crisis* is commonly understood as 'an extremely difficult or dangerous point in a situation' or 'a time of great disagreement, confusion, or suffering'.[5] However, the meaning of crisis is not straightforward and varies across disciplines and contexts (Abdelrahman, 2022; Dafermos, 2024; Freeden, 2017). We take up an alternative meaning of the concept, rooted in its ancient Greek etymology, viewing crisis as a 'turning point' (Dafermos, 2024), where the outcome is critical but still uncertain:

> According to the Hippocratic treatise 'On Affections', crisis 'occurs in diseases whenever the diseases increase in intensity or go away or change into another disease or end altogether.
>
> (Dafermos, 2024; citing; Starn, 1971, p. 4)

Borrowing from Vygotsky's perspective on crisis, as presented by Dafermos (2018, 2024), we understand it as 'not only something negative or positive itself but a critical moment of a dynamic, contradictory, developmental process' (Dafermos, 2024):

> The crisis was defined by Vygotsky as a situation of the contradictory co-existence between the destruction of old, previous, concepts on the one hand and the emergence of new concepts on the other. The old concepts have been hopelessly compromised, while the new concepts have not yet been created.
>
> (Dafermos, 2024)

Ultimately, a crisis signals that *something meaningful needs to be heard and addressed*. And something needs to change.

Adolescence as a period of crisis, change, and transition

Adolescence is a critical phase marked by many changes (Bleiberg, 1988; Blos, 1967; A. Freud, 1958), involving the gradual 'shedding of family dependencies' and 'loosening of infantile object ties' (Blos, 1967), a journey marked by back-and-forths. It is also a time of significant vulnerability, including mental health challenges such as suicide and self-harm, which, as we've mentioned, have sharply increased over the past two decades (Haidt, 2024; Sharma & Fowler, 2018). Contemporary adolescence has become further complicated by shifts in attitudes towards mental wellbeing, with young people increasingly engaging with psychiatric diagnoses, moving from stigmatisation to heightened awareness and strong interest (Acheson & Papadima, 2023). While these shifts have benefits, they also bring unintended, complex consequences (Foulkes, 2022; Foulkes & Andrews, 2023). The immersive nature of online life adds another layer of complexity, contributing to the rise in emotional and behavioural difficulties (Fowler & Vinson, 2020; Haidt, 2024; Nesi et al., 2020).

All this has a direct impact in the way adolescents interact with us as clinicians as well as how they engage with their families and friends. When we encounter the adolescent in the room, talking to us during a crisis, we must consider all these factors: what do they have in mind when they refer to a 'breakdown'? How would they describe it? What does suicidality look like in detail? What do they think is the meaning of the self-harm? What does it offer them? For example, does it occur in isolated moments of very low mood? Is it a coping mechanism? Does it happen within a friendship group? Does it lead to family clashes? And how does this occur in the context of their online and offline experiences?

Viewing a crisis in adolescence through this lens reframes it as a transformative, meaningful process that pushes towards change: it's not yet clear, when a crisis is happening, what this change will be. We can think of the crisis as a temporary deviation from the developmental path, where for a period of time various possibilities are open. The goal is to help the adolescent and family move back to ordinary development, avoiding further escalation into crisis.

Relational, psychodynamic risk management

Traditional risk assessments often use structured questionnaires and safety plans created with the family and network. While these aim to capture a comprehensive picture of risk, they can easily become standardised, with compartmentalised risk stratification (e.g. low, medium, high risk). Moreover, procedures that don't focus on continuity of care, and often alternate between practitioners, fail to build on previous therapeutic progress.

Safety planning, as described by the Royal college of psychiatrists (2020), typically involves practical problem-solving, such as identifying coping strategies and reducing access to lethal means. In our own project, we have focused instead on the current NICE guidelines on self-harm and risk, which invite clinicians to 'focus . . . on the person's needs and how to support their immediate and long-term psychological and physical safety' (NICE, 2022).

Suicide and self-harm, in any case, can be challenging or impossible to fully understand and prevent when it comes to the individual level, as each case is different and the causes are multifactorial, but prevention becomes more feasible on a population level (Gibbons, 2023). Risk-taking can be better understood as 'acting out behaviours' (Gibbons, 2023), expressing something (or a number of things) beneath the surface.

In our pilot project, we have focused on the adolescents' narrative and their family relationships to achieve effective risk reduction, rather than relying on a structured risk assessment approach. Anderson (2000) offered a psychoanalytic perspective on understanding and working with risk in adolescence that we have kept in mind, while De Kernier (2012) emphasises the 'latent meaning of the suicidal gesture'. Lybbert et al. (2019) explain that even brief therapeutic encounters should 'promote the exploration and development of meaning . . . relative to behaviours and factors related to suicidality'.

Two key psychoanalytic principles: the distinctiveness of each family and the importance of the obvious

We adopt two key principles from our psychoanalytic tradition. First, we focus on the simple fact that each patient and family are different, rather than being preoccupied with surface symptoms and risks. It can be hard to stay with this, given the anxiety risk evokes and the emphasis on diagnostic explanations. But as many psychoanalysts and systemic clinicians have demonstrated, paying attention to the nuances of a narrative can bring substantial relief, including not just individual aspects but also contemporary sociocultural elements, all of which come together into the young person and parents' narrative and meaning-making. Bion's words come to mind:

> The most important assistance that a psychoanalyst is ever likely to get is not from his analyst, or supervisor, or teacher, or the books that he can read, but from his patient. The patient – and only the patient – knows what it feels like to be him or her . . . That is why it is so important that we should be able to hear, see, smell, even feel what information the patient is trying to convey. He is the only one who knows the facts.
>
> (1977/2005 CWB Vol. IX pp. 103)

The second principle is the importance of the *obvious or common-sense*. These common-sense elements, often hiding in plain sight, can be overshadowed by loud symptoms and conflict and acting out behaviours. Bion stressed this idea:

> One is usually so busy looking for something out of the ordinary that one ignores the obvious as if it were of no importance.
>
> (1973/2005 CWB Vol. VII p. 67)

Inspired by this, we deliberately steered away from viewing crises solely through a mental illness lens, instead focusing on discussions devoid of professional jargon (Shedler, 2023). Wondering simply, 'What's going on?' or 'What might this mean?' can bring relief and can, surprisingly, represent a radical departure from the current norm.

The central involvement of parents

Ruth Schmidt Neven (2010, 2017) emphasises the critical role parents play in therapy with adolescents. She has long critiqued the artificial and excessive, as she sees it, psychoanalytic focus on adolescent independence, often at the expense of thinking about togetherness and attachment as they occur during these years. Others, amongst them psychoanalysts Novick and Novick (2013) and child psychotherapist Deborah Marks (2020), have also stressed the importance of involving parents much more directly in therapy with adolescents.

Adolescents, of course, *are* moving towards greater independence and *do* need separate spaces. However, as Schmidt Neven reminds us, separating adolescents from their parents at this critical juncture is premature. Adolescence may provide the last window of opportunity for therapy involving both parents and the young person together to understand the crisis in the context of earlier developmental experiences.

Involving parents at the heart of crisis work with adolescents, we have found, enriches the therapeutic work and makes it more possible to move beyond something merely supportive, to something exploratory that has a chance to lead to lasting change. For example, on numerous occasions we found that parents were able to help by identifying elements that their son or daughter could not at first articulate in moments of high anxiety. The parents did this through having access, it seemed to us, to their own version of countertransference, which the crisis and the adolescent's behaviour evoked in them. What surprised us was how open adolescents were to these moments, perhaps because during crises defences break down to some degree, offering more access to previously unseen personality and family issues: this is true both for parents and for the adolescents themselves (Campbell & Hale, 2017; Yakeley, 2018).

The active involvement of parents thus enables therapists and parents to build an awareness of what might be going on, which may have become obscured by the anxiety of the crisis. By becoming familiar with previously unknown details of their child's struggles, which may also relate to their own experiences, parents can become more able to respond. In turn, this increased openness can help adolescents feel more secure, enabling them to move towards independence with greater confidence.

Parents often feel shocked and unsure how to react when they discover their teenager is self-harming or expressing suicidal thoughts. They may fear making the situation worse and, as a result, may refrain from setting ordinary boundaries. Others may become angry, not understanding why their child feels and behaves the way they do, or may perceive these actions as an attack on them, becoming confrontational or controlling in response. Frequently, parents share that *they* also struggled as teenagers yet, they add, they *'just had to get on with it: why can't their teenager do the same?'* It's easy to lose sight of what it is like to be a teenager amid the emotional turmoil of a crisis.

Through close work with parents, we have observed that crises often de-escalate when the young person feels that something has been heard. Primarily, that they have understood something about themselves, but importantly, that their parents have recognised this as well.

This understanding can happen even in situations when the parents and adolescent continue not to see eye to eye on what all this means. This is where the therapists can help in the 'translation' process. For example, a young person may view their self-harm as indicative of an underlying disorder, while the parent may see it as 'doing it for attention'. The critical point here is the mutual effort to appreciate each other's perspective, which often has cultural as well as personal roots. A parent from a traditional, stricter background may struggle to understand the fluid way today's adolescents slip in and out of diagnostic language and may equally feel unclear on whether this language indicates something serious or not. This can lead to either dismissing the problem altogether or panicking about it. Similarly, an adolescent who feels stuck in their internal self-attack or rumination and expresses it in intense, diagnostic-heavy, or risk-laden language may not realise how their words impact their parents.

Expanding the field of inquiry: broadening circles around the adolescent and parents

To understand a crisis in the context of the young person's life and make a meaningful difference within a short period, going beyond the symptoms, close collaboration with schools and other agencies is essential, widening the teenager's safety net. This perspective is well-established in CAMHS work, recognising that teenagers are embedded within interconnected systems, as described in Urie Bronfenbrenner's Ecological systems theory (Bronfenbrenner, 1979).

Sometimes, a positive relationship with a keyworker can make all the difference; other times, complications may arise: a 'good teacher' can become idealised, while a 'bad parent' can become demonised. We integrate these circles of support into our work, considering both the home and school-based spheres. We see this as a broader application of Bion's container/contained environment (Cartwright, 2014), like Russian matryoshka dolls, with different levels of holding for the teenager at the centre. Bronfenbrenner described this as 'a set of concentric circles representing nested systems'[6] (Gerrard, 2012).

Schmidt Neven (2017) also highlights that widening the field of enquiry around the young person is an essential part of the therapeutic endeavour at times of crisis; she uses the term 'leverage' to evaluate where and how positive change can be effected in the system to support the adolescent.

In contrast with other similar models, we place special emphasis on the particular sociocultural context in which adolescents live today. This includes their daily experiences; the diagnostic ways they interpret their psychological symptoms; their friendships, both online and offline; and the ways they care for and impact each other's mental health within peer groups. All this comes into their experience of themselves and, in turn, comes into their crises as well. Recognising these factors is crucial for addressing risk, as peer group dynamics can significantly impact teenagers and family life, often without the parents' awareness. Schmidt Neven highlights this, stating:

The individual's life cannot be separated from the relational, family, systemic and wider organisational, social and political environment. Predominantly pathology-driven diagnosis associated with these problems has not led to hoped-for outcomes with respect to improvements in child and family mental health. In fact, we can argue that narrow pathology-centred diagnosis not only compromises the child and young person, but also the ability of professionals to offer meaningful treatment and care.

(2017, p. 6)

Two therapists working together

As mentioned earlier, this project emerged when we, as therapists in a crisis team, felt the need to pull together and support each other amidst the influx of referrals and the Covid-19 crisis. Typically, our team would assign one clinician to manage a case at the assessment stage, with additional resources (e.g. psychiatric input) sought later if necessary. In our project, however, we opted for collaboration between two clinicians from the outset.

The benefits of co-working in crisis are threefold. First, it creates a containing framework for therapists, which is vital when addressing self-harm or suicidal ideation. In such cases, meaning often emerges through actions rather than words or is revealed through powerful countertransference. Jointly conducting reviews with the adolescent and parents allows contemplation on what is observed, fostering the sharing of perspectives within the family and the therapy dyad.

Second, the adage 'Two minds are better than one' applies particularly well in managing risk and crisis given the intense emotions these situations evoke for families and therapists alike. Joint efforts can accelerate shifts in understanding and lead to better outcomes. Having two therapists for each case helps identify blind spots, considering the tendency for splitting that can occur when there is heightened emotion. Further, liaison with external networks is inherently time-consuming for a single psychotherapist to manage alone, but co-working allows tasks to be shared, providing more robust and safer care.

Third, co-working helps avoid over-identification with either the young person or the parents, allowing therapists to maintain a balanced perspective. This ensures that family dynamics are understood from multiple perspectives.

Finally, the peer support and supervision we offer each other enrich and deepen the therapy. When under pressure, we can easily neglect the time needed to discuss the work with colleagues. However, we stress the importance of protecting this time for regular meetings to process what is taking place.

A psychoanalytic psychotherapy perspective

The framework we present broadens the scope of enquiry across two dimensions. Horizontally, it extends beyond the parents to include wider support circles surrounding the young person. Vertically, within the adolescent's intrapsychic dynamics, a psychodynamic perspective ventures beneath observable behaviour to uncover unconscious forces that drive symptoms. By exploring defences, identifying anxieties, and revealing underlying patterns, we gain a deeper understanding of the crisis at hand, which is necessary to successfully address it. We take it as a given that what we see on the surface is not always what drives the problem (Shedler, 2023).

Central to the psychodynamic approach is that we expect resistance to change, along with an investment in symptoms, negativity, and acting out behaviours, even though on the surface the stated purpose of those who come to therapy is to change. We don't assume that teenagers and parents will automatically *want this change* or, for that matter, that they want to be safe and reduce the risk, and this needs to be understood and respected. The investment in what's familiar – even if dysfunctional – is a longstanding psychoanalytic insight:

> [N]o one who has any experience of the rifts which so often divide a family will, if he is an analyst, be surprised to find that the patient's relatives sometimes betray less interest in his recovery than in his remaining as he is. When, as so often, neurosis is related to conflicts between members of a family, the healthy party will not hesitate long in choosing between his own interest and the sick party's recovery.
>
> (S. Freud, 1917)

A psychodynamic lens allows the exploration of unstated death wishes, suicidal fantasies, projective processes that may play a role in risk, and the fluid boundary between thought and action. It could be, for example, that the passive, self-destructive wish of a parent who's incapacitated by depression or addiction may get acted out through loud, risky behaviour on the part of the adolescent. And vice versa (sometimes the parent may be the risky one!). Keeping these possibilities in mind is crucial when considering how to approach a family in crisis and how to gradually build sufficient trust to point out these patterns when they emerge.

A time-limited but flexible therapy

Contrary to the misconception that short-term psychotherapy is 'second best' when compared to the 'gold standard' of long-term therapy, Schmidt Neven argues that it is a valuable and fitting approach, matching the young person's natural trajectory of growth. Brief therapy is especially well suited to risky situations, where events move quickly and where understanding and containment are needed within a short timeframe.

In some of the brief psychoanalytic approaches on which we've drawn (e.g. Bronstein & Flanders, 1998; Searle et al., 2011; Winnicott, 2018), the common thread is attention to the uniqueness of each family while ensuring the young person feels heard in their distress, whether expressed through self-harm, parasuicidal actions, or delinquent behaviour. There is a strong element of individualising the treatment to each case in these ways of working. In this spirit, our intervention, while specifying an approximate number of 12 sessions including both parent and adolescent meetings, holds a firm position of flexibility, as we are not aiming to produce a manualised way of working. Sometimes we see families for just a few sessions, while other times we see them for more than 12 sessions.

Interestingly, by looking at the numbers of what was actually offered over the two and half years, we noticed that the average number of sessions offered and taken up was indeed 12, hence suggesting this number as a benchmark to start from, rather than something to stick rigidly to.

We now move on to the practical details of the time-limited psychodynamic crisis therapy we have piloted.

The two-year pilot project

While we cannot comment on the specifics of cases, in this section we will offer an overview of the pilot project and will then present a composite example. The overview with which we start includes information on:

- Sources of referrals
- Reasons prompting referrals
- Demographics of the cases
- Common overarching themes observed
- How we formulate the presenting problems
- Any observed reductions in the risk of self-harm or suicidality

Context and demographics

The project has run for three years in a London specialist CAMHS clinic that offers community-based, rapid support to adolescents aged 13 to 18 in need of urgent care. This often includes young people who have harmed themselves or are at risk of suicide. Referrals frequently follow visits to the Emergency Department, sometimes after a suicide attempt, or they may be referred by their general practitioner (GP), school, or social worker. SAFE also offers specialist assessment and treatment for teenagers experiencing complex or severe difficulties, such as emerging psychosis, or where there is ongoing risk.

The group running the project

Referrals to our clinic typically belong to two categories: those experiencing temporary crises linked to age-specific concerns, and those dealing with acute versions of longstanding problems. Our multidisciplinary team, which includes psychiatrists, psychologists, nurses, systemic family therapists, and psychoanalytically trained child and adolescent psychotherapists, aims to respond promptly to referrals and assess adolescents and their families within two weeks.

The pilot project has involved the cohesive effort of a closed group of professionals at the clinic. The group includes child and adolescent psychoanalytic psychotherapists, both qualified and in training, as well as assistant psychologists who have supported the work. Together and over time, we have worked towards defining the framework, aims, goals, and key principles of the treatment. This has involved dedicating time to review relevant literature and presenting our evolving work to the wider CAMHS team.

The first steps of the intervention

When starting each intervention, we first need to ensure that it aligns with the presenting problems of the family. For example, in cases where parent participation hasn't proven possible (which can be for a variety of reasons), we don't proceed with offering this intervention, and other members of the wider team work with the family.

Before the first meeting, all young people complete the RCADS forms, as is standard in our team. We ensure that all families are seen within two weeks of referral and then continue with the brief therapy aimed at risk reduction, without any intervening waiting time. The vast majority of referrals in our team, including in this intervention, involve female adolescents, mirroring the broader pattern of referrals to teams like ours, where young women constitute the bulk of referrals.[7] The families we have seen spanned a wide range of socioeconomic backgrounds, encompassing both disadvantaged families and some on the other end of the economic spectrum. In addition to the crises these families faced, a recurring theme that came up involved the *disconnect* between adolescents and parents. Both parties usually felt misunderstood, with parents experiencing fear and uncertainty about how to care for their adolescent during the crisis, which often involved language and behaviour they could not comprehend and follow. Some parents felt 'paralysed' by the stress of the situation, leading them to refrain from setting regular boundaries out of fear of further escalation. Other parents, on the opposite end, imposed strict measures, such as removing bedroom doors or closely monitoring their adolescent's every move. Our work aimed to address these relational difficulties, facilitating a gradual easing of tensions.

As we have outlined earlier in this chapter, one psychotherapist primarily works with the young person, while the other focuses on the parents and broader network liaison. We aim for approximately 12 sessions, but with an emphasis on flexibility, depending on what fits for each family. Sometimes this may mean spreading out the sessions over a much longer period; other times we have opted for different combinations of individual adolescent sessions, parent sessions, and joint reviews. We have had a few cases, for example, where the two therapists did almost all the work together with both adolescent and parent(s) because that was deemed clinically most helpful.

First appointment

In the first appointment, the two therapists introduce the framework. After spending about 15 minutes jointly as a group, one therapist then meets separately with the adolescent, while the other remains with the parents or carers.

After this first meeting, each therapist independently notes their observations, feelings, and thoughts. To help with this, we use a grid based on the Milan family therapy group's structure (Selvini et al., 1980), which focuses on creating a provisional working hypothesis at the outset of the work. This allows us to craft a psychodynamic formulation that is adapted and reconsidered over time. Specifically, each therapist writes:

- Sentence A: 'I have a hunch that . . .' (explaining the presence of the problem or symptom)
- Sentence B: 'And therefore, I am interested in finding out more about . . .' (identifying avenues of enquiry)

Within two days of the first meeting, the two therapists meet to share their thoughts and formulate a unified plan. Individual sessions for the adolescent are then scheduled weekly at first to build momentum; they either continue weekly or shift to fortnightly intervals to ensure continuity. In parallel, sessions with the parents are offered (a minimum of four, but usually more). Sometimes, again in the spirit of flexibility, we have opted for a larger number of joint meetings rather than separating the adolescent and the parents. Ongoing liaison with the school or other relevant networks is maintained throughout.

Midway review

Around the sixth session mark, a review meeting is scheduled with the young person, parents, and the two therapists, followed by a discussion between the two therapists. This stage involves revisiting and potentially reformulating our initial working hypotheses, built on the progress so far and our observations. In this and all similar phases of the therapy, we actively use the emotions and reactions we have in appointments, recognising that in cases where acting out and projective processes are prominent, much of the formulation work hinges on carefully noting our countertransference and learning from it.

Final sessions and review

Next, there are approximately six more sessions, concluding with a closing review where the parents, young person, and two therapists come together again. At this point, we consider whether to end the work or whether further support is needed for the young person and/or their family. This decision will have been discussed in advance with both the adolescent and the parents or carers. While sometimes further work is offered, such as ongoing parent support, family therapy, group therapy, or individual longer-term psychotherapy, often the 12 sessions prove to be enough. We have found in this way of working that risk levels can diminish within a short period of time.

A composite case example[8]

Case overview

Melissa, aged 15, was referred by her GP for self-harm through cutting. The self-harm had started after she failed an exam for which she had prepared extensively.

Melissa, we were told, had a sibling with profound disabilities, and when she would become angry with her parents for (inevitably) focusing more of their time on her sister, she told them she felt depressed, couldn't see the point of it all, and wanted to die.

Her school and parents were alarmed by the escalation in Melissa's behaviour, the deterioration in her mood, and the overall sense of things being stuck. It seemed that Melissa was dealing with multiple stressors simultaneously; as a result, there had been frequent trips to A&E and repeated calls to the crisis line whenever she expressed suicidal thoughts or after incidents of self-harm. At first, these contacts provided relief for Melissa, but over time, their usefulness waned, and her frustration with her parents and school grew. She felt that no one and nothing could help.

Therapists' initial reflections

Following the first meeting, the two therapists involved in Melissa's case documented their initial hunches and expressed what they were curious about.

Parent therapist's reflections

Hunches:

> *The mother seems eager to fix everything at once, likely because of the guilt she feels about possibly contributing to Melissa's self-harm.*
>
> *It could also be that her guilt stems from resentment towards Melissa for 'creating problems' when her sister 'has it so much harder'.*
>
> *Both parents were brought up in traditional Middle Eastern families, where mental health isn't talked about: it's a taboo. I have a hunch that Melissa's parents struggle to understand the mental health–oriented language she uses. They swing between feeling panicked at the risk and frustrated with her when she talks about feeling suicidal.*

I have a hunch there might be an unconscious attack on Melissa by the parents due to the confusion they feel, which perhaps Melissa internalises as anger towards herself.

What am I curious about?

I am curious to hear about the parents' background, the function of guilt within the family, and Melissa's relationship with her sibling.

Adolescent therapist's reflections

Hunches

Melissa seems to struggle with expressing her feelings and appears suspicious of me.
    I suspect she harbours strong feelings of anger about being sidelined – sometimes directing this anger outward, other times inward.
    There are frequent miscommunications with friends and family.
    She is particularly furious with her mother for prioritising her sibling and feels disconnected from her.

What am I curious about?

I'm curious about Melissa's place in the family, particularly with a sibling who has disabilities and requires a lot of attention.
    I'm interested in her relationship with her parents. How do they talk about mental health?
    I am curious to understand how the family communicates thoughts and feelings.

When the two therapists met to discuss the first appointment, they shared their thoughts about the session, their working hypotheses, and what they were curious about. The therapist working with Melissa reported a feeling of heaviness at times, with moments of blankness, or disconnect. The therapist working with the parents noticed an intense wish to provide immediate solutions, coupled with a feeling of being ineffective. Following this discussion, the two therapists together planned the next steps.

As the work progressed, one day Melissa's school called to say they were considering sending her to A&E: she had told a member of staff that she felt suicidal. It occurred to us, while listening, that if this went ahead, it would be the third visit to the hospital in a month. If it was necessary, it should happen, of course: but what was going on?

Melissa's therapist spoke to her on the phone and asked how she was doing. Melissa expressed that she couldn't see the point in living. The therapist enquired about what might have led to these feelings, asking Melissa to just talk about the events leading up to this moment of despair, even if she didn't know how they were connected. Melissa at first didn't know what to say, but later in the conversation, she mentioned a small argument with her mother that morning. Initially, Melissa rejected any connection between the argument and her suicidality. However, after thinking together about the details of the argument, she eventually came to see she had felt sad and angry since the morning. She paused and added, 'In truth, I don't want to die, but I feel so stuck. No one understands how I feel, and my parents get frustrated with me: they understand nothing about mental health'.

What she wanted, she said, was for someone to just listen and understand, but that felt impossible; she also wanted the feelings to go away. She didn't really know what to do.

Subsequent sessions were held jointly with Melissa and her parents, allowing the therapists and family to explore family communication and the underlying meaning of Melissa's suicidal language and self-harm. Rather than immediately contacting the crisis line whenever Melissa struggled, her parents started sitting with her and simply listened to what she was saying, sometimes going through the day's events.

Over time, the parents grew in their ability to view the self-harm and suicidality as a communication of distress, which helped contain their own responses as well as Melissa's. Although further difficulties arose, the self-harm and crisis calls ceased. Melissa and her parents spoke on several occasions about feeling better connected as they now had a narrative that helped them understand each other's perspective to some degree.

The case was closed after 12 sessions, which was a joint decision.

Preliminary findings and clinical implications

In this section, we share some thoughts about the efficacy of this brief therapy and identify the types of clinical presentations where it might be most useful. After the first year of running the project, one of the co-authors conducted a qualitative service evaluation looking at clinicians' reflections on the project up to that point. Findings from the service evaluation, as well as findings from our continued observations and learning from the pilot project, indicated a number of themes which we will summarise in this section.

At the time of finalising this chapter, we have offered this brief psychotherapy to 22 adolescents and their parents. In some cases, it was determined that this treatment was not appropriate due to factors such as the nature of the family's trauma and loss, or that the parents chose not to engage. From the cases where we proceeded, all the young people were self-harming, either through cutting or through deliberately mismanaging serious health conditions. The majority also expressed suicidal thoughts, and a considerable number had taken an overdose.

One of the primary aims when we first started working this way was to find effective but also clinically meaningful ways to reduce risk by establishing the driving forces behind a crisis. At the end of the two and a half years, in all cases, we observed a clear reduction in risk following this intervention. While this was a pilot study, the conclusions indicate a positive outcome based on the clinical observation of far fewer incidents of self-harming behaviours and visits to A&E in these cases.

More meaningfully, we also observed a noticeable shift in how the young person and parents understood their situation and communicated their problems to each other. We see this improved understanding and communication as the most critical outcome, as it was generally coupled with an increased sense of self-efficacy and confidence in the parents, when it came to making sense of and responding to the crisis.

The findings from the pilot project may be considered aligned with those of the *practitioner research model* of translational research that has the potential to create immediate application to the practical field circumstances (See: Translational Research: American Institutes of Health NIH, Rubio et al., 2010).

Key findings

- Based on the service evaluation, exploring the experiences of the clinicians involved in the project, the reality of working within a pressured service landscape came up as a main overarching theme, echoing in a way the crisis faced by families coming to the service.
- The case for the value of time-limited psychodynamic work in crisis, for adolescents and their families, emerged as a strong central theme in the service evaluation.
- We were reminded, as a central finding, of something we knew but that was illustrated vividly in the project: that the crises presented by adolescents are diverse, each with different traits; we cannot generalise them and treat them all in the same way, so each crisis (and thus each family) needs its own approach. This point may seem obvious, until we pause to remember the unifying, repetitive approach structured risk assessments and safety plans take, and the way they rely on certain assumptions that, in many cases, may prove untrue.
- Understanding and normalising the adolescent process, particularly the changes and transitions it involves, and avoiding pathologising and premature fixing of the problems observed, leads to better outcomes for the adolescent and parents.
- Including parents leads to far better outcomes, as shown clearly in the service evaluation and subsequent work. It helps the young person feel better understood, it contextualises the crisis symptoms within a framework that expands beyond the individual teenager, it offers scaffolding for parents' sense of authority, and most importantly, it creates a unique opportunity for a therapeutic intervention that can have long-lasting effects in the parent–adolescent relationship, as the young person moves towards adulthood.
- Establishing links with critical networks broadens the help available to the adolescent for a supportive therapeutic scaffold, leading to better outcomes.

- When two therapists co-work on cases involving self-harm and suicidality, a more intensive approach to brief work is enabled, avoiding the risk of splitting. It also provides better containment for the therapists themselves to recognise and articulate what is being enacted.
- Central to understanding the meaning of the crisis within a fairly short period of time was attention to the immediacy of the relationship between the therapist and the adolescent, and the therapist and the parent–carer working together in open dialogue.

Questions for future research

Exploring the thoughts and feelings of adolescents and their parents, how meaning is made by them, is an invaluable dimension of this work. Our goal has always been to move beyond symptoms and uncover some of the previously unconscious elements driving a crisis, making a fuller picture of what's happening possible. Involving the young person and their parents in shaping future steps, both in research and clinical directions, would help us understand what aspects work particularly well for them, delineating the different priorities of patients and clinicians and shedding light on whether our own perceptions of the work 'fit' for families too. This could transform the project into an action research forum, which is our initial hope for a next step.

Advocates of time-limited therapy, particularly for adolescents with complex vulnerabilities referred to CAMHS (Abbass et al., 2013; Schmidt Neven, 2017; Trowell et al., 2007), recognise its potential to help adolescents 'confront [the] specific developmental tasks, thereby enabling the developmental process to proceed' (Laufer, 1975, p. 525). Despite its potential, this way of working presents its own challenges, such as negotiating the end of treatment and timing it well – a common issue in all brief psychotherapy (Della Rosa & Midgley, 2017). Issues specific to short-term therapy have started to be researched (e.g. Briggs et al., 2015, p. 314). Continued exploration by psychoanalytic psychotherapists working with children and young people in crisis is needed to better establish when and how brief models can be effective and when they might not be indicated.

By adopting a phenomenological perspective and exploring how people attribute meaning to what happens to them, we can also consider broader sociocultural shifts and how they impact adolescents. This might include the influence of social media on adolescents' everyday life and relationships, the erosion of parental authority and the confusions many parents feel as to how to respond to the different world their children inhabit, the higher percentage of self-harm among girls, or the distinct meanings of overdosing and suicide attempts in different social groups, as well as gender differences in these particular areas.

Another area we would like to develop and research, and which would be a promising avenue for psychoanalytic clinicians in other CAMHS teams, is whether this way of working can apply to other types of crisis, beyond suicidality and self-harm. This intervention stands in the area of overlap between the individual, often unconscious reality of each adolescent we see and the concentric circles around them, including family, friendship group, parents, wider society, and the internet.

Further, this is a pragmatic intervention, created in the context of the realities of working at CAMHS, and could be applied as one of the frontline services for a wider range of crises without relying on formal diagnosis. While we consult with schools about safety planning, we don't create written crisis plans, except if a family explicitly requests this. Instead, we rely on clinical engagement, continuity of care, interest in the psychodynamics of the individual and the family, and a belief that symptoms have a meaning and tell a story.

Conclusion

Looking back on the past three years, we have grown increasingly confident in the applicability and potential of brief psychodynamic crisis work for adolescents and their parents. This work has proven helpful in most of the cases, provided the main principles are kept in mind, the parents are closely involved, and the emphasis is placed on uncovering meaning rather than on reducing symptoms. We concentrate on engagement, the active involvement of parents and the broader network, and verbally agreed-upon plans to monitor risk – all grounded in uncovering meaning and building trust.

We believe, based on the pilot project, that this method of working with adolescents in crisis can be manageable and straightforward to implement, working well in the context of strained NHS services. It is also therapeutically effective. By centring the work on understanding the underlying meanings behind the crisis, involving parents as key partners, and fostering trust through continuity and consistency over a period of time, we have observed promising positive outcomes.

Notes

1 This chapter is based on an article originally published in the *Journal of child psychotherapy*, 50, 3, 2024, pp. 470–496.
2 The views and opinions expressed in this chapter are those of the authors and do not necessarily reflect the official policy or position of the NHS or the team within which the authors work.
3 Children and Adolescents Mental Health Services within the NHS (National Health Service) in the UK.
4 Association of Child Psychotherapists, the regulatory body in the UK for psychoanalytic child and adolescent psychotherapists.
5 https://dictionary.cambridge.org/dictionary/english/crisis.
6 'Bronfenbrenner's model begins by recognising that young people's personal experiences and development are shaped by their interactions with the people around them; that is, they react to and act on their immediate environment of familial and peer relationships (microlevel). These interpersonal relationships are also influenced by neighbourhood and community dynamics and exposure to institutions and policies (mesolevel). These, in turn, are nested within the organisational, political, historical, cultural (for example, values, norms and beliefs) and physical environments (macrolevel) whose interplay directly or indirectly affects the adolescent's mental health and well-being. A high court ruling (policy

environment) could have direct or indirect effects on the community, household and personal well-being of a young person seeking asylum. The socioecological framework encompasses the dynamic relationships of an individual with the social environment' (Collins et al., 2024).

7 It's beyond the scope of this chapter to explore the reasons for this striking gender disparity, but it's something that is reflected widely across the relevant literature of referrals to CAMHS adolescent services and, particularly, in crisis services.

8 This is not based on any of the existing – past or present – cases we have worked with. To create it, we have combined some overarching themes that occur repeatedly in this type of work.

References

Abbass, A., Town, J. M., & Driessen, E. (2013). Intensive short-term dynamic psychotherapy: A treatment overview and empirical basis. *Research in Psychotherapy: Psychopathology, Process and Outcome*, 16(1), 6–15.

Abdelrahman, M. (2022). COVID-19 and the meaning of crisis. *Development & Change*, 53(6), 1151–1176. https://doi.org/10.1111/dech.12744

Acheson, R., & Papadima, M. (2023). The search for identity: Working therapeutically with adolescents in crisis. *Journal of Child Psychotherapy*, 49(1), 95–119. https://doi.org/10.1080/0075417X.2022.2160478

Adini-Spigelman, E., Gvion, Y., Haruvi Catalan, L., Barzilay, S., Apter, A., & Brunstein Klomek, A. (2024). Comparative effectiveness of ultra-brief, IPT-a based crisis intervention for suicidal children and adolescents. *Archives of Suicide Research*, 1–14. https://doi.org/10.1080/13811118.2023.2298499

Anderson, R. (2000). Assessing the risk of self-harm in adolescents: A psychoanalytical perspective. *Psychoanalytic Psychotherapy*, 14(1), 9–21. https://doi.org/10.1080/02668730000700021

Axelrod, S. D., Naso, R. C., & Rosenberg, L. M. (eds.). (2018). *Progress in psychoanalysis: Envisioning the future of the profession*. Routledge.

Bion, W. R. (1973/2005). *Attention and interpretation (CWB)* (Vol. 7). Karnac Books.

Bion, W. R. (1977/2005). *Clinical seminars and four papers (CWB)* (Vol. 9). Karnac Books.

Bleiberg, E. (1988). Adolescence, sense of self, and narcissistic vulnerability. *Bulletin of the Menninger Clinic*, 52(3), 211.

Blos, P. (1967). The second individuation process of adolescence. *The Psychoanalytic Study of the Child*, 22(1), 162–186. https://doi.org/10.1080/00797308.1967.11822595

Bommersbach, T. J., Olfson, M., & Rhee, T. G. (2024). National trends in emergency department visits for suicide attempts and intentional self-harm. *The American Journal of Psychiatry*, 181(8), 741–752. https://doi.org/10.1176/appi.ajp.20230397

Bouter, D. C., Zarchev, M., de Neve-Enthoven, N. G. M., Ravensbergen, S. J., Kamperman, A. M., Hoogendijk, W. J. G., & Grootendorst van Mil, N. H. (2023). A longitudinal study of mental health in at-risk adolescents before and during the COVID-19 pandemic. *European Child & Adolescent Psychiatry*, 32(6), 1109–1117. https://doi.org/10.1007/s00787-021-01935-y

Briggs, S., Maxwell, M., & Keenan, A. (2015). Working with the complexities of adolescent mental health problems: Applying time-limited adolescent psychodynamic psychotherapy (TAPP). *Psychoanalytic Psychotherapy*, 29(4), 314–329.

Briggs, S., Netuveli, G., Gould, N., Gkaravella, A., Gluckman, N. S., Kangogyere, P., & Lindner, R. (2019). The effectiveness of psychoanalytic/psychodynamic psychotherapy for reducing suicide attempts and self-harm: Systematic review and meta-analysis. *British Journal of Psychiatry*, 214(6), 320–328. https://doi.org/10.1192/bjp.2019.33

Bronfenbrenner, U. (1979). *The ecology of human development: Experiments by nature and design.* Harvard University Press.

Bronstein, C., & Flanders, S. (1998). The development of a therapeutic space in a first contact with adolescents. *Journal of Child Psychotherapy,* 24(1), 5–36. https://doi.org/10.1080/00754179808414803

Campbell, D., & Hale, R. (2017). *Working in the dark: Understanding the pre-suicide state of mind.* Routledge.

Cartwright, D. (2014). *Containing states of mind: Exploring Bion's "container model" in psychoanalytic psychotherapy.* Routledge.

Catty, J. (2021). Out of time: Adolescents and those who wait for them. *Journal of Child Psychotherapy,* 47(2), 188–204. https://doi.org/10.1080/0075417X.2021.1954977

Collins, P. Y., Sinha, M., Concepcion, T., Patton, G., Way, T., McCay, L., Mensa-Kwao, A., Herrman, H., de Leeuw, E., Anand, N., Atwoli, L., Bardikoff, N., Booysen, C., Bustamante, I., Chen, Y., Davis, K., Dua, T., Foote, N., Hughsam, M., Juma, D., Khanal, S., Kumar, M., Lefkowitz, B., McDermott, P., Moitra, M., Ochieng, Y., Omigbodun, O., Queen, E., Unützer, J., Uribe-Restrepo, J. M., Wolpert, M., & Zeitz, L. (2024). Making cities mental health friendly for adolescents and young adults. *Nature,* 627(8002), 137–148. https://doi.org/10.1038/s41586-023-07005-4

Cummins, I. (2018). The impact of austerity on mental health service provision: A UK perspective. *International Journal of Environmental Research and Public Health,* 15(6), 1145. https://doi.org/10.3390/ijerph15061145

Dafermos, M. (2018). *Rethinking cultural-historical theory: A dialectical perspective to Vygotsky.* Springer.

Dafermos, M. (2024). Discussing the concept of crisis in cultural-historical activity research: A dialectical perspective. *Human Arenas,* 7(2), 273–292. https://doi.org/10.1007/s42087-022-00289-4

De Kernier, N. (2012). Suicide attempt during adolescence a way of killing the "Infans" and a quest for individuation-separation. *The Crisis,* 33(5), 290–300. https://doi.org/10.1027/0227-5910/a000135

De Maat, S., de Jonghe, F., de Kraker, R., Leichsenring, F., Abbass, A. A., Luyten, P., Barber, J. P., van, R., & Dekker, J. (2013). The current state of the empirical evidence for psychoanalysis: A meta-analytic approach. *Harvard Review of Psychiatry,* 21(3), 107–137. https://doi.org/10.1097/HRP.0b013e318294f5fd

Dekel, R., Lebowitz, E. R., & Feldman, R. (2021). Combining parenting training with cognitive-behavioral therapy for adolescents: A short-term intervention. *Cognitive Therapy and Research,* 45(3), 439–450. https://doi.org/10.1007/s10608-021-10204-3

Della Rosa, E., & Midgley, N. (2017). Adolescent patients' responses to interpretations focused on endings in short-term psychoanalytic psychotherapy. *Journal of Infant Child, & Adolescent Psychotherapy,* 16(4), 279–290.

Edlund, J. N., & Carlberg, G. (2016). Psychodynamic psychotherapy with adolescents and young adults: Outcome in routine practice. *Clinical Child Psychology and Psychiatry,* 21(1), 66–80. https://doi.org/10.1177/1359104514554311

Edwards, D., Carrier, J., Csontos, J., Evans, N., Elliott, M., Gillen, E., Hannigan, B., Lane, R., & Williams, L. (2024). Review: Crisis responses for children and young people – a systematic review of effectiveness, experiences and service organisation (CAMH-Crisis). *Child and Adolescent Mental Health,* 29(1), 70–83. https://doi.org/10.1111/camh.12639

Esman, A. H. (1998). What is 'applied' in 'applied' psychoanalysis? *The International Journal of Psycho-Analysis,* 79(4), 741.

Fonagy, P., Rost, F., Carlyle, J., McPherson, S., Thomas, R., Fearon, P., Goldberg, D., & Taylor, D. (2015). Pragmatic randomized controlled trial of long-term psychoanalytic psychotherapy for treatment-resistant depression: The Tavistock Adult Depression Study (TADS). *World Psychiatry,* 14(3), 312–321. https://doi.org/10.1002/wps.20267

Foulkes, L. (2022). *What mental illness really is . . . (and what it isn't)*. Random House.

Foulkes, L., & Andrews, J. L. (2023). Are mental health awareness efforts contributing to the rise in reported mental health problems? A call to test the prevalence inflation hypothesis. *New Ideas in Psychology*, 69, 101010. https://doi.org/10.1016/j.newideapsych.2023.101010

Fowler, B., & Vinson, S. Y. (2020). Digital media, culture, and child and adolescent mental health. In: *Cultural psychiatry with children, adolescents, and families*, 231. American Psychiatric Publishing.

Freeden, M. (2017). Crisis? How is that a Crisis!?: Reflections on an overburdened word. *Contributions to the History of Concepts*, 12(2), 12–28. https://doi.org/10.3167/choc.2017.120202

Freud, A. (1958). On adolescence. *The Psychoanalytic Study of the Child*, 13(1), 255–278. https://doi.org/10.1080/00797308.1958.11823182

Freud, S. (1917). Introductory lectures on psycho-analysis. In: *The standard edition of the complete psychological works of Sigmund Freud* (Vol. 16, pp. 241–463). Hogarth Press.

Garland, A. F., & Zigler, E. (1993). Adolescent suicide prevention: Current research and social policy implications. *The American Psychologist*, 48(2), 169.

Gatta, M., Miscioscia, M., Svanellini, L., Spoto, A., Difronzo, M., De Sauma, M., & Ferruzza, E. (2019). Effectiveness of brief psychodynamic therapy with children and adolescents: An outcome study. *Frontiers in Pediatrics*, 7, 501. https://doi.org/10.3389/fped.2019.00501

Gerrard, S. (2012). The big picture: Do mothers cause social problems? *Moving on from Bowlby: Theories about child development blog*. Retrieved May 6, 2024, from https://movingonfrombowlby.wordpress.com/2012/07/24/the-big-picture/

Gibbons, R. (2023). Eight 'truths' about suicide. *BJPsych Bulletin*, 1–5. https://doi.org/10.1192/bjb.2023.75

Gibbons, R. (2024). Someone is to blame: The impact of suicide on the mind of the bereaved (including clinicians). *BJPsych Bulletin*, 1–5. https://doi.org/10.1192/bjb.2024.37

Ginnis, K. B., White, E. M., Ross, A. M., & Wharff, E. A. (2015). Family-based crisis intervention in the emergency department: A new model of care. *Journal of Child & Family Studies*, 24(1), 172–179. https://doi.org/10.1007/s10826-013-9823-1

Glenn, C. R., Franklin, J. C., & Nock, M. K. (2015). Evidence-based psychosocial treatments for self-injurious thoughts and behaviors in youth. *Journal of Clinical Child & Adolescent Psychology*, 44(1), 1–29. https://doi.org/10.1080/15374416.2014.945211

Goodyer, I. M., Tsancheva, S., Byford, S., Dubicka, B., Hill, J., Kelvin, R., Reynolds, S., Roberts, C., Senior, R., Suckling, J., Wilkinson, P., Target, M., & Fonagy, P. (2011). Improving mood with psychoanalytic and cognitive therapies (IMPACT): A pragmatic effectiveness superiority trial to investigate whether specialised psychological treatment reduces the risk for relapse in adolescents with moderate to severe unipolar depression: Study protocol for a randomised controlled trial. *Trials*, 12, 1–12.

Haidt, J. (2024). *The anxious generation*. Penguin Random House.

Hanna, S. M. (2018). *The practice of family therapy: Key elements across models*. Routledge.

Haruvi Catalan, L., Levis Frenk, M., Adini Spigelman, E., Engelberg, Y., Barzilay, S., Mufson, L., Apter, A., Benaroya Milshtein, N., Fennig, S., & Klomek, A. B. (2020). Ultra-brief crisis IPT-A based intervention for suicidal children and adolescents (IPT-A-SCI) pilot study results. *Frontiers in Psychiatry*, 11, 553422. https://doi.org/10.3389/fpsyt.2020.553422

House of Commons Health and Social Care Committee. (2021). *Children and young people's mental health: Time to deliver*. Eighth Report of Session 2021–22. House of Commons. Retrieved September 1, 2024, from. https://publications.parliament.uk/pa/cm5802/cmselect/cmhealth/17/report.html

Hunter, S. (2018). Dangerous times for looked-after children: Austerity cuts risking the lives of the most vulnerable. In: *Austerity policies: Bad ideas in practice* (pp. 221–240). Cham: Springer International Publishing.

Jones, P. B. (2013). Adult mental health disorders and their age at onset. *British Journal of Psychiatry*, 202(s54), s5–s10. https://doi.org/10.1192/bjp.bp.112.119164

Kelleher, I., Murtagh, A., Molloy, C., Roddy, S., Clarke, M. C., Harley, M., & Cannon, M. (2012). Identification and characterization of prodromal risk syndromes in young adolescents in the community: A population-based clinical interview study. *Schizophrenia Bulletin*, 38(2), 239–246. https://doi.org/10.1093/schbul/sbr164

Lång, U., Yates, K., Leacy, F. P., Clarke, M. C., McNicholas, F., Cannon, M., & Kelleher, I. (2022). Systematic review and meta-analysis: Psychosis risk in children and adolescents with an at-risk mental state. *Journal of the American Academy of Child and Adolescent Psychiatry*, 61(5), 615–625. https://doi.org/10.1016/j.jaac.2021.07.593

Laufer, M. (1975). Preventive intervention in adolescence. *The Psychoanalytic Study of the Child*, 30(1), 511–528. https://doi.org/10.1080/00797308.1975.11823317

Lemma, A., & Patrick, M. (eds.). (2010). *Off the couch: Contemporary psychoanalytic applications*. Routledge.

Lia, M. (2017, April). Reflections, and relative examples, regarding countertransference, empathy, and observation. *International Forum of Psychoanalysis*, 26(2), 85–96. Routledge. https://doi.org/10.1080/0803706X.2016.1200197

Luborsky, L., & Barrett, M. S. (2006). The history and empirical status of key psychoanalytic concepts. *Annual Review of Clinical Psychology*, 2(1), 1–19. https://doi.org/10.1146/annurev.clinpsy.2.022305.095328

Lybbert, R., Ryland, S., & Bean, R. A. (2019). Existential interventions for adolescent suicidality: Practical interventions to target the root causes of adolescent distress. *Children & Youth Services Review*, 100, 98–104. https://doi.org/10.1016/j.childyouth.2019.02.028

Marks, D. (2020). Fostering parental growth and enhancing the therapeutic alliance: Key tasks for the child psychotherapist. *Journal of Child Psychotherapy*, 46 (1), 20–34.

Massey, R. F. (1986). What/Who is the family system? *The American Journal of Family Therapy*, 14(1), 23–39. https://doi.org/10.1080/01926188608250230

Mees, P. (2015). A psychoanalytic child psychotherapy contribution to generic assessments. *Clinical Child Psychology and Psychiatry*, 21(1), 1–12. https://doi.org/10.1177/1359104514567580

National Institute for Health and Care Excellence. (2022). Self-harm: Assessment, management and preventing recurrence. *NICE Guideline*. https://www.nytimes.com/2023/05/01/health/adolescents-mental-health-hospitals.html

Nesi, J., Telzer, E. H., & Prinstein, M. J. (2020). Adolescent development in the digital media context. *Psychological Inquiry*, 31(3), 229–234. https://doi.org/10.1080/1047840X.2020.1820219

NHS Digital. (2020). *Mental health of children and young people in England, 2020: Wave 1 follow up to the 2017 survey*. https://digital.nhs.uk/data-and-information/publications/statistical/mental-health-of-children-and-young-people-in-england/2020-wave-1-follow-up

The NHS Long Term Plan. (2019). https://www.longtermplan.nhs.uk/

Novick, K., & Novick, J. (2013). Concurrent work with parents of adolescent patients. *The Psychoanalytic Study of the Child*, 67(1), 103–136. https://doi.org/10.1080/00797308.2014.11785491

Ormel, J., Raven, D., van Oort, F., Hartman, C. A., Reijneveld, S. A., Veenstra, R., Vollebergh, W. A. M., Buitelaar, J., Verhulst, F. C., & Oldehinkel, A. J. (2015). Mental health in Dutch adolescents: A TRAILS report on prevalence, severity, age of onset, continuity and co-morbidity of DSM disorders. *Psychological Medicine*, 45(2), 345–360. https://doi.org/10.1017/S0033291714001469

Panchal, U., Salazar de Pablo, G., Franco, M., Moreno, C., Parellada, M., Arango, C., & Fusar-Poli, P. (2023). The impact of COVID-19 lockdown on child and adolescent mental health: Systematic review. *European Child & Adolescent Psychiatry*, 32(7), 1151–1177. https://doi.org/10.1007/s00787-021-01856-w

Poyraz Fındık, O. T., Erdoğdu, A. B., Fadıloğlu, E., & Rodopman Arman, A. (2022). Emergency department visits for non-suicidal self-harm, suicidal ideation, and suicide attempts in children and adolescents. *Child Psychiatry and Human Development*, 53(2), 289–299. https://doi.org/10.1007/s10578-021-01125-6

Rossouw, T. I. (2013). Self-harm in young people: A randomised control trial comparing mentalization based treatment against treatment as usual (Doctoral dissertation, UCL University College London).

Rossouw, T. I., & Fonagy, P. (2012). Mentalization-based treatment for self-harm in adolescents: A randomized controlled trial. *Journal of the American Academy of Child and Adolescent Psychiatry*, 51(12), 1304–1313. https://doi.org/10.1016/j.jaac.2012.09.018

Rowan, A. (2003). *Applied psychoanalysis in mental health: Can we reconcile the pragmatism and the poetics of practice?* Retrieved September 1, 2024, from https://jcfar.org.uk/jcfar-bookshop/digital-editions/jcfar-issue-13-digital-edition/

Royal College of Psychiatrists. (2020). https://www.rcpsych.ac.uk/improving-care/campaigning-for-better-mental-health-policy/college-reports/2020-college-reports/cr229

Rubio, D. M., Schoenbaum, E. E., Lee, L. S., Schteingart, D. E., Marantz, P. R., Anderson, K. E., Platt, L. D., Baez, A., & Esposito, K. (2010). Defining translational research: Implications for training. *Academic Medicine*, 85(3), 470–475. https://doi.org/10.1097/ACM.0b013e3181ccd618

Salinger, J. D. (1951). *The catcher in the rye*. Little, Brown and Company.

Salisbury, L., Baraitser, L., Catty, J., Anucha, K., Davies, S., Flexer, M. J., Moore, M. D., & Osserman, J. (2023). A waiting crisis? *Lancet*, 401(10375), 428–429. https://doi.org/10.1016/S0140-6736(23)00238-6

Sandler, J., Holder, A., & Dare, C. (1970). Basic psychoanalytic concepts: IV, counter-transference. *The British Journal of Psychiatry*, 117(536), 83–88. https://doi.org/10.1192/S0007125000192189

Schmidt Neven, R. (2010). *Core principles of assessment and therapeutic communication with children, parents and families: Towards the promotion of child and family wellbeing*. Taylor and Francis.

Schmidt Neven, R. (2017). *Time-limited psychodynamic psychotherapy with children and adolescents: An interactive approach*. Taylor and Francis.

Searle, L., Lyon, L., Young, L., Wiseman, M., & Foster-Davis, B. (2011). The young people's consultation service: An evaluation of a consultation model of very brief psychotherapy. *British Journal of Psychotherapy*, 27(1), 56–78. https://doi.org/10.1111/j.1752-0118.2010.01222.x

Selvini, M. P., Boscolo, L., Cecchin, G., & Prata, G. (1980). Hypothesizing – circularity – neutrality: Three guidelines for the conductor of the session. *Family Process*, 19(1), 3–12. https://doi.org/10.1111/j.1545-5300.1980.00003.x

Sexton, T. L., & Stanton, M. (2016). Systems theories. In: J. C. Norcross, G. R. VandenBos, D. K. Freedheim, & B. O. Olatunji (eds.), *APA handbook of clinical psychology: Theory and research* (pp. 213–239). American Psychological Association. https://doi.org/10.1037/14773-008

Sharma, S., & Fowler, J. C. (2018). Restoring hope for the future: Mentalization-based therapy in the treatment of a suicidal adolescent. *The Psychoanalytic Study of the Child*, 71(1), 55–75.

Shedler. (2023). https://www.tandfonline.com/doi/abs/10.1080/00107530.2022.2149038

Starn, R. (1971). Historians and "crisis". *Past & Present*, 52(1), 3–22. https://doi.org/10.1093/past/52.1.3

Trowell, J., Joffe, I., Campbell, J., Clemente, C., Almqvist, F., Soininen, M., Koskenranta-Aalto, U., Weintraub, S., Kolaitis, G., Tomaras, V., Anastasopoulos, D., Grayson, K., Barnes, J., & Tsiantis, J. (2007). Childhood depression: A place for psychotherapy: An outcome study comparing individual psychodynamic psychotherapy and family therapy. *European Child & Adolescent Psychiatry*, 16(3), 157–167. https://doi.org/10.1007/s00787-006-0584-x

Uh, S., Dalmaijer, E. S., Siugzdaite, R., Ford, T. J., & Astle, D. E. (2021). Two pathways to self-harm in adolescence. *Journal of the American Academy of Child and Adolescent Psychiatry*, 2021(12), 1491–1500. https://doi.org/10.1016/j.jaac.2021.03.010

Washburn, J. J., Richardt, S. L., Styer, D. M., Gebhardt, M., Juzwin, K. R., Yourek, A., & Aldridge, D. (2012). Psychotherapeutic approaches to non-suicidal self-injury in adolescents. *Child and Adolescent Psychiatry and Mental Health*, 6(1), 1–8. https://doi.org/10.1186/1753-2000-6-14

Wharff, E. A., Ginnis, K. B., Ross, A. M., White, E. M., White, M. T., & Forbes, P. W. (2019). Family-based crisis intervention with suicidal adolescents: A randomized clinical trial. *Pediatric Emergency Care*, 35(3), 170–175. https://doi.org/10.1097/PEC.0000000000001076

Wharff, E. A., Ginnis, K. M., & Ross, A. M. (2012). Family-based crisis intervention with suicidal adolescents in the emergency room: A pilot study. *Social Work*, 57(2), 133–143. https://doi.org/10.1093/sw/sws017

Wijana, M. B., Feldman, I., Ssegonja, R., Enebrink, P., & Ghaderi, A. (2021). A pilot study of the impact of an integrated individual-and family therapy model for self-harming adolescents on overall healthcare consumption. *BMC Psychiatry*, 21, 1–13.

Winnicott, D. W. (2018). *Therapeutic consultations in child psychiatry*. Routledge.

Wolf, K., & Schmitz, J. (2024). Scoping review: Longitudinal effects of the COVID-19 pandemic on child and adolescent mental health. *European Child & Adolescent Psychiatry*, 33(5), 1257–1312. https://doi.org/10.1007/s00787-023-02206-8

World Health Organization. (2014). *Preventing suicide: A global imperative*. World Health Organization.

World Health Organization. (2021). *Suicide worldwide in 2019: Global health estimates*. Retrieved September 1, 2024, from https://www.who.int/publications/i/item/9789240026643

Yakeley, J. (2018). Psychoanalytic contributions to risk assessment and management. In: *Lectures on violence, perversion and delinquency* (pp. 59–82). Routledge.

Chapter 14

Playing with fire

Or how do we play when we're scared? the nature and function of play in psychotherapy with high-risk adolescents

Kate Mills

Introduction

Before we get stuck in, a few provisos. This chapter will in no way provide a manual or any clear answers or guidelines. These are active questions in my mind, ideas to play with and to be explored in supervisory spaces and in our own minds as therapists. If we are to find our own way with each patient, as the Independent psychoanalytic tradition encourages us, this is nowhere more vital than in the area of play, or indeed of risk.

Play and risk can't be decoupled from each other, for they share an important quality: something to do with the unknown, the unpredictable, but also of being on the edge, bordering a potential space of either destruction or creativity. In therapy, when faced with challenging situations involving risk, we must lean more heavily than ever on our countertransference feelings and reactions. As we will discuss, the need to think with others is also paramount.

Here are some further starting points to frame the chapter. When I talk about work with a young person, I am specifically referring to work within a psychoanalytic psychotherapy treatment, where the therapist is able to see the young person on a weekly basis for an agreed length of time (this may be short-, medium-, or long-term work). This treatment setting is crucial, because it is the containment provided by the boundaries of the psychoanalytic frame that allows thinking about play and risk to take place.

In CAMHS work (Child and Adolescent Mental Health Services), high-risk adolescents sometimes have another clinician acting as their care coordinator,[1] and perhaps also a psychiatrist supporting them. This is particularly helpful, so that the therapist is free to work psychoanalytically, knowing that the care coordinator is providing a more formal type of risk assessment and safety planning. Ideally, the two roles go hand in hand, and one usually informs the other.

Although I am writing here about psychotherapy treatment, the ideas and ways of thinking about risk and play might also be helpful for more generic CAMHS work, or for other professions working with high-risk adolescents. The chapter consists of three main sections: the role of play in psychotherapy; risk, institutional anxieties, and their impact on play; and finally, the challenge of maintaining a playful approach as a psychotherapist when working with adolescents.

DOI: 10.4324/9781003592778-19

The role of play in psychotherapy with adolescents

Adolescents come to psychotherapy with a range of symptoms, diagnoses (or wishes for them), backgrounds, and histories. They may have been severely neglected or abused, or they may come from good enough homes, free from the worst kind of relational trauma. However, as Winnicott reminds us, even the latter offers no guarantee against adolescent distress (Winnicott, 1971). There is, of course, great variability in the adolescents referred for psychotherapy treatment. Some may have genuine hopes for the work, while others may be profoundly hesitant or ambivalent about engaging in the process.

But I think what most adolescent patients have in common is the painful and challenging search for their own identity. 'Where am I going?' 'Do I want to go there?' 'Who am I?' 'How can I be separate?' 'Am I okay?' These questions lie at the core of adolescent therapy and may link directly to the increase in suicidality and risk in adolescents. The adolescent search for identity is essentially a quest for the 'true self', and according to Winnicott, the true self can only develop if aggression is acknowledged, expressed, and survived (Winnicott, 1971). The challenge for many adolescents experiencing mental distress and engaging in risk-taking behaviours is that, in their struggle to play or find creative outlets for their aggression, their aggression remains unintegrated: it is split off and directed inward, towards the self.

In 'Playing and reality', Winnicott puts play firmly at the heart of the therapeutic process. Playing takes place in a third space, an intermediate space between internal and external, fantasy and reality. In the consulting room, play exists – or doesn't – between patient and therapist. Play is closely linked to other key Winnicottian concerns – transitional phenomena (Winnicott, 1953), the capacity for concern (Winnicott, 1962/2016), and the capacity to be alone (Winnicott, 1958). Through the transitional (and increasingly playful) space of therapy, conflicts and anxieties can be played out, worked through, and understood. Thus, play can provide a space where murderousness can be expressed symbolically, allowing the patient to process aggression without acting it out destructively. The therapist's survival of these symbolic acts of murder becomes the proof that aggression does not have to result in real violence, paving the way towards emotional maturity.

But crucially, Winnicott also sees play as a 'thing-in-itself' and not only a route into the unconscious. 'Playing is itself a therapy', he asserts (Winnicott, 1971), and it is the experience of playing itself, rather than the interpretation of it, that matters. Playing offers a new creative experience: 'it is in playing and only in playing that the individual child or adult is able to be creative and to use the whole personality, and it is only in being creative that the individual discovers the self' (Winnicott, 1971).

Play is integral to the development of the ego, helping to build ego strength and capacity. It fosters skills such as delay of gratification, reality testing, impulse control, problem-solving, and mental flexibility. According to Winnicott, the ability to play creatively is a developmental achievement that may be compromised by impingements, whether these be in the form of external traumas, such as experiencing war or illness, or relational traumas, if a child's carer has not been able to provide the 'facilitating environment' necessary for healthy growth and development (Winnicott, 1965). In these cases, it is the therapist's job to bring the patient 'into a state of being able to play' (Winnicott, 1971). Truly creative play works towards anti-rigidity and can open up a way out of the stasis and stuckness we see so often in our work. Where the patient can initially feel that the way forward is impossible to find, creative play may allow the therapist to become a 'transformational object' (Bollas, 1987), a person or experience that can profoundly alter the self to create deep emotional change: transformation through relationship.

But what does play look like when it doesn't involve doll's houses, lions and dinosaurs, strings, Play-Doh, and the other contents of the traditional psychotherapy box? Or when it doesn't involve the free association of adults on the couch? Of course, some adolescents will still have and use a box; others will make creative use of art materials, card games, or Jenga. Perhaps this says something more about me as a therapist, but in my experience, most boxes I have provided to adolescents have gone unopened, the paintboxes left strikingly clean and dry. Perhaps the defences against what feel like 'childish things' are too prohibitive. But also, play for adolescents is different in other ways, as I hope to explain. It can come through intellectual discussions, playing with ideas or fantasies (what I call *making space*), and through how playful the adolescent and therapist together can be allowed to become, for example, allowing themselves to talk about or enjoy movies, music, computer games, fashion.

Adolescent play may look different from play with younger children, but you will feel it when it's present, and almost certainly when it's not! With an adolescent who is well enough, play can take many forms – though this list is by no means exhaustive. It can involve imagination, holding uncertainty, creativity, humour, and improvisation. There is a certain fluidity, a 'going with', that allows for a dynamic back-and-forth in the interaction. Adolescent play often involves a capacity to flirt with the fundamentals of the adolescent process – sexuality and aggression (anger, rage, and murderousness) – and to playfully explore identity. Play can also involve challenge, with challenge itself becoming a form of play. There is the potential for more childish forms of play – such as pretend play or displacement – to return, allowing the adolescent to regress temporarily, but with more flexibility, slipping in and out of these phases of development. Play creates space for exploration, growth, and the handling of complex emotional states that are part of the adolescent experience.

Risk behaviours and the collapse of play

We might all be familiar with how sessions feel when there is a real absence of play. We recognise a feeling of rigidity, concreteness, a sense of impasse, or a marked lack of reciprocity. In our countertransference, we might experience feelings of boredom, frustration, or irritation. Sessions might be dominated by 'here and now' questions about diagnoses or symptoms. There might be a strong pull towards offering solutions, and ways of fixing things:

Clinical vignette[2]

Leah comes into the room and sits slumped in the chair, hood up, arms folded. She doesn't look like she wants to talk much. She starts to tell me she's angry with the psychiatrist, who won't increase her meds. She's visibly frustrated at any attempt to open this up for exploration. She tells me she just needs a diagnosis; she knows she's got personality disorder, and there's no point talking about other stuff. She doesn't need to be here: it's a waste of time. She says, if she doesn't get a diagnosis, she is going to 'do it'.

The therapist feels anxious and asks her what she means: is she thinking about suicide? Does she have a method in mind? Leah says she wouldn't tell the therapist anyway if she did, because she knows how all this works. She says it's her right to kill herself if she wants to; she doesn't see why she should stay alive for everyone else.

The therapist asks about self-harm, and Leah says of course she's cutting – that's nothing new. The therapist asks, 'Why do you think you cut yourself yesterday?' Leah says, 'To feel something'.

The therapist can't get a sense where Leah is emotionally: it feels very blocked. What the therapist is aware of is their own anxiety, the way their thoughts have turned to the risk assessment that hasn't been updated. The therapist asks what Leah uses to cut herself, and as she says this, she realises she is now operating in a much more concrete mode and notices that the 'play' of exploration feels missing. She is aware of her own anxiety, and the list of questions needing to be asked dominating her own mind.

I imagine most psychotherapists working with risky adolescents have been here, and in this instance, things become more concrete on the therapist's part first. It can feel very difficult for the adolescent who finds themselves locked in cycles of self-harm and suicidal thoughts to communicate in a way that feels flexible and playful and that can result in some kind of psychic change. The risky adolescent is not simply being difficult or stubborn in their refusal to engage more playfully with the therapist (this refusal can, of course, also be an important communication of anger and aggression in itself). Their difficulty in playing is indicative of an internal world where the fluidity and flexibility of symbolic thought is no longer possible, if indeed it ever was.

Self-harm can, of course, have many different meanings (see chapter 6 in this book). For some adolescents, self-harm is something they try out as a coping mechanism, or as a way to regulate feelings. They may be influenced by the group and by their peers, and 'trying on' the identity of 'someone who self-harms' can be, in itself, a form of identity play. Adolescents are generally more prone to expressing themselves through the body, and self-harm can be seen as part of the adolescent acting out experience (Winnicott, 1968/1971; Freud, 1958). For others, however, the self-harm can become more entrenched and may be understood as the antithesis to play and as a failure of symbolisation.

Symbolisation is the process by which emotions, thoughts, and experiences are translated into symbolic representations that can be understood, allowing the individual to express and process inner experience (Segal, 1957). For some of the adolescents who self-harm, inner distress can no longer be effectively symbolised or articulated but instead becomes a physical, and therefore concrete, action inflicted on the body. In these cases, self-harm represents a return to primitive ways of managing internal states, inscribing pain onto the skin, rather than communicating it to others, or putting it into words, internal images, or symbols.

A suicide attempt is frighteningly real. But is there a way in which suicidal thinking can also be thought of as a form of play, however dangerous? The adolescent may, for example, 'play' with the question: 'What would it be like if I weren't here anymore?' This can be a way of exploring a death wish and 'play it out' in fantasy, thinking about the imagined impact on others, exploring the wish to hurt or escape, expressing the intensity of distress internally before – hopefully – recognising the wish to remain living and finding ways to manage the psychic pain that is experienced.

This form of *playful experimentation* with the idea of death doesn't sound like most of the adolescents who come to us for therapy, and certainly not at the beginning of treatment. What we tend to get is adolescents for whom the suicidal idea is not a fantasy to explore with curiosity (in a way that could be described as 'playful'). The suicidal fantasy has instead become rigid, and as with some cases of self-harm, it can indicate a state of mind where play has altogether collapsed. Where play offers something transformative, open-ended, and improvised, the suicidal fantasy represents a desire to end, control, or remove oneself from possibility – from the chance or hope for change. While play engages with uncertainty and risk in a way that opens doors to exploration and new beginnings, suicidal fantasies often signify an overwhelming sense of hopelessness and a desperate desire to escape pain, without seeing any avenue for transformation:

Clinical vignette

Alex says if they don't get a place on an army scholarship, they will kill themselves. They already know how they would do it.

> The therapist doesn't know where to go from here; it is as though all routes of enquiry have now been closed. Alex doesn't seem particularly emotional, and the therapist observes that she is finding it hard to access any feeling within herself, other than this dead-endness.

The playful multiplicity of outcomes, and the ability to *not know* (so essential to any form of improvised play), has here been lost. The collapse of play may exacerbate feelings of inner emptiness, alienation, and despair, as individuals lose access to the symbolic resources necessary to process their distress in a constructive way. Without the capacity for symbolic expression and play, which allow for exploration, flexibility, and transformation of difficult emotions, suicidal fantasies can become pervasive and entrenched. Such fantasies can further reinforce the sense of hopelessness and isolation, creating a cycle where escape seems the only option, and the capacity for change becomes utterly out of reach.

For some young people, the suicidal belief – the notion that there is only one way to end their suffering – can feel incredibly real and overwhelming. This belief, rooted in a lack of symbolic outlets and a narrowed sense of possibility, is, I believe, a driving force behind suicide attempts and the suicides that are completed. When the mind is unable to see alternative pathways, and when play and creativity – essential elements of self-expression and self-discovery – are absent, the only option may seem to be an irreversible act of finality. Psychotherapy must work to rebuild the capacity for play – the ability to hold uncertainty, engage with imagination, and explore different possibilities – as a way to foster hope, connection, and the belief that *change is always possible.*

Risk, institutional anxieties, and their impact on play

As we have seen, it is not only the patient who can lose their capacity to play. The therapist, too, can experience moments where they feel as though they are losing their own ability to think symbolically or engage in the creative, flexible thinking that play requires, as we saw in the clinical vignette with Leah. As therapists, we, too, can get stuck in 'too much reality', leading to a collapse of play.

When it comes to risk in particular, the experience of *managing it* can feel like a straitjacket that prohibits a playful approach in both patient and therapist. It might feel impossible to maintain playfulness in the face of suicide attempts, deliberate self-harm, risky sexual behaviour, and crucially, high levels of anxiety in the network. The rules, the fear, the worry – it all gets in. As in the clinical vignette with Leah, the reverie of the therapist can be easily interrupted by anxiety in such situations, about the risk assessment that needs to be updated, or about the questions the multidisciplinary team will want to know the answers to.

Most difficult of all is the anxiety that if something happens to the young person, it will be the therapist's fault for not saying or doing *the right thing* in the session.

In these moments, curiosity and playfulness can feel as impossible for the clinician to reach as they are for the patient. David Bell offers a powerful description of these anxieties:

> I have described a common central structure in suicidal patients, a primitive psychotic superego which demands omnipotence, not knowledge. It is easy for such disturbed modes of thinking to find a home, not only in the staff but in the institution itself, especially when this is backed up by an external world that demands the impossible. To insist that mental health personnel accept a level of responsibility that is quite unrealistic, seems increasingly · to be a part of mental health policy. Such policies, based less on thought and more on the wish to project unmanageable anxiety into those faced with an already very difficult task, set the scene for a deterioration in the real care of these patients. Management plans come to serve as a defence of the self against any possible blame, rather than acceptance of the complexities of the task. An attitude of enquiry is transformed into one of protection of the self from the Inquisition.
>
> (Bell, 2001, p. 35)

The current NHS workplace in the UK is facing considerable pressures and challenges: a surge in referrals and an increase in the complexity of presentations, coupled with under-staffing, long waiting lists, rigid structures of bureaucracy, and what can feel like an increasingly litigious and complaints-saturated culture:

> [T]he CAMH services we work in are often extremely high-pressured environments – arguably more complex now, post-austerity, post-Brexit, and post-Covid, than ever in some locations. I think it is rare to be able to rely on them for any form of professional containment as qualified clinicians, but we must then find the right support elsewhere in order to maintain our analytic frames, that is, without our training schools and our analysts.
>
> (Smith, 2004)

The 'Zero Suicide Policy', whilst not adopted by all NHS trusts, nonetheless promulgates the idea that all suicides can be prevented through systematic, evidence-based interventions, leadership commitment, staff training, patient engagement, and continuous quality improvement. There is no mention here of the effects of socio-economic factors, austerity, educational challenges, scarcity of social care provision, the impact of social media, or the ease of access to illegal substances. As Bell (2001) argues, the very idea of the policy seems to put responsibility solely in the hands of mental health services and clinicians, rather than seeing us as a crucial but small part of a larger puzzle.

These institutional anxieties can get into the therapist and can easily turn a psychotherapy session into a risk review. The danger, then, is that the unconscious fantasies underneath the behaviour are not given an opportunity to come to light: in the short term, the clinician can feel reassured, but perhaps in the long term, their anxiety increases as the patient fails to make progress.

This is not the only consequence of the institutional anxiety state of mind. I know I have pulled back from asking difficult questions, in certain situations, for fear of making things worse or triggering a risk incident. I think there are frequently times when therapists feel constrained from following their own therapeutic lines of curiosity or enquiry out of a fear of the consequences; this is particularly true, I think, when working with young people who are both suicidal and experiencing gender-related distress, where therapists are so worried about *doing the wrong thing* that they can become profoundly inhibited in having access to their ordinary therapeutic process.

Of course, we need to be mindful and use our countertransference as sensitively as we can to guide us. But there are times when being direct, asking the difficult questions – particularly around suicide – can be a form of *very serious playing*, if we take *playing* to mean enquiring, questioning, offering, improvising, rather than turning to the much more standardised questions of the typical risk review:

Clinical vignette

Jack had been in psychotherapy for several months, and a strong and trusting therapeutic alliance with the therapist had been co-created. Nonetheless, his therapist felt alarmed and rather lost when he started to talk about suicidal fantasies, in the context of a great deal of risky drug-related behaviour and hedonistic partying. He described a fantasy of jumping from a bridge into water. The therapist wondered what he thought would happen once he had jumped. And what would happen next? Why that way of ending his life?

The therapist noticed the sense of excitement described by Jack: the moment of release. She wondered aloud how this might link to another sort of release or climax; perhaps it was more difficult to name. And she noticed aloud that he had said very little about the girls he had once hoped these parties would allow him to meet.

This brings us to sex and sexuality, which are also a crucial part of the 'serious-play-world' when working with older adolescents and young adults: an area of exploration that can get particularly restricted where there are high levels of risk. I wonder if risk, worry, and institutional anxiety can all get into the therapist and make any exploration of sex and sexuality feel even more dangerous than it normally would – as though talking about it could further push the adolescent patient towards dangerous acting out, or even that talking about sex could be a safeguarding concern in itself. Yet I have found it often hugely relieving to adolescents to name the absence of sex and sexuality in a straightforward way, giving a sense of permission for sex to be talked about. We need to work hard to keep institutional anxieties from inhibiting therapeutic exploration.

Maintaining a playful approach as a psychotherapist when working with adolescents

From a state of crisis towards a state of becoming able to play again

Understanding the interplay between suicidal fantasy, self-harm, and the collapse of play underscores the importance of psychoanalytic interventions aimed at facilitating symbolic expression, resolving unconscious conflicts, and restoring the capacity for creative and imaginative engagement with the world. How can the play-space of the therapy, even within crisis teams, be used to resurrect a psychic structure that is able to manage (sublimate) psychic pain? And how do we bring an adolescent in crisis into a state of being able to play again (or for the first time)? But if we can't play, particularly during the transitional space/time that adolescence itself represents, the hope of nurturing this capacity in the patient can become severely compromised. So how, in the first place, do we maintain playfulness in ourselves as therapists?

There are probably many answers to these questions – and these are just some of the ideas that have helped me in my own clinical practice and that have been helpful to consider in supervising others.

The importance of authenticity

I think what playing requires on the part of the therapist is primarily the capacity to respond and react with authenticity and to make use of 'what is unique and idiosyncratic to each of them'[3] (Gabbard & Ogden, 2009, p. 311). Monica Lanyado addresses the importance of authenticity in the chapter 'The playful presence of the therapist' (2017), and I am indebted to her ideas, which do so much to highlight the need for ordinary, sensitive responsiveness. She refers to the transformative effect of 'moments of meeting', where something new is created in the present relationship between therapist and patient (Stern et al., 1998). Lanyado argues that you can't pretend, or play, until you are able to find your authenticity within the uniqueness of each patient–therapist dyad: 'The moment of change notably is a two-way process. Without the openness of heart that playfulness requires on both sides, I think it is much less likely to happen' (Lanyado, 2017, p. 97).

Something I have been playing with in my own mind is the question of authenticity in relation to work with adolescents. Is there a need to be more real with adolescents compared to other age groups? Is there a need to nudge the dial from *blank slate* to *real human* just a little further towards the latter? This is potentially controversial, and I am not entirely sure what I think: I certainly don't imagine it would apply to all therapeutic dyads. But adolescents can smell out a fake with terrier-like efficiency and perhaps require a greater emphasis on the realness of the therapist to begin to trust them.

Being real feels particularly significant in the case of working with a suicidal adolescent. This might mean being real about your wish for them to choose to live, and also being real about why you think this is a good idea. I am sure there have been many times when I have said something like, 'I don't want you to hurt yourself, but I am here to understand the pull towards it, and what in those moments it gives you'. In this sense, Bion's prescription to go into each session 'without memory or desire' strikes me as particularly problematic when working with high-risk adolescents (Bion, 1965/1984). Inevitably, we have a desire, a wish: we want them to stay alive, to start to value life over death. We are invested in a particular outcome, and I will argue later that it is of little therapeutic value to hide this from the patient in the name of psychoanalytic neutrality. Playing means feeling real, for both therapist and patient, and is part of what sustains therapists through years of challenging work.

Feeling real for the self-harming adolescent might have a particular resonance. Adolescents often tell me they self-harm to *feel something* (or to stop feeling something else for a time). Sometimes they describe a bleak internal landscape of feeling numb, empty, or dead inside. To feel real, in the play-space, is a step towards re-discovering their will to live, despite the pain and challenges that life will inevitably involve:

Clinical vignette

Amos has been feeling suicidal for some time. His suicidality is partially linked to deprivation in his relationships and to parental mental health difficulties that make it difficult for his parents to always express the love and care that he needs. Amos has poor self-esteem and has lost all hope that things can be different.

He tells me that he has been thinking about ending his life and says that he doesn't think anyone would care. I reply, 'I would care': a genuine response. There is a moment of meeting. I feel something in him shift ever so slightly with the recognition that perhaps he is important to me.

I simultaneously ask myself why I responded in that way. Was it okay? Was this expressing my own need, or was it an offer to him? What if he now feels he has to be okay for me – which would not be helpful? What if I have paved the way for him to express his anger towards me through an act of self-violence? I feel the 'supervisor on my shoulder' bristling, telling me this is not psychoanalytic enough!

Later, after the session, I reflect further. Perhaps there can be a place for this kind of real, live response and encounter. He saw me as human; he saw my wish for him to stay alive.

The risk here is that the patient might stop sharing suicidal thoughts for fear of making the therapist feel bad, which would be unhelpful at best, and dangerous at worst. If this had been the case, it would have needed much thinking about together to find a way back to the patient feeling able to express truthfully how they felt. For Amos, however, there was something within my expression of my own feelings about his suicidal fantasy that did promote change in him, and thus it was helpful. I am reminded here of Nina Coltart's words quoted by Lanyado in her chapter on playfulness:

> I am now of the opinion that I deprived both him and me unnecessarily by being so prim. I think I might have got nearer to some true shape or pattern in him faster, by responding with a natural reaction and then talking about it. If we are too protective of our self-representation and of what we consider grimly to be the sacred rules of True Psychoanalysis, then we may suffocate something in the patient, in ourselves, and in the process.
>
> (Lanyado, 2017, p. 86)

I love the capitalisation of 'True Psychoanalysis', and find I often want to remind 'Child and Adolescent Psychoanalytic Psychotherapists' that we are trying to *do something different* in our work with young people. Particularly within the Independent tradition, we have argued for the flexibility to meet the needs of the patient, as long as this is done with thought and awareness. It is my experience that working with high-risk adolescents will push us to the edge of our comfort zone, and frequently out of it. We might find ourselves having to bend and stretch the therapeutic frame in ways that might make us uncertain about whether we are doing the right thing: sending an email to try to reach an ambivalent adolescent; speaking to the teenager who turns up in distress a few days after their missed session; answering provocations like 'Give me a reason to live' or 'You wouldn't care if I died' or 'This is just your job' with an authenticity that might take us by surprise.

Not only do I believe that this kind of *off-script improvisation* can be helpful to the patient, but it is also part of the pleasure of working with adolescents, even those at risk. In the current context of mental health services, maintaining that capacity for pleasure is more important than ever. Adam Phillips writes:

> The adolescent, unlike any other patient group I would suggest, makes us acutely aware of our limitations as therapists. . . . And the pleasure here could be the pleasure of being let off the hook, of realising how inappropriate, how unrealistic our standards may be; as if we have been playing draughts with the rules of chess; and that we can be good, or good enough therapists to adolescents only by not being excellent therapists, by not being so sure of ourselves that we know what is best for them. I am talking about the possible pleasures of (relative) powerlessness here . . . the pleasures of not trying to be something that one can't be. And that is precisely what the adolescent, developmentally, is having to work out; what he or she can realistically be?
>
> (Phillips, 2011)

By allowing more of our authentic selves – our *realistic selves* – to emerge in the therapeutic encounter, we invite our adolescent patients to do the same. This way of interacting can skate close to the edge, and the need to draw on past or present personal analysis and supervision is key.

Working authentically with adolescents is risky, and many therapists would argue powerfully and persuasively against such moments of candour, as when I told Amos quite explicitly that I would care. By embracing our own risks of authenticity, we may sometimes tip the balance, making what Gabbard and Ogden (2009) describe as 'errors' – colluding with the patient, arriving late, ending a session early.[4]

But these 'errors' may be exactly what is needed: Goddard and Ogden end their article with a powerful reflection: 'It has been our experience that, when the analyst is off balance, he does his best analytic work' (Gabbard & Ogden, 2009, p. 324). Playful authenticity keeps us alive and developing as people and as therapists, a vivacity crucial in working with young people at an apex of development themselves. There may indeed be a place for these 'errors, or moments of candour', especially when the reality of relationships is often denied for some adolescents. I am reminded of patients who express with conviction, 'No one would care if I died' or 'They would care for a bit, then they would get over it'. For these adolescents, the reality of our relationship and the therapeutic care we offer can be profoundly transformative.

When working with adolescents at risk of self-harm or suicidality, moments of meeting and authenticity can 'cut through' the language of risk-taking threats and risk management plans, creating something more connected, a 'special moment' where 'something new in the present starts to tip the internal balance of the patient towards greater emotional health and well-being' (Lanyado, 2017, p. 96). The freedom within the technique that as therapists we need to find in such moments could be seen as a metaphor for the freedom the adolescent is struggling to find within the rigidity of an internal structure that says suicide or self-harm is the only solution. In this sense, we are also offering 'developmental therapy' (Hurry, 1998): modelling a way of being spontaneous but in control, authentic but reflective, showing our patients that it is okay to express genuine feeling.

Making friends with our internal adolescent

I love working with adolescents, and I have wondered whether that's partly to do with the fact that my adolescent self has never felt too difficult to access – sometimes I wish it were more so! As clinicians we will all be very different, with unique patterns of strengths and weaknesses, blind spots and areas that are easier or more difficult to access. I include this section because I used to feel rather ashamed of the adolescent part of me that would pop up in the work – and outside it! – perhaps by using language that I might not normally use at work (swear words or slang, idioms, or song lyrics) or raging emotively against some system or another. I have questioned at times whether I am colluding with the adolescent, trying to 'get them on my side', in ways that could be unhelpful and non-therapeutic.

But over time I have begun to see that perhaps it was exactly these 'shameful' things that have made me well-suited to working with adolescents. Adam Phillips argues that this is also part of the pleasure:

> Working with adolescents more often, in my experience, exposes us to the parts of ourselves, the versions of ourselves that we are most troubled by. And that is the point and not the problem. The pleasure, and of course the pain, of this very demanding work is that it exposes us to ourselves.
>
> (Phillips, 2011)

I have realised that there are times when being too adolescent myself might be acting out in an unhelpful way to an adolescent patient, but there are many more times when it is a way of joining their world, of playing alongside, much like we might take our shoes off and kneel on the floor to join the play of an under-five. It feels to me a bit like balancing on a wobble board, which is how working with risky adolescents can often make us feel. After all, the therapist of the adolescent 'is always a double-agent, on the side of the parents and the state, and on the side of the child's rebellious desire' (Phillips, 2011).

With risky adolescents in particular, it seems to me vital that we join them in the precariousness – the risk – of their current situation. If we feel too comfortably safe, even within our therapeutic technique, we may be denying them the chance to work through the wobbles, the risks, the 'not-knowings', and the 'getting-it-wrongs', which might eventually nudge them towards greater emotional health.

I am reminded of an excellent supervisee who, in one meeting, was reading aloud her process notes on a recent session with an adolescent patient. During the session, she had laughed spontaneously at a patient's joke. When she came to this part of the session, she rushed to explain that she knows she shouldn't have laughed – she knows she should have remained 'blank slate', and that her laughter was an act of collusion. But slowing things down, we realised that her laughter hadn't been collusion. The joke *had* been funny, if a little dark, and the therapist's laughter had been genuine. I was struck by how unhelpful it was for her to feel so persecuted as a therapist, particularly when her patient was grappling with her own internal persecutory anxiety of having damaged her internal objects, so common to those in states of suicidal despair (Campbell & Hale, 2017). And it reminded me that we might still need permission to be our authentic selves.

What we need as therapists in order to play – the role of supervision

In this chapter, I have argued so far that we can think of play itself as a form of risk-taking, which can become inhibited in therapist–patient dyads where there is a high level of risk in the young person's behaviour and a good deal of worry and institutional anxiety affecting the therapist.

We know that young children need to feel safe before they are able to play freely and creatively, and that the capacity to play can be affected by trauma, fear, and anxiety. We are no different as clinicians: we need to feel safe in our practice so that we can take the risk of being playful in the ways described earlier: without feeling that we have institutional protection and support for our ways of working, defensive practice becomes much more likely. This feels particularly important in the current social and political context, where there are enormous pressures on mental health staff, limited resources, and a culture that can feel litigious and blaming.

So how can the institutions in which we work enable playfulness in clinicians? This could be a chapter in itself, where we might think about the way in which Serious Case Reviews are conducted, or how learnings following patient deaths are shared with staff. What I do want to think about in this chapter, though, is the role of supervision and other creative thinking spaces in providing opportunities for clinicians to continue to engage playfully and creatively, no matter how seriously.

Supervising playfully

Supervising playfully means, I think, facilitating a supervisory space where the supervisee feels confident to try things out and where, much like with a patient, there is a co-created sense of what works with a particular patient and what doesn't. Supervision can be a teaching and learning opportunity for both parties, and even with a trainee, the supervisor has a duty to find a way to be non-persecuting and, broadly speaking, non-directive.

Ideally, supervisee and supervisor can play with ideas collaboratively, whether these be theoretical perspectives or practical ways to manage a situation, reaching an understanding that feels rooted in a joint endeavour of playful exploration. Questions like 'What do you think?', 'How does that feel?', and 'What does that make you think?' can help establish the supervisory play-space, as can a stance that *plays with an idea*, rather than assuming that our interpretations are correct or not. There is no such thing as a correct interpretation; rather there are interpretations that work (and lead to change) and interpretations that don't!

Outside of supervision, we can encourage our workplaces to establish more playful thinking spaces, which don't need to be focused on care planning, decision-making, or risk management. In the NHS clinic where I work, there is a long-established psychotherapy workshop that aims to do just this. It meets weekly for an hour, and clinicians from any discipline can present a case to be thought about in a free associative, and therefore playful, way. Risk or case management issues are directed back to the MDT meeting or to the care coordinator, so that this space remains as free as possible from anxieties around treatment, waiting lists, progress, and risk.

Conclusion

This chapter began with the question of play and identity. The therapist helps the adolescent play, in order to explore who they are, just as the supervisor helps the supervisee play with ideas – not only to support their work with patients but also to help them continuously evolve as a therapist. Every therapist–patient dyad is unique, and each therapist must find their own way of playing with their patients. What feels natural and effective with one may not work with another.

It is this playfulness, creativity, and flexibility that makes the Independent Psychoanalytic Tradition so stimulating and creative. And play is not just for children. It remains a vital tool for adolescents in psychotherapy, a bridge between internal experience and external reality.

Adolescence is a time of boundary-testing, where young people *play with fire* to explore autonomy. In psychotherapy, we, too, must play with fire, taking risks with our patients and working to maintain our own playfulness in the face of anxiety. Because of course, not all playing with fire is dangerous, and taking risks is essential for development. Therapists working within the Independent tradition do not extinguish the fire of adolescence; rather, they help shape it into something constructive. By allowing for play, exploration, and symbolic expression, we create a therapeutic play-space where adolescents have the chance to transform risk and self-hatred into growth and self-discovery.

Notes

1 A *care coordinator* is the clinician responsible for the young person's care within CAMHS, and for maintaining all clinical standards, such as updated risk and care plans. Sometimes, due to necessity and lack of resources, the psychotherapist also acts as the care coordinator.
2 Please note, all case examples and clinical vignettes in this chapter are imaginary and fictional, inspired by ideas or details from composite cases over many years.
3 In this 2009 paper, Gabbard and Ogden describe the development of 'a voice of one's own' as the analyst's primary maturational task and consider the processes by which this may happen.
4 Gabbard and Ogden clearly distinguish these errors from outright boundary violations like breaching confidentiality, having an inappropriate relationship with a patient, and so on.

References

Bell, D. (2001). Who is killing what or whom? Some notes on the internal phenomenology of suicide. *Psychoanalytic Psychotherapy*, 15(1), 21–37.
Bion, W. (1965/1984). *Transformations*. Routledge.
Bollas, C. (1987). *The shadow of the object: Psychoanalysis of the unthought known*. New York, NY: Columbia University Press.
Campbell, D., & Hale, R. (2017). *Working in the dark: Understanding the pre-suicide state of mind*. London, UK: Routledge.
Freud, A. (1958). Adolescence. *Psychoanalytic Study of the Child*, 13, 255–278.
Gabbard, G., & Ogden, T. (2009). On becoming a psychoanalyst. *International Journal of Psychoanalysis*, 90(2), 311–327.
Hurry, A. (1998). *Psychoanalysis and developmental therapy*. Routledge.
Lanyado, M. (2017). *Transforming despair to hope: Reflections on the psychotherapeutic process with severely neglected and traumatised children*. Routledge.

Phillips, A. (2011). The pleasures of working with adolescents. *Psychodynamic Practice*, 17(2), 187–197.

Segal, H. (1957). Notes on symbol formation. *International Journal of Psychoanalysis*, 38(6), 391–397.

Smith, T. (2004). What is the journey that follows our personal training analyses? Reflections on the post-analytic phase of development and some of the challenges of the modern NHS workplace. *Journal of Child Psychotherapy*, 50(3), 2024.

Stern, D., Sander, L., Nahum, J., Harrison, A., Lyons-Ruth, K., Morgan, A., Bruschweiler-Stern, N., & Tronick, E. (1998). Non-interpretive mechanisms in psychoanalytic therapy: The "something more" than interpretation. *International Journal of Psycho-Analysis*, 79, 903–921.

Winnicott, D. W. (1953). Transitional objects and transitional phenomena. *International Journal of Psychoanalysis*, 34, 89–97.

Winnicott, D. W. (1958). The capacity to be alone. *International Journal of Psychoanalysis*, 39, 416–420.

Winnicott, D. W. (1962/2016). The development of the capacity for concern. In: *The collected works of D. W. Winnicott: Volume 6, 1960–1963* (pp. 73–82). Oxford University Press.

Winnicott, D. W. (1965). *The maturational processes and the facilitating environment: Studies in the theory of emotional development*. Routledge.

Winnicott, D. W. (1968/1971). Contemporary concepts of adolescent development and their implications for higher education. *Playing and Reality*, 139.

Winnicott, D. W. (1971). *Playing and reality*. London: Tavistock Publications.

Chapter 15

'To dream is to live'

The therapist's function for representation in work with at-risk adolescents

Nikolaos Tzikas

When working with adolescents in crisis, therapists often encounter challenging times, when simply being present with them can feel almost unbearable. Words, however carefully chosen, may seem to fall into an abyss, failing to reach the adolescent or dissipating entirely.

This mirrors the profound despair these young people frequently endure, a state where they and those around them can feel at a loss, unable to communicate, think clearly, or represent their inner world. This cuts young people off from vital capacities for connection, reflection, and meaning-making. In these moments, we might ask: how can a therapist working in these conditions dream and engage in the symbolic and imaginative processes necessary for emotional growth and integration when so much feels lost?

To explore this question, we must examine the unique developmental processes of adolescence – a turbulent stage marked by both vulnerability and potential. Crises during this period may signify not just breakdowns but also opportunities for breakthroughs. With this foundation, I will share my experiences as a child psychotherapist working with at-risk adolescents, demonstrating how adopting a playful and imaginative therapeutic stance can help them feel contained, reawaken their capacity for dreaming, and ultimately represent and make meaning of their unprocessed experiences.

Additionally, I will include an example where this approach has proven ineffective, discussing the limitations and challenges involved. It's important to note that in some cases, I encountered adolescents whose emotional difficulties seemed rooted in very early developmental deficits. In these instances, I found it helpful to introduce a box of toys typically used for much younger children – to allow them to re-engage in foundational forms of play within a safe therapeutic space, offering a way to reconstruct early experiences that may have been missed or interrupted.

Exploring adolescent development: a brief journey

Adolescence is a transitional phase and one of the most radical developmental periods in our lifespan. It is the time when the sense of self needs to adapt to physical changes, such as size, shape, strength, build, appearance, voice, and new

DOI: 10.4324/9781003592778-20

sexual desires. The social corollaries of this involve developing the capacity for intimacy, forming sexual relationships, becoming gradually less dependent on parents, and moving towards separation from the family.

During the latency period (between the ages of 5 and 10), children achieve a degree of emotional balance as their body and emotional world are not in total chaos, which also depends upon their internal and external worlds being stable. When they enter adolescence, huge changes occur both internally and externally. The young adolescent's mind goes through significant re-negotiation of every aspect of relationships with the self, as well as with external and internal objects. There is a constant interplay between the development of new internal structures and the experience of loss. Therefore, adolescents often struggle between the wish to achieve some balance while simultaneously experiencing feelings of instability.

Erikson (1968) defined adolescence as an experimental period or 'moratorium', wherein adolescents gradually discover and develop various aspects of adult identity. In parallel, Blos (1965) described this period as the second individuation stage, characterised by heightened vulnerability in personality organisation and changes in psychic structure that align with maturational progress. The developmental transition from infancy, marked by emerging from symbiosis to becoming an individuated toddler (Mahler & Furer, 1963), evolves into adolescence, involving the reduction of family dependencies and the relinquishment of infantile object ties in order to integrate into society and the adult world.

Significant neurological, physical, and emotional changes occur in infancy and adolescence (Stortelder & Ploegmakers-Burg, 2010). Neurologically, adolescents undergo rapid development, forming new synapses and neural programming, with maturity not being reached until age 25 (Sowell et al., 2007). Adolescence is often a turbulent chapter in life, with intense transformations within both the body and the mind. Adolescence involves something that can at times be experienced as chaotic, with adolescents feeling uncomfortable about the strange body shape they are developing and sometimes feeling the world around them can appear equally strange. This sense of chaos or strangeness requires construction and reconstruction, allowing for the integration of the internal and external image of the self.

Thus, adolescence is marked by considerable turmoil, leading to the deployment of complex defence mechanisms. During this time, the defence of intellectualisation may continue to play a role, but adolescents also rely heavily on kinetic discharge, symbolic inhibition, and psychosomatic expression. Ladame (1995) drew a parallel between the central role of dreaming in adults and the prominence of action and enactments in adolescence. He suggested that physical expressions help adolescents shift from immediate gratification (pleasure ego) towards a more realistic and adaptive perspective (reality ego). Ladame also emphasised that this return to physical action and expression plays a vital role in therapy, placing the body at the centre of the therapeutic process during adolescence.

This constant attempt by young people to find independence away from adults and family is a persistent challenge that professionals have to manage, as they also represent adult figures whom adolescents sometimes want to run away from.

Engaging with young people thus often feels hard-won. They frequently want to avoid pausing and thinking about themselves, with action becoming their preferred mode of communication.

At the crossroads: a breakdown or an opportunity for a breakthrough?

The extended period of plasticity and the late maturation of the adolescent brain and psyche contribute to an increase in vulnerability to the development of psychopathology. Recent epidemiological research supports the psychoanalytic notion that many adolescents encounter temporary emotional turbulence during this time. Moses and Eglé Laufer (1995) conceptualised pathology in adolescence as a 'developmental breakdown' during this crucial developmental phase, which occurs when the physical and emotional changes of puberty generate unbearable anxiety, resulting in a disavowal of the sexually mature body and genital sexuality. A breakdown:

> appears to occur in the necessity for an object into which the patient feels he can project parts of his personality for their development and manipulation. If he feels there is no such object and no such possibility as splitting off parts of his personality, disturbance is set up.
>
> (Bion, 1965, p. 41)

Therefore, the capacity to use thoughts and function symbolically is impeded.

Breakdowns undermine the apparatus for thinking, weaken the psyche's organisational structures, and signify an inability to use an object of containment. In the face of profound vulnerability and risk often experienced by adolescents, reminiscent of the vulnerability seen in infants, the initial sense of aliveness, comparable to the infant's 'holding' experience, is disrupted. The feeling of 'going-on-being' can then become severely interrupted in this delicate state (Winnicott, 1962/1965).

When navigating the complex emotional and psychic experiences of adolescents, the therapist must enter what we could term a state of *secondary parental preoccupation*. This involves being fully immersed in the adolescent's emotional world, attuned to their infantile needs, while simultaneously fostering a space that encourages separation and independence. This dual stance supports the adolescent in developing new internal structures during this critical stage.

A unique challenge when working with adolescents is to remain in touch with their internal conflict between the wish to remain a dependent child, and the wish to become an independent adult. It's important to exercise caution and avoid actions that might further disrupt the delicate psychic fabric of these vulnerable patients, so it's important to refrain sometimes from directly referring to their infantile needs for dependence and safety, which they might be trying to defend or rebel against. The therapist is tasked here with the challenging responsibility of psychologically 'holding' the patient, safeguarding their sense of 'going-on-being' as an individual beyond symptomatology and risk. By encompassing all facets of the adolescent's self, rather than fixating solely on risky behaviours, the young person can hopefully feel held and gradually more able to develop object-related ways.

During times of crisis, clinicians often feel the instinctual urge to act swiftly, driven to extinguish the metaphorical fire or 'driven by the imperative of the transference', as Peter Wilson (2009) has said, in some cases transforming the breakdown into a potential *breakthrough*. After a psychic breakdown or a suicide attempt, ego defences can be at a low point, providing an opportunity to help the patient rebuild their defences and develop a narrative regarding their sense of self. From a Winnicottian perspective, a breakthrough can only emerge when clinicians cultivate an unobtrusive presence and create a *holding environment* for their patients. This space allows adolescents to feel that their actions and feelings are taken seriously. It also reassures them that their therapist is not just another adult overwhelmed by their crisis, but can remain steady, contained, and present while listening to their worries as they attempt to communicate.

Every interaction with adolescents in crisis represents a valuable therapeutic opportunity (Anderson, 1997; Ruggiero, 2006), influencing whether the subject's psychic reality is recognised and understood. This supports the gradual emergence of creativity (Winnicott, 1958), a breakthrough acting against the inner urges of death and punishment.

The therapist both as the subject and the object of analysis – mirroring the patient's fragments

To effectively treat our patients, it is important to understand our own emotional reactions and responses arising when working with young people who present with risk. The challenge lies in finding a starting point for this process, navigating the barriers created by the adolescent's sense of isolation, need for independence, and scepticism towards adult figures. One possibility for us as clinicians in finding a starting point is described by Christopher Bollas:

> It is a feature of our present-day understanding of the transference that the other source of the analysand's free association is the psychoanalyst's countertransference, so much so that in order to find the patient we must look for him/her within ourselves. This process inevitably points to the fact that there are two 'patients' within the session and therefore two complementary sources of free association.
>
> (1987, p. 135)

Taking the time to look within ourselves is often the initial step in connecting with our patients' emotional experiences and finding their projected fragments. While allowing such experiences to touch us might feel overwhelming, given the rattled states of our patients, it is still important to allow our ego capacities to regress to a degree, in order to meet our patients where they are emotionally.

Winnicott (1986) knew that to understand our patients, we, as therapists, need to adapt to their ego defects and characterological biases. Botella and Botella (2005) emphasise the significant role played by the analyst's bodily experiences, in response to the feelings and expressions of the analysand. They suggest that what cannot be represented within the subject itself, including its inability to form an idea of its identity, is projected onto the analyst. In this way, the body of the analysand, together with the body and psyche of the analyst, become a privileged space, a container, where anxiety can manifest and where intangible objects can be given form.

In the case of Alex that I will present now,[1] my mind became the theatre of his projected eerie and disturbing thoughts. Alex was a 16-year-old boy and an only child who had been taken into care at five, following neglect and emotional and physical abuse. He was moved into a long-term foster placement, where he improved academically. He was referred to our clinic at 15 because of appearing emotionally cut off, and because also of concerns in his support network about how his extensive early trauma might affect him in all areas of his life. There were also allegations of past sexual abuse by male figures he had experienced.

In the course of therapy, Alex talked about his self-harming (by cutting his fingers) and his feelings of emptiness during adolescence, which often led to feelings of isolation and withdrawal. He resorted to spending most of his time in his room, away from peers and supportive figures. This led the professional network to conclude that Alex's experience of prolonged depression was leaving him stranded in a negated emotional place.

From our first contact, it was evident to me that, in Alex's mind, I represented not just a *bad figure* but, even worse, a person who could potentially bring death and darkness. As we entered the therapy room one time, Alex noticed a dead fly on the floor, which I had not seen and had accidentally stepped on. He immediately jumped behind me, screaming that I was a killer: *I had killed that poor fly on purpose.*

After that incident, Alex seemed quiet for a few weeks, exploring the box with the toys in the room silently. In one session:

Alex sits quietly and goes through his box in a calm and controlled manner. He picks a number of objects from his box and keeps dropping them by accident, moving around the room.

Various thoughts suddenly enter my mind, which I find disturbing. My mind feels as if it's invaded by cataclysmic, violent, vivid images of unknown figures in destroyed worlds, with an image of a burnt field that looks like the aftermath of a war. My mind feels intruded relentlessly by uncanny and violent scenes of humans tearing bodies apart, with their bare hands. Images of Kronos2 ripping his sons apart and eating them were dramatically and vividly represented in my mind.

> I become aware as this is going on in my mind that I struggle to focus on Alex's actions, and I make a conscious effort to do so. The only thing I remember of him at this point is his calm manner of trying to hold on to something. He becomes more withdrawn, and his affect becomes flat.
>
> The phantasies invading my mind feel so powerful and disturbing that it's as if I am losing touch with reality, a real struggle to keep thinking, and an anxiety about losing my mind in madness.

I was struck by the violent thoughts entering my mind in this moment, contrasting with the calmness Alex was displaying in the room. I felt that I was in contact with the disturbed part of his psyche, reflecting the aftermath of his experience of abuse that had left him with a shattered world full of *dead bodies and destroyed fields*. The therapy room and I represented Alex's perilous internal world – a psychological void and an unsafe internal space.

These projected *beta elements* mirrored, I think, Alex's deep anxieties and fragmented internal world. Although these images and violent thoughts kept returning in subsequent sessions, their intensity eventually diminished. The decreasing intensity of these thoughts entering my mind indicated to me when it might be the right time to address these unrepresented states.

> After a few sessions, Alex picked up some art materials but found it difficult to draw anything. He made squiggles, became frustrated, and then would rip each piece of paper apart, throwing them away.
>
> I realised that these unmapped parts of him, projected and communicated to me, were those parts that could not take the form of images and create internal coherence. Did I represent a frightening and abusive male figure in the transference, prompting in him fears of being devoured and annihilated? These inexplicable shared experiences affected my mind as well as Alex's ability to assemble anything on paper or in words.
>
> During such times, I continued experiencing uncanny and violent thoughts in my mind and feared that Alex would drop out of therapy, but he continued coming to every session. Although it took me some time to understand the violent images in my head and to get a sense of why I kept having them, I was certain that Alex was unconsciously communicating something within the unique environment we had created together in therapy. My mind had become the vessel for all these uncanny and violent images, with Alex making me feel something of what he was experiencing.

Alex's material illustrates the importance of unconscious communication in accessing the feelings of adolescents, who often communicate their experience through emotions rather than words. On various occasions, Freud (1912a, 1913, 1921) drew attention to communication *from unconscious to unconscious*, with the analyst becoming aware of the derivatives of these unconscious communications, referring to ideas that come into our head without us knowing where from, and expressed in intellectual conclusions that we arrive at, without fully knowing how.

For the therapist to receive such communications, Freud (1912b, 1923) emphasised the attitude of *evenly suspended attention*. The therapist listens to the patient without directing their attention to anything in particular. This helps them avoid premature selection of this or that material, which would foreclose the possibility of surprise and discovery.

The concept of the 'analytic field', extensively developed by Willy Baranger and Madeleine Baranger (2017), elaborates on this deeply involved thinking and relational involvement between two people. The Barangers define the *analytic situation* as a 'field' where unconscious thoughts and fantasies become known and structured through the contribution of intersected mental lives and projective identifications between patient and therapist. In this configuration, the therapist's mind needs to maintain free-floating attention and to allow themself to regress, but only partially, to avoid being overwhelmed by the projected parts of the patient.

Enough time must also be allowed for metabolisation. The therapist's mind acts as a container for the patient's beta-elements, transforming them into alpha-elements, and returning those processed thoughts to the patient (Bion, 1962). Our adolescent patients enact and project fragments of their mind and unconsciously invite us to *learn through experience* how it feels to be them. The therapist, as such, is invited when meeting each patient to enter a process of creating a unique environment and to inhabit different identities that are presented in the transference–countertransference matrix. Thus, patient and therapist enter a total situation together, creating a unique environment with each other, where the feelings, thoughts, fantasies, and images that emerge can be thought about and processed within their dyad.

In the unique therapeutic environment that is created, the therapist allows the patient to use them as an object (Winnicott, 1969). Slowly, by drawing on our subjective experiences of how we, as therapists, are feeling used, we can understand our patient's communications. Then, by drawing on our own emotional experience and on how we experience the feelings our patients project as the object of our observation, we can gain some understanding of the patient's transference (Symington, 1983).

Regressions do not only occur in the patient but also within us in the therapeutic situation, enabling the more disturbed part of our patient to be received by us while maintaining and observing the analytic attitude. Hence, the genuine process of healing and emotional connection is fundamentally an intersubjective experience.

From fragments to representation:
on the construction of meaning

During adolescence, the mind undergoes a significant transition, often finding itself unprepared to process this new developmental stage. The preconscious, where word representations are linked with object representations, may not perform its function adequately. This can result in a heightened risk of suspension of preconscious function, leading to an overwhelming influx of stimuli and acting out. To navigate this developmental stage, therapy interpretations must focus on the significance of the representations and constructions proposed by the therapist. A processing model is offered to create a mental space where patients can explore and use representations in the form of our interpretations, rather than accepting them as ultimate truths. The therapist's mind becomes, in this way, the stage where primitive experiences and feelings can take the form of images and eventually be represented.

One of the most challenging aspects of psychoanalytic therapy, and one that we constantly confront in our work especially with more disturbed patients, is the existence of experiences that cannot be verbalised. Because of all this, the concept of representation is central to what I'm expressing in this chapter. The capacity to symbolise depends on the formation of internal representations.

At times of crisis, such as severe self-harming incidents, overdoses, or suicide attempts, it is often observed that internal representations fade and weaken. This leaves the ego depleted and unable to protect the psyche of young people, which is already vulnerable due to their developmental stage. Therefore, it becomes crucial to re-establish an internal representation and coherence to ensure the survival of our patients.

Every meeting with a young person offers an opportunity for reconstructing and re-establishing meaning amidst the chaos and void they may be feeling during times of crisis or rapid change. During these transitions, characterised by fast internal and external movements, we often rely on interpretations, a common therapeutic practice. But we may overlook the reality that certain aspects can't be represented.

For severely disturbed young people, particularly those presenting with significant risk, verbal representations often appear disinvested, resulting in a disconnect from the representational world. This may manifest as rapid, incoherent speech or, conversely, prolonged and profound silences. Consequently, the therapist is confronted with something that, by its very nature, cannot be represented. Both patients and therapists experience this, and what is at stake is nothing less than psychic survival itself.

Due to all this, sometimes working with adolescents presenting with high risk can feel like a riddle, as they may demonstrate serious difficulties in symbolisation and representational function. Under these circumstances, how do we establish contact with adolescents whose ability to assign personal meaning to their experiences is compromised? Emotional connections and building some threads from experience can only be represented and emerge from shared experiences with another, often based on mutual suffering or connection between two people. But what can be done when both therapist and patient struggle to use language to represent an unspeakable, unrepresented experience with which they could build a connection?

I will now present further clinical examples where such experiences emerged and explore how communication through *playful action* – including the use of metaphor and the therapist's capacity to dream – can support adolescents in entering a *dreaming state*: by this I'm referring to a psychic process that enables the emotional experience to be processed, symbolised, and made meaningful (Ogden, 2004a, 2004b).

Filtering through the dark waters

When an adolescent we see has suffered severe traumas in early childhood, such as in the case of Alex, their self-concept can become hidden behind a wall of chaos and split-off debris. In response, our own emotional aliveness may become curtailed, with projective and introjective processes impeded.

In Alex's case, these destructive projections could be seen as attacks on linking (Bion, 1959); however, interpreting them in such terms to Alex would only have made them stronger. Identifying and addressing the unrepresented states of our patients require our capacity to survive the breakdown of the defensive, protective walls, which may seem catastrophic but can ultimately allow both the therapist and the patient to create new threads and meaningful representations.

This more disturbed part of Alex was projected into me, allowing me to experience and discover it. When we, as therapists, begin to feel and understand these more vulnerable parts of our patients, young people can sometimes respond with anger or distress, as if threatened by the sense that someone else has accessed something deeply personal. Often, the closer we come to grasping the underlying meaning of their actions, the more resistance we may encounter. At such moments, some young people might react with threats of suicide or escalate self-harming behaviours – signals that the strong defensive wall they've built for protection is beginning to crumble. Those are the moments when we may see an excess of acting out, where bodily discharge becomes an attack on the therapist, so that they can keep thinking and experiencing those disturbing parts within our patient's mind.

We need to find and meet these actions with our own action – the action of play. In my practice, I've noticed that when adolescents have experienced early trauma and there is a deficit in their developmental trajectory, it can help to offer them a box of toys typically given only to young children. I always place the box discreetly in one corner of the room, to avoid making the adolescent feel threatened at the outset. During our first session, I'll make a slight remark that there is a box of toys for them, which I do not mention again. To my surprise, I've noticed that all adolescents who have faced significant adversity earlier in life eventually play with the toys during therapy.

Going back to Alex: after some time of staying with various deep, dark thoughts in my mind and puzzling over them, he provided me with an opportunity to transform these experiences. This wasn't through words and interpretations, but through play, a form of action.

A few sessions after what I previously described, I kept experiencing similar violent and intense thoughts.

In one session, Alex looks for the drawing materials again. This time, the violent thoughts intrude upon my mind to a less intense level. He keeps making lines on the paper and throwing each piece of paper in the bin, and I have a sense that he can't hold himself together. I take two of the pieces of paper and glue them together in such a way that the lines he drew on each piece of paper make a shape. Then, I put them on the table in front of him.

I notice that my anxieties and phantasies feel less intense, and I am able to stay with my thoughts, while also focusing on Alex. He takes the two pieces of paper glued together and tells me that he sees a body part in them and that he will draw a robot. I observe closely and ask him what I should do now. He suggests that I draw a robot too.

We end up with two robots. He appears more responsive and able to keep eye contact with me, discussing the robots.

Instead of interpreting verbally, in this case I actively participated in Alex's play by connecting the two pieces of paper, hoping to contain his anxiety about fragmentation and represent the connection of his unintegrated parts. This action was also my way of building our therapeutic alliance and of showing him that he was not alone in holding these scary parts, establishing trust and connection. This helped Alex feel contained and create something out of the 'spontaneous gesture' of the play (Winnicott, 1962/1965), showing me that he was beginning to represent his feelings through the robot, a mechanical creature without emotions, something not yet embodied.

In the next session, Alex takes the two robots we drew and glues them together, making them one. The uncanny and dark phantasies I experience become intrusive again, more intense. I feel baffled by his communication, as he becomes withdrawn and fidgety in the room. I can sense that something terrifying is enacted both in his play and in my own mind.

> I take the combined robot he made and start to unglue it. I separate the two pieces, and then he joins in the game. We both together draw on the pieces of paper, since some of the glue has ripped the paper and changed the figures on each page. He shows relief and becomes involved in this in an excited, engaged way.

The patient's experiences and their deepest anxieties can be found, as I've tried to show, via our own introjective identification. I came to understand, in Alex's case, that the uncanny thoughts intruding upon my mind and the representation of the two robots in the play stood for two figures: by making them into one, Alex was communicating his fear of potential sexual abuse. These profound anxieties (Winnicott, 1974) were dramatised in my own mind and then represented in the play: they were about life and death, existence and nonexistence.

What happens when a body and mind penetrate another? What happens when two bodies violently become one? Alex's defence was to withdraw and freeze emotionally, mutilating a part of himself to survive psychically. In the *here and now* of the therapy session, Alex experienced me in the transference as an abusive and terrifying object that would engulf him, overpowering and annihilating his psyche by coming too close, the two figures joining into one in his mind.

It is through this kind of spontaneous gesture in the play that one can begin to understand transference and countertransference. By separating the two, I had tried to 'interpret in action' (Ogden, 1994), formulating the scary transference Alex had developed towards me but also trying to convey the opposite, as a new object that is not there to engulf and destroy him, creating a representation of separateness. As such, I was trying to express through play thoughts and experiences that could not be conveyed through words.

> He draws the sea on another sheet of paper, depicting it with a very dark, deep bottom. I wonder aloud what's happening down there. He says that it is scary: dark and frightening things live down there. In my countertransference, I experience some apprehension and vivid images of darkness. I don't know what may emerge in my mind. I draw a tiny submarine, cut it from my paper, and place it at the bottom of the sea in his drawing. I tell him that we can look together at those dark and scary things at the bottom of the ocean.

With Alex feeling more separate now, he was able to enter a realm where more symbolisation could occur, allowing me to understand that the bottom of the ocean's sea, representing the dark and deep corners of his mind, was inhabited by uncanny experiences.

By becoming aware of my thoughts and phantasies and allowing his intrusive projections to enter my phantasy world, on my part I was able to enter into a process of metabolisation and reverie. Being attuned with those parts of Alex and getting a better understanding of scary thoughts, I could try to 'interpret in action' through the play, where both self and other are relevant, separate and co-existing, rather than violently merging into one.

A boy with luggage and the broken home

With panicked, acting-out adolescents, as therapists we can struggle to find the right words or actions.

Alex's material evokes Cassorla's (2005) concept of the *'non-dream-for-two'*. By this, Cassorla refers to a psychological and relational state within the analytic dyad in which the capacity for dreaming, understood as the symbolic elaboration and transformation of emotional experience, is suspended or reversed. In such states, both patient and analyst become mutually entangled in a kind of enactment, where meaning-making breaks down. What emerges is often confusing, stereotyped, or bizarre material that lacks emotional resonance or symbolic potential, reflecting a shared collapse in the dreaming function of the analytic couple. This creates an environment analogous to an early situation, where the primary object is unable to contain affects, inducing a state of terror experienced as 'nameless dread' by the infant (Bion, 1965). Such attacks can at times transform the parent-analyst's dreams into terrifying nightmares (Bion, 1965).

Cassorla's description demonstrates the impact on the therapist of excessive projective identification and psyche discharge, attacking the capacity for connection and genuine emotional experience between two people. What I want to describe now is the way that an idea of connection can be born through actual play, as well as through *word and idea play* between two people. This connection comes in the form of images that don't belong either within the therapist or within the patient but in the space between the two.

I will now discuss the case of Jack, a 17-year-old engaging in high-risk behaviour. He was involved in gangs and often got into fights with knives. As he told me, he felt excited by the idea of getting hurt, and even of dying. I soon found out in sessions that his parents had been violent towards him when he was younger.

Jack was initially defensive when it came to therapy, finding it difficult to attend regularly in the first months. He often spoke to me with a mechanical tone of voice. He appeared depressed and faced many difficulties in his interpersonal relationships at school and with his parents. He often isolated himself in his room, sleeping for extended hours when not in school, or stayed out until late. At other times, he would run away from home and would disappear, sometimes for days.

His voice and statements often contradicted his bodily demeanour, which indicated hypervigilance, such as fidgeting. For a number of months in the therapy, I felt flat, sleepy, and withdrawn. But after a while, there was this moment in a session:

I invite Jack to make something for me with the Lego pieces he is fidgeting with in his hands. He makes a shape out of bricks, and I invite him to share his thoughts about what this reminds him of. He tells me that it reminds him of a house, and I invite him to make a home together. I join him in building this house together.

I notice a striking contradiction in my mind: he is 17 years old but seems much younger and more alive; his voice undergoes a noticeable change, and he narrates the process of constructing the house, telling me step by step how he does it, adding the door and windows, etc.

As demonstrated in the case of Jack, interpretations are often not the most effective approach. Jack required an environment, symbolised by the house the two of us built together, in which he could feel emotionally nurtured.

In the vignette I've presented, I know that Jack's demeanour resembles that of a much younger child. I was aware at that time of the potential danger inherent in our (unusual for his age) activity of playing with Lego and the possibility that Jack might feel vulnerable doing this, pushing him closer to a need to act out. Despite the risks in our playing together, I felt that inviting Jack to share his thoughts about the game was a way to signal that we were separate entities working together to build something – a house. It was within the confines of this house we created that things could be dramatised, represented, and explored safely.

In the next session, Jack came to the room seeming more alert, as if picking up from where we had left off.

Jack tells me for the first time about the difficulties he's having with his parents. He recounts that he often leaves his house to stay with a supportive family member who takes care of him.

As I attentively listen to Jack, I notice a shift within myself. For the first time in several months of therapy, my mind starts to conjure vivid images in response to what he is saying. I feel alive as he talks excitedly and appears filled with joy describing this nurturing family figure.

However, despite his happiness, a wave of intense sadness washes over me too. The mental image that crystallises in my mind depicts a young boy standing at a crossroads, appearing lost and clutching a small, empty suitcase.

I decide to share this mental tableau: 'Jack, as you were speaking, I thought of a boy standing lost at crossroads and clutching on his small suitcase'. He unexpectedly bursts into tears and, in that moment, sheds his guarded exterior and reveals the vulnerability of a much younger child. While sobbing, he talks about his wish for parents who would be softer and kinder to him.

Towards the end of the session, he shares a thought/image he has had for a very long time, of being held strongly by his parent when he was a young child and feeling scared.

Jack's capacity for symbolic thinking seemed to increase as the therapy progressed. As we (metaphorically and actually) built a house together, he began to feel safer and trust me as another object. It is within the safety of the therapeutic environment that both therapist and patient can regress into a state of fantasising and dreaming, and within those states, evocative images can be born in the intersubjective field. Such internal images often reflect the spontaneous, internal working through of the patient's projected emotions and the therapist's responses.

Rather than just mirroring our patient's fragmented experiences, we must strive to be reflective, introducing our mind as a space where unconscious dimensions can be explored and understood. My image of the young boy clutching onto his suitcase at the crossroads strongly represented Jack's loneliness. Moreover, the crossroads seemed to symbolise the unknown path of emotional connection, being touched by another mind within the transference.

Both Jack's and Alex's cases highlight the intricate psychic movements through the exchange of ideas and actions, revealing glimpses of the interlinked subjective experiences between therapist and patient. This was achieved either through playful interaction with toys, figurines, or art materials, or through the use of metaphors and internal imagery that was evoked within the therapist's mind.

However, after the experience of overdose or engaging in excessive self-harm, young people often find their senses and ego capacities dismantled, blurring the lines between separateness and unity with others. In the aftermath of such crises, some adolescents retreat into an illusory world overwhelmed by their somatic and emotional experiences. As therapists, we then keenly feel the dread of trying to reach out to them, constantly sensing that we are up against a wall, sometimes as powerful as an 'autistic barrier' (Tustin, 1986).

Sessions with such patients may feel monotonous, continuous, with no end in sight. The passage of time may sometimes seem the only viable solution to this impasse, as any premature attempt at thinking together could further entrench them in their stuckness.

Fergie, who I will now describe, was unfortunately a young person who fit this more stuck description. She came to me in a state of despair, following a worrying overdose and excessive self-harming, expressing a strong wish not to overcome her severe emotional pain but to cease feeling altogether.

For some time during the initial sessions, Fergie neither looked at me, spoke to me, nor even acknowledged my presence in the room. I found myself unable to think, 'dream', or feel anything physically or emotionally. It was as if all my senses had shut down, as if any crack in what felt like a formidable wall would unleash dread and breakdown, and as if my own psychic survival was at stake.

After a few sessions, I invited Fergie to engage in a game of squiggle with me. The drawings that emerged reminded me of those made by young children, and I remember seeing her smile. However, instead of feeling pleased that she was opening up, I found myself feeling overwhelmed by the multitude of colours she had used in such a simple drawing. It wasn't until much later in our work together that I better understood this detail of my experience, which had possibly mirrored Fergie's overwhelming feelings, giving me a clue as to why she was emotionally shutting me out.

In a subsequent session, feeling drained and devoid of energy, I decided to draw by myself, recognising the need to counteract the deadening effect of my own experiences.

> After finishing the drawing, we both sit in silence. As I look at the piece of paper, I notice that my drawing depicts a closed square shape composed of differently coloured bricks. I find myself thinking that it could easily break, as if made of fragile material.
>
> The subsequent thought of this square shape shattering into a million pieces if it dropped on the floor fills me with a wave of panic. I comment on the fragility of the shape I drew, mentioning how scary it would be if it were to fall and break into a million pieces. I notice Fergie's body tense up, her movements becoming agitated, as if she's trying to stop something. In response, she becomes more closed off, curling up in her chair and remaining motionless for the rest of the session.

I hope this vignette, despite its playful and creative elements, demonstrates that Fergie's capacity for representation and symbolisation felt deeply threatening to her sense of self. Because of her extreme fragility, my attempt to introduce something new into her mental arena was experienced as painful and dismantling. Fergie appeared lost in an intersubjective realm where ideas, images, thoughts, and feelings lacked vitality. Her mind felt like an empty space, with emotions adrift in a void. While I was trying to serve as a container and bring in some vitality, it felt as though I was inadvertently contributing to a catastrophe.

Alex's, Jack's, and Fergie's experiences illustrate the different levels at which we, as therapists, can engage with our adolescent patients. In the work we do together, we become part of their landscape, actively participating in 'playful action', 'dreaming', and 'reverie', as we try to understand, process, and engage in their world, even while also facing failures and difficulties. Both Alex and Jack offer us insights. Vividly, Winnicott's words come to mind: 'It is a joy to be hidden, but a disaster not to be found.' Despite being hidden, both Alex and Jack seemed to have found some joy and vitality in being discovered by me as another mind. In contrast, Fergie's experience of being found seemed to hint at a catastrophe. Her fragile psyche perceived being discovered as a threat, causing her to retreat further into her inner world.

What is required with patients like Fergie is the passage of time and patience, keeping in mind also the fragile narcissism characteristic of adolescence. It's essential to respect their hypersensitive defences and avoid overstimulating them. My comment on the fragility of the square I drew in Fergie's presence, though an interpretation in displacement, brought to the surface her anxiety of breaking down into a million pieces.

Ferro (2009) has described that when working with those who have defences similar to autistic barriers, the therapist's intervention is akin to becoming a transformer to the intensity of the 'voltage'. In Fergie's case, my interpretation of displacement, which represented her ego's fragility, created a high-voltage situation, infusing an unsustainable tension into the 'field' between us. She had experienced significant trauma early in her life, leaving her already with an overwhelming sensory influx, hindering her mind's capacity for representation. Therefore, there was a need to focus on her defence mechanisms and on strengthening her ego.

In retrospect, I think that in Fergie's case, I should have noted and held on to the first raw images evoked in my mind, representing her fear of breakdown and instead commenting on her capacity to hold everything together and how vital that would be for her stability and wellbeing. That way, I could have helped her build a more stable and secure ego capacity before going near her deepest anxieties.

The flipbook: interpreting the moving images

What becomes clearer and clearer to me is that, as therapists, we need to be able to adapt to our patients' specific needs and deficits. Similar to the metaphor that Ferro (2009) has given us about being the transformers of intensity, we need to transform our capacities for thinking, representation, and symbolic functioning according to our patients' capacities. But we also need to trust our intuition and psychic experiences and not be afraid of saying something in a clumsy way, allowing for continuous trial and error.

As Winnicott has described in many different ways, the therapist needs to play with the patient. We can remember Winnicott's (1971b) idea on the 'squiggle game'; the therapist puts an idea forward, as an object that exists in the potential space between them and the patient, passing that object back and forth, playing with it, kicking it, running with it, and doing anything the patient wants. If the patient can use it, then there can be a form of creativity between patient and therapist.

The aim of such acts is not for us to talk as if we hold the truth of the patient's unconscious life, but to release our own subjective state and offer it to be played with. To do this is an effort to reach the patient and provide him with material that can be used to facilitate a growing understanding about unique parts themselves.

Anzieu (1969) saw the act of interpretation as akin to a musical or theatrical performance. When we talk to our patients, our aim is not merely to explain but to represent and strike a sensitive chord through what is being discussed. As interpreters, we adhere to the notes, respecting the melody and the text, while also striving to uniquely convey meaning within the scene. The initial encounter with a patient, especially an adolescent at risk, can evoke intense emotions within a story that has not yet been written, making interpretation challenging. Therefore, to create a framework for understanding, the therapist must delve into their own reservoir of experiences and theoretical knowledge alongside the adolescent's perspective.

Reflecting on our own experiences, we begin by listening with all our senses. When facing an adolescent in crisis, it can feel like stepping into an unknown world, where we may feel isolated. Emotions such as fear, anger, and pain may surface in us, revealing our patient's deep-seated experiences too. The bodily sensations we experience, imprinted in our mind and body, form the foundation of our therapeutic work. Consequently, emotions gradually take shape as images, eventually transforming into objects and representations that we can address to the adolescent.

The therapist may at times perceive these strange states as a regression of their ability to symbolise. Yet coherence is not lost; instead, a dichotomous dynamic gradually emerges. While the therapist's 'observing ego' (Sandler & Freud, 1980) continues its work, albeit in a murky landscape, the experiencing ego is left to explore. But what is created is unique to the moment and time where patient and therapist meet, becoming a distinctive organism comprising elements of both of them, at the boundary of the unconscious and preconscious.

As therapists, we follow emotional cues and seek signs of representation work. We dismantle the text, distort it, and then reorganise it into a new composition. We become both the subject and the object of a fantasy scenario that emerges in a space belonging neither to us nor to the adolescent. By perceiving and experiencing what arises, we can find words to offer to our patient.

This was similar to the case of Ryan, a 17-year-old adolescent boy who had attempted suicide. He reached our service in a state of calmness, 'cool' with everything that had happened. His capacity for symbolism and representation was more developed than that of Alex, Jack, and Fergie.

Ryan came to the clinic without any request for therapy and no verbal acknowledgment that anything felt bad or difficult in his life. In the first sessions, he appeared defended and kept minimising all the underlying issues that might have contributed to his attempted suicide. At a conscious level, I also struggled to see beneath the surface of what was going on. Ryan seemed to have a good relationship with both parents, who were concerned about him. He was doing well in school and appeared to be a sociable young man, with an active sex life. He seemed content, and his language was well structured.

In most of the sessions, he came across as well presented, and in a seductive way, asked a lot of personal questions about me. At first, I felt flattered. But at the end of most sessions, I wondered what the point of the sessions were. Ryan appeared to be making a defensive manoeuvre, by driving attention to me and making me feel seduced. I said quite a few times that he seemed curious about me, but that it was important for us to keep thinking about him.

In one session, Ryan starts talking about all the things that are going well and also references his future. Although a sense of hopefulness is evoked in me, I feel puzzled why he is even there to see me. An image emerges in my mind of me struggling to go through a swamp, moving through debris, trees, and dirt.

I think that although there is something beneath the surface with Ryan emotionally, his ego appears contained at a superficial level. I feel that I can share with him the following thought: 'There is a feeling that we cannot go through the swamp, pass all the debris and the muddy water, and see clearly why we are having these sessions'. Ryan ignores my metaphor at first, and then after a few seconds of silence, he starts talking about his parents and how emotionally disconnected he is from them. He describes his difficulty to even be with them and how lonely he feels at times to a point of even having thoughts of suicide and self-harm.

I am struck by his sudden change of narrative and mood. After a few minutes of describing his experience from a young age and how he has hardly ever felt warmth, he also talks about a couple that, although living together, are absent: both as a couple and as parents. His father is described as physically absent and uncaring, in combination with a depressed mother, leaving Ryan with no choice than to be dependent on himself only.

I have this image in my head of moving images like a flipbook: a boy screaming 'Mum, Dad!' at the top of his lungs, looking for them. I share this in the session, saying, 'And all you want to do, Ryan, is to scream 'Nik, MUM, DAD, where are you?' Ryan's eyes become watery, and he bursts out crying, telling me how he never referred to his parents as 'Mum' and 'Dad'. I feel emotionally touched by his raw emotional expression.

Ryan's longing for connection was expertly concealed beneath his cool, seductive exterior, masking his loneliness and isolation under a chaotic pile of debris. This debris created a labyrinth, concealing all that was painful. Though I initially believed that my interpretation, illustrating the evocative images of swamps and debris, had been overlooked, it nonetheless seemed to have had an impact on Ryan. My interpretation centred on both of us, struggling together to navigate the debris,

Ryan not alone in his struggle. This fostered a sense of togetherness and connection as we confronted the difficulty together. At that moment, Ryan edged closer to the reality of his experience, but not close enough to his emotional response to this reality.

My interpretation had been influenced by the powerful, moving images in my mind, representing Ryan's emotional experience that needed to be put in words. Through the transference, I was able to subtly address his true need for care, going beyond the facade of self-sufficiency he presented. By phrasing my interpretation as a question, using simple language, I tried to capture his longing for connection, as well as his anxiety about feeling lonely and struggling to connect with his parents, through the presence of a caring object in the here and now that was listening to and trying to represent Ryan's experience.

Figuring the unspoken: from dreaming to representation – venturing reflections

Working with at-risk adolescents in this way hinges on the therapist's capacity to internalise and embody a playful and 'evocative' object (Bollas, 2009). This capacity is informed by the therapist's own analytic experience, requiring not only intellectual understanding but also emotional resonance. This moves beyond mere interpretation or passively 'sitting with the silence'. It involves helping adolescents move away from the influence of internalised parental objects, fostering their ability to rebel, seek new objects, and transform their psychic landscape during a stage of profound vulnerability.

Adolescence is a period of destabilisation, where regression often threatens – but as Winnicott (1961/2012, 1967) reminds us, regression is not only inevitable but also essential. It is not only the patient that needs to regress but the therapist also, meeting the adolescent where they are. This shared, hopefully playful regression creates a collaborative and exploratory dyad where unspoken fears and terrors, 'nameless dread' (Bion, 1965), can be articulated, understood, and transformed into something representable. This shared process helps adolescents feel heard, contained, and supported in their capacity to 'go on being' (Winnicott, 1960).

Roussillon's (2018) concept of the 'objeu' – or 'the object of play' – resonates here. He argues that for transitionality to be achieved, the object must transform the subject's concrete thoughts and actions into more symbolic forms, through the processes of playing and naming. This places the 'object therapist' at the centre of the development of the capacity for symbolisation when working with adolescents at risk. The therapist becomes the container, holding and transforming overwhelming experiences into tolerable and meaningful representations.

Winnicott (1971a) in his chapter 'Dreaming, fantasying and living', draws a clear distinction between dreaming and fantasying. *Dreaming*, for him, is a creative and symbolic process deeply connected to emotional life and real relationships, whereas *fantasying* is a dissociated, isolated activity that drains psychic energy and blocks integration. For Winnicott, dreaming is closely allied with living.

This transformative potential of dreaming resonates with the concept of *figurability* proposed by Botella and Botella (2005), which describes the mind's capacity to generate mental images and symbolic forms that can process unconscious material. They emphasise dreams as a key site where figurability operates, producing images and narratives that process and transform unconscious material. They liken the state of dreaming for both therapist and patient to the analytic space itself – a shared field of creativity and transformation. However, when figurability is impaired, as often seen in at-risk adolescents, the mind may experience blank spaces or fragmented imagery, mirroring its internal chaos and difficulty integrating experiences.

Figurability is critical in working with at-risk adolescents, as their minds often struggle to integrate fragmented and chaotic experiences, leaving behind raw sensations that manifest in destructive behaviours, like self-harm or repeated suicide attempts.

In these moments, the therapist's role is to restore figurability by engaging in dreaming and reverie, generating squiggles, ideas, thoughts, and mental imagery, all born within the analytic field. These are offered back to the adolescent through interpretations in action-play, metaphor, and symbolic thinking. By entering such states, the therapist aids adolescents in processing unspoken and unprocessed experiences, enabling them to reclaim their capacity for representation, connection, and meaning-making, ultimately facilitating emotional integration.

Notes

1 All cases presented in this chapter are composite case examples, constructed to protect confidentiality.
2 In Greek mythology, Kronos (Cronus) was the youngest of the Titans, born to Gaia (Earth) and Uranus (Sky). Fearing a prophecy that his children would overthrow him, Kronos swallowed each of his offspring at birth. However, his wife, Rhea, saved their youngest, Zeus, by hiding him and tricking Kronos with a stone wrapped in swaddling cloth. Zeus later overthrew Kronos, forcing him to regurgitate his siblings, and the Olympian gods rose to power, marking the end of the Titan's reign and the beginning of a new divine order.

References

Anderson, R. (1997). Assessing the risk of self-harm in adolescents. In: E. Quagliata, & M. Rustin (eds.), *Assessment in child psychotherapy* (1st edition) Karnac Books.
Anzieu, D. (1969). Dificultades de un estudio psicoanalítico sobre la interpretación [Difficulties of a psychonalytic study on interpretation]. *Revista de Psicoanalisis*, 29, 253–282. [Difficulté d'une étude psychanalytique de l'interpretation. *Bulletin de l'Association Psychanalytique de France*, 5, 12–32].
Baranger, M., & Baranger, W. (2017). The analytic situation as a dynamic field. *The International Journal of Psychoanalysis*, 89(4), 795–826. https://doi.org/10.1111/j.1745-8315.2008.00074.x
Bion, W. R. (1959). Attacks on linking. *International Journal of Psychoanalysis*, 40, 308–315.
Bion, W. R. (1962). *Learning from experience*. London: Routledge.

Bion, W. R. (1965). *Transformations: Change from learning to growth*. London: Butterworth-Heinemann.

Blos, P. (1965). The universal experience of adolescence. *Psychoanalytic Quarterly*, 34, 296–298.

Bollas, C. (1987). *The shadow of the object: Psychoanalysis of the unthought known*. New York, NY: Columbia University Press.

Bollas, C. (2009). *The evocative object world*. London: Routledge.

Botella, S., & Botella, C. (2005). *The work of psychic figurability: Mental states without representation*. London: Routledge.

Cassorla, R. M. (2005). From bastion to enactment: The "non-dream" in the theatre of analysis. *International Journal of Psychoanalysis*, 86, 699–719.

Erikson, E. H. (1968). *Identity, youth, and crisis*. W. W. Norton & Company.

Ferro, A. (2009). Transformations in dreaming and characters in the psychoanalytic field. *International Journal of Psychoanalysis*, 90, 209–230.

Freud, S. (1912a). A note on the unconscious in psycho-analysis. *The Standard Edition*, 12, 255–266.

Freud, S. (1912b). Recommendations to physicians practising psycho-analysis. *The Standard Edition*, 12, 109–120.

Freud, S. (1913). An evidential dream. *The Standard Edition*, 12, 267–278.

Freud, S. (1921). Group psychology and the analysis of the ego. *The Standard Edition*, 18, 65–144.

Freud, S. (1923). Two encyclopaedia articles. *The Standard Edition*, 18, 233–260.

Ladame, F. (1995). The importance of dreams and action in the adolescent process. *International Journal of Psychoanalysis*, 76, 1143–1153.

Laufer, M. E., & Laufer, M. (1995). *Adolescence and developmental breakdown: A psychoanalytic view*. London: Routledge.

Mahler, M. S., & Furer, M. (1963). Certain aspects of the separation-individuation phase. *The Psychoanalytic Quarterly*, 32(1), 1–14.

Ogden, T. H. (1994). The concept of interpretive action. *Psychoanalytic Quarterly*, 63, 219–245.

Ogden, T. H. (2004a). On holding and containing, being and dreaming. *The International Journal of Psychoanalysis*, 85(6), 1349–1364. https://doi.org/10.1516/T41H-DGUX-9JY4-GQC7

Ogden, T. H. (2004b). This art of psychoanalysis: Dreaming undreamt dreams and interrupted cries. *International Journal of Psychoanalysis*, 85, 857–877.

Roussillon, R. (2018). *Primitive agony and symbolization*. Routledge.

Ruggiero, I. (2006). Consultation in adolescence: Hurried, terminable, interminable. *International Journal of Psychoanalysis*, 87(2), 537–554.

Sandler, J., & Freud, A. (1980). Discussions in the hampstead index on "the ego and the mechanisms of defence": I. The ego as the seat of observation. *Bulletin of the Anna Freud Centre*, 3, 199–212.

Sowell, E. R., Thompson, P M., & Toga, A. W. (2007). Mapping adolescent brain maturation using structural magnetic resonance imaging. In: D. Romer, & E. F. Walker (eds.), *Adolescent psychopathology and the developing brain: Integrating brain and prevention science*. Adolescent Mental Health Initiative (online edition. New York: Oxford Academic, May 1, 2009). https://doi.org/10.1093/acprof:oso/9780195306255.003.0003

Stortelder, F., & Ploegmakers-Burg, M. (2010). Adolescence and the reorganization of infant development: A neuro-psychoanalytic model. *Journal of the American Academy of Psychoanalysis and Dynamic Psychiatry*, 38(3), 503–532. https://doi.org/10.1521/jaap.2010.38.3.503

Symington, N. (1983). The analyst's act of freedom as agent of therapeutic change. *International Review of Psycho-Analysis*, 10(3), 283–291.

Tustin, F. (1986). *Autistic barriers in neurotic patients*. London: Routledge.

Wilson, P. (2009). Winnicott and the psychoanalytic tradition: Interpretation and other psychoanalytic issues. *British Journal of Psychotherapy*, 25(1), 110–116. https://doi.org/10.1111/j.1752-0118.2008.01104_1.x

Winnicott, D. W. (1958). The capacity to be alone. *International Journal of Psychoanalysis*, 39, 416–420.

Winnicott, D. W. (1960). The theory of the parent-infant relationship. *International Journal of Psychoanalysis*, 41, 585–595.

Winnicott, D. W. (1961/2012). Adolescence. In: *The family and individual development*. Routledge.

Winnicott, D. W. (1962/1965). Ego integration in child development. In: *The maturational processes and the facilitating environment: Studies in the theory of emotional development* (Vol. 64, pp. 56–63).

Winnicott, D. W. (1963/1965). The development of the capacity for concern. In: *The maturational processes and the facilitating environment: Studies in the theory of emotional development* (Vol. 64, pp. 73–82). International Universities Press.

Winnicott, D. W. (1967). Delinquency as a sign of hope. In: *Home is where we start from: Essays by a psychoanalyst by Winnicott, D. W.* (pp. 90–100).

Winnicott, D. W. (1969). The use of an object. *International Journal of Psychoanalysis*, 50, 711–716.

Winnicott, D. W. (1971a). *Playing and reality*. London: Routledge.

Winnicott, D. W. (1971b). *Therapeutic consultations in child psychiatry*. London: Karnac.

Winnicott, D. W. (1974). Fear of breakdown. *International Review of Psychoanalysis*, 1, 103–107.

Winnicott, D. W. (1986). *Holding and interpretation: Fragment of an analysis*. London: Routledge.

Index

For Product Safety Concerns and Information please contact our EU
representative GPSR@taylorandfrancis.com
Taylor & Francis Verlag GmbH, Kaufingerstraße 24, 80331 München, Germany

www.ingramcontent.com/pod-product-compliance
Lightning Source LLC
Chambersburg PA
CBHW050332270326
41926CB00016B/3424

9 781032 972237